THE GLASGOW ENLIGHTENMENT

THE GLASGOW ENLIGHTENMENT

Edited by
Andrew Hook and Richard B. Sher

TUCKWELL PRESS
in association with the
Eighteenth-Century Scottish Studies Society

First published in 1995 by Tuckwell Press Ltd, The Mill
House, Phantassie, East Linton, East Lothian, EH40 3DG,
Scotland

ISBN 1 898410 18 6

Published with support from the University of Glasgow
Publications Committee and from the MacFie Fund

British Library Cataloguing-in-Publication Data
A catalogue record for this book is available on request
from the British Library

Typeset from disk supplied by Light Technology Ltd,
Fife, Scotland
Printed and bound by
Cromwell Press, Melksham, Wilts

Contents

II BEYOND THE ACADEMIC ENLIGHTENMENT

Acknowledgements

This collection of essays, the fourth volume in the 'Studies in Eighteenth-Century Scotland' series sponsored by the Eighteenth-Century Scottish Studies Society, originated in a conference on 'Glasgow and the Enlightenment' held at the University of Strathclyde in the summer of 1990. In that year, when Glasgow succeeded Paris as 'European City of Culture', what could have been more appropriate than to direct attention to the period when Glasgow first began to establish itself as a city worthy of European attention? For most of us in attendance, a more memorable conference would be difficult to imagine. Besides the conference papers, highlights included an evening walk along the Forth and Clyde Canal; an outing to Burns and Boswell country in Ayrshire, with an excursion to Robert Adam's Culzean Castle; a magnificent dinner and reception at Glasgow City Chambers, hosted by the Lord Provost of Glasgow; and a trip to Smollett country near Loch Lomond, concluding with dinner at Ross Priory, the University of Strathclyde's eighteenth-century estate on the banks of the loch, where guests heard a lecture-recital of Burns songs by John Davison, Shoshana Shay, and the late John Ashmead.

On behalf of the Eighteenth-Century Scottish Studies Society, the editors are happy to acknowledge the gracious hospitality and support that was given to our conference and our volume by a variety of individuals and organizations, including the city of Glasgow itself. We are particularly grateful to the University of Strathclyde — especially Hamish Fraser, Andrew Noble and the conference co-ordinator, Richard L. Peddie — for hosting the 1990 conference with so much style, and to the University of Glasgow both for sponsoring Ian Ross's Stevenson Lecture and for providing generous financial support from its Publications Committee and MacFie Fund. Finally, we wish to thank John Tuckwell of Canongate Academic for giving us the opportunity to put the Glasgow Enlightenment into print.

Contributors

Andrew Hook is the Bradley Professor of English at the University of Glasgow and the immediate past president of the Eighteenth-Century Scottish Studies Society. Among his many publications is *Scotland and America: A Study of Cultural Relations 1750–1835* (1975).

Richard B. Sher is professor of history at New Jersey Institute of Technology and the graduate school at Rutgers University-Newark, and the founding executive secretary of the Eighteenth-Century Scottish Studies Society. His publications include 'Commerce, Religion and the Enlightenment in Eighteenth-Century Glasgow' in *The History of Glasgow*, vol. 1, ed. T. M. Devine and Gordon Jackson (1994).

John W. Cairns is senior lecturer in private law at the University of Edinburgh and the author of many articles on legal education in Scottish universities during the eighteenth century.

Robert Kent Donovan is associate professor of history at Kansas State University. He is the author of *Radicalism and No Popery: Opposition to Roman Catholic Relief in Scotland, 1778–1782* (1987) and articles in the *Historical Journal* and other publications.

Roger L. Emerson is professor of history at the University of Western Ontario and the author of *Professors, Patronage and Politics: The Aberdeen Universities in the Eighteenth Century* (1992). He is a past president of the Eighteenth-Century Scottish Studies Society.

H. L. Fulton, professor of English at Central Michigan University, is completing a biography of the eighteenth-century Scottish novelist and travel writer John Moore.

Kathleen Holcomb is the Lee Drain Professor in English at Angelo State University in San Angelo, Texas. She is currently editing the papers that Thomas Reid read at the Aberdeen Philosophical Society and the Glasgow Literary Society.

Thomas D. Kennedy, associate professor of philosophy at Valparaiso University in Indiana, is currently director of that university's Overseas Study Program in Cambridge, England. He has written articles and presented papers on the interplay of philosophy, rhetoric, and religion in the works of eighteenth-century Scottish ministers such as William Leechman and David Fordyce.

Ned C. Landsman is associate professor of history at the State University of New York at Stony Brook. He is the author of *Scotland and Its First American Colony* (1985) and numerous articles on Scottish and American religious culture in the eighteenth century.

Thomas P. Miller is associate professor of English at the University of Arizona. His publications include *Selected Writings of John Witherspoon* (1990), several articles on the rhetoric of the Scottish Enlightenment, and a forthcoming volume entitled *The Formation of College English Studies: Rhetoric and Belles Lettres in the British Cultural Provinces*.

Ian Simpson Ross is professor emeritus of English at the University of British Columbia and founding president of the Eighteenth-Century Scottish Studies Society. He has published extensively on the Scottish Enlightenment and is the author of a forthcoming *Life of Adam Smith*.

Gordon Turnbull has published several articles on James Boswell, about whom he is writing a book. A native of Australia, he has taught at Yale University and is currently a lecturer in the English Department at Smith College in Massachusetts.

Paul Wood is a member of the History Department at the University of Victoria, British Columbia, and a specialist in the history of science and philosophy in the universities of eighteenth-century Scotland. He has recently published *The Aberdeen Enlightenment: The Arts Curriculum in the Eighteenth Century* (1993).

Illustrations
(between pages 116 and 117)

PORTRAITS

1. Francis Hutcheson. By Allan Ramsay.

2. William Leechman. Painter unknown.

3. Robert Simson. By William Cochrane after De Nune.

4. William Cullen. Painter unknown.

5. Joseph Black. By Sir Henry Raeburn.

6. William Hunter. By Allan Ramsay.

7. Adam Smith. By Hans Gasser.

8. Thomas Reid. By Sir Henry Raeburn.

9. John Anderson. By William Kay.

10. John Millar. Tassie medallion.

11. James Boswell. By John Jones after Reynolds.

12. John Moore. By Thomas Lawrence.

The University of Strathclyde is thanked for permission to reproduce Kay's John Anderson and the Scottish National Portrait Gallery for the reproduction of Lawrence's portrait of Dr John Moore. The Hunterian Museum and Art Gallery, University of Glasgow are thanked for permission to reproduce the other portraits.

SCENES

13. The College of Glasgow. John Slezer, 1693.

14. A View of the Middle Walk in the College Garden. Robert Paul, 1762.

15. A View of the Trongate of Glasgow from the East. Robert Paul, ca. 1760.

16. The entrance to Glasgow College in the High Street. Swan's *Select Views of Glasgow*, 1828.

With acknowledgements to the Glasgow Room of the Mitchell Library, and Special Collections, Glasgow University Library.

Abbreviations

AUL   Aberdeen University Library
EUL   Edinburgh University Library
GLS   Glasgow Literary Society
GUA   Glasgow University Archives
GUL   Glasgow University Library
NLS   National Library of Scotland
SRO   Scottish Record Office

Introduction: Glasgow and the Enlightenment

Richard B. Sher and Andrew Hook

The Scottish Enlightenment was overwhelmingly concentrated in Scotland's three largest cities: Edinburgh, Glasgow and Aberdeen. These diverse urban settings encouraged the sociability for which eighteenth-century Scotland was justly famous. Clubs flourished, some formal and academic, others social and convivial. Taverns and bookshops were close at hand, and easy access to the sea and to frequently published newspapers and pamphlets put the inhabitants in close touch with the world. The leading literati of the Scottish Enlightenment were for the most part engaged, cosmopolitan townsmen, employed (with rare exceptions, such as David Hume) in the learned professions of law, medicine, the church and academia. Of the five Scottish universities that helped to nurture and sustain the Enlightenment during the eighteenth century, only St Andrews, and perhaps King's College in the village of Old Aberdeen, followed the pattern of the great English centres of learning at Oxford and Cambridge — small towns dominated by their ancient universities. The other three Scottish universities were urban institutions: the University of Edinburgh in the capital, Marischal College in the New Town of Aberdeen and the University of Glasgow in western's Scotland's largest city. Not coincidentally, they were also more progressive and dynamic institutions than St Andrews or King's. In these urban-academic environments, native Scottish students mixed with young men sent to Scotland for their education from as near as England and Ireland, and as far as America and Russia.

It follows that an appreciation of the unique character of cultural, intellectual and social life in each of Scotland's three major cities and their surrounding regions is critically important for developing a deeper, comparative perspective on the nature of the Scottish Enlightenment. Yet scholarship of this kind is still in its infancy. It is true that the Enlightenment in Edinburgh has been the focus of numerous studies in recent years, and that the long neglected Aberdeen Enlightenment has suddenly spawned a formidable secondary literature.[1] But much remains to be done along these lines before a truly comparative study of the Scottish Enlightenment in its urban and regional contexts can be seriously contemplated. In the case of Aberdeen, for example, we now know a great deal about certain topics concerning three particular institutions — King's College, Marischal College and the Aberdeen Philosophical Society or Wise Club — but precious little is known about most of the Aberdeen literati themselves or about the relationship of the Scottish Enlightenment to other key institutions, such as the church and the town council.

It is in regard to Glasgow, however, that the inadequacy of scholarship on the discrete urban contexts of the Scottish Enlightenment is most evident. Despite a veritable publishing industry devoted to its most famous professor, Adam Smith, and modest amounts of specialist literature on some of its other thinkers and institutions, the Glasgow Enlightenment as such has been virtually ignored.[2] The purpose of this volume is to begin the process of making up for past neglect by examining some of the principal people and developments that made the Glasgow Enlightenment interesting and distinctive. Towards that end, we have focused this collection on interactions among individuals, institutions, ideas and ideologies, particularly in so far as these seem to have some bearing on the peculiar cultural makeup of the Enlightenment in Glasgow.

I

WHAT KIND OF CITY was Glasgow in the eighteenth century, and how did its character affect the Enlightenment there? In the first place, it was a town of considerable vitality and growth. Around the middle of the century, Glasgow's population of perhaps 30,000 was roughly twice the size of Aberdeen but scarcely half that of Edinburgh. By 1800, however, the population had grown to about 80,000 — almost three times the size of Aberdeen and, for the first time, slightly more than Edinburgh.[3] Demographic increases were matched by the physical expansion of the city, especially towards the west. This process of enlargement encompassed not only famous streets like Virginia Street (1753), Queen Street (1762) and Buchanan Street (1771) but also a broader, grid-like network of at least forty-eight new streets constructed between 1779 and 1815.[4]

It is tempting to attribute these developments to industrialization, since nineteenth-century Glasgow would become one of the great urban centres of the Industrial Revolution. David Dale — owner of the cotton spinning mill at New Lanark that would be made famous by his son-in-law, Robert Owen — and James Watt, of steam engine fame, are among the eighteenth-century residents of the city who may be cited in support of this claim. It should be remembered, however, that Dale was essentially a merchant-entrepreneur engaged in rural industry,[5] and that Watt had to go to his partner Matthew Boulton's Birmingham in order to see his technological innovations machined into reality. Though manufacturing was increasingly important during the second half of the eighteenth century, the key to Glasgow's prosperity and growth lay not in heavy /industry of the nineteenth-century variety but in small-scale industry and commerce, especially the carrying trade with the New World.

This point has important implications for understanding the disposition and even the very appearance of Glasgow. A commercial ethos permeated the city, giving it a much different atmosphere from the professional-aristocratic ambience [7] that characterized Edinburgh. The direction of Glasgow's commercial life is also significant: to a greater degree than east-coast cities that faced Europe, Glasgow had a western, Atlantic orientation. This distinction manifested itself in various ways, such as in the contrast between Aberdeen's extensive Scandinavian connections or Edinburgh's enormous Dutch influences — which generally encouraged politeness, toleration, social stability and sober religion and learning — and Glasgow's often unstaid relations with Ireland and the Americas. Finally, since eighteenth-century Glasgow possessed substantial commercial wealth without the heavy industry of later times, and since, in contrast to Edinburgh, relatively few physical remnants of the old city now exist, it is necessary to use one's visual imagination when trying to recapture the look and feel of Glasgow during the age of the Enlightenment. Rather than conjure up an image of the grimy industrial city of the early twentieth century, we must picture eighteenth-century Glasgow as a clean, prosperous and exceptionally handsome town.

That is how Daniel Defoe saw it as early as the mid-1720s. In *A Tour Through the Whole Island of Great Britain* (1724–26), he praised the streets and buildings of Glasgow and called it 'the cleanest and beautifullest and best built' of British cities, London excepted. Defoe had a sharp eye for Glasgow's enormous commercial potential, particularly in regard to the growing trade with America. Leaving the Firth of Clyde, he noted, Glasgow's ships were able to sail directly and without interruption to the American colonies; often they were at the capes of Virginia before London ships were clear of the English Channel. The shorter voyage meant significantly lower costs of transatlantic transportation for merchants from Glasgow, as opposed to London: 'Nay even in Times of Peace, [when there is no danger from privateers in the English Channel] and take the Weather to happen in its usual Manner, there must always be allow'd one Time with another, at least fourteen or twenty Days Difference in the Voyage, either Out or Home.'[6] Defoe's estimate was correct, and its further implication was that in the summer sailing season vessels from Glasgow, unlike those from London and other English ports, could fit in two out-and-back Atlantic crossings, with obvious economic benefits.

The merchants of Glasgow, and the smaller ports further down the Clyde estuary, had not been backward in exploiting the advantages pointed out by Defoe. Even before the legalizing Act of Union of 1707, they had begun to develop their trade with America; since the latter part of the seventeenth century, the Clyde had been the centre of a profitable transatlantic contraband trade, particularly in tobacco. After the Union, the pace of development quickened. The London merchants' fear of this growing northern competition began to appear in the form of complaints about alleged irregularities in the Glasgow trade: custom dues, it was asserted, were not collected on the Clyde with the same rigour as in the South. In the end the government acted on these complaints, tightening up the Scottish revenue organization and replacing local Scottish officials with English ones.

The Glasgow tobacco trade continued to grow, however. In the early post-Union years, Glasgow's tobacco imports averaged about one and a half million pounds per annum. In the 1720s this figure climbed to six million pounds. But the most startling development began in the 1740s, when tobacco imports rose from eight million pounds in 1741 to a record forty-seven million pounds in 1771. Two years earlier, Glasgow had become the leading tobacco port in the British Isles, importing just over half of Britain's supply. This highly profitable economic connection between the Firth of Clyde and the Chesapeake Bay played a crucial part in the material and commercial development of western Scotland. In Glasgow itself, it created the famous tobacco aristocracy, a group exercising enormous influence over nearly every aspect of the city's life.[7] The so-called 'tobacco lords' built their splendid mansions on Virginia Street and were distinguished by their scarlet cloaks, curled wigs, cocked hats and gold-headed canes.

More was at issue, however, than the creation of a wealthy commercial élite. The link between economic prosperity and cultural vitality may not be an automatic one, but the two phenomena frequently do seem to sustain each other. For both the city and the colonies, the effects of Glasgow's American trade transcended purely material factors. Scotland imported tobacco, but its exports included news, letters, books, politics, religion, ideas. The trading link made an interweaving of Scottish and American culture almost inevitable, with consequences that are still being explored by scholars.[8] Moreover, Glasgow's role as a commercial entrepôt, processing and warehousing tobacco, sugar and other New World products for resale throughout the British Isles and Europe, encouraged still broader cultural contacts and influences.

Glasgow's commercial prosperity also provided opportunities for the development of notions of enlightened progress and improvement, in all aspects of the polite civic culture of an increasingly civilized modern world. Progress could be seen in economic life, stimulating the dissemination of new, progressive ideas. Yet the process also worked in the reverse direction, as enlightened intellectual values provided a stimulus to economic success. It is entirely possible to see in the Glasgow merchant community a demonstration of the view that enlightened values in education could and should have a practical application. In Philadelphia, that centre of Enlightenment in America, Benjamin Franklin had asked the question: 'What signifies Philosophy that does not apply to some Use?'9 The professors of Enlightenment Glasgow would certainly have understood the force of the question, and to a degree they provided an appropriate answer. No fewer than 36 of the 166 tobacco merchants identified in Glasgow between 1740 and 1790 had matriculated at Glasgow University, and there is evidence that many other merchants attended university classes without matriculating.10

Few merchants were members of the Glasgow Literary Society, or the more convivial Friday and Anderston Clubs, which were dominated by professors from the university. But Glasgow's merchant community was involved in other clubs and societies with loose links to the Enlightenment. As early as the 1740s some merchants were active in a political economy club. At least twenty-five Glasgow merchants were members of the Hodge Podge Club, which was founded in the early 1750s as a literary society, even though its activities soon became strictly social. After the outbreak of the American Revolution, local businessmen founded the Morning and Evening Club, meeting in a tavern in the merchant city; members assembled before breakfast to read the latest newspapers from Edinburgh and London and discuss the American war and the affairs of Parliament. Other clubs, such as the Glasgow branch of the Cape Club and My Lord Ross's Club, combined conviviality with some literary conversation.11 It would seem, then, that Glasgow's mercantile community was reasonably well educated and engaged in enlightened club life.

Throughout the century, foreign visitors to Glasgow continued to register their delight that such a bustling, prosperous city, one dedicated so largely to merchant enterprise, was also so attractive in its layout and appearance. The description that the English traveller Henry Penruddocke Wyndham sent to his father on 19 July 1758 is typical, differing from Defoe's earlier account only in detail and degree:

> Glasgow . . . is a large, handsome, & populous city. The Streets are strait, very broad & long; the houses are lofty & uniform and well built with good stone. I never saw in any Town in England, four such fine & elegant streets as run imediately from the Market place to the Four Points. The lower stories near the Market place are supported with handsome Piazzas in the manner of Covent Garden. The public Edifices are very handsome such as the Guild hall, & several good Hospitalls. There are nine Parishes in this city besides an English Chapell, & the inhabitants of the Town are computed to be 50,000. A vast deal of Trade is carried on here, & the streets are as much crowded by Passengers as they are about Charing Cross in London.

In his next letter home, dated 25 July 1758, Wyndham, an Oxford man himself, picked up the same theme, contending that neither 'the high street of Oxford nor any one in London is so good, as the great street in Glasgow.'¹²

The impressions of Glasgow registered by some of the fictional English travellers in Tobias Smollett's *Humphry Clinker* (1771) are not unlike the views of Wyndham and other actual English visitors. Although scholars have repeatedly cited Matthew Bramble's characterization of Edinburgh as 'a hot-bed of genius', few have quoted his glowing description of Glasgow:

> I am so far happy as to have seen Glasgow, which, to the best of my recollection and judgment, is one of the prettiest towns in Europe; and, without all doubt, it is one of the most flourishing in Great Britain. In short, it is a perfect bee-hive in point of industry . . . . The number of inhabitants is said to amount to thirty thousand; and marks of opulence and independency appear in every quarter of this commercial city.

After pointing out the beauty of the streets and houses, the cathedral, the Cross, and the college, as well as two of the town's 'defects' (the poor quality of the water and the shallowness of the River Clyde), Bramble launches a discussion of some of Glasgow's foremost citizens — the medical men John Moore and John Gordon, and the merchants Andrew Cochrane and John Glassford — by observing that 'the people of Glasgow have a noble spirit of enterprise'. Bramble's nephew Jery Melford is equally enthusiastic, praising not only Glasgow's 'trade and opulence' but also its 'gaiety and diversions'. 'Glasgow is the pride of Scotland,' Jery declares, 'and, indeed, it might very well pass for an elegant and flourishing city in any part of Christendom.'¹³

In 1777 the Glasgow success story was enshrined in a historical account of the town's progress in *The History of Glasgow*, written by John Gibson, a local merchant. 'An extending commerce and increasing manufactures, joined to frugality and industry' had generated wealth, Gibson explained, and wealth in turn had stimulated the growth not only of banking, credit and more ambitious 'schemes of trade and improvement', but also of a wide range of changes in areas well outside the economic sphere: 'a new stile was introduced in building, in living, in dress, and in furniture; the conveniences, the elegances of life began to be studied; wheel-carriages were set up; public places of entertainment were frequented; an assembly-room and a play-house were built by subscription.' What all this amounted to was nothing less than a Glaswegian cultural revolution during the third quarter of the eighteenth century:

> It may be confidently asserted, that, since the year 1750, a total change has been effected, not only in Glasgow, but over the whole country around it; the manners of the people have undergone an alteration greatly for the better; a spirit of industry and activity has been raised, and now pervades every order

of men; commerce has been increased, manufactures have been carried on to a considerable extent, and they are still extending; every person is employed, not a beggar is to be seen in the streets, the very children are busy.[14]

Because they had greatly improved the inhabitants' 'manner of living' and contributed 'in a very great degree, to health and happiness', these immense changes constituted, in Gibson's opinion, an unmitigated blessing.

Much of what Gibson had to say was accurate. Yet matters are usually more complicated than booster histories would lead us to believe, and the topic at hand is no exception. The year before Gibson's *History of Glasgow* appeared, Adam Smith's *Wealth of Nations* singled out urban merchants for some harsh criticism, not only for their materialistic self-interest but also for their tendency 'to deceive and even to oppress the publick'.[15] It seems likely that Smith formulated his views on these matters on the basis of his experiences with Glasgow merchants, with whom he associated during the 1750s and early 1760s. Other members of the Glasgow academic community were privately still more critical of the town's merchants. Writing in 1787 to his former student, the Englishman Samuel Rose, the Glasgow humanity (Latin) professor and poet William Richardson made fun of the popularity of Robert Burns's poetry among 'the Glasgow Manufacturers & merchants, persons who never read a verse before in their days'. As a student in Glasgow three years earlier, Rose himself had written an angry letter home to England to describe the hostile reception accorded to the staunch Foxite professor John Millar when he attempted to convince the citizens of the town of the inadvisability of sending up a loyal address in support of the younger Pitt's government:

> But what can possibly be expected from a parcel of Merchants, whose every Thought turns upon the *one* thing useful? Whose acquaintance with Books is confined to the cash-Book and Ledger? . . . To see men, who often cannot write their own names, who more frequently cannot spell them with propriety, and who sometimes cannot read them after they are written, to see such men in possession of *plums*, it must naturally excite one's Indignation.[16]

Rose claimed to have been present when wealthy Glasgow merchants harangued on the advantages of an 'Illiterate Education' over a 'Literary' one.

Rose's depiction of the merchants of Glasgow as so many cultural Philistines is an overdrawn stereotype, but then so is the opposite conception of them as thoroughly enlightened. In reality, the commercial character of Glasgow created both cultural opportunities and hazards for the Enlightenment. In the same way, Rose's suggestion that the self-interest and general ignorance of the Glasgow merchants fuelled a crude variety of political conservatism is at best only one side of the story. Against this view, it could be argued that the percolation of

Enlightenment values down into the professional and mercantile middle class lay behind Glasgow's increased political awareness, which historians have traditionally seen as a straightforward product of the American crisis. It goes without saying, of course, that Glasgow would take an intense and continuing interest in the dispute between Britain and the American colonies, and that the town's economic interests would lead the Glasgow merchants as a whole to speak for compromise and reconciliation. Glasgow was flourishing as a result of existing conditions; change could only be for the worse. As a result, up to and even beyond the point when the Revolution began, Glasgow was one of the few places in the United Kingdom where war with America was openly opposed. Only when it became clear that the war would be fought to a finish did Glasgow shift its ground. If a quick British victory would be the best protection for its investments in the colonies, Glasgow would do all in its power to achieve that end.

However, even if Glasgow's initial concern over the dispute between Britain and the American colonies was based chiefly on economic self-interest, the diffusion of Enlightenment values seems to have ensured that the larger political, ideological and philosophical issues involved in the American Revolution would not go unnoticed. Some of the occasional material printed in Glasgow during and immediately after the American War lends credence to this point of view. In 1778 Revd William Thom of nearby Govan, a supporter, like John Witherspoon before him, of the Popular party in the Church of Scotland, was still able to publish his pro-American sermon, *The Revolt of the Ten Tribes*, originally delivered on 12 December 1776. Still more significant was the publication in Glasgow in 1783 of *A Collection of the Constitutions of the Thirteen United States of North America*, first printed in Philadelphia late in 1780 by order of Congress. The Glasgow edition contains a prefatory set of 'Verses on the Constitutions' that contains the following lines:

> But now, behold, a set of new-born states
> (Their western shores the vast Atlantic beats)
> Whose constitutions have no other plan,
> Nor aim than this — the happiness of man.

The echo of the Declaration of Independence is clear, but the basic error in geography suggests that the writer was more familiar with American ideals than with the physical reality of the United States.

The poet goes on to ask of the newly-created nation, 'Whence they their institutions drew?' — and proceeds to attempt an answer:

> Perhaps their wisdom's borrowed from the store
> Of civil policy in ancient lore;
> From Him who knew to form a warlike race;
> Or Solon who excell'd in arts of peace:
> Perhaps they've culled from states of modern days

> Whate'er was best and most deserving praise:
> Perhaps, in fine, they've search'd Utopian schemes
> From Grecian Plato's down to David Hume's.

The final poetic judgement is that the American constitutions were directly inspired by the goddess of liberty. It is interesting that the poet approaches the subject of the American state constitutions from the perspective of the Enlightenment. The references to 'civil policy', the 'arts of peace', and the classical lawgivers Lycurgus and Solon, not to mention David Hume, all underline the point. Perhaps it is not too much to say that the existence of these verses demonstrates that there were those in Glasgow in the 1780s who were prepared to see the successful conclusion of the American Revolution as an endorsement and vindication of Enlightenment values.

II

HALF A CENTURY AFTER Defoe's tour, and fifteen years after Henry Wyndham's visit, Glasgow was visited by another distinguished English literary figure. Samuel Johnson, returning with James Boswell from their tour of the Hebrides, spent 28 and 29 October 1773 in the city. Boswell recalls a day in London when Johnson, hearing Adam Smith praise the beauty of Glasgow's buildings, turned to him and asked, 'Pray, sir, have you ever seen Brentford?' Now, listening to Johnson express admiration for the elegance of Glasgow's streets, Boswell slyly reminds him of this episode.[17] In his published comments in the *Journey to the Western Isles of Scotland*, Johnson does seem to allow Glasgow a somewhat grander status than that of Brentford: 'To describe a city so much frequented as *Glasgow*, is unnecessary. The prosperity of its commerce appears by the greatness of many private houses, and a general appearance of wealth.'[18] On the other hand, the social and intellectual life of the city does not appear to have elicited quite so positive a response. Johnson met several of the university's leading men, including Thomas Reid, John Anderson and William Leechman, then principal of the college, as well as Robert and Andrew Foulis, the printers to the university. But Boswell tells us that their conversation was not to Johnson's taste. The Foulis brothers, indeed, clearly upset their famous guest by arguing and answering back — 'I found that, instead of listening to the dictates of the sage, they had teased him with questions and doubtful disputations' — and Johnson had to turn to Boswell to cope with such an unprecedented situation. The university professors appear to have been more cautious; Boswell suggests that they were reluctant to expose themselves in conversation to Johnson's 'superior powers' (*Tour*, 365). Perhaps in truth, having learned from the Foulis experience, they were simply being polite.

These conversational encounters with the literati of the Glasgow Enlightenment may well lie behind Johnson's far from enthusiastic assessment of the Scottish universities. He allows that Glasgow and the other universities have chosen to divide up the academic year in a more rational manner than their English counterparts; but in all other respects the Scottish universities are deemed inferior. Because the Scottish grammar schools are in his view inadequate, students entering university are too young and ill-prepared. Johnson concludes:

> Men bred in the universities of *Scotland* cannot be expected to be often decorated with the splendours of ornamental erudition, but they obtain a mediocrity of knowledge, between learning and ignorance, not inadequate to the purposes of common life, which is, I believe, very widely diffused among them, and which countenanced in general by a national combination so invidious, that their friends cannot defend it, and actuated in particulars by a spirit of enterprise, so vigorous, that their enemies are constrained to praise it, enables them to find, or to make their way to employment, riches, and distinction. (*Journey*, 134)

This complex sentence finally draws a distinction between knowledge pursued for its own sake and knowledge put to use. The emotional thrust of the passage seems to require us to acknowledge the 'mediocrity' of the more utilitarian approach to learning. Yet the actual language employed seems almost to undermine that position: 'the splendours of ornamental erudition' do not appear to be self-evidently more valuable than the kind of knowledge which, allied to 'a spirit of enterprise', allows men bred in the Scottish universities to gain the strongly positive benefits of 'employment, riches, and distinction'.

In spite of Johnson, and a stubborn preoccupation with internal bickering and litigation among the faculty, the University of Glasgow was certainly one of the leading academic centres of the Enlightenment in eighteenth-century Europe. It was also impressive physically, as Henry Wyndham's letter to his father of 25 July 1758 makes clear. After briefly describing Glasgow Cathedral and 'the stately remains of the Arch Bishop's Palace', he continues:

> But the chief ornament of the Town is the College. It consists of 3 neat Courts & has a pretty front towards the street. The members of the College are 16 Professors & about 300 students. Here is no Chapell or common Hall as at Oxford for the Students to attend, but ev'ry member dines & lodges where he pleases, & is only expected to be present at the proper Lectures. Over the entrance of this College in a long Room is an extraordinary good collection of all the best old Painter's pictures. Painting is very much encourag'd here, for there is a school on purpose for it, another for Sculpture & another for Engraving.[19]

At the time of Wyndham's visit, there were actually only twelve academic chairs at Glasgow University, but if one counts the principal, an important lectureship in chemistry and the lecturers in the Foulis brothers' affiliated fine arts academy, to which Wyndham drew his father's attention, the figure of sixteen professors is near enough the truth. The professors included such luminaries as Adam Smith in moral philosophy, Joseph Black in medicine, James Moor in Greek, John Anderson in natural philosophy, Robert Simson in mathematics and William Leechman in divinity. By the time of Johnson's visit in October 1773, Smith, Black and Simson were gone; but Leechman had become principal, and the university could now boast of Thomas Reid in the moral philosophy chair, James Williamson in mathematics, William Richardson in humanity, William Wight in church history, John Millar in civil law, William Irvine in chemistry and Alexander Wilson in the new chair of practical astronomy.

III

THE ENLIGHTENMENT AT GLASGOW, then, even more than at Edinburgh, appears to have been centred around the university. Accordingly, the first part of this volume focuses on the academic component of Glasgow's Enlightenment. The composition of the Glasgow professoriate and the ways in which Glasgow professors obtained their academic positions, thanks in large measure to enlightened patrons such as Lord Ilay, third duke of Argyll, is the subject of the book's opening essay, by Roger L. Emerson. The authors of chapters 2–7 focus on aspects of particular Glasgow professors during the age of the Enlightenment: Thomas P. Miller on the civic humanist rhetoric of the Irish 'father' of the Glasgow Enlightenment, Francis Hutcheson; Thomas D. Kennedy on the divinity teaching and pious character of Hutcheson's protégé and friend, William Leechman; Ian Simpson Ross on the Glasgow years of the university's brightest light, Adam Smith; Kathleen Holcomb on the contributions of Thomas Reid to the university's philosophical club, the Glasgow Literary Society; Paul Wood on the scientific outlook of the much-maligned professor of natural philosophy, John Anderson; and John W. Cairns on the remarkable achievement of John Millar as a one-man school of law. In keeping with the general purpose of the book, the aim of these chapters is not to present comprehensive analyses of the theories of important thinkers but rather to explore some of the ways in which the lives, teachings, ideas and outlooks of prominent Glasgow professors can be used to enhance our understanding of the distinctive academic culture that existed at Glasgow University during the eighteenth century.

Henry Wyndham may have slightly underestimated the number of students attending Glasgow University in the 1750s,[20] but his comments on the freedom of students to dine and lodge where they please are accurate and significant. The urban character of Scottish universities like Glasgow and Edinburgh was largely responsible for this feature, so different from the residential system that Wyndham had known at Oxford. Samuel Rose found this freedom to his liking but wondered whether he would have fared as well had he studied at Edinburgh, where a bigger and more varied metropolis offered diversions that could easily lead unsupervised students astray:

> I cannot sufficiently rejoice at my Good-fortune, in residing at Glasgow instead of Edinburgh. In the former of the places I meet with no temptations to which I should not be exposed in the most retired situations. A student, who prosecutes his Studies with attention and diligence at Edinburgh must possess the greatest degree of fortitude, self denial, and Resolution. Since that place abounds with many Amusements, and avocations from Business, . . . the greatest praise is due to that young man, who performs his college-Business without stumbling.[21]

No wonder that Alexander Boswell, Lord Auchinleck abruptly transferred his son James to Glasgow University in 1759, after the younger Boswell had rebelled against his father by taking up with stage-players and Roman Catholics while a student at Edinburgh. After matriculating at Glasgow, Boswell came under the unlikely influence of Adam Smith, establishing a relationship that, according to Gordon Turnbull's chapter in this volume, had an influence on the pupil which lasted far beyond his student days.

If Boswell was an outsider who spent a short but perhaps significant time at Glasgow University, Dr John Moore was a native who left Glasgow in part because he could not get a position in the university there. In his chapter on Moore in this volume, H. L. Fulton provides a look at the Glasgow medical profession from the standpoint of a medical man who had literary ambitions that Glasgow simply could not fulfill. Like his kinsman and biographical subject, Tobias Smollett, Moore became a Glaswegian cultural exile — first on the Continent and subsequently in London. His initial decision to give up his medical practice in Glasgow was prompted by a generous offer to become travelling tutor to the duke of Hamilton at £300 a year for life, but the decision not to settle there permanently after his tutoring days were over had deeper foundations that were both social and intellectual. The imaginative literature that Smollett and Moore wished to write was never Glasgow's strong suit. Yet by the 1770s and 1780s Glasgow itself was a modest source of poetic inspiration, as men such as John Mayne and Robert Galloway put their visions of the city into verse. Their poetic images of Glasgow form the subject of Richard B. Sher's chapter in this book.

We have seen that in one way or another both Wyndham in 1758 and Johnson in 1773 encountered the remarkable Foulis brothers, who not only dominated the Glasgow book trade during the third quarter of the eighteenth century but also established in Glasgow a short-lived fine arts academy for painting, sculpture and engraving. These seemingly unrelated activities were in fact closely connected. As printers and publishers, the Foulis brothers were famous for their magnificent editions of the classics, such as their splendid folio editions of the *Iliad* and *Odyssey* (1756–58). Such books were truly works of art. On the other hand, the great majority of the Foulis brothers' book output consisted not of sumptuous showcase quartos and folios but of workmanlike octavo and duodecimo editions of classical and modern authors. Prominent among the latter were their mentor Francis Hutcheson and another of Hutcheson's protégés, William Leechman, whose moderate occasional sermons were among the most frequently printed works on the Foulis list. It can be argued that the Foulis brothers' achievement was to translate into print culture the values of the classical, aesthetic, moralistic, Hutchesonian Enlightenment in Glasgow.[22]

The development of Enlightenment print culture by the Foulis brothers and a handful of other Glasgow printers and booksellers, such as Robert Urie, was notable, but so was the rise of evangelical print culture associated with devout Presbyterian printers and booksellers such as John Bryce, Glasgow's most active producer and purveyor of pious Calvinist books and pamphlets. In a career that stretched from the 1740s through the mid-1780s, Bryce had his name in the imprint of well over two hundred titles. Only a handful of them were not religious or ecclesiastical in nature. More than thirty of his titles were works by Ralph or Ebenezer Erskine, the leading mid-eighteenth-century seceders from the Church of Scotland in the name of evangelical Calvinist purity. Pious sixteenth- and seventeenth-century authors were also popular, and larger works, such as John Howie's account of Scottish Presbyterian 'worthies', *Biographica Scoticana* (1775), were sometimes published by subscription, with pious Paisley weavers and other workers and tradesmen from the Glasgow region making up a large proportion of the subscribers. Bryce printed pamphlets directed against Roman Catholic relief and against the dreaded law of ecclesiastical patronage, which, by giving patrons the power to nominate or present parish ministers, effectively deprived local heritors, elders and congregations of an active voice in the ministerial selection process. And he printed several works having to do with America, including the previously mentioned *Collection of the Constitutions of the Thirteen United States of North America*, as well as critical speeches on the Union of Parliaments by Lord Belhaven, the Scottish Presbyterian patriot, whose writings were deemed 'Very Necessary for These Times' on the title page of Bryce's 1784 edition.[23]

What this added up to was a commitment to a radical, pious, evangelical brand of Scottish Presbyterianism that was particularly strong in Glasgow and the West of Scotland, just as it was unusually weak in the more Episcopalian and Jacobite Northeast. When the common sense philosopher and moderate Presbyterian minister Thomas Reid left Aberdeen to replace Adam Smith as professor of moral philosophy at Glasgow in 1764, he was startled at the extent to which the 'common people' of Glasgow were involved in religion of 'a gloomy, enthusiastical cast'.[24] Within a year he was telling the same correspondent in Aberdeen that the clergy of Glasgow worked to keep the common people 'fanatical in their religion' (13 July 1765, *Works*, 1:41). Had Reid gone to Glasgow about twenty years earlier, when enthusiasm over the Cambuslang Revival was at its height, he would have been still more distressed at the intensity of popular Presbyterianism in the Glasgow vicinity. From the seventeenth through the eighteenth centuries, America, Ulster and greater Glasgow experienced a remarkable transatlantic upsurge of evangelical Calvinism that had no equivalent in Edinburgh and Aberdeen.[25] From an east-coast perspective, the 'holy fairs' and mass conversions of the early 1740s sometimes seemed to be little more than mass hysteria, and it is noteworthy that one of the most popular orthodox Presbyterian pamphlets of the age, the anonymous *Letter from a Blacksmith to the Ministers and Elders of the Kirk of Scotland* of 1758, was directed against revivalism.

The intensity and extent of evangelical Presbyterianism in Glasgow often worked against the Enlightenment. The theatre, for example, had a difficult time of it in Glasgow, and on more than one occasion pious zeal seems to have provoked acts of arson against playhouses there. Similarly, the Enlightenment's sacred principle of religious toleration was not always popular in Glasgow, which became the centre of Scottish opposition to the modest proposals for Roman Catholic relief that came under consideration during the late 1770s. In religion as in commerce, however, a simplistic dichotomy of light versus darkness fails to capture the complexity of the situation. Despite their opposition to some of the principles of the Enlightenment, Popular party clergymen in the Glasgow vicinity were often among the most aggressive spokesmen for principles of liberty, both at home and in the colonies. In his chapter on contested clerical calls, Ned C. Landsman further develops an argument, begun in two previous contributions to volumes in this series,[26] which contends that the evangelical Presbyterian movement in Glasgow and the West of Scotland constituted an alternative form of the Enlightenment rather than an anti-Enlightenment. Perhaps the most interesting figure in this context is William Thom, the tenacious foe of the Glasgow professoriate and the subject of the final chapter in this book, by Robert Kent Donovan. Landsman and Donovan force us to reconsider the relationship of enlightened principles and popular Presbyterian piety, with results that may pose a serious challenge to the prevailing conception of the Scottish Enlightenment as fundamentally academic and religiously moderate.

IV

OUR THREE ENGLISH VISITORS to Glasgow — Defoe in the 1720s, Wyndham in the 1750s and Johnson in the 1770s — encountered a city unlike any other. Prosperous from its burgeoning commerce, rapidly expanding in population and size, handsome in appearance, oriented towards the west, rich with clubs and bookshops, possessed of a fine university with a respectable philosophical or 'literary' society, and imbued with evangelical Presbyterianism in religion — Glasgow in the eighteenth century was a fascinating place. Depending on whom you asked, its inhabitants were characterized by industry and useful knowledge or greed and ignorance, by piety and devotion or fanaticism and bigotry. It was amid these dynamic, sometimes contradictory elements of urban growth, wealth, beauty, learning and piety, that the distinctive voices of the Glasgow Enlightenment could be heard.

Notes

1. P. B. Wood, *The Aberdeen Enlightenment: The Arts Curriculum in the Eighteenth Century* (Aberdeen, 1993); Roger L. Emerson, *Professors, Patronage and Politics: The Aberdeen Universities in the Eighteenth Century* (Aberdeen, 1992); *Aberdeen and the Enlightenment*, ed. Jennifer J. Carter and Joan H. Pittock (Aberdeen, 1987); *The Minutes of the Aberdeen Philosophical Society 1758–1773*, ed. H. Lewis Ulman (Aberdeen, 1990); Stephen A. Conrad, *Citizenship and Common Sense: The Problem of Authority in the Social Background and Social Philosophy of the Wise Club of Aberdeen* (New York, 1987).

2. See, however, R. H. Campbell, 'Scotland's Neglected Enlightenment', *History Today* 40 (1990): 22–28, and David Daiches, *Glasgow* (London, 1982), chaps. 6 and 7. Richard B. Sher, 'Commerce, Religion and the Enlightenment in Eighteenth-Century Glasgow', in *The History of Glasgow*, vol. 1, ed. T. M. Devine and Gordon Jackson (Manchester, 1995) contains a fuller account of several of the topics discussed in this Introduction, and the book in which it appears provides the most complete and up-to-date coverage of the story of Glasgow in the eighteenth century.

3. See the demographic charts in T. C. Smout, *A History of the Scottish People 1560–1830* (London, 1969), 243.

4. Frank Arneil Walker, 'The Glasgow Grid', in *Order in Space and Society: Architectural Form and Its Context in the Scottish Enlightenment*, ed. Thomas A. Markus (Edinburgh, 1982), 155–99; Andrew Gibb, *Glasgow: The Making of a City* (London, 1983), 95.

5. David J. McLaren, *David Dale of New Lanark* (Milngavie, 1983); Ian Donnachie and George Hewitt, *Historic New Lanark: The Dale and Owen Industrial Community since 1785* (Edinburgh, 1993).

6. Daniel Defoe, *A Tour through the Whole Island of Great Britain* (Harmondsworth, 1971), 605, 610.

7. T. M. Devine, *The Tobacco Lords: A Study of the Tobacco Merchants of Glasgow and their Trading Activities, c. 1740–90* (Edinburgh, 1975); Carolyn Marie Peters, 'Glasgow's Tobacco Lords: An Examination of Wealth Creators in the Eighteenth Century' (Ph.D. thesis, Glasgow University, 1990).

8. William Brock, *Scotus Americanus: A Survey of the Sources for Links between Scotland and America in the Eighteenth Century* (Edinburgh, 1982); *Scotland and America in the Age of the Enlightenment*, ed. Richard B. Sher and Jeffrey R. Smitten (Edinburgh, *1990*); Andrew Hook, *Scotland and America: A Study of Cultural Relations, 1750–1835* (Glasgow, 1975).

9. See Andrew Hook, 'Philadelphia, Edinburgh and the Scottish Enlightenment', in *Scotland and America*, ed. Sher and Smitten, 227–41.

10. Brock, *Scotus Americanus*, 19. According to Devine, *Tobacco Lords*, 8, 'between 1728 and 1800 . . . at least sixty-eight tobacco and West Indies merchants had been students at Glasgow University.'

11. John Strang, *Glasgow and Its Clubs* (Glasgow, 1856), 43–66, 120–22; Daiches, *Glasgow*, 70–72; Davis D. McElroy, *Scotland's Age of Improvement: A Survey of Eighteenth-Century Literary Clubs and Societies* (n.p., 1969), 162–64; *The Autobiography of Dr. Alexander Carlyle of Inveresk, 1722–1805*, new ed., ed. John Hill Burton (London and Edinburgh, 1910), 81–82.

12. Richard B. Sher, 'Wyndham's Letters on Scotland and Northern England, 1758', *Yale University Library Gazette* 65 (1991): 146–58, quoting 150 and 152. Wyndham's population estimate of 50,000 people is unusually high, and no source is given for it.

13. Tobias Smollett, *The Expedition of Humphry Clinker*, ed. Thomas R. Preston (Athens, Ga., 1990), 238–39, 230. Smollett himself was no stranger to Glasgow, having been born and raised in nearby Dunbartonshire, and educated and apprenticed in Glasgow itself.

14. John Gibson, *The History of Glasgow, from the Earliest Accounts to the Present Time* (Glasgow, 1777), 115, 120.

15. Adam Smith, *An Inquiry into the Nature and Causes of the Wealth of Nations*, ed. R. H. Campbell, A. S. Skinner, and W. B. Todd, 2 vols. (Oxford, 1976), 1:267, and n. 12. See John Dwyer, 'Adam Smith in the Scottish Enlightenment', in *Adam Smith: International Perspectives*, ed. Hiroshi Mizuta and Chuhei Sugiyama (London, 1993), 153–54.

16. Richardson to Rose, 1 Jan. 1787, and Rose to ?, 24 Feb. 1784, Samuel Rose Papers, GUL, uncatalogued. The rough treatment accorded to Millar on this occasion was supposedly the first time that hissing was heard at a public meeting in Glasgow. See Henry W. Meikle, *Scotland and the French Revolution* (Glasgow, 1912), 5.

17. *Boswell's Journal of a Tour to the Hebrides with Samuel Johnson, 1773*, ed. Frederick A. Pottle and Charles H. Bennett, new ed. (New York, 1961), 364.

18. Samuel Johnson, *A Journey to the Western Islands of Scotland*, ed. J. D. Fleeman (Oxford, 1985), 133.

19. Sher, 'Wyndham's Letters', 152. In this letter Wyndham also discusses the college's impressive collection of Roman antiquities.

20. Roger L. Emerson, 'Scottish Universities in the Eighteenth Century, 1690–1800', *Studies on Voltaire and the Eighteenth Century* 167 (1977): 473, accepts Henry Grey Graham's figure of four hundred students in 1750. We are probably safe to say that the actual number of students during the 1750s lay between three and four hundred.

21. Samuel Rose to ?, 20 Jan. 1784, Samuel Rose Papers, GUL, uncatalogued.

22. This argument is developed in Sher, 'Commerce, Religion, and the Enlightenment in Eighteenth-Century Glasgow'.

23. John Hamilton, Baron Belhaven, *A Speech of Lord Belhaven, in the Scotch Parliament, at the Making of the Union* (Glasgow, 1780) and *The Late Lord Belhaven's Memorable Speeches in the Last Parliament of Scotland, Holden at Edinburgh, in November 1706, on the Subject-Matter of the then Projected Union of Both Kingdoms. . . With an Occasional Preface, by the Editor. Very Necessary for These Times* (Glasgow, 1784). On Bryce and evangelical publishing generally, see Ned C. Landsman, 'Presbyterians and Provincial Society: The Evangelical Enlightenment in the West of Scotland, 1740–1775', in *Sociability and Society in Eighteenth-Century Scotland*, ed. John Dwyer and Richard B. Sher (Edinburgh, 1993), 194–209, esp. 199–200.

24. Reid to Andrew Skene, 14 Nov. 1764, in Reid's *Philosophical Works*, ed. Sir William Hamilton, 2 vols. (1895; rpt. Hildesheim, 1967), 1:40.

25. Leigh Eric Schmidt, 'Sacramental Occasions and the Scottish Context of Presbyterian Revivalism in America', in *Scotland and America*, ed. Sher and Smitten, 65–80, and *Holy Fairs: Scottish Communions and American Revivals in the Early Modern Period* (Princeton, 1989); Marilyn J. Westerkamp, *Triumph of the Laity: Scots-Irish Piety and the Great Awakening* (New York, 1988); Arthur Fawcett, *The Cambuslang Revival: The Scottish Evangelical Revival of the Eighteenth Century* (London, 1971).

26. Landsman, 'Presbyterians and Provincial Society', and 'Witherspoon and the Problem of Provincial Identity in Scottish Evangelical Culture', in *Scotland and America*, ed. Sher and Smitten, 29–45.

PART I

The University and Enlightenment Culture

I

Politics and the Glasgow Professors, 1690–1800

Roger L. Emerson

The cultural politics of eighteenth-century Scotland focused principally on two related sets of institutions: those of the established church and those of the schools, including the colleges and universities. In both sets the determination of policy and the recruitment of staff slipped after 1690 from the hands of clerics into those of laymen, especially politicians.[1]

In the kirk, this process began in 1690 with the Erastian settlement imposed by William and his advisors, who were not willing to follow the extreme policies urged upon them by devout and fanatical elements. By 1712 the Barrier Act (1697) and the Toleration and Patronage Acts (1712) had restored the process of recruitment to the gentry, prevented the zealous and bigotted from harrassing dissidents, and made it difficult for a popular party to dominate the church. Increasingly, political manipulation of presbyteries, synods and the annual General Assembly imposed moderation on the kirk. The cases brought against the Glasgow divinity professor John Simson on grounds of heresy (1714–29), the various secessions (e.g., 1733, 1761), the failure of strict Presbyterians to discipline the three Homes (John, Henry and David Hume) for their philosophical and theatrical indiscretions during the 1750s, and the ability to use the church for the purposes of government, which was so greatly facilitated by the Moderates after the mid-1750s, all point to the kirk's loss of independence. As this happened its clergy also changed, but not in ways the Moderates had expected. The failure of the heritors and taxpayers to raise clerical stipends lowered the quality of the ministers and let into the parishes men whose social antecedents made them more docile and deferential towards those who had appointed them.

In the schools something similar happened. Those founded and staffed by the Scottish Society for the Propagation of Christian Knowledge (SSPCK) imposed anglicizers upon reluctant Highland parishes. Lowland heritors tended to employ and pay right-thinking young men, many of whom would trim their views because they aspired to promotion into better livings in the kirk. In the colleges and universities the pressures were equally clear. These institutions were visited between 1690 and 1702 by a parliamentary visitation commission, a committee of which attempted to standardize a new and reformed curriculum. Further visitations were contemplated in 1708 at St Andrews,[2] and were carried out in 1716–17 at Aberdeen, 1717–18 at St Andrews and Glasgow, and again in 1726–27 at Glasgow. Similar political interference was sought by Foxite Whigs such as the earl of Buchan at Edinburgh in 1782–83, Professor John Anderson at Glasgow in 1783–84, and Buchan's friend William Ogilvie at Aberdeen in 1786.[3].

The Crown increased its ability to interfere in collegiate matters by awarding grants that were usually of limited duration or contingent upon the life of the monarch. At Glasgow, these are to be seen in the grant of the tack of Bishop's teinds, in Queen Anne's Bounty and other particular grants that lapsed with the death of the sovereign, and in other sinecure offices used to reward academics. The establishment of regius chairs, grants for facilities and extraordinary purchases and favours, such as the making of their libraries deposit libraries for copyrighted materials, all showed the increasing reliance of the universities upon the state. But nowhere was this dependence more apparent than in appointments. As the real value of university livings at Glasgow rose on average from about £100 per annum to over £200,[4] the concern to control these positions grew and became rooted in considerations other than ideology and orthodoxy in religion and politics. The politicians were eager to monopolize such patronage; and, as they organized increasingly effective machines, they were able to do so. None did so better than Archibald Campbell, first earl of Ilay and, after 1743, third duke of Argyll (1682–1761), and Henry Dundas, first Viscount Melville (1742–1811). When there were no strong political managers, however, corporations like Glasgow University went their own ways and talked of their independence.

In the long run, the politics of the church and the universities were tremendously important because they shaped the attitudes, values and ideas of Scots, particularly those of the educated élite. It is extremely difficult to believe that Scots would have exhibited so much interest in improvements, science and technology, politeness and enlightenment had not patronage in the kirk and schools come to rest in the hands of many individuals who were already committed to those ends because they saw them as intrinsically good or as necessary to the making of political careers in a British state. The pressures to control zealous Presbyterians in 1712 came from Anglicans more than Scottish Episcopalians, and the need to exercise moderation in the church was also as much English as Scottish. The politicians favoured by the English were the polite, cultivated men already like their better selves, but also men whose positions in Scotland made them capable of securing political support for Whig governments and, after 1707, for a United Kingdom.

This is not to say that the roots of the Scottish Enlightenment were

English, but it is to suggest that English political needs and pressures made it possible for men like William Carstares; James Ogilvy, first earl of Seafield; John Kerr, first duke of Roxburghe; John Hay, second marquis of Tweeddale; Ilay and others to come to power and to place in the church and universities men who shared their outlooks and aspirations. Ilay, the most effective of these men, became the great creator of the Scottish Enlightenment because politics required someone like him — a capable organizer with both Highland and Lowland connections who could get things done. It was largely accidental that this great patron was also a lover of learning, an amateur scientist and an enthusiastic improver who liked the company of intellectuals, or that he came to power in the early 1720s.

I

BETWEEN 1690 AND 1704, Scottish political factions fell into court and country parties that looked to 'great men' for leadership. By 1705 one fairly stable political group, the Squadrone, had emerged under the leadership of the first dukes of Montrose and Roxburghe, in whose wake followed the second marquis of Tweeddale, the earls of Rothes, Leslie, Melville, Leven, Marchmont and Haddington, and lairds such as Maxwell of Pollock, Dundas of Arniston, Baillie of Jarviswood and a host of related men whose acres were more or less broad. During the debates over the Union of 1707, the Squadrone tended to pursue a policy of independence for a reformed Scotland. After the Union, for which most of its members voted, the Squadrone was sometimes in office but more often was allied with English country party politicians, with whom it was associated throughout most of the period of power enjoyed by Sir Robert Walpole (c. 1722–42). For most of that era, it was opposed in Scotland by the friends of the second and third dukes of Argyll. They formed a court party, which dominated Scottish politics between 1725 and 1742 and again from 1746 to 1760. Walpole and the Pelhams found the Argathelians indispensable. Although principles mattered to both these sets of Whigs, their lust for office and spoils mattered even more.

Every political manager in eighteenth-century Scotland sought to control as many places of honour, profit and power as he could. They all had interests in the universities' valuable livings as well as in what was said and done within their walls. The long-run effects of these concerns included keeping the colleges open to new ideas and responsive to the classes whose sons they educated. The Scottish colleges became not merely clerical institutions but also institutions engaged with a secular world that they sought to improve. If politicking in the universities produced some bitterness and litigation, it also produced progress. When Ilay sought to discipline Glasgow University in the mid-1720s, he also tried to raise its academic standards and to force its medical professors to teach. Moreover, most chairs created in the eighteenth-century universities were also founded in years when factions newly come to power, or threatened by opponents, were trying to consolidate their hold on institutions. In Glasgow, it seems likely that the chairs of law (1713), medicine (1714), ecclesiastical history (1716) and botany (1720) owed their creation at least in part to considerations of this sort.5

University politics were seldom as simple as naming a new professor. Even if the post was a regius chair, the Crown had probably been solicited by several important people whose candidates had at least to be considered. Other chairs involved legal patrons jealous of their rights to appoint, who would take suggestions only if it were clearly in their interest to do so. The kirk everywhere had a right to inquire into the religious beliefs and morals of prospective professors. Professors whose incomes depended on fees could be expected to oppose appointees likely to diminish enrolments. They were litigious, and that mattered. Academic recruitment was a matter for negotiation, but those who had to be consulted differed from one university to another, as becomes clear from a brief comparison of Edinburgh and Glasgow.

At Edinburgh, the town council was by 1800 the legal patron to eighteen of the university's twenty-six chairs, and it still protested appointments it did not make. The city fathers controlled the college funds and throughout most of the eighteenth century supervised the university through a town council committee chaired by the university or college bailie. The Senatus Academicus at Edinburgh counted for little before 1763. Even as late as 1789 that university had to seal its diplomas with 'one of the City Seals', a procedure described by its professor of Greek as 'inconvenient and unsuitable to the dignity of the University'.6

Glasgow knew nothing of such subservience to a merchant oligarchy. Its professors were also freer from interference by the town council than were those at Marischal College, Aberdeen where the professors of divinity and mathematics were chosen by the council, albeit after an allegedly open and competitive examination of candidates. There, too, the council had some say about the Crown's choice òf a principal because his salary was largely derived from a church living in the gift of the town. Although Glasgow's town fathers could and did act as trustees for some bursaries and other funds, they did not have much purchase on the college livings. Nevertheless, more sons of merchants and artisans held professorships at Glasgow between 1690 and 1800 than in any other Scottish university — a sign of the degree to which professorial recruitment was locally based.

Glasgow University also did not have to contend with powerful external corporations that could influence appointments to its chairs. Edinburgh judges, advocates and writers to the signet had a hand in appointments to the chair of humanity, and advocates had a say in appointing professors of history, civil law and Scots law. Lawyers were sometimes successful lobbyists for those seeking other chairs and often had some input into decisions about the regius chair of public law. By contrast, as John W. Cairns shows in chapter 7 below, Glasgow lawyers had no say about that university's regius chair, even though the regius professor's courses reflected concerns with the topics of extramural lecturers catering to the needs of Glasgow's legal writers (solicitors).

Similarly, the Glasgow Faculty of Physicians and Surgeons appears to have had no say about the appointees to medical chairs at the university, though they did have a role to play in the establishment of a botanical garden.[7] At Edinburgh, the Edinburgh Incorporation of Chirurgeons played a far more important role in the university: because they were the premier trade, and usually represented on the town council, the surgeons were heard when medical school appointments were made. The incorporation (known after 1779 as the Royal College) could also dictate with whom those 'booked' as servants and apprentices could study botany, anatomy and midwifery. Thus, the Edinburgh surgeons were in a position to render worthless any appointments to university chairs in those fields that were made without their consent. Since they also sponsored an extramural medical school for much of the eighteenth century, their recommendations were heeded.

So, too, were those made by the Royal College of Physicians. Between 1713 and 1724 they approved appointments made to Edinburgh medical chairs. After the 'founding' of the medical school in 1726, and especially after about 1740, there was simply too much money at stake for the Edinburgh city fathers to ignore the doctors.[8] From 1726 until 1778 the fellows of the Royal College of Physicians recommended to all the Edinburgh medical chairs and seem to have given in only one name when they did so. By contrast, Glasgow University's lecturers in chemistry (1747), *materia medica* (1766), and midwifery (1790) were chosen by its masters (i.e., those professors who managed the business of the college and university), and its two regius professors (anatomy and botany, and medicine) were usually men picked by the masters after consultations with politicians and medical men in Edinburgh. Because Glasgow University was free from the influence of local corporations, its medical chairs could be filled by outsiders without effective protests and obstruction from local medical men. Furthermore, Glasgow avoided costly and protracted struggles over appointments to the law chair, such as occurred at King's College, Aberdeen — struggles waged in part to preserve a sinecure post for a member of the Aberdeen Society of Advocates.

In Glasgow, only the presbytery and one of its ministers exercised by right an authority within the college; the Minister of Glasgow was *ex officio* a Visitor. In addition, every new professor had to sign the Westminster Confession of Faith before the presbytery — a requirement that embarrassed William Leechman and may have cost David Hume his prospects of a professorship in the college.9 Some of the problems encountered between 1714 and 1729 by John Simson, the professor of divinity, emanated from the presbytery and synod, which resented the university's assertion of corporate privilege to protect an unsound if not heretical teacher of divinity.10 Here Glasgow University did resemble its companion institutions, which had experienced similar difficulties. It was doubtless a sign of changing times that Simson was not deprived of his academic salary and that elsewhere Alexander Scrimgeour (1713–32), John Lumdsden (1733–35), William Wishart (1736–38) and Archibald Campbell (1736) all survived attacks upon them by local clerics, thanks to politicians eager to keep the kirk quiescent.11

Glasgow University also had a unique relationship to the local gentry. At the beginning of our period, the Earl Marischal named six of the eight professors in what was very much his college at Aberdeen. After 1717, these rights were vested in the Crown, which used its patronage power during the political regimes of the first duke of Roxburghe (1715–23), Ilay (1724–42, 1746–61) and Henry Dundas (c. 1778–1805) to control the burgh's parliamentary vote, and occasionally to gratify a local aristocrat. At neighbouring King's College, most professors throughout the period 1690–1717 were related to local landed families — Middletons, Frasers, Moirs, Gregories, Gordons, Urquharts — or owned small properties themselves. From 1704 to 1715 new professors were recruited from the dependents of the Jacobite earls of Erroll or from Whig families named Gordon and Grant. This state of affairs continued throughout much of the century, with 41 percent of King's men showing relations to the landed classes — the highest percentage of all the universities and more than twice that of their counterparts at Glasgow.

At St Andrews, genteel private patrons such as the Kennedys of Cassillis and the Scotts of Scotstarvit appointed to two chairs that served as springboards to more lucrative ones. Correspondence regarding other posts often came from the earls of Crawford, Rothes, Haddington and Kinnoull, and from untitled landed families in Fifeshire. Other influences can be inferred from the fact that about half the St Andrews professors themselves came either from landed families or from cadet branches that had declined into the ministry or professoriate; hence the prominence of Craigies, Pitcairnes, Hadows, Haldanes, Ramsays, Tullidelphs, Hills and Cooks, who filled chairs in more than one generation. At Edinburgh, where the professorial recruitment pool was national and not local, the landed gentry furnished nearly a third of the professors.

This situation may explain why throughout the century Glasgow University was less concerned with agrarian issues and more oriented towards the professions and polite subjects. But Glasgow teachers had served the gentry more than those elsewhere, even if they had not come from its ranks. One indicator is that fully 32 percent of Glasgow's professors had earlier tutored or taught aristocratic boys. Elsewhere this figure does not appear to have risen above 17 percent, and at Edinburgh only 14 percent, for the period 1690–1800. This circumstance may explain why until about 1760 Glasgow College had a better reputation than the other arts colleges, and why it is said to have educated more aristocratic boys. Since many of the tutors had also travelled with their charges, it is not surprising that far more Glasgow professors throughout this period are known to have been abroad (60%) than those who taught elsewhere in Scotland (c. 24%).

At Glasgow, particularly after about 1725, no one local family or set of families could dominate the college. Although the dukes of Montrose were chancellors for four long generations (1714–1875), in our period no member of that family lectured in any classroom. The dukes and other gentlemen belonging to the Squadrone party placed protégés in the university, but no one family monopolized places in the Glasgow corporations, not even the powerful Campbells of Argyll. Because the college meeting (the masters) and the senate (the masters plus the rector and dean of faculty) were strong and capable of independent action, outside interference tended to come through the managers of the Scottish political factions and their Edinburgh deputies or, at both ends of the eighteenth century, through politically important chancellors. These men could argue and persuade, but appointments arranged by them had to pay a decent regard to professorial interest as well as to the demands of clamorous political supporters outside the college. At St Andrews, which in many ways resembled Glasgow, professorial poverty and the fact that the Crown appointed to the most prestigious and lucrative livings — the principalships and the divinity chairs — meant that the faculty could not resist pressures the way Glasgow professors sometimes did.

If masters at Glasgow appointed men favoured by politicians, professors in return got pensions, sinecure offices and sometimes appointments to better chairs. They also did fairly well for their children, though less well for other relatives. At King's, 78 percent of the masters were related to someone who taught with them or who recently had preceeded them as a teacher in the college; neighbouring Marischal, at 40 percent, had the low figure for our period. The frequency of such appointments was almost as low at Glasgow (42%), and most of them occurred during the first quarter of the century, when Principal Stirling and his friends in the kirk and the Squadrone party built up an interest in the college that was familial as well as ideological. Ilay's visitations of Glasgow in 1726 and 1727 were aimed at breaking this Squadrone-connected interest; he had been, and continued to be, engaged at Aberdeen and Edinburgh on similar tasks.

The recruitment pattern of Glasgow's professors from 1690 to 1800 reflects what has been said above. Only one of its seventy-eight professors seems to have been a lawyer's son. Very few had fathers who were physicians (12%) or surgeons (8%), and even fewer were the sons of civil officials (4%). None of the professors came from titled families who used their titles but, as the century wore on, a small but increasing number were drawn from landed and merchant backgrounds (20%), sometimes from the intersect of those groups. Over a third of the professors had clerical fathers — roughly the Scottish average if King's College is excluded.[12] Glasgow, too, had had some academic inbreeding: eleven men (38%) born before 1700 were related to at least one other professor teaching during their tenure in a chair. The comparable figures elsewhere were higher: 50 percent at King's, 47 percent at Edinburgh and 41 percent at St Andrews. For men born after 1700, the proportion at Glasgow fell to 10 percent, while remaining generally higher elsewhere: 59 percent at King's, 32 percent at St Andrews, 23 percent at Marischal and 15 percent at Edinburgh. Glasgow's openness was due largely to the meddling of politicians and to the decline of the Squadrone party after 1725. Although Glasgow University could be autonomous, there was more to be gained by co-operation with 'great men' like Montrose or Ilay.

II

I SHALL NOW LOOK more closely at the clerical and lay politicians who shaped Glasgow during the eighteenth century. The Revolution of 1688–89 brought to power one brilliant clerical politician, William Carstares. He was a moderate evangelical, a fairly tolerant and reasonable man of wide interests, a reformer and improver whose model universities were Dutch. Carstares's outlook was to affect more than the kirk and Edinburgh University, of which he became principal in 1703. In 1690 his brother-in-law, William Dunlop, became principal of Glasgow University and Carstares's man on the scene. By 1715, when Carstares died, he had a nephew each at Glasgow (Alexander Dunlop, professor of Greek) and Edinburgh (William Dunlop, professor of ecclessiatical history), a brother-in-law at St Leonard's College, St Andrews (Principal Joseph Drew) and a clutch of distant relatives and relations by marriage, including at least half the professors at Glasgow. By 1720 the principal of Glasgow University, John Stirling, was at the centre of this connection, with kinship ties to seven of the professors there.

Under the influence and during the regime of Carstares at Edinburgh, there were a number of new initiatives in teaching. Ecclessiastical history was taught after 1702, and Carstares attempted to found 'a History Professorship' in 1707. The principal managed to create a professorship of civil law in 1710 and three years later the first permanent chair of medicine — the professorship of chemistry and medicine. Carstares's emulous friends at Glasgow did as much, founding a professorship of history in 1716 and others in botany (1704, 1720), law (1713) and medicine (1714). Both colleges acquired better botanical gardens and new collections of instruments, Edinburgh in 1708, Glasgow around 1712.[13] Both found men excited by the new science and able to teach it with enthusiasm: Robert Steuart at Edinburgh and Robert Simson and Robert Dick the elder at Glasgow. Both colleges sought to modernize and expand in order to attract students from England and Ireland, and both recognized that a politer and more useful kind of education would have to be created. That ideal found an exemplum in the Glasgow humanity course of Andrew Ross.[14] No doubt some of these developments would have come about anyway, as the institutions sought to make themselves attractive to students; but some were the result of Carstares's influence, which was felt more at Glasgow than anywhere else outside Edinburgh.

As Carstares and his friends built up a following in the universities, they also created their own 'patriot party' or Squadrone interest, which would long be loyal to politicians following the first duke of Montrose and his successor, the first duke of Roxburghe.[15] Montrose became chancellor of Glasgow University in 1714. He joined an institution whose rector since 1691 had been Sir John Maxwell of Pollock, and whose vice-rector was a Squadrone lawyer and judge, Mungo Graham of Gorthy, a cadet of the duke's family. Pollock was also related to Principal Stirling; the duke placed more than one protégé in the college. The deans of faculty in these years, usually local ministers, also tended to have relatives in the college and to be under obligation to the local Squadrone gentry. When the Squadrone party was ousted from the exercise of patronage by the Argathelians between 1721 and 1725, the college was upset. The visitations of 1726 and 1727 and the threats to extrude Professors Anderson (Montrose's old tutor), Brisbane and Johnston were meant to cow a recalcitrant majority.[16] In 1727 the appointment of Neil Campbell to the principalship wrested control of the college meeting from unfriendly hands. Alexander Dunlop and possibly Andrew Ross were bought, and the appointment of Francis Hutcheson in 1729 consolidated the Argathelian hold on this college, where only one other appointment would be made before 1740. Factionalism would flare up again in disputes over the divinity chair in 1740 and 1743, but from 1725 until his death in 1761 Ilay was the chief patron and guide of his *alma mater*.

Scotland was fortunate to have had for so many years a politician of the calibre of Ilay involved in the bestowal of patronage.[17] He was a tolerant, humane, practical, compromising and improving sort of man whose temper was generally unruffled and whose own interests and knowledge made him a good judge of those who sought chairs of classical languages, mathematics, natural philosophy, medicine, law and fields related to these specialties. Ilay had no great liking for clerics — he called them 'Levites' — but the men who formed the leadership of the Moderate Party in the kirk were mostly noticed and patronized by him before 1760–61, when they became protégés of his nephew, the third earl of Bute.[18] Among them were Robert Hamilton, Adam Ferguson,

William Wilkie, William Robertson, Alexander Carlyle, John Home and John Jardine. All had approached him about jobs in the universities by 1759, and three of them (Ferguson, Wilkie and Robertson) had sought a Glasgow post. Three had been rewarded elsewhere; two had obtained Edinburgh pulpits.

Ilay was the chief broker for Scottish university chairs. Between 1723 and 1761 he is known to have had a hand in at least fifty-five appointments, including twenty at Glasgow, and he tried to prevent several more there (see Appendix). Another thirty or so men he permanently kept out of the universities. But Ilay's attentions went beyond patronage. In the 1720s his friends forced Glasgow College to 'fix' its professors to specialized chairs. Later he helped the university to secure funds and saw to it that some professors — at least Principal Neil Campbell and Alexander Dunlop — got pensions.[19] He was clearly friendly with 'Robin' Simson, with whom he discussed mathematics.[20] He encouraged the Foulis brothers' press and inveigled its typefounder, Alexander Wilson, to settle and remain in Glasgow, eventually creating for him the chair of practical astronomy (1760).[21] The duke probably gave plants to the botanical garden (Boney, *Lost Gardens*, 88), and he helped the masters to sort out their dispute with Balliol College, Oxford, concerning the Snell Exhibitions. It was appropriate for Carlo Denina to observe in 1768 that the duke 'patronized the ingenious with a bounty worthy of himself, and paid particular attention to the University of Glasgow, which has since become one of the most renowned in Europe'.[22]

Ilay's importance as an academic patron at Glasgow can be traced in the papers of his Edinburgh *sous-ministre*, Andrew Fletcher, Lord Milton, and in manuscripts at Glasgow. Between 1717 and 1762, thirty-four academic appointments going to eighteen individuals were made in the college or university. Discussions of all but five of the appointments show up in Lord Milton's papers. In three or four cases Ilay opposed the men ultimately chosen by Squadrone politicians between 1742 and 1746.[23] In at least twenty-five cases men were appointed with his blessings, sometimes because they were his choices. Over the years men with his countenance filled every chair but that of divinity, and did so on average for better than ten years per appointment. In 1761 only three of the fifteen professors in the university did not owe their places to Ilay.

Many of the professors also shared his interests. Robert Simson dedicated to him a mathematical book. James Moor, James Buchanan, James Williamson and probably John Anderson were also mathematicians whom the duke helped. Ilay was an amateur chemist who botanized and concocted his own medicines. It was fitting that William Cullen got his chair in 1750 with the duke's aid and that Joseph Black's regius appointments in 1756 and 1757 were secured by him. Though Thomas and Robert Hamilton belonged to a family which had sometimes opposed Argathelian interests, the duke was willing to promote these men in 1756 and 1757.

John Anderson was not his candidate for the chair of natural philosophy in 1757 because Ilay had hoped to find a better man, a 'young man of Genius and who had already acquired some reputation for Astronomy'.[24] The duke's choice seems to have been John Bevis, a London physician and astronomer. When the masters elected Anderson, the duke got a chair created for his old protégé, Alexander Wilson, who shared his interests in chemistry and who had long supplied him with scientific instruments. He was also friendly with three other men with some interests in science and furthered their careers: Robert Dick, Francis Hutcheson and Adam Smith.[25] Only after Ilay began to act as a patron at Glasgow did its medical school begin to flourish. His interests extended to history and law, and there, too, he patronized good men. William Ruat's surviving lecture notes suggest that he was a polite historian.[26] James Moor wrote about history,[27] as did Smith in both *The Theory of Moral Sentiments* and *The Wealth of Nations*.

Of the eighteen men whom Ilay allowed to come into the university, a surprisingly high number were, or later became, famous beyond the Glasgow region: Francis Hutcheson, James Moor, William Cullen, Adam Smith, Alexander Wilson and John Anderson (whose grandfather had been the tutor of the second duke of Argyll and whose father had held a kirk living in the duke's gift). All of them had some knowledge of science, and four were expert in either mathematics or a science of particular interest to Ilay. The latter's nephews, the third earl of Bute and James Stuart-Mackenzie, who followed him as the government's Scottish managers, continued to favour science and medicine at Edinburgh and Marischal College, where Bute became chancellor, but not at Glasgow, where there were few vacancies for them to fill.

After Ilay's death in 1761, control of Glasgow livings for nearly twenty years was divided between the masters and government functionaries such as Bute and Stuart-Mackenzie (1761–65) and William Mure of Caldwell (1765–76). Because of the instability of ministries in London, the masters found and exerted a new freedom. For science and medicine, the professors' patronage was of great importance. They kept alive the lectureship in chemistry begun in 1747 and bestowed it upon a succession of distinguished men: William Cullen, Joseph Black, John Robison, William Irvine, Thomas Charles Hope and Robert Cleghorn. As John Christie has pointed out, the first four of these scientists made it possible to carry out a sustained investigation of heat, one which constituted a paradigmatic research tradition in chemistry.[28] In 1766 the masters created a lectureship in *materia medica* for Irvine, who would be followed by Hope, Cleghorn and Richard Millar. Finally, in 1790 they completed their medical school with the appointment of John Tower to a lectureship of midwifery. All of these scientific and medical lectureships appear to have been filled without outside interference.

In 1756 even the regius chairs of medicine and botany went to men whom the masters had recommended — Joseph Black and Robert Hamilton. Ten years later Alexander Stevenson obtained the medicine chair through the influence of the masters and the Royal College of Physicians of Edinburgh.29 In the arts faculty, independence was used less creatively; there the professors arranged for themselves retirement deals of varying sweetness. These gratified some gentlemen with protégés to place and brought into the college George Jardine (logic, 1772), John Young (Greek, 1771), Hugh McLeod (ecclesiastical history, 1778) and Archibald Arthur (moral philosophy, 1780).30

By this time, however, the masters' days of independence at Glasgow University were nearly at an end, for Henry Dundas was then busy creating a political machine that would once again monopolize almost all the country's patronage. In 1781 the professors chose as their new chancellor James Graham, third duke of Montrose. The duke was a friend of Dundas and eager to be used. He began to intervene in appointments even before his own election, and he continued to do so throughout a long term of office that ended only in 1836.

The change in control of appointments was significant for the college generally, but it was especially so for the science chairs, three of which (botany, medicine and astronomy) were in the gift of the Crown. In the period 1780–84 the chancellor interfered in the filling of the astronomy and anatomy chairs. He opposed the appointment of Patrick Wilson to the former in 1782 and initiated a struggle with the faculty that ended in 1784, when Wilson was finally allowed to succeed his father, Alexander, who would resign for no one else.31 The anatomist in 1780, Thomas Hamilton, had been similarly positioned (Boney, *Lost Gardens*, 185–86). Once again an ageing professor had employed his son as an assistant with the faculty's permission. Here, too, the college was concerned to keep cultural property — specimens and preparations which, though not so valuable as the Wilson's type foundry and instruments, they did not wish to see sold outside Glasgow. Montrose acquiesced in their desires about Hamilton in 1781, as he would about Wilson three years later. In 1786, however, the principalship went not to the masters' choice, the Glasgow minister William Taylor, D.D. and Minister of Glasgow, but to Montrose's candidate, Archibald Davidson.32

From that point on, the masters were no longer able to control their own affairs. A concession was made to John Millar in 1789, when his son James succeeded James Williamson in the mathematics chair,33 but discipline tightened considerably with the French Revolution. Even men whom the masters had earlier elected to lectureships were now found suspect and ineligible for promotion. Most of the professors opposed the Revolution, but Reid, Millar, Anderson, Jardine and Arthur constituted a minority whose support for it divided the faculty. By the mid-1790s the college had split into a Whiggish party that wanted professorial independence within the corporation and a Tory group, led by the principal, which was willing to accept the leadership of Montrose and Henry Dundas. The result was a series of nasty contests in the latter 1790s.

In January 1796 James Brown was chosen professor of natural philosophy in a five-man race. Although the government's candidate did not win, his backers blocked the election of several men better than Brown, including John (later Sir John) Leslie, Thomas Jackson and Robert Cleghorn, then the lecturer in chemistry. Brown's election was unanimous, but against him at one time or another had been John and James Millar, James Mylne and Patrick Wilson, as well as Principal Davidson, William Richardson and the rest of the ministry's supporters (Robert Freer, Hugh McLeod and William MacTurk) — in all, nine of the twelve on the faculty.[34] Earlier that year Freer had been preferred over Cleghorn and James Jaffray for the chair of medicine. Something of the flavour of the times is captured in the following excerpt from a letter of George Jardine, the professor of logic:

> Dr. Cleghorn from a General conviction of his fitness, could almost have no Competitor even though it be in the Gift of the Crown — if it had not been [for] his alleged attachment to Modern Politics and his connexion with that Party here. This at present [25 January 1795] seems likely to cast the balance against him — though not absolutely certain. No General Recommendation on the above account and others could be got from the College — A majority but not without great opposition appointed him to teach the [medical] class in the meantime. Though I disapprove of his Politics, yet I was ready to support that point as the best recommendation we could give him, and some have no doubt blamed me for it — But I do not care — I can never allow Politicks to get the better of every consideration; and I was piqued that Dr. Jeffry with no other motive but to disappoint C. offered to teach the Class. We have now heard that a Dr. Freer from Edinburgh is likely to it.[35]

Three years later the political atmosphere had worsened. When Patrick Wilson resigned the astronomy chair in that year, he and six of his colleagues recommended Thomas Jackson as his successor. This recommendation was opposed by Principal Davidson and four others, who cast aspersions upon Jackson's loyalty and petitioned for the appointment of William Meikleham. Chancellor Montrose refused to transmit Jackson's name to the home secretary, and his candidacy failed.[36] Jackson later had a distinguished career at St Andrews, whereas Meikleham was a lacklustre professor who possessed the Glasgow chair until 1846.[37] Political interference of this sort was very different from that practised by Ilay or Bute, and it damaged all the Scottish universities during the 1790s. It also led to intramural bitterness and contention. The observations of George Jardine are once again interesting. His letters in 1800 and 1801 are full of politics and rumours concerning the real and alleged views of his colleagues and the chancellor. By mid-1801 he could write of the latter: 'Our Chancellor now is an absolute Dictator — and I have no kind of Connection with him.'[38] Glasgow University had been soured by politics.

III

EIGHTEENTH-CENTURY GLASGOW functioned in the same political world as the other Scottish universities, but its charter and location made it unique. Its professors were more often sons of the manse and the counting house than those elsewhere, and they came less often from the landed classes or the ranks of artisans and farmers. They tended to be local men, but they were the best educated and most widely travelled members of the eighteenth-century Scottish professoriate. They consequently began their careers and entered their classrooms at a slightly higher age than professors elsewhere, and they tended to publish more and marry less.

They were a singularly innovative group throughout the century. At Glasgow, it was the professors, not the Crown, the Faculty of Advocates, or private patrons, who contributed most to the university. The modern chairs of mathematics, oriental languages, humanity, history, law, medicine, botany, chemistry, *materia medica* and midwifery were all created by them. Indeed, of the new chairs added in this period, only those in Greek and astronomy were created by outsiders. The Glasgow medical school was a professorial creation and might have had a more illustrious career had the masters made all the appointments to its chairs. That was not possible, and the school suffered from political appointees until the period of dominance by Ilay during his tenure as third duke of Argyll, from 1743 to 1761. Ilay's record was not sustained by those whose control of Scottish patronage from 1780 to 1805 was equally great. The Glasgow professors also found distinguished men to fill the arts chairs and, in the person of William Leechman, at least one notable professor of divinity. The masters looked after the college fabric, collected a great library, founded collections of instruments and a botanical garden and became relatively wealthy as their enrolments and endowments grew. Professors elsewhere were often as independent, but nowhere else did they use their freedom as responsibly as at Glasgow University.

Notes

1. For a detailed account of this process in the academic life of one Scottish town, see Roger L. Emerson, *Professors, Patronage and Politics: The Aberdeen Universities in the Eighteenth Century* (Aberdeen, 1992).
2. See William Carstares to John Erskine, earl of Mar, 30 Nov. 1708, SRO, Mar and Kelly Papers, GD 124/15/765/3; James Erskine, Lord Grange to Mar, 4

Dec. 1708, Historical Manuscripts Commission, *Report on the Manuscripts of the Earl of Mar and Kellie* (London, 1904), 475–76.

3. For Edinburgh, see Roger L. Emerson, 'The Scottish Enlightenment and the End of the Philosophical Society of Edinburgh', *British Journal for the History of Science* 21 (1988): 33–66; for Glasgow, see chap. 6 below; for Aberdeen, see *A Complete Collection of the Papers Relating to the Union of the King's and Marischal Colleges of Aberdeen* (Aberdeen, 1787), 16, 30, 32

4. All statistics about Scottish professors are drawn from the appendices in Emerson, *Professors, Patronage and Politics*.

5. See R. L. Emerson, 'Medical Men, Politicians and the Medical Schools at Glasgow and Edinburgh, 1685–1803', in *William Cullen and the Eighteenth-Century Medical World*, ed. A. Doig et al. (Edinburgh, 1993), 186–215.

6. *Charters, Statutes, and Acts of the Town Council and the Senatus, 1583–1858*, ed. Alexander Morgan and Robert Kerr Hannay (Edinburgh, 1937), 244, 257.

7. By the mid-eighteenth century their apprentices probably learned botany from Dr John Wodrow, to whom the Faculty of Physicians and Surgeons made a yearly payment. See A. D. Boney, *The Lost Gardens of Glasgow University* (London, 1988), 31, 288–89.

8. Alexander Monro *secundus* estimated in 1764 that since 1725 'the town had received from anatomy students at least £300,000'. Quoted in J. B. Morrell, 'The Edinburgh Town Council and Its University, 1717–1766', in *The Early Years of the Edinburgh Medical School*, ed. R.G.W. Anderson and A.D.C. Simpson (Edinburgh, 1976), 46–57, esp. 56.

9. The presbytery initially refused Leechman the right to subscribe to the creed in 1744, as discussed in chap. 3 below. Fear of a controversy over the placement of Hume led the duke of Argyll to veto his appointment in 1751–52.

10. The Simson cases agitated the kirk for more than fifteen years. Despite the interest and importance of this business, it has lacked a historian, as has the somewhat comparable case of Alexander Scrimgeour, the St Andrews University professor of divinity who was suspended from his chair between 1719 and his death in 1732.

11. Though the kirk did not interfere with any Glasgow appointments between 1743 and 1800, it had often done so so elsewhere in Scotland. Examples include the divinity chair at King's College between 1690 and 1711, involving James Garden and others (Charles Gordon, Thomas Hogg, Allan Logan, George and David Anderson); Principal George Chalmers at King's, 1728–29; Patrick Sibbald, professor of divinity at Marischal College, 1690s; Thomas Blackwell, Jr., at Marischal, 1731–32; Thomas Black in ecclesiastical history at St Andrews, 1707–8; and David Hume's bid for the moral philosophy chair at Edinburgh in 1744–45.

12. At King's the figure was 20 percent, reflecting the inbreeding that characterized an institution in which chairs were frequently passed from father to son. Marischal College also had a low rate because of the politicians' preferences for secular teachers.

13. Boney, *Lost Gardens*, 88. For accounts of the importance of a growing interest in science, see Roger L. Emerson, 'Natural Philosophy and the Problem of the Scottish Enlightenment', *Studies on Voltaire and the Eighteenth Century* 242 (1986): 243–91, and 'Science and Moral Philosophy in the Scottish Enlightenment', in *Studies in the Philosophy of the Scottish Enlightenment*, ed. M. A. Stewart (Oxford, 1990), 11–36.

14. See 'The Method in which Humanity is taught in the University of Glasgow', GUL, MS Gen. 357; 'Mr. Andrew Ross Regent of Humanity . . . his directions to his scholars . . . Oct. 10 1709', GUL, MS Murray 410.

15. The best accounts of the Scottish Whig political factions of the period 1700–60 are in works by P.W.J. Riley, Alexander Murdoch and John Stuart Shaw, which are all cited in Ronald M. Sunter, *Patronage and Politics in Scotland 1707–1832* (Edinburgh, 1986).

16. On 2 December 1727 Ilay wrote to Lord Milton: 'I am preparing some measures to make uneasie some of the foe at Glasgow Colledge. There are (among other matters) two of them Law & Medicine who have been elected, & I think The Exchequer has made some memorandum upon payment of their money containing it[s] reservations of the right of the Crown; the medicine Dr. Johnson [*sic*] is for us, the law, Forbes agt us, pray send me the name of A proper person in case I should happen to molest knave Forbes' (NLS, Saltoun Correspondence, MS 16,535, fol. 133.) This and other letters from 1727 define the atmosphere in which the 1726–27 visitation commission worked.

17. There is a fuller account in Roger L. Emerson, 'The Scottish Scientific and Medical Patronage of Archibald Campbell, 3rd Duke of Argyll, 1723–1761', unpublished.

18. See Roger L. Emerson, 'Lord Bute and the Scottish Universities, 1760–1792', in *Lord Bute: Essays in Re-interpretation*, ed. Karl W. Schweizer (Leicester, 1988), 147–79, esp. 150–51.

19. Campbell had to give up part of his salary (£25) to the other masters as well as £50 *per annum* to Alexander Dunlop. In return, Ilay gave him the principalship, a royal chaplaincy and possibly a gratuity or pension (NLS, MS 16,535, fols. 124, 131, 180, 182, 206, 208, 210.

20. For Simson's contacts with Lord Milton and Ilay himself, see Simson's letters in the NLS, GUL and GUA.

21. William Ruat to Robert Simson, 30 June 1757, GUA, 17,983 A GS; see also GUA, 17,982 GS; 17,984 GS; 17,985 GS; 17,986 GS; 30,522; and 30,525; and NLS, 16,708, fol. 56; J. D. Mackie, *The University of Glasgow, 1451–1951: A Short History* (Glasgow, 1954), 193.

22. Carlo Denina, *An Essay on the Revolution of Literature*, trans. John Murdoch (London, 1771), 276–77.

23. The men were Robert Hamilton (1742), William Leechman (1743), William Cross (1746) and probably Thomas Craigie (1746). For an account of Cross's appointment, see John Cairns, 'William Crosse, Regius Professor of Civil Law in the University of Glasgow, 1746–1749: A Failure of Enlightened Patronage', *History of Universities* 12 (1993), 159–96.

24. William Ruat to Robert Simson, 9 June 1757, GUA 17,982 GS. There was a good deal of correspondence about this appointment, and seven applicants for it. See GUA 17,983A-86 GS, 30,522, 30,525; Andrew Wilson to David Erskine, earl of Buchan, 30 Nov. 1808, GUL, MS 1087; NLS, MS 16,700, fols. 104, 106, 198; MS 16,702/72, fols. 83–84, 99.

25. Francis Hutcheson was called to Glasgow in 1729 at least partly through the good offices of Ilay; see Robert Wodrow, *Analecta*, 4 vols. (Edinburgh, 1842–43), 4:99. Smith was similarly circumstanced; see *The Correspondence of Adam Smith*, ed. Ernest Campbell Mossner and Ian Simpson Ross, 2nd ed. (Oxford, 1987)335. Robert Dick, Jr., came to the chair of natural philosophy in 1751 when the masters allowed him to replace his father. Ilay is not known to have been involved in that appointment, but he was very much involved in others in 1750 and 1751 and very likely approved of an appointment that would keep in the college some apparatus and bring to it an M.D. who had studied at Leyden and had an interest in botany. Dick's appointment would not have had the unanimous endorsement of the masters if Ilay had opposed it.

26. In 1750 Ruat was unanimously elected to the chair of oriental languages, although others had also applied to Ilay for it. The duke's silence implies his consent to that appointment. Two years later Ruat had the backing of Lord Hyndford and Ilay for the regius chair of ecclesiastical history. Ruat was related to the Maxwells of Pollock, the Mures of Caldwell and the Dunlops of Dunlops, and his grandfather had been a tutor in Ilay's family. Between 1752 and 1757 Ruat saw a good deal of Ilay in London. His lecture outlines and some of his notes are preserved at NLS, MS 4992 and GUL, MS Murray 660, no. 24.

27. E.g., James Moor, 'An Essay on Historical Composition', in his *Essays; Read to a Literary Society; at their Weekly Meetings, within the College at Glasgow* (Glasgow, 1759), 126–78.

28. J.R.R. Christie, 'William Cullen and the Practice of Chemistry', in *William Cullen*, ed. Doig et al., 106–7.

29. *Selections from the Family Papers Preserved at Caldwell*, 3 vols. (Glasgow, 1854), 2:301, 83.

30. On Jardine: *Caldwell Papers*, 2:83; Jardine to Robert Hunter, GUL, MS Gen. 507, box 1. Young was the nominee of the retiring professor, James Moor, who would resign for no one else. Hugh MacLeod got his regius chair through the patronage of Charles Fitzroy, whose son he had tutored (GUA, MSS 2040 and 43,163). Archibald Arthur was the assistant and successor to Thomas Reid and had already acted as librarian and chaplain.

31. James Coutts, *A History of the University of Glasgow* (Glasgow, 1909), 319.

32. SRO, MS GD 26/260/2. The principalship was also sought by Henry Grieve, who had some Moderate party support; see Joseph MacCormick to Alexander Carlyle, 10 Feb. 1784.

33. James Millar was the cashier for the Greenock Banking Company. He was able to give a practical turn to mathematics but seems to have been known for lectures on law given after his father's death in 1801. James Williamson is

said to have named his successor in a retirement deal. See *Fortuna Domus: A Series of Lectures Delivered in the University of Glasgow in Commemoration of the Fifth Centenary of Its Foundation* (Glasgow, 1952), 68.

34. Besides the faculty minutes, this contest can be followed in: SRO, GD 51/6/1141; George Jardine to Robert Hunter, GUL, MS Gen. 507, box 3; John Leslie to James Brown, 20 Jan. 1796, EUL, Dc.2.57.

35. Jardine to Hunter, 25 Nov. 1795, GUL, MS Gen. 507, box 3.

36. George Jardine to Robert Hunter, 15 Sept. 1799, GUL, MS Gen. 507, box 3: 'You would probably see a Dr. Meikleham appointed Peter Wilsons successor — We know him well — He was brought up with us — Many of us however wished for a Young man of much greater Genius & Fitness [Jackson] — But a disappointed party raised a Cursed & false insinuation about Politicks which so terrified the D. of Montrose, that he would not hear his name mentioned.' See also SRO, GD 51/6/1297, 1334, 1338, and Coutts, *University of Glasgow*, 319.

37. For a more sympathetic treatment of Meikleham, see David Murray, *Memories of the Old College of Glasgow* (Glasgow, 1927), 263.

38. George Jardine to Robert Hunter, 16 July 1801, GUL, MS Gen. 507, box 3.

Appendix

A. Glasgow University Appointments Made with the Approbation of Lord Ilay, Third Duke of Argyll (or without opposition from him or his faction)

1.	1728	Neil Campbell	Principal
2.	1729	Francis Hutcheson	Moral Philosophy
3.	1735	George Ross	Humanity
4.	1744	Alexander Dunlop	Oriental Languages
5.	1746	William Cross	Law
6.	1746	James Moor	Greek
7.	1747	William Cullen	Medicine
8.	1750	William Rouet	Oriental Languages
9.	1750	Hercules Lindsay	Law
10.	1751	Adam Smith	Logic
11.	1751	Robert Dick, Jr.	Natural Philosophy
12.	1752	George Muirhead	Humanity
13.	1752	James Clow	Logic
14.	1755	John Anderson	Oriental Languages
15.	1756	Joseph Black	Botany
16.	1757	James Buchanan	Oriental Languages
17.	1757	Joseph Black	Medicine
18.	1757	Thomas Hamilton	Botany and Anatomy

| 19. | 1760 | Alexander Wilson | Astronomy |
| 20. | 1761 | James Williamson | Mathematics |

B. Glasgow University Appointments Ilay Tried to Stop

1740	Michael Potter	Divinity
1742	Robert Hamilton	Botany
1743	William Leechman	Divinity
1757	John Anderson	Natural Philosophy

Note: Although Ilay knew of the candidacies of James Moor, Robert Dick, Jr., Thomas Craigie and James Clow, there is no indication that he did more than allow these men from Squadrone families to be elected. Ilay knew of Thomas Craigie's candidacy but did not act to stop it. James Williamson's appointment was made after Ilay's death in 1761, but with his prior support.

2

Francis Hutcheson and the Civic
Humanist Tradition

Thomas P. Miller

For most people, 'rhetoric' is a dirty word, used to describe a
political speech that is long on appeals to emotions and short on
facts. Although negative attitudes to rhetoric have been deepened
by today's television politicians, rhetoric was first identified with 'mere
language', as opposed to logical reasoning from factual evidence, by such
critics as Bacon and Locke. To be sure, philosophers have always been
able to find sufficient reasons to hate rhetoric, which they have typically
condemned as the art of pandering to public ignorance. However, classical moral philosophers such as Cicero and Aristotle viewed rhetoric as
important precisely because it provides a public voice for rational inquiry.
The tradition of civic humanism that was founded by Aristotle and Cicero
portrays educated individuals as citizen orators — rhetoricians whose
authority is signified by their ability to speak with wisdom and virtue
to public problems.[1] Aristotle and Cicero founded the dominant classical
traditions in both rhetoric and moral philosophy on the assumption that
the two disciplines served a common purpose: the preparation of citizens
who could speak with *phronesis*, practical wisdom or prudence. Such
general concepts figure prominently in eighteenth-century Scottish moral
philosophy, but the traditional relationship between rhetoric and moral
philosophy undergoes fundamental changes in response to the moral
philosophers' ambivalent attitudes to the rhetoric of practical politics.

Every moral philosophy contains a rhetoric in two respects. First, even
those theories that idealize disinterested reason make at least implicit
judgements about the value and social role of persuasion. Such judgements reveal important insights into the political practices that are legiti-
mized by a particular theory. For example, moral philosophers' attitudes
to public debate provide a good indication of how democratic their
theories will be in practice because democratic ideals must be combined
with a commitment to open, public dialogue if they are to be democratic
in practice. Second, a perspective on rhetoric is inscribed in how moral
philosophers argue their positions, as well as whom they choose to argue

for and how they claim authority for their arguments. Before they became social scientists, moral philosophers generally did not use a specialized language to communicate with an audience of professional academics. According to J.G.A. Pocock, before politics became a specialized science, political theorists assumed that they spoke in the language of practical politics, a language they understood to be 'rhetoric, the language in which men may be found articulating and communicating as part of the activity and the culture of politics'.[2] Even rhetoric's worst critics have themselves been rhetoricians in quite basic respects. In fact, Locke lectured on rhetoric and moral philosophy for a time at Oxford, and he was himself an active public rhetorician on the political issues of his day.[3]

Although every moral philosopher may in some respects be a rhetorician, the rhetorical exhortations of traditional moral philosophers are an embarrassment to contemporary ethicists and social scientists. University English teachers of today view rhetoric's traditional interest in political discourse as similarly unrelated to their concerns. Such views were first institutionalized by the Scottish professors who introduced British society and culture into the university curriculum. Scottish moral philosophers such as George Turnbull and Francis Hutcheson were among the first to lecture in English on British life and letters, and Scottish rhetoricians founded the study of English literature, composition and rhetoric.[4] Scholars have long recognized that moral philosophers' interest in contemporary social experience gave the Scottish Enlightenment its characteristic tenor and that Scottish moral philosophers contributed to the origins of the social sciences in the nineteenth century.[5] Scottish rhetoricians made an even more definitive contribution to college English studies, which were dominated by Hugh Blair's *Lectures on Rhetoric and Belles Lettres* into the middle of the nineteenth century in most of the English-speaking world, if not in England itself.[6] The Scottish Enlightenment's broad influence on American higher education has also been widely recognized.[7] Because of these broad influences, the Scottish transformation of philosophical and rhetorical studies from a classical to a contemporary frame of reference represents a formative movement in the development of the modern humanities, and it deserves to be carefully examined in order to see what was involved in translating the classical tradition into a contemporary context.

The translation of moral philosophy and rhetoric into the contemporary idiom involved closely related changes in basic assumptions. While the moral philosophers who first lectured in English were influenced by the assumptions and goals of classical civic humanism, Hutcheson and Turnbull had an ambivalence about public conflicts that was ill-suited to a practical engagement with politics, and their attention to human nature can be seen as an effort to resolve the kind of conflicts of interest that civic humanists had identified with the art of rhetoric. Against advocates of self-interest such as Mandeville, Scottish moral philosophers sought to demonstrate that the moral sensibility was in harmony with the larger natural order. Such developments in philosophy were paralleled within language studies by a movement away from political rhetoric towards belles lettres — a movement that shifted the focus from public conflicts to the literary concerns of the republic of letters. These developments helped to create a gap between the humanities and public life that became a virtual chasm in the nineteenth century, when moral philosophy transformed itself into a political science and English studies came to confine itself to aesthetic discourse. Today English is studied in academic departments of literature that are cut off from the language of political affairs, which became part of the domain of the social sciences. Within that domain, philosophies of public discourse and public life have been translated into the language of the sciences, which have traditionally assumed that facts speak for themselves. The trend towards aestheticism in language studies and towards the disinterested perspective of the social scientist can be traced back to the eighteenth century, when rhetoric and moral philosophy lost their shared concern for practical political debate.

In order to provide a sense of the significance of the traditional relationship between rhetoric and moral philosophy, this chapter will begin by summarizing the central role that rhetoric played in classical civic humanism and will then analyse the attitudes to rhetoric that were involved in Hutcheson's departure from the civic humanist tradition. Although Cicero and Aristotle provided some of the basic assumptions of Hutcheson's moral philosophy, Hutcheson was also deeply influenced by the natural law tradition and by Shaftesbury. It was from the modern sources that he developed the goal of reducing human nature and political economy to a system that would establish the continuity between disinterested benevolence and the natural order of society. This system of thought valorizes the polite sentiments of belletristic studies and a disinterested perspective on politics, but it has little place for civic rhetoric, or for the citizen who will use it with practical wisdom to negotiate legitimate conflicts of interest in public forums. The subsequent transformation of moral philosophy into the social sciences was consistent with Hutcheson's effort to apply the perspective of natural philosophy to politics, and the subordination of rhetoric to belles lettres was also justified by Hutcheson's tendency to discuss practical morality in aesthetic terms. The position of rhetoric within Hutcheson's works provides useful insights into the origins and practical implications of these broader developments in the humanities.

I

THE CIVIC HUMANISM of Aristotle, Isocrates and Cicero represented a practical compromise between absolutism and scepticism, and the art of rhetoric was central to that compromise. Aristotle and other civic humanists developed a social philosophy that emphasizes *phronesis*, practical wisdom or prudence, in an effort to mediate between the abstract idealism of Plato, which they perceived to be inapplicable to the uncertainties of public life, and the relativism of the Sophistic perspective, which they believed reduced practical political arts like rhetoric to amoral *techne*.[8] Aristotle distinguishes practical wisdom or prudence from theoretical and technical knowledge in order to argue that political practice is guided by knowledge in context, which cannot be translated into universal generalizations, nor merely methodically applied to particular situations, but rather must be gained from political involvement with the means and ends of human action.[9] Aristotle's teleological perspective led him to view the state as a means to fulfill the civic potential of humanity, which he saw as essentially political in nature (*Politics*, 1263b:36). Politics includes within its purview ethics, practical reasoning and rhetoric because the individual's ability to speak with practical wisdom is both a sign of his civic virtue and the means through which that moral and rational ideal is put into political practice. Aristotle's *Rhetoric* addresses the ethical, emotional and logical elements of public discourse because he assumes that practical wisdom is holistic, and not purely rational. Aristotle discusses forensic, deliberative and ceremonial discourse because he knew that his students would become citizens who would need to resolve public conflicts, persuade others to follow their policies, and celebrate the traditional values of the community. Isocrates, another civic humanist who sought to mediate between the Platonic and Sophistic perspectives, founded the liberal arts or humanities educational tradition upon the assumption that a broad understanding of the shared values and wisdom of the community would prepare the citizen to speak to the uncertain affairs of public life.[10]

Throughout the tradition shared by rhetoric and moral philosophy, Cicero has personified the common ideal of the good man speaking well on issues of public importance. Cicero identifies himself with his predecessors by criticizing Plato for separating the study of philosophy from political arts like rhetoric because wisdom without the ability to make it persuasive has little impact on public life (*De Oratore*, 3:16). Elsewhere he follows civic humanists like Isocrates and Aristotle in arguing that the ability to reason together through language is the foundation of civilized society and the characteristic that most clearly distinguishes the civilized individual from the barbarian (*De Officiis*, 1:16:50). Cicero consistently identifies rhetoric with the prudential, practical reason that is basic to society: speaking with wisdom (*modo prudenter*) 'is better than speculation', he asserts; '. . . for mere speculation is self-centered, while speech extends its benefits to those with whom we are united by the bonds of society'.[11]

Civic virtue is the central practical ideal for civic humanists, and it is also characteristic of their general commitment to practice. For Aristotle in particular and civic humanists in general, virtuous acts are not a matter for abstract speculation but means and ends that can only be understood and realized through actual political action. Rhetoric is central to both this practical ideal and to the idealization of practice, not just because it is the art that makes virtue and wisdom persuasive in public life, but also because the art of rhetoric itself shows that practical action can neither be reduced to an amoral *techne* nor elevated to the level of theoretical certainty. Aristotle, Isocrates and Cicero consistently opposed those who would reduce rhetoric to mere technique or absorb it into some theory of logic because they recognized that rhetoric must be learned from practical experience and is essential to it. Aristotle defined rhetoric as the art of discovering the available means of persuasion in a given situation, and Isocrates and Cicero also understood rhetoric to be the art of saying the right thing at the right time. For Aristotle, the effective rhetorician must have practical wisdom to be able to speak effectively to the situation. This view became idealized as the complete orator, the broadly educated citizen who knows how to speak to shifting situations by drawing on the values and wisdom of the community. Such ideals show how civic humanists placed rhetoric at the intersection of language, practical understanding and social experience in order to mediate between absolutism and relativism.

According to Pocock, civic humanism exercised a dominant influence on European moral philosophy until the Scots replaced the philosophy of civic virtue with the science of political economy; other researchers have detailed the specific debts of Smith, Hume and others to Cicero and Aristotle.[12] However, scholars have generally ignored the parallels between the departure from civic humanism in moral philosophy and the subordination of civic rhetoric to belles lettres, even though similar developments have been observed in other periods when access to direct political expression became limited.[13] In both fields, the tradition founded by Cicero and Aristotle remained dominant until the Scots absorbed and supplanted the classical tradition in the latter half of the eighteenth century. With the transition to the contemporary idiom, the relationship between moral philosophy and language studies was no longer based in their shared concern for practical political discourse but rather in their common interest in polite literature and moral sensibility. This transition can be traced back to the generation who taught Blair, Smith and Reid. In the teaching of John Stevenson, John Pringle, George Turnbull and Hutcheson, one can see the classical tradition being translated into a new cultural and political idiom.[14]

Cicero's influence on Hutcheson has long been recognized, as have his debts to James Harrington, who like other commonwealthmen drew on civic humanist sources.[15] Hutcheson was a practical moralist in the Ciceronian tradition, a teacher of virtue who sought to persuade his students at Glasgow University and his reading public not just to understand the good life but to live it. The transition from Hutcheson to his successors can appear to be quite dramatic on this point. While Hume might well be the 'sceptical metaphysician' and 'common-sense moralist' presented by recent scholars, he claimed to belong to that 'species of philosophers' who regard 'human nature as a subject of speculation', philosophers who are to be distinguished from those who 'paint her in the most amiable colors, borrowing all helps from poetry and eloquence and treating their subject in an easy and obvious manner, and such as is best fitted to please the imagination and engage the affections'.[16] For Hume, at least in this speculative mode, moral philosophers do not need rhetorical 'eloquence' because their method is rational inquiry. One would expect a different attitude from a practical moralist like Hutcheson. In just the way Hume criticized, Hutcheson used a highly rhetorical style to appeal to the imagination in order to move the will to action, which is how the persuasive process was understood from the time of Bacon. According to Leechman, in the classroom and in his public lectures Hutcheson was an engaging orator who regarded 'the culture of the heart as the main end of all moral instruction', a viewpoint that is consistent with his emphasis on sentiment as a motivating force in ethical behaviour.[17] Yet for all his reliance on the art of rhetoric to move his audience to practical virtue, Hutcheson generally ignores rhetoric in his philosophy of society. Why is this the case? Why does a Ciceronian like Hutcheson ignore the civic philosophy of rhetoric in his own social theory?

II

THE INTRODUCTIONS TO Hutcheson's works provide one of the best opportunities to assess his rhetorical practice. In an introduction an author must create a relationship with the reader, establish authority and set out the argument — in other words, create the rhetorical situation to which the reader will respond. The openings of works that address formative developments in a discipline are particularly noteworthy because writers in such situations do not have an accepted set of conventions and authorities on which to rely. Faced with such uncertainty, a writer must reinterpret authorized sources and methods or establish the relevance of new modes of thought by showing how they serve the basic values or goals of the audience. Hutcheson addressed two main audiences: *A Short Introduction to Moral Philosophy* (1747) was a classroom text for students, and the posthumous *A System of Moral Philosophy* (1755) was intended for a broader reading public.[18] These works provide an opportunity for a comparative analysis of how he understood the role of moral philosophy in contemporary education and public life.

Hutcheson opens the *Short Introduction* with an advertisement that identifies the work with the tradition of Cicero and Aristotle among the ancients, and Pufendorf among the 'moderns' (*Works*, 4:i). He justifies publishing a compend by arguing that each teacher must decide on the method 'best suited to the apprehensions of the students, and aptest to touch their hearts on such subjects' (*Works*, 4:ii). To accomplish his purpose of both informing and moving his audience, he begins with a grand preoration addressed 'To The Students in Universities'. He presents the lectures as merely an introduction to the far more important works of 'the inventors and improvers of all ingenious arts, the Greek and Roman writers', which along with the Bible will help you to 'adorn your souls with every virtue, prepare yourselves for every honourable office in life, and quench that manly and laudable thirst you should have after knowledge'. Hutcheson further counsels his students not to let 'philosophy rest in speculation' but rather to act in accordance with 'right reason' (*Works*, 4:iv).

The lectures begin with the teleological approach to moral philosophy first established by Aristotle's *Ethics*:

> As all other arts have in view some good to be obtained, as their proper end, Moral Philosophy, which is the art of regulating the whole of life, must have in view the noblest end; since it undertakes, as far as human reason can go, to lead us into that course of life which is most according to the intention of nature, and most happy, to which end whatever we can obtain by other arts should be subservient. Moral Philosophy therefore must be one of these commanding arts which directs how far the other arts are to be pursued. And since all Philosophers, even of the most opposite schemes, agree in words at least that 'Happiness either consists in virtue and virtuous offices, or it is to be obtained and secured by them:' The chief points to be enquired into in Morals must be, what course of life is according to the intention of nature? wherein consists happiness? and what is virtue? (*Works*, 4:1–2)

Many of these comments remind one of classical sources, particularly the Stoics' emphasis on living in accordance with right reason to accomplish the ends of human nature, which is also mentioned in the prefatory advertisement. Most important is the assumption that moral philosophy is one of the 'commanding arts' because it is concerned with basic practical questions about how to live well. The identification of happiness as the 'intention of nature' is tentative, and the point is made in terms taken from a general sense of traditional assumptions, which are presented within quotation marks even though no specific source is cited, as if Hutcheson were speaking for the collective wisdom of tradition.

The prefatory materials in the *System of Moral Philosophy* do not identify the work as merely an introduction to the classical tradition. Rather than opening with a grand preoration, the work begins with a dedication to a lord, an account of the author and a list of noteworthy subscribers — materials that serve to introduce the writer to his polite reading public in a quite different manner. Hutcheson begins the *System* itself with a paragraph stating the methods and assumptions of his system of thought:

> The Intention of Moral Philosophy is to direct men to that course of action which tends most effectually to promote their greatest happiness and perfection; as far as it can be done by observations and conclusions discoverable from the constitution of nature, without any aids of supernatural revelation; these maxims or rules of conduct are therefore reputed as laws of nature, and the system or collection of them is called the LAW of NATURE. (*Works*, 5:1)

Hutcheson thus claims the authority of natural laws and the method of data collection and synthesis associated with natural philosophy. In the very next paragraph, he in fact claims a 'science' of human nature.

Similar differences in emphasis can be seen at other junctures in the two works. The first books of the *Short Introduction* and *System* both move from the individual, to society, to God in order to show the continuity of the natural order and divine providence. The *Short Introduction* concludes the first book with the same emphases that it opened with: a long quotation from Cicero is followed by a paragraph presenting 'a grand view of the good man' that emphasizes his necessary engagement with the 'general interest' of society, which like him must follow the 'dictates of right reason' that make up the '*Law of Nature*' (*Works*, 4:107). This synthesis of civic humanist ideals and Stoical natural rights doctrines popularized by Cicero takes a different form in the conclusion of the first book of the *System*. Considerable stress is given to the 'moral faculty', the closely related finer senses and 'the more extensive interest of the system', and this emphasis on human faculties and the abstract system pushes the concern for the social context of human action into the background. While prudential reasoning about means and ends is added, it is not identified with the public sphere, which has virtually disappeared from the discussion. Instead, Hutcheson argues that while few people have the opportunity to act in 'public offices of virtue' and achieve 'external success', virtue can still be attained 'in all the lower private offices; in a constant sweetness of deportment in obscurity; and a constant resignation to the *Supreme Mind*' (*Works*, 4:107, 5:225). A Stoic acceptance of the larger good of the system makes public virtue accessible to private members of society, for there is not 'any station of life excluded from the enjoyment of the supreme good' (*Works*, 5:226).

Stoic resignation to lowly private status is here supplanting the traditional civic humanist commitment to an active political life. Hutcheson's 'science' of moral philosophy has little place for the political art of rhetoric, as is evident in his treatment of another sort of introduction, the introduction of society. Civic humanism idealized the source of civilized society as *logos*, understood as both language and reason, or rather reason shared through language. According to Isocrates, 'because there has been implanted in us the power to persuade each other and to make clear to each other whatever we desire, not only have we escaped the life of wild beasts, but we have come together and founded cities and made laws and invented arts'.[19] Civic humanists generally agreed that our ability to persuade each other makes social unions possible by providing a civilized alternative to barbaric violence.

Hutcheson occasionally acknowledges this line of reasoning, even using the term 'prudence' for the practical wisdom that led to the creation of political institutions, and he regularly endorses the related conclusion that the purpose of the social union is to fulfill our natural potential for civic virtue (*Works*, 5:34–35). But whereas Isocrates identified practical wisdom with the art of persuasion, on the assumption that 'the power to speak well is taken as the surest index of a sound understanding (*tou phronein eu*)' ('Antidosis', 327), Hutcheson bases society not on the rhetoric of practical reason but on the more certain foundation provided by the social contract. Drawing on the natural law tradition, he reasons that the institution of 'arbitration' marks the transition from natural liberty to civil polity. He describes the first rudimentary system of law, overseen by 'disengaged' 'arbitrators'. Although 'of equal prudence with . . . the contending parties', these arbitrators would have been able to make a disinterested judgement of the case (*Works*, 6:141–42). With the institution of a legal system, people came to see 'the order, grandeur, regular dispositions and motions, of the visible world', and this recognition of the larger system leads to the establishment of religion (*Works*, 5:35). Hutcheson specifically rejects the view that people could have resolved conflicts through debate among themselves, and he turns to the image of the disinterested observer, which would become characteristic of Scottish moral philosophy, in order to create a more certain standard for social justice.[20] At this and other points, the ideal of engaging in prudential debate is supplanted by a natural system of jurisprudence that is shown to be consistent with the divine order of nature.

The *Short Introduction* and the *System* share a common organization and purpose: first a basic theory of human nature is introduced, and then theories of ethics and politics are established that are shown to be consistent with the law of nature as ordained by natural theology. The purpose, which becomes more evident in the *System*, is to develop a consistent system of thought founded upon natural philosophy. Hutcheson, like most eighteenth-century moral philosophers, was very interested in the method of natural philosophy, which he saw as yielding more reliable knowledge than the rationalist speculations of moral philosophers like Clarke. Leechman emphasizes that Hutcheson's whole approach was based on the assumption that 'in the same way that we enquire into the structure of an animal body, of a plant, or of the solar system, a more exact theory of morals may be formed' (*Works*, 5:xiv-xv).[21] However,

Hutcheson's application of natural philosophy to moral philosophy often amounts to little more than a rhetorical strategy to claim authority for a universalized sense of experience against deductive reasonings from outmoded metaphysical assumptions. The object of investigation is not the social experience, but an idealized system of human nature and the natural order of society.

In a letter to Hutcheson, Hume objected to just this reliance on some abstract concept of nature:

> I cannot agree to your Sense of *Natural*. 'Tis founded on final Causes, which is a Consideration, that appears to me pretty uncertain & unphilosophical. For pray, what is the End of Man? Is he created for Happiness or for Virtue? For this Life or for the next? For himself or for his Maker? Your Definition of *Natural* depends on solving these Questions, which are endless, & quite wide of my Purpose.[22]

Hutcheson's tendency to universalize both individual and social experience often leads him to deemphasize practical political affairs, as is evident in how he defines politics itself, the third part of moral philosophy, as 'shewing the various plans of civil government, and the rights of states with respect to each other' (*Works*, 4:i). Such topics might help to support an abstract theory of natural laws, what Hutcheson terms 'the general Rights of Human Society, or Mankind as a System' (*Works*, 6:104). However, such topics are far removed from the practical art of political action presented by seminal civic humanist texts like Aristotle's *Politics*, which was based on an actual survey of the existing constitutions.

Hutcheson developed an eclectic system, incorporating the values of civic humanism and the methods and principles of the natural rights tradition, but the model for the system itself came from Shaftesbury, who also provided the basic concept of a moral sense. Shaftesbury describes human nature and social relations in terms of the aesthetic harmony or balance of a larger system, or 'economy'. The 'economy of the passions' (the balance of selfish and benevolent feelings within human nature) is the microcosm of the 'economy of the species or kind' wherein 'the *private interest* and *good* of every-one . . . work towards the *general good*'.[23] As developed by Hutcheson, the microcosm and macrocosm are linked in practice by feelings of benevolence, sympathetic feelings that evolve naturally from one's family, to neighbours, to fellow citizens, to all humanity (*Works*, 4:79–80). These feelings are strengthened by 'frequent impartial meditation' on the larger system (*Works*, 4:12). Ethics and politics tend to become defined in terms of aesthetic values like balance and harmony, and the moral sense becomes modelled upon aesthetic judgement.

In line with this approach, the perspective of the critic, not the agent, becomes central. Hutcheson assumes the perspective of the 'spectator' when he recommends calmly assessing the larger good to refine

one's 'benevolent' passions and aesthetic sentiments, and he begins to
sound very much like later moral philosophers when he states that a
'*sympathetick*' sense prompts 'fellow-feeling' in the '*observer*' (*Works*,
5:19–21). This abstraction from the perspective of the agent is an attempt
to answer Mandeville and those who saw self-interest as the controlling
motive of social action: though 'the agent himself perhaps may be moved
by a view of advantages', 'such advantages won't engage the approbations
of others' (*Works*, 4:18).

Hutcheson is clearly trying to create a holistic model of practical
apprehension that has a place for both feeling and reason, but he does
not focus upon purposeful practical action because purposeful acts are
interested acts, and he wants to valorize disinterested sentiments. The
dislocation from practical political action is evident in numerous aspects
of Hutcheson's works on moral philosophy. Although Hutcheson treats
many practical matters, such as the status of women or the need to
maintain a contract, he tends to slip into moralizing when confronted
with legitimate political conflicts with no clear moral answers: 'such as
sincerely aim at acting the virtuous part, will always easily discern what
equity and humanity require, unless they are too much influenced by
selfishness' (*Works*, 4:155). Although he emphasizes that human beings
have a natural propensity to social action, even in his description of
that propensity he slips into the spectatorial perspective by citing such
examples as children's delight in discovering how things work, 'publick
shows', 'but above all, the important actions of great characters; the
fortunes of such men, and the states where they lived' (*Works*, 5:23).

Thus, civic virtue itself becomes an event to be observed. The ability to
distance oneself from the event and appraise its larger order and harmony
is fundamental to Hutcheson's basic conception of rational social action.
Natural sentiments provide the foundation for practical judgement, but
educated people have the responsibility to step back and appraise the
larger system, and it is this critical detachment that gives them superior
authority. Although the disengaged, objective perspective becomes the
privileged vantage point of enlightened reason and the sciences generally,
this perspective assumes that one can and should divorce oneself from the
practical situation in order to make an objective, rational judgement. This
fundamental assumption of enlightened reason has been challenged by
those interested in the social construction of knowledge, and Hutcheson
himself became disenchanted with the project of applying enlightened
reason to social practice.[24]

III

LIKE CIVIC HUMANISTS faced with the extremes of Platonic absolutism
and Sophistic relativism, Hutcheson sought to mediate a position that

would be both consistent with traditional ideals and applicable to practical problems. Whereas civic humanism recommends the art of arguing and reasoning together about practical political issues, Hutcheson turns inward, positing an innate moral sense that operates in concert with the laws governing human nature and society. Civic humanism defines human beings as political animals and develops a philosophy of political practice centred on the art of persuading one's fellow citizens to act with civic virtue and practical wisdom. Hutcheson faced a less unified political community in need of a more certain grounding, a political world in which the art of heated oratory had become associated with the divisive interests of religious and political factions, not the common good. Hutcheson and his successors dreamed of developing a science of politics, and they defined civic virtue in terms of the sentiments of the literati, who might not have access to distant political forums but could resign themselves to their private labors and become active participants in the republic of letters. Although Hutcheson and his successors were practical spokesmen for the civic value of polite sensibility, their disinterested perspective on rhetoric created the gap between the individual and the larger political system that would eventually separate the domain of political theory from practical political action. Ever since the classical age, rhetoric was defined as the art of persuasively advancing one side of a conflict; as such, it was threatening to those who based their authority on claims to be disinterested observers of the political system. For this reason, it was the advocate of self-interest, Thomas Hobbes, who first translated Aristotle's *Rhetoric* into English in order to teach young lords the political art of rhetoric, and it was preachers of virtue like Hutcheson and the Scottish literati who first subordinated rhetoric to belletristic literary studies.[25]

Scottish belletristic rhetoricians like Hugh Blair were very concerned with aesthetic sentiments and the republic of letters, but they showed very little interest in the rhetoric of practical politics. In his *Lectures on Rhetoric and Belles Lettres* (1783), which had a major impact on the introduction of the vernacular into higher education, Blair ignored the political oratory then shaping the future of the British Empire because he believed that political debate was less important than ministerial influence, and he was probably right when it came to Scottish politics.[26] Rather than emphasizing political discourse, Blair turned his students' attention to the style of periodical essays like those in the *Spectator*. The only treatise that came close to rivalling the influence of Blair's *Lectures*, George Campbell's *Philosophy of Rhetoric* (1776), drew on contemporary efforts to develop a science of human nature in an effort to compose a rhetorical theory more concerned with epistemology than with politics. In their common inattention to public controversies, Blair and Campbell helped to institutionalize the spectatorial perspective on politics that eventually reduced the study of English to the study of literature.

Notes

I would like to thank Knud Haakonssen for his helpful responses to an earlier draft of this essay.

1. In the classical context, civic humanism is a broad political and cultural philosophy, not Pocock's clearly defined 'paradigm'. Roger L. Emerson, 'Science and Moral Philosophy in the Scottish Enlightenment', in *Studies in the Philosophy of the Scottish Enlightenment*, ed. M. A. Stewart (Oxford, 1990), 33, argues that this paradigm misrepresents the diversity of Scottish moral philosophy, and John Robertson, 'The Scottish Enlightenment at the Limits of the Civic Tradition', in *Wealth and Virtue: The Shaping of Political Economy in the Scottish Enlightenment*, ed. Istvan Hont and Michael Ignatieff (Cambridge, 1983), 137–78, suggests using the broader term 'civic tradition'. However, civic humanism had a strong influence on Hutcheson, and the term helps to distinguish three traditions of humanism, with three related views of rhetoric: Platonic humanism, which dismissed rhetoric as concerned with mere opinion and appearance (*doxa*), rather than with knowledge of universals; civic humanism, which defined rhetoric as the art of speaking to the uncertainties of practical affairs; and the sceptical humanism of the Sophists, who took a figurist approach to rhetoric.
2. J.G.A. Pocock, *Politics, Language and Time: Essays on Political Thought and History* (New York, 1971), 17.
3. Wilbur Samuel Howell, *British Logic and Rhetoric in the Eighteenth Century* (Princeton, 1971), 265.
4. For a summary of contemporary reports on Hutcheson's being the first to lecture in English, see Richard B. Sher, 'Professors of Virtue: The Social History of the Edinburgh Moral Philosophy Chair in the Eighteenth Century', in *Studies in the Philosophy of the Scottish Enlightenment*, ed. Stewart, 97n.
5. See Gladys Bryson, 'The Emergence of the Social Sciences from Moral Philosophy', *International Journal of Ethics* 42 (1932): 304–23.
6. In addition to Howell, *Eighteenth-Century British Logic and Rhetoric*, see James Berlin, *Writing Instruction in Nineteenth-Century American Colleges* (Carbondale, Ill., 1984) and Thomas P. Miller, 'Where Did College English Studies Come From?' *Rhetoric Review* 9 (1990): 50–69.
7. See, for example, Andrew Hook, *Scotland and America: A Study of Cultural Relations* (Glasgow, 1975) and Thomas P. Miller, Introduction, *Selected Writings of John Witherspoon* (Carbondale and Edwardsville, Ill., 1990).
8. The standard history is George A. Kennedy, *Classical Rhetoric and Its Christian and Secular Tradition from Ancient to Modern Times* (Chapel Hill, N.C., 1980). For a broader perspective, see Werner Jaeger, *Paideia: The Ideals of Greek Culture*, 3 vols. (New York, 1939–40).
9. Aristotle's concept of practical wisdom is a key concern in Hans-Georg Gadamer, *Truth and Method*, ed. Garrett Barden and John Cumming (New York, 1975) and Alasdair MacIntyre, *Whose Justice? Which Rationality?*

(Notre Dame, Ind., 1988). See also Lois S. Selfe, 'Rhetoric and *Phronesis*: The Aristotelian Ideal', *Philosophy and Rhetoric* 12 (1979): 130–45. The centrality of prudence or practical wisdom to the civic humanist tradition is suggested by the fact that Harrington introduces *Oceana* by dividing the history of political thought into 'ancient prudence' and 'modern prudence'; see *The Political Works of James Harrington*, ed. J.G.A. Pocock (Cambridge, 1977), 161, 163. See also Victoria Kahn, *Rhetoric, Prudence, and Skepticism in the Renaissance* (Ithaca, N.Y., 1985).

10. On the contrast with the specialized philosophical education of Plato, see Henri-Irenee Marrou, *A History of Education in Antiquity* (New York, 1956) and Ernesto Grassi, *Rhetoric as Philosophy: The Humanist Tradition* (University Park, Pa., 1980).

11. Cicero, *De Officiis*, trans. Walter Miller (London, 1913), 161 (1.44.156).

12. See particularly J.G.A. Pocock, 'Cambridge Paradigms and Scotch Philosophers: A Study of the Relations between the Civic Humanist and the Civil Jurisprudential Interpretations of Eighteenth-Century Social Thought', in *Wealth and Virtue*, ed. Hont and Ignatieff, 235–52. For Hume and Smith, see Peter Jones, *Hume's Sentiments: Their Ciceronian and French Context* (Edinburgh, 1982); David Fate Norton, *David Hume, Common-Sense Moralist, Sceptical Metaphysician* (Princeton, 1982); and Nicholas Phillipson, 'Adam Smith as Civic Moralist', in *Wealth and Virtue*, ed. Hont and Ignatieff, 179–202.

13. The emphasis on polite self-improvement within the two fields can be understood as part of the tendency of rhetoric and practical philosophy to become more literary and speculative, with decreased opportunities for political expression. This movement from primary to secondary rhetoric is termed *letteraturizzazione* in Kennedy, *Classical Rhetoric*, 110–15.

14. One can see the interests of Scottish moral philosophy begin to emerge out of the classical tradition in the records of logic and moral philosophy courses taught by Stevenson and Pringle at Edinburgh. Stevenson lectured on Cicero, Aristotle and Quintilian, but he also included the works of Locke and Bacon as well as those of Dryden, Pope, Addison and other contemporary critics, as discussed in Miller, Introduction, *Selected Writings of John Witherspoon*. Pringle was less eclectic, but one can see the transition to the concerns of Scottish moral philosophy in his 'Lectures on Cicero' (EUL, MS 1741), where he mediates the conflict between 'self love' and 'benevolence' with the concept of a 'moral sence'.

Turnbull's works provide the clearest example of how the influence of classical civic humanism was complicated by natural rights sources. In his edition of Heineccius, *Methodical System of Universal Law*, 2 vols. (London, 1741), Turnbull comments upon and corrects the continental jurisprudence tradition in long notes, interspersed sections responding to key points, and a lengthy concluding discourse titled 'A Discourse Upon the Nature and Origine of Moral and Civil Laws'. Turnbull's dialogue with the natural rights tradition is one of the best examples of the rich interactions among competing traditions that tend to be ignored by those who would locate Scottish moral philosophy within a single tradition such as civic humanism.

15. See William Robert Scott, *Francis Hutcheson: His Life, Teaching and Position in the History of Philosophy* (Cambridge, 1900) and Caroline Robbins, *The Eighteenth-Century Commonwealthman* (Cambridge, Mass., 1959).

16. Jones, *Hume's Sentiments* and Norton, *David Hume* both generally describe Hume as a Ciceronian humanist, but Hume clearly distinguishes himself from practical moralists in the opening paragraph of the *Enquiry concerning Human Understanding*.

17. Preface, *A System of Moral Philosophy*, in *Collected Works of Francis Hutcheson*, 7 vols. (Hildesheim, 1969), 5:xxi. Subsequent references to Hutcheson's *Works* are cited parenthetically in the text. *The Autobiography of Dr. Alexander Carlyle of Inveresk, 1722–1805*, new ed., ed. John Hill Burton (London and Edinburgh, 1910), 78, also praises the 'fervent and persuasive eloquence' of Hutcheson's teaching.

18. James Moore compares the two works in 'The Two Systems of Francis Hutcheson: On the Origins of the Scottish Enlightenment', in *Studies in the Philosophy of the Scottish Enlightenment*, ed. Stewart, 37–59.

19. 'Antidosis', *Isocrates*, 3 vols. (London, 1958), 2:327.

20. Hutcheson may have been unwilling to make a place for rhetoric in the founding of society because he wanted to defend the social contract against criticisms that no record of such a contract existed and that it was far more likely that social unions resulted from the superior force or craft of a dominant few. See James Moore and Michael Silverthorne, 'Gershom Carmichael and the Natural Jurisprudence Tradition in Eighteenth-Century Scotland', in *Wealth and Virtue*, ed. Hont and Ignatieff, 73–87.

21. One could easily conclude from such statements that natural philosophy provided scientific methods that came to be recognized as more reliable than moral philosophers' traditional metaphysical speculations, but Locke believed that 'Morality is the proper Science, and Business of Mankind', and that 'Natural Philosophy is not capable of being made a Science'. In the *Essay concerning Human Understanding*, ed. Peter H. Nidditch (Oxford, 1975), 646, Locke maintains that our knowledge of physical experience is fundamentally uncertain, but 'our faculties can plainly discover to us the Being of a God, and the knowledge of our selves, enough to lead us into a full and clear discovery of our Duty'. A shared belief in the reliability of a philosophy of human nature did come to link natural and moral philosophy, but often this belief was verified with only the most speculative arguments about human understanding. As in Leechman's comment, such beliefs were frequently validated by rhetorical appeals to advances in the physical sciences. Leechman states that Hutcheson first entered Glasgow as 'a student in The Natural Philosophy class', and that he turned from rationalism 'to treat morals as a matter of fact' largely because he wanted to apply the methods of natural philosophy to moral issues (5:iii-iv).

22. *The Letters of David Hume*, ed. J.Y.T. Greig, 2 vols. (Oxford, 1932), 1:33.

23. Anthony Ashley Cooper, Lord Shaftesbury, *Characteristics of Men, Manners, Opinions, Times* . . ., 2 vols. (Indianapolis, 1964), 1:336, 338.

24. In a letter to Hume written late in life, Hutcheson remarked that he had been turning more and more to 'the Old Academy, despairing of Certainty in the most important Subjects, but satisfied with a sort of Probable knowledge'. In Ian Ross, 'Hutcheson on Hume's *Treatise*: An Unnoticed Letter', *Journal of the History of Philosophy* 4 (1966): 71.

25. On Hobbes, see John T. Harwood, ed. *The Rhetorics of Thomas Hobbes and Bernard Lamy* (Carbondale, Ill., 1986). On the public discourse of the literati, see John Dwyer, *Virtuous Discourse: Sensibility and Community in Late Eighteenth-Century Scotland* (Edinburgh, 1987).

26. For a discussion of the influence of the civic humanist tradition on Hugh Blair and John Witherspoon, see Thomas P. Miller, 'Witherspoon, Blair and the Rhetoric of Civic Humanism', in *Scotland and America in the Age of the Enlightenment*, ed. Richard B. Sher and Jeffrey R. Smitten (Princeton, 1990), 100–14.

3

William Leechman, Pulpit Eloquence and the Glasgow Enlightenment

Thomas D. Kennedy

On 23 November 1743, Michael Potter, professor of divinity at Glasgow University, died at the age of seventy-three. Potter had been selected for the chair in 1740 over the much younger and healthier John MacLaurin, minister of the Ramshorn Church in Glasgow. There is reason to believe that Francis Hutcheson's support for Potter in that contest occurred not because Hutcheson considered Potter a more able theologian than MacLaurin but because he foresaw that the probable brevity of Potter's tenure would enable him to prepare for the professorship William Leechman, whom Hutcheson identified some months before Potter's death as 'the man I wished to be, in the first place, our Professor of Theology'.[1]

So it was that in 1743, upon Michael Potter's death, the wheels that would drive William Leechman's succession to the divinity chair were quickly set in motion. For the past seven years Leechman had been serving as minister at the nearby parish of Beith in the Presbytery of Irvine in Ayrshire. Hutcheson had met him in the early 1730s, when the younger man attended some of his lectures in Glasgow. Shortly before Potter's death, Hutcheson had been touting Leechman for a parish in Belfast, a position he deemed more consistent with his friend's character and manners. Apparently puzzled by Leechman's reluctance to leave Beith, Hutcheson wrote to his friend Thom Drennan in Belfast on 5 August 1743 that Leechman was 'well and happy tho' preaching to a pack of horse copers and smugglers of the rudest sort' (*FH*, 88).[2] In the same letter Hutcheson expressed some obligation to see to it that Leechman was better placed: 'If the field be clear, it would be *peccare in publica commoda* [to sin against public interest], not to force him out of that obscure hole, where he is so much lost.' But Leechman did not share his friend's enthusiasm about Belfast, and on 29 October Hutcheson regretfully informed Drennan that the Belfast congregation need pursue Leechman no further (*FH*, 89).

A month later Hutcheson reported Michael Potter's death to Drennan and confided hopefully that he and some of his colleagues were campaigning for Leechman as his successor, believing that 'if he succeeds, it will put a new face upon Theology in Scotland' (*FH*, 89). Leechman did succeed Potter in the chair of divinity, but he was not the uncontested choice of the faculty. There were at first three candidates for the position: Leechman, the Moderate Glasgow minister William Craig (who withdrew his candidacy early on, thus strengthening Leechman's hand) and, once again, John MacLaurin. Leechman's contemporary biographer, James Wodrow, describes well both the significance of this election for the people of Glasgow and the division of support for the candidates:

> The people of the city and neighbourhood interested themselves warmly in the fate of this election; as it was indeed an event of no small consequence to the future education of their clergy. They befriended one or the other candidate according to their acquaintance with him, and their opinion of the conformity of his religious sentiments to their own. Mr. Leechman had the good wishes of all the hearers of his friend Craig who considered themselves as the people of taste and education; and Mr. MacLaurin the good wishes of a much larger body, even all the rest of the town.[3]

Faculty support for MacLaurin was led by the professor of church history, William Anderson, who, like MacLaurin, had had some involvement in the religious revivals of the Southwest; as Hutcheson put it in a letter to Leechman's patron William Mure of Caldwell, Anderson had 'made himself ridiculous to all men of sense by dangling after Whitefield and McCullogh'.[4] Other supporters of MacLaurin on the Glasgow faculty were John Loudon (logic), John Johnstone (medicine), William Forbes (civil law), Robert Dick (natural philosophy) and the principal, Neil Campbell. Leechman was supported by the avowed friends of taste and education: Hutcheson (moral philosophy), Alexander Dunlop (Greek), Charles Morthland (oriental languages), Robert Simson (mathematics), Robert Hamilton (anatomy) and George Ross (humanity).[5] When the election was held in the faculty meeting on 13 December, the university rector, George Bogle, broke a tie by casting the deciding vote in favour of Leechman.

Even then the sailing was not smooth for Leechman. Anderson protested the legality of the rector's vote, and later the Presbytery of Glasgow refused to accept Leechman as a member, charging that his published sermon *On the Nature, Reasonableness, and Advantages of Prayer* (1743) was heretical. The presbytery was not inexperienced in pursuing heresy, having hounded a former divinity professor, John Simson, until the General Assembly of the Church of Scotland suspended him from teaching in 1729, and having harassed Hutcheson, unsuccessfully, a decade later. The dispute over Leechman's sermon was filled with bitterness and acrimony. Leechman and his defenders regarded it as but one more attack of the ill-educated and feverish presbytery upon those of more moderate tastes and dispositions. Those who forwarded the case against Leechman, however, maintained that the moderates were not entirely moderate, and one alleged that the members of the prosecuting committee had themselves been intimidated:

> There were Scandalous Libels and Advertisements spread against some of them; there were incendiary anonymous Letters written to others, threatening, that, in case the Committee, or Presbytery, should find any Thing culpable in the Sermon, they would make Reprisals, and publish Slanderous Falshoods (they condescended on, or insinuate) at London, against several they particularly named, in the University and Presbytery.[6]

Having failed with the Presbytery of Glasgow, appeal was made by Leechman and his supporters to the Synod of Glasgow and Ayr. Leechman defended himself against the charges of heresy to the satisfaction of the synod and was eventually accepted as a member of the presbytery. Hutcheson, in a letter to Drennan written late in 1744, proudly boasted that 'we have at last got a Right Professor of Theology, the only right one in Scotland' (*FH*, 93). This chapter seeks to account for Hutcheson's words by looking at the career of the man who inspired them.

I

IN RETROSPECT, IT SEEMS difficult to understand or substantiate Hutcheson's glowing estimation of Leechman. After all, Leechman left behind precious little by which to evaluate his religious and theological views. Besides James Wodrow's edition of his *Sermons*, some of which were originally published individually, we have only two student notebooks of Leechman's 'Lectures on Pictet's System of Theology' (1747 and 1748, GUL, MS Gen. 111 and 61), an unpublished 'Treatise of Rhetoric, especially as it regards the Pulpit' (GUL, MS Gen. 51), completed in 1763, and a student notebook of Leechman's lectures on composition (EUL, MS Dc.7.86). In some respects, we are in a better position to evaluate the intellectual contribution of the twice unsuccessful candidate for the divinity chair, John MacLaurin.

MacLaurin was a well-known figure in Glasgow, but he travelled in different circles from the Glasgow intellectual and cultural élite. For a number of years he conducted services in Gaelic for Highlanders resident in Glasgow. More significant, perhaps, was his concern for public morals in Glasgow and his championing of religious orthodoxy. MacLaurin's son-in-law John Gillies mentions the sermons he preached before the societies for reformation in Glasgow. In those sermons MacLaurin 'made it his business to inculcate upon the conscientious inhabitants the necessity of doing their part to bear down wickedness by giving information against offenders'[7] — a message not likely to endear him to the hearts of everyone. He was also a champion of orthodoxy in Glasgow. Robert Wodrow mentions 'a light-headed metaphisicall lad at Glasgow', an Arian who, desiring to receive communion, had been sent to John MacLaurin for correction of his wayward Simsonite beliefs. Fearing an outbreak of Arianism in Glasgow, MacLaurin accepted the young man's challenge to a series of public debates.[8] And MacLaurin was one of three members of the Presbytery of Glasgow to evaluate John Simson's responses to the presbytery's heresy charges. (This, in itself, may have been sufficient to turn Hutcheson and his colleagues against MacLaurin.)

MacLaurin was noted for his involvement in the revivals at Cambuslang, about which he corresponded with the American philosopher-theologian Jonathan Edwards. Indeed, John's involvement in the revivals in the West of Scotland was a matter of some concern to his brother Colin, the famous Newtonian mathematician, and caused him to waver somewhat in his support for John's candidacy for the chair. Although he considered John to be 'really over Orthodox', he finally decided that John's honesty and sincerity adequately compensated for this shortcoming, 'considering how much that College suffered formerly by a Professor of D—y'.[9]

Like Edwards, MacLaurin was not merely a revivalist. Perhaps his nineteenth-century editor overstated the case in describing him as 'the evangelical Butler'. All the same, he was a well-educated and thoughtful Presbyterian, having studied theology at Leyden after earning his M.A. from Glasgow University in 1712. His essays and works were first published in 1755, following his death in the preceding year. His intellectual acumen is particularly evident in his 'Philosophical Inquiry into the Nature of Happiness', written sometime before the mid-1730s for a Glasgow philosophical society. There he develops a Christian neo-Platonic theory of happiness not unlike that of Edwards in *The Nature of True Virtue*, though lacking Edwards's grace and profundity.[10]

What should be made of Hutcheson's preference for Potter and Leechman in light of John MacLaurin's ostensible philosophical and theological abilities? Why, with MacLaurin available, did Hutcheson prepare the chair for Leechman, and Leechman for the chair? The answer to this question may be critical for understanding the character of the Glasgow Enlightenment. If we cannot establish Leechman's superior theological abilities by inference from his writings, we need not despair at understanding Leechman's role in the Scottish Enlightenment, and particularly in grasping the part he played in putting a new face upon theology in Scotland. Hutcheson's description of Leechman and comments by the latter's students, together with the dearth of Leechman's theological writings, suggest an explanation for Hutcheson's views and actions: Leechman put a new face upon theology in Scotland not by what he thought, but by who he was, not by his theological acumen, but by his personal character. Leechman was a man of 'moderate and charitable sentiments in religious matters', as Hutcheson told Thomas Steward in a letter of 12 February 1740 (*FH*, 134). Well-educated and refined, yet pious, he embodied the virtues that Hutcheson and the Moderates thought commendable in the clergy.

Leechman's education, manners and style, his eloquence and his deep concern for eloquence, were no small part of his character. But his influence — first as professor of divinity, and later as preacher and principal of Glasgow University — was due not to these attributes alone, but to what his students called a godly and pious character. Without such a character, Leechman believed, true eloquence, which was requisite for successful preaching, could not be attained. If Leechman was influential, it was not merely because he imitated the refinement and sophistication of Hutcheson, but also because he exuded, albeit with a bit too much sternness, the Moderate character. Learned, but more concerned with moral virtue than with theological subtleties; well read, but reserved in his enthusiasm for popular authors such as Voltaire and Hume; not given to religious fervour, yet unmistakable in his piety — Leechman's was indeed a new face upon theology, especially in Scotland's West.

To obtain a better understanding of Leechman's public character, and thus the critical role he played in changing the face of religion in Glasgow, we must consider his education at the University of Edinburgh. There he studied with William Hamilton, to whom, he told his biographer, he was 'under great obligations' (*Sermons*, 1:4). Hamilton's influence on his students was extensive. John Ramsay of Ochtertyre wrote of him: 'There was a sincerity, a kindness and a vein of liberality in all that he did and said that gained him the hearts of his students and made them enter with warmth into his views and sentiments.'[11] Hamilton's 'liberality' was not welcomed by all. As early as 1728, Robert Wodrow suspected him of 'favouring Mr. Simson'; by 1730 he was sure that Hamilton had 'departed from the Calvinisticall doctrine' and was taking his students with him (*Analecta*, 3:485, 4:139–40).

As Henry Sefton has pointed out, Hamilton was noted for his silence on theological issues, a noticeable reluctance to reveal his own position on controversial theological matters.[12] Robert Wodrow assumed that Hamilton's silence was not primarily a pedagogical technique, but rather a way of declining 'to dip into hazardous points' (*Analecta*, 3:486). Whatever his intention, Hamilton's practice of silence was found especially striking and intriguing by his student, William Leechman. Leechman professed to have learned from Hamilton not only when the professor spoke his mind on a subject, but also when he was silent, because the latter pattern of behaviour drove him to 'investigate the causes' of Hamilton's silence. The effect of his professor's practice of silence is evident in Leechman's discussion of the sublime in his unpublished

'Treatise of Rhetoric, especially as it regards the Pulpit', where Leechman examines the ability of silence to express the sublime.[13] In such cases, he argues, silence raises the souls of men 'above the ordinary pitch', enabling them to conceive higher ideas and instilling in them a conciousness of the mind's 'natural grandeur' ('TR', 92).

To what extent did Leechman successfully imitate Hamilton's silence? We have testimony that Leechman practised the same impartiality that he attributed to Hamilton's teaching. James Wodrow notes that Leechman 'never offered a dictatorial opinion, an infallible or decisive judgment' (*Sermons*, 33–34) and was scrupulous about presenting both sides fairly, leaving it to the students to make up their own minds on the issue at hand. This is confirmed by another of Leechman's students, William M'Gill, who credited Leechman's reputation as a teacher to his practice of 'stating different opinions with fairness and perspicuity, encouraging literature and free inquiry, exciting his pupils to the love of christian truth and piety, and directing them how to form right sentiments for themselves.'[14]

It was the opening and enlarging of minds that Alexander Carlyle found most memorable about Leechman's teaching.[15] "That this trait was one of Leechman's foremost concerns is clear from the student notebooks of his lectures on Pictet's theology. During a discussion of. . . the books of Exodus and Leviticus, Will Campbell records the following words of his professor:

> There is one caution here necessary and which every one should observe; that is 'to keep a largeness of Mind, to take in a Knowledge of Antiquity, and of Customs that then prevailed in the World and of capacities of the people to which Moses certainly made great condescensions,' otherwise they might have rejected in bulk that divine religion which he was establishing: For its certainly 'Bigotry to judge of all things by Morals, but we should keep a great largeness of Mind in order to judge of Many things.' (GUL, MS Gen. III, fol. 31)

James Wodrow asserts that Leechman himself was free of the bigotry that he warned his students about and was attached to no systems of theology or philosophy, 'that of Hutcheson his beloved friend not excepted' (*Sermons*, 1:68). This same evenhandedness and fairness of mind, along with his affability and a 'perfect simplicity of manners' and, 'above all, his earnest and animated manner in the public offices of religion, especially the devotional part of them', led to a continuing dialogue between Leechman and various secession ministers, some of whom even attended his lectures at the university (*Sermons*, 1:15–16, 70). Leechman had ample opportunity to display his evenhandedness and impartiality in theological discussion. He was responsible for a one-hour lecture four days a week during a six month session. It was

customary for him to present a critical lecture on the New Testament
on Mondays. On Tuesdays, Thursdays and sometimes Fridays he would
lecture on polemical divinity. (These sessions are the origin of the student
notebooks on Leechman's lectures on Pictet's theology.) On Wednesdays
he would lecture in alternate years on the evidences of Christianity and
the composition of sermons (*Sermons*, 30–35).

It is not unusual that Leechman was responsible for lectures on preaching. Hutcheson had been in the habit of instructing divinity students in
. the art of preaching, and Leechman presented an account of this practice
in his biographical preface to Hutcheson's posthumous *System of Moral
Philosophy*, published in two volumes in Glasgow in 1755 (1:xxxviii-xl).
At Aberdeen David Fordyce, regent at Marischal College, presented
lectures on the art of preaching to his students, and these became the
basis for his *Theodorus: A Dialogue Concerning the Art of Preaching*
(1752). A few years later Hugh Blair began giving lectures on this topic
at Edinburgh, and they were eventually published as chapters 29 and 30
in his *Lectures on Rhetoric and Belles Lettres* (1783).

Leechman was well suited to this task. When promoting him for
the Belfast congregation, Hutcheson had written to Thom Drennan
on 5 August 1743: 'You never knew a better, sweeter man, of excellent
literature and except his air and a little roughness of voice, the best
preacher imaginable' (*FH*, 88). He reaffirmed this opinion in his letter
to William Mure of 23 November, when campaigning for Leechman for
the chair of divinity: 'You may represent, what is abundantly known, that
he is universally approved for literature and eloquence' (*FH*, 90). Lord
Woodhouselee maintained that Leechman's style and composition 'with
equal purity, had more elegance than Hutcheson's'.[16] Alexander Carlyle's
voice may be added to those who praised Leechman's eloquence: 'His
appearance was that of an ascetic, reduced by fasting and prayer; but
in aid of fine composition, he delivered his sermons with such fervent
spirit, and in so persuasive a manner, as captivated every audience'
(*Autobiography*, 75).

Carlyle's praise for Leechman's eloquence was not, however, without
qualification. Carlyle remarks that, during term, Leechman devoted one
evening a week to conversation with six or seven students, but that
Leechman's eloquence did not extend to that mode of discourse. Indeed,
Leechman could hardly carry on an ordinary conversation, and tended
instead to deliver a short lecture whenever he spoke: 'This was therefore
a very dull meeting, and everybody longed to be called in to tea with Mrs.
Leechman, whose talent being different from that of her husband, she was
able to maintain a continued conversation on plays, novels, poetry and the
fashions' (*Autobiography*, 93). Despite his failures at repartee, however,
Leechman was by common testimony a gifted and eloquent preacher,
both a model preacher for his students and a qualified teacher of the art
of preaching.

II

IN HIS SERMON, 'The Temper, Character and Duty of a Minister of the Gospel', preached in 1741, Leechman presented his views on the relation between eloquence and moral character — views he would later reassert in his 'Treatise of Rhetoric'. Ministers must be blameless in their outward behaviour as well as their inward character. To achieve this end they must attempt to improve their understanding and to store their minds with 'a large treasure of the best moral and divine sentiments' through a study of scripture, Christian doctrine, natural religion, right reason, the original languages of the sacred authors and history (*Sermons*, 1:109). Having accomplished this, they are fit for teaching the truths of religion and inculcating morals, the primary goals of preaching. Thus, Leechman preached:

> If then we would attain true eloquence, we must cherish an inward sense of the importance and excellency of sacred truths and cultivate a strong feeling of all the virtues . . . . The inward feelings of a good heart have a natural eloquence accompanying them, which can never be equalled by laboured and studied ornament. The heart really and justly moved never fails to dictate a language plain and easy, full of natural and continued vigour . . . . All is nervous and strong, and does not so much please the ear as fill and ravish the soul. (*Sermons*, 159–60)

The same point, that true eloquence cannot exist independent of true virtue, is repeated in the 'Treatise of Rhetoric':

> Men who are thoroughly sincere, never think of studied eloquence: their chief aim is to gain the heart, and to make it be justly moved, which never fails to dictate plain, easy, natural, nervous and strong language, which will be accomplished with such power, as will never be equalled by laboured and studied ornaments. ('TR', 119)

'Corruption of the human heart', Leechman maintains, 'is as bad for stile as false taste and want of genius' ('TR', 95). To be a just speaker one must be a just person. For Leechman, then, rhetoric is, as Aristotle had stated, 'an offshoot of ethical studies' (*Rhetoric*, 1356a25). Any approach to rhetoric that consists of nothing more than an elaboration of rules for the composition and presentation of speeches is doomed to failure. A knowledge of rules of composition and speech might make one a clever speaker, but those who would be truly eloquent need more than a mere mastery of the rules.

Leechman's 'Treatise of Rhetoric' does attend to rules for composition and speech, although these rules receive only modest attention. Leechman would, in any case, have been sensitive to rules and means for the achievement of eloquence. Commenting on Leechman's sermon on prayer in 1743, David Hume remarked that although the author 'has a very clear manly Expression, . . . he does not consult his Ear enough, nor aim at a Style that may be smooth & harmonious; which next to Perspicuity is the chief Ornament of Style.'[17] He referenced this criticism to Cicero, Quintilian and Longinus.

Apparently, some thought Leechman took Hume's advice too seriously. Twenty-one years later, William Thom attacked the Glasgow faculty for constructing a college chapel, where William Leechman would share preaching duties with John Hamilton, rather than continuing the tradition of college members worshipping at Blackfriars Church, where John MacLaurin's son-in-law John Gillies preached. Thom accused the faculty of, among other things, trying to bring about 'a reform in the matter and method of preaching' by adherence to the rules of Aristotle, Cicero and Quintilian.[18]

Knowledge of the rules of Cicero and Quintilian, especially, was important to Leechman, but because the fundamental role of a good speaker is to 'move the passions and affections of the hearers', to raise some passions and to lower others, there is yet a more important kind of knowledge. Only one with a knowledge of human nature and an understanding of the Divine intentions for human life can be truly eloquent ('TR', 5). Only one who *knows* the divine intention of our passions and affections and *possesses* those passions and affections, appropriately raised, will be eloquent.

Leechman commends to his students meditation upon religion and morality as a means of developing the appropriate moral sentiments. Meditation gives 'clearer and more striking views' on the sentiments than do either books or an examination of the sentiments of others. Upon deep meditation, the would-be preacher will 'feel an inward flame and warmth in his Mind which will suggest the most proper and touching sentiments' ('TR', 65). Leechman was a pious man, but he is not here suggesting a mystical piety that is repelled by rationality. Books are, indeed, to be consulted; he here commends the Bible as containing a 'fuller collection of sentiments, moral and divine, than any other book'. Books of morality and sermons ought also to be consulted, especially the works of the heathen moralists Marcus Antoninus, Simplicius, Epictetus, Hierocles and Plato, in whom one can discover various and 'abounding sources of devout and pious thoughts' ('TR', 66). Books may provide the material for meditation, Leechman seems to suggest, but they are no substitute for meditation itself, from which the sentiments follow.

Although *feeling* the right sentiments is critical, so is *understanding* the passions and affections. The ancient orators, Leechman contends, knew well the human heart, and their success in oratory was based on this knowledge. Leechman especially recommends Aristotle's *Rhetoric* as a guide to the passions and the objects suited to them ('TR', 52). But to acknowledge some insightful moral psychology in Aristotle is not to endorse the rhetorical theory of the ancients. Indeed, *contra* Cicero, Leechman argues for the legitimacy of addressing the passions in preaching. The passions, after all, have been placed in human nature by God, each passion having an appropriate object and use. The preacher must work upon these passions and affections so that they obey the ordinances of reason and conscience, thus fulfilling their divinely ordained functions.

Eloquent and effective preaching, then, is dependent upon a knowledge of moral psychology. Leechman details this knowledge requisite for preaching. First of all, one must know 'for what ends nature has implanted the passions in Mankind and to what objects they are ultimately directed by Nature, what is the Supreme Object of those passions and affections of the human mind and what their various uses' ('TR', 63). One must also understand how the passions can go wrong, how they can be directed to improper objects, and what the consequences of misdirected passions are for happiness and purity. Not only must preachers understand the passions themselves, but they must also learn the method for working upon the passions, for redirecting misdirected passions, for 'reducing' wrong passions and awakening or exciting affections which are too 'low' ('TR', 63).

A related concern, frequently mentioned by Leechman, is the 'wrong associations of ideas'. As a result of education, custom and general opinion, ideas that are deleterious to piety and virtue can be joined together. This, Leechman believed, was precisely the problem with religion in Scotland. Religion can become wrongly associated with superstition, with the result that God is believed to be an unforgiving, severe, inexorable deity 'whose favour is extremely difficult to be gotten'. Or religion can come to be thought of as a dull, heavy, melancholy affair, lacking the joy and good pleasure that are its true essence. Similarly, a false association of ideas can lead one to confuse virtues with vices: pride is thought to be 'greatness of mind'; zeal for God is thought to entail sourness towards neighbours. In light of this common problem of the false associations of ideas, sermons must work upon the human imagination; 'indeed,' Leechman asserts, 'the chief business of Sermons is to break these wrong associations of ideas' ('TR', 25).

Preachers must be scholars, then, wise in their understanding of human nature and the workings of human passions, affections and imagination. This demand for an in-depth knowledge of moral psychology in order to preach is quite similar to what one finds in David Fordyce's *Theodorus*.[19] Fordyce satisfies this demand by providing a developed Baconian taxonomy of the passions and affections. His is a careful, painstaking observation of the affections and passions and a deliberate cataloging of the multitude of the passions and their objects. 'It is from a full and exact detail of the process of Nature and the Structure and Operations of its leading Powers', Fordyce argues, 'that we must deduce the true healing Art, or the surest Rules for restoring and perfecting the human constitution' (*Theodorus*, 175).

Leechman, however, denies the effectiveness of this 'scientific' approach. Leechman's approach is a more 'intuitive' analysis of human nature, apposite of a student of Hutcheson. It is more the method of Aristotle, a method of common sense reflection upon human nature, than the method of Bacon or Newton. We gain the requisite knowledge of moral psychology not by a detailed listing of affections and their objects following a lengthy observation of human beings from childhood to adulthood, as Fordyce supposed. Rather, Leechman contends, the knowledge needed can be gained

> from the history of mankind and from observations on human life and from what we see passing about us. *It does not* consist in making an enumeration of the several powers and passions of the human heart; but it consists in knowing the real characters of mankind ('TR', 63, emphasis added).

The similarity of vocabulary, the talk of 'observation', ought not mislead us. Although Leechman and Fordyce both deny any innate moral knowledge, their methods of gaining knowledge of human moral psychology are radically different: the difference between a common sense approach typical of Aristotle and Francis Hutcheson and the 'scientific' or empirical approach that characterized the Enlightenment philosophers of Aberdeen.[20] Leechman not only affirms Aristotelian common-sense observation but also commends Aristotle's own understanding of the passions and their objects in the *Rhetoric*.

Knowledge of the real characters of mankind is necessary for proper preaching, Leechman contends, and this knowledge is most readily acquired in conjunction with a knowledge of God and self revealed in the Holy Scriptures. What does he see as the 'real characters of mankind'? Discernment of moral character is not easy, Leechman argues, due to the 'unfathomableness' of the human heart. But what Leechman does notice, in addition to the mixtures of good and evil in all persons, is an 'inexhaustible fund of self-love' that prevents us from even knowing our own characters. Of his thirty-two collected sermons, no fewer than five explicitly address this problem of self-love: 'The Necessity of Self-Denial as the Foundation of Virtue', 'Practical Lessons to the Young, founded on the Necessity of Self-Denial', 'On the Sources of Humility', 'The Excellence and Advantages of Humility' and 'On Humility'. James Wodrow notes that Leechman's willingness to affirm this apparently orthodox Calvinist doctrine of the fallen and self-interested character of human beings did not go unchallenged at the college. One of these sermons, 'The Necessity of Self-Denial', preached in the college chapel sometime after 1764, was, because of its emphasis on the character and extent of self-love in all persons, misconstrued and 'too keenly opposed' by an unnamed professor in a public lecture (*Sermons*, 2:297).

Leechman was cautious, however, lest he be accused of painting too dark a picture of human nature. We know from inspection of our natural sentiments, from consideration of the received wisdom of humanity, and from the teachings of Christianity, as well as from daily observation that, although we may be disposed towards selfish pursuits, we are 'capable of exercising generous affections in a variety of ways; that we are capable of and designed for very high improvements'. 'It must be admitted', Leechman remarks, 'that there is a mighty, an essential difference, between a Cato and a Cataline, between a Marcus Antoninus and a Nero' (*Sermons*, 2:157). Our self-interested nature is not, by any means, an excuse for wrong-doing. Self-interested we may tend to be, but this limitation does not preclude genuine beneficence to others.

If Leechman wished his preachers and parishioners to be aware of their intractably self-interested characters, he wanted them also to be on guard against seductive pleasure and dangerous passions, particularly those most common to youth. He therefore offered 'Motives and Directions to Restraining Youthful Passions', 'A Worthy Plan of Life Recommended to Youth', 'Youth Guarded Against hurtful Maxims and Books' and two sermons on 'Youth Guarded against licentious Pleasure'. Leechman's comments on pleasure are as instructive about the nature of his moral thought as they are eloquent:

> Pleasure is a Demonness of a very malignant kind, that haunts, infests and fascinates, particularly those places of the earth which have carried their improvements and refinements highest; and that, if a vigorous stop be not put to her incantations, she will lead them (amidst all their admired and boasted advancements in arts and sciences) blindfolded to their utter destruction. Here we may observe and admire the wisdom of Providence, which has placed the great bulk of mankind in a situation in which the necessity of labouring secures them, in some measure, against the enchantments of this sorceress. (*Sermons*, 2:140)

Here we find the grand themes of Enlightenment religion in mid-eighteenth-century Glasgow. Here is the cautious embracing of improvements, refinements and 'advancements in arts and sciences', with the awareness that even in the secret places of modernity an illegitimate pleasure tempts us. Here is the confidence in the wisdom of God, providentially ordering nature in such a way that the order and happiness of society is attained, and at the same time ensuring that no one need fall prey to pleasure. Here is the affirmation of the goodness of labour. And here is the conviction that the 'lower ranks of people', those most likely to be distracted from their labour, are those most liable to the lure of the seductress, pleasure, and in need of special assistance.

Students, therefore, must keep busy and be ever watchful. Those who would guard themselves against licentious pleasures should be careful in their choice of books, of plays, of poetry, lest their minds be 'polluted with lust and lasciviousness'. They should disavow any instruction that commends the life of mere pleasure as the happy life, should embrace only those sentiments and opinions which encourage the heart's ardour for 'the good, the generous, and the great', and should beware of any suggestions that 'lessen our veneration for the sacred Scriptures', or suggest that religion is a joyless thing.

In order to secure oneself against false opinions such as these, and thus to control and regulate the passions properly, Leechman proposes adherence to six rules.[21] First, we should be suspicious of any principle that recommends indulging the passions, mindful always that the passions are more than ready to justify themselves without warrant. Secondly, we should remember that the principles we embrace are matters of extreme importance; this should preclude a rash or careless endorsement of principles. Thirdly, in reading books, even the 'geniusses of the age' (Leechman mentions Voltaire, Rousseau, Bolingbroke and Hume), one is to read critically, 'to exercise judgment in the most cool and deliberate manner . . . with candour and modesty indeed, but at the same time with firmness' (*Sermons*, 2:183–185). Fourthly, our desire for developing our reasoning powers ought not lead to a neglect of our critical powers. Fifthly, we are to study and judge 'the temper and spirit of the work', not just its arguments. Finally, Leechman admonishes his congregation to 'preserve an habitual and humble sense of the weakness and foibles of the human life and to ask God for guidance' (*Sermons*, 2:177–193).

William Leechman, like Francis Hutcheson, believed that God, in creating the world, had equipped all humans with a moral faculty, a power by which to distinguish good and evil in dispositions and actions. Furthermore, humans are constructed in such a way as naturally to feel approbation in the presence of human excellence, to feel abhorrence of evil actions, and to feel 'complacency' when we do no wrong. A third part of this moral power is a sense of moral desert, a feeling, when we do good, that we 'deserve the approbation of God and all good beings and that we may depend securely on happiness in the divine moral government' ('TR', 31–32). In the presence of persons of excellent character we feel not only esteem and approbation but also pleasure and delight in their moral excellence, and we wish them happiness and prosperity. Before such people we feel humble, desire their approbation and seek to act in ways that will win their favour.

How important, then, if preachers are to be the shapers and molders of moral character, that they themselves be people of virtue! Those who possess a virtuous moral character cannot fail to be noticed and approved of. 'A human mind can scarcely be so entirely corrupted, as not to own and acknowledge, not be smitten with the beauty, and struck with the reverence, of pure and unaffected piety and goodness' (*Sermons*, 2:15). The congregations of such ministers will not only approve of their characters but will believe their words, and will endeavour to pursue those actions and to form in themselves those virtues that the minister endorses and exemplifies. But if the preacher is not possessed of true goodness, that too will be noticed, his words resounding as a clanging gong as the congregation is left to its own devices.

Leechman himself preached the personal virtues of humility, piety, equity of disposition, wisdom and greatness of mind, and the social virtues of love, magnanimity, courage and politeness. He warned his congregations, usually college youth, of the vices of self-love, pride, envy, meanness and intemperance, as well as the vicious effects of guilt and melancholy. By almost all accounts, despite his rather stern countenance, his words were eloquent and rang true, for he was perceived as embodying the virtues of which he spoke.

III

WILLIAM LEECHMAN PLAYED an active part in the life of the college at Glasgow for a quarter of a century following his appointment to the faculty in 1744. He edited a work by his former student, James Geddes, *An Essay on the Composition and Manner of Writing of the Ancients, particularly Plato*, which was published posthumously by Robert Foulis in 1748. In addition to his divinity teaching, Leechman was among the four Glasgow professors who filled in for Hutcheson's successor, Thomas Craigie, when Craigie fell ill in 1751, taking personal responsibility for lectures on natural theology and the first book of Hutcheson's *System of Moral Philosophy*. He was a founding member of the Anderston Club and was active in the Glasgow Literary Society. The extent of Leechman's stature in the church was revealed in 1757, when he was elected moderator of the General Assembly.

Illness forced Leechman to give up teaching in 1759. He recovered, at least moderately, and was made principal of the university in 1761. For the next few years he preached at the college chapel and held open lectures on Sunday evenings. He died towards the end of 1785, at almost eighty years of age.

Leechman's rival for the chair of divinity, John MacLaurin, acknowledged that, whatever his own gifts, he was not a master stylist, his style being 'not so polite as to please the palates of some' (quoted in Ramsay, *Scotland and Scotsmen*, 1:272). Leechman, by contrast, remained until his death concerned with style, but not only style. Elizabeth Mure recalled that in Leechman's 'speech' to her as he lay dying he complained that men had become so preoccupied with style that they had abandoned truth. Hume and Voltaire, he believed, were the dangerous models for far too many (NLS, MS 5003, fol. 15).

The kind of style that attracted Leechman was natural, meaning that it was dependent upon piety and moral virtue — a style that was the fruit of moral goodness rather than the tool of cleverness. Leechman was, we may surmise, what Hutcheson took to be a moral model for clergy and aspiring

clergy. It is no surprise that Hutcheson found the character and style of
Leechman to be his most important qualification for the professorship
of divinity. There is, in the ancient philosophers so much loved by
Hutcheson, a 'great man' tradition in ethics. The two Stoics most dear
to Hutcheson, Cicero and Marcus Aurelius Antoninus, were themselves
individuals who combined practical wisdom and the moral virtues, private
and public, with eloquence. Aristotle also embraces such a model of virtue
in his *phronimos*, the person of practical wisdom, and the *megalopsuchos*,
the 'great-souled' person who, because of his greatness of soul, moves
slowly and communicates with a 'deep voice and calm speech' (*Ethics*,
1125a15). Hutcheson hoped that the men of the Glasgow Enlightenment
would emulate these individuals, whose example was required if a 'new
face' was to be put not only upon Scottish theology, but upon Scotland
itself. In Glasgow and the West of Scotland, the charitable, pious,
refined, eloquent and fair-minded William Leechman did much to bring
about the realization of Hutcheson's vision.

Notes

I am deeply indebted to Richard Sher and Roger Emerson for their generous
assistance with references, to Anthony Weston and the special collections staff
at the GUL and to Iain G. Brown of the manuscripts division of the NLS.

1. Hutcheson to Thomas Drennan, 5 Aug. 1743, in William Robert Scott,
   *Francis Hutcheson: His Life, Teaching and Position in the History of
   Philosophy* (1900; rpt. New York, 1966) (hereafter cited as *FH*), 88.
   Robert Wodrow's suggestion that John MacLaurin was among the chief
   friends of Hutcheson shortly after his arrival in Glasgow in 1730 seems
   unlikely in light of Hutcheson's failure to support Maclaurin in 1740 and
   his disdain for the evangelical revivalism with which MacLaurin would later
   be associated (*FH*, 62).
2. I have corrected Scott's transcription of this letter, as well as others from
   Hutcheson to Drennan, using the originals in GUL, MS Gen. 1018.
3. James Wodrow, 'Account of the Author's Life and of His Lectures', prefixed
   to William Leechman, *Sermons*, 2 vols. (London, 1789), 1:18–19.
4. Hutcheson to Mure, 23 Nov. 1743, in *FH*, 90. The references are to George
   Whitefield and William McCulloch, who attracted thousands of worshippers
   to the Cambuslang Revivals near Glasgow in 1742. Leechman had served as
   Mure's tutor after graduating from Edinburgh University in the 1720s.
5. *FH*, 92. Ross had supported MacLaurin in 1740, and his was considered
   the critical vote in the 1743 election. Even after Ross had cast his vote for
   Leechman, he promised his support to MacLaurin should there be some
   difficulty in loosing Leechman from his presbytery. See Archibald Campbell
   of Succoth to Archibald Campbell, Dec. 1743, NLS, MS 16,591, fol. 199.
6. James Robe, *The Remarks of the Committee of the Presbytery of Glasgow*,

William Leechman, Pulpit Eloquence

upon Mr. Leechman's Sermon on Prayer, with His Replies Thereunto (Edinburgh, 1744), 9–10.

7. John Gillies, 'Some Account of the Life and Character of John Mac-Laurin', in *The Works of the Reverend John MacLaurin*, ed. W. H. Goold (Edinburgh, 1860), xv.

8. Robert Wodrow, *Analecta*, 4 vols. (Edinburgh, 1842–43), 3:257.

9. Colin MacLaurin to Andrew Mitchell, 17 Dec. 1743, in *The Collected Letters of Colin MacLaurin*, ed. Stella Mills (Exeter, n.d.), 86–87.

10. Goold's 1860 edition of MacLaurin's *Works*, cited earlier, includes the latter's *Sermons and Essays* (1755), where the 'Philosophical Inquiry into the Nature of Happiness' was first published, and *An Essay on the Prophecies Relating to the Messiah* (1773).

11. John Ramsay, *Scotland and Scotsmen in the Eighteenth Century*, ed. Alexander Allardyce, 2 vols. (Edinburgh, 1888), 1:227ff.

12. Henry Sefton, "Neu-lights and Preachers Legall': Some Observations on the Beginnings of Moderatism in the Church of Scotland', in *Church, Politics and Society: Scotland 1408–1929*, ed. Norman Macdougall (Edinburgh, 1983), 189.

13. The manuscript of the 'Treatise of Rhetoric' (hereafter cited as 'TR'), dated 16 May 1763, is in the GUL, MS Gen. 51 (another copy is in the EUL). It is most likely a revised version of Leechman's lectures on preaching.

14. William M'Gill, *A Practical Essay on the Death of Jesus Christ* (Edinburgh, 1786), 185n.

15. *The Autobiography of Dr. Alexander Carlyle of Inveresk, 1722–1805*, new ed., ed. John Hill Burton (London and Edinburgh, 1910), 94.

16. Alexander Fraser Tytler, Lord Woodhouselee, *Memoirs of the Life and Writings of the Honourable Henry Home of Kames*, 2 vols. (Edinburgh, 1807); *Supplement* (1809), 14.

17. Hume to Mure, 30 June 1743, in *New Letters of David Hume*, ed. Raymond Klibansky and Ernest C. Mossner (Oxford, 1954), 12.

18. *The Works of Rev. William Thom* (Glasgow, 1799), 231–55. I am indebted for this reference to Richard B. Sher, 'Commerce, Religion and the Enlightenment in Eighteenth-Century Glasgow', in *The History of Glasgow*, vol. 1, ed. T. M. Devine and Gordon Jackson (Manchester, 1994).

19. It is more than a little surprising that Leechman makes no mention of Fordyce. Not only were they similar in age and religious disposition, but there is also a strong resemblance between Fordyce's *Theodorus*, published in 1752, and Leechman's 'Treatise of Rhetoric', which was completed eleven years later. Whenever they discuss the same topic, which is frequently, Fordyce is always the more penetrating and perceptive thinker.

20. On the Baconian-Newtonian orientation of Aberdonian moral philosophy, see P. B. Wood, 'Science and the Pursuit of Virtue in the Aberdeen Enlightenment', in *Studies in the Philosophy of the Scottish Enlightenment*, ed. M. A. Stewart (Oxford, 1990), 127–49.

21. It is worth noting that Leechman embraces an intellectualist notion of moral motivation more in keeping with Aristotle than with Hutcheson. We are not

unavoidably led by operative passions or affections, 'enslaved to no passion'; rather, reason is in control ('TR', 130). For Leechman, then, wisdom is chief among the virtues, the preacher's authority resting, in part, in his knowledge of what ideas are correctly associated. In addition, reason and conscience have it within their power to correct the reigning affection and, thus, to direct human action. In preaching, ministers wrongly direct their attention only to working on the passions, but must likewise present arguments to convince the judgement of their audience ('TR', 42).

4
Adam Smith's 'Happiest' Years as a Glasgow Professor

Ian Simpson Ross

In 1750, young Adam Smith began a third year in Edinburgh as a freelance lecturer on rhetoric, law and possibly the history of philosophy.[1] Born in Kirkcaldy in 1723, where he was educated at the burgh school, Smith had spent three stimulating years as a Glasgow student, from 1737 to 1740, and then six mainly unhappy ones as a Snell Exhibitioner at Balliol College, Oxford. Nothing came of family hopes that he would secure a position as a travelling tutor, but the Edinburgh lectures brought him recognition. Then his former logic teacher at Glasgow, John Loudon (or Loudoun), died on 1 November 1750, and at a university meeting on 19 December it was decided to elect a successor on 9 January 1751. There were at least two 'able candidates' for the post: George Muirhead, subsequently professor of oriental languages and still later professor of humanity (Latin), and Smith, the unanimous choice.[2]

The faculty clerk, Robert Simson, Smith's former mathematics teacher, was instructed to inform Smith of his election, to ask him to come to Glasgow 'as soon as his affairs can allow him, in order to be admitted'; and to require him to present a dissertation, 'De Origine Idearum', as a trial of his qualifications (Scott, 137–38). Smith accepted his new position on 10 January, presumably 'by first post', as requested, and went on to say that he would try to get to Glasgow 'on Tuesday night', but that he would have to return to Edinburgh within two days, adding that he could not 'even be very certain if that absence will be consented to by my friends here' (*Corr.*, 4). This reference is probably to his commitment to Henry Home of Kames and others who wanted him to give his Edinburgh lectures during the winter months.

Smith attended a university meeting at Glasgow on 16 January 1751, read the dissertation expected of him, to unanimous approval, and having signed the Calvinist Confession of Faith before the Presbytery of Glasgow, he took the 'usual Oath de Fideli' to secure admission as a professor of Glasgow University. After he 'was solemnly received by all the members', he was permitted to return immediately to Edinburgh. With the agreement of the university meeting, he appointed Hercules Lindesay, professor of civil law since 1750, to teach the 'Semi' class in his absence (*Scott*, 139).

Despite the show of unanimity alluded to in the minutes of these university meetings, there seems to have been some feeling about Smith's election. This can be deduced from a draft letter to Smith in the hand of the recently admitted professor of medicine, William Cullen, who is believed to have been a friend from his Edinburgh lecturing period and who later treated Smith for the lifelong 'hypochondriasis' that afflicted him.[3] Cullen's letter was written some time before April 1751, when poor health forced Thomas Craigie, professor of moral philosophy, to cease teaching and live in the country. Cullen suggests that Smith had been troubled by divisions among the Glasgow faculty, and he hopes matters will improve when his friend comes to Glasgow 'to live among us'. Craigie and six other professors apparently supported Smith 'without regard to any great man whatever', whereas William Ruat, the professor of oriental languages appointed on 31 October 1750, made out that Craigie's vote for Smith, along with that of William Leechman, professor of divinity, was a 'compliment to Lord Hyndford and [the] Duke of Argyle'. Cullen also intimates that Smith had written to London to the third duke of Argyll and to his cousin and guardian, William Smith (the second duke's secretary) about his election, and that these efforts had been taken amiss in Glasgow (*Corr.*, 334–36). Competition for Scottish university chairs was intense at this time, and there was a great deal of jockeying for advantage among the candidates and their supporters.

Once the political maneuvering was behind him, Smith finally settled at Glasgow, where he would live from 1751 to 1764. This chapter will sketch some of the highlights of those years, with particular emphasis on Smith's role as a professor. Part I treats Smith's teaching of logic and rhetoric, part II his teaching of moral philosophy — including ethics, jurisprudence and political economy, and part III his lecturing style, influence on students and administrative activities.

I

THE GLASGOW LOGIC CHAIR that Smith filled had been created in 1727 as a result of a commission that recommended reform in the manner of teaching the philosophy curriculum. It appeared that Glasgow was following the example of Edinburgh in abandoning the regenting system, in which a master would take a class of students through the work in philosophy over a period of three or four years, without specializing in one part of the subject. However, the *nova erectio* (new foundation) of Glasgow in 1577 had envisaged specialist teaching on the model of contemporary European developments, including fixing public chairs to different subjects and requiring the holders to give prescribed courses of lectures. As principal of Glasgow University from 1574 to 1580, Andrew Melville had sought to carry out this plan, with his nephew James Melville teaching dialectic and rhetoric in the Ramist tradition to first-year students and the principal himself teaching Aristotle's logic and ethics to the second-year class.

These innovations were abandoned during the seventeenth century, and the regents reverted to teaching scholastic logic in order to provide students with an intellectual approach that was considered fundamental to all fields of inquiry. The regent read out portions of Latin texts or notes on them, and the students accustomed themselves to the terminology by recording the dictation. The regents also provided questions and a commentary as a focus for study, encouraging students to answer questions in Latin and to take sides over 'disputed questions'. The increasing availability of books took away much of the need for dictation, and the commentary and disputation had a tendency to degenerate into quibbling over terms and definitions.[4] According to an account given by John Millar, when Smith began teaching logic at Glasgow in October 1751, he 'soon saw the necessity of departing widely from the plan that had been followed by his predecessors' (Stewart, 273). These included John Loudon, whose scholastic approach is reflected in extant sets of his 'Dictata'.[5] In the *Wealth of Nations*, Smith was to sum up logic on the ancient model as the 'science of the general principles of good and bad reasoning' (*WN*, 2:770). For his students, however, he was content to paint the syllogistic formulations of Aristotle as an 'artificial method of reasoning', about which curiosity should be gratified, since it had formerly taken up the attention of learned men. Apparently deciding that new times demanded a new approach, he proposed to turn to 'studies of a more interesting and useful nature' by presenting a 'system' of rhetoric and belles lettres. Millar's defence of this procedure, which was probably that of Smith himself, runs as follows:

> The best method of explaining and illustrating the various powers of the human mind, the most useful part of metaphysics, arises from an examination of the several ways of communicating our thoughts by speech, and from an attention to the principles of those literary compositions which contribute to persuasion or entertainment. By these arts, every thing that we perceive or feel, every operation of our minds, is expressed and delineated in such a manner, that it may be clearly distinguished and remembered. There is, at the same time, no branch of literature more suited to youth at their first entrance upon philosophy than this, which lays hold of their taste and their feelings. (Stewart, 274)

Smith's revolutionary decision to reform formal logic teaching may have been determined by a critical view of Loudon's performance as a professor, memories of the wearisome insistence on Aristotelian logic during his student days at Oxford, and demands on his time when he arrived in Glasgow. We have evidence about the content of his innovative course in the two slim volumes of the 'Notes of Dr Smith's Rhetorick Lectures' that John M. Lothian discovered in 1958 and published in 1963. There survives in this form an expansion of rather full notes on what Smith said in teaching rhetoric to a 'private' class in 1762–63, when he was professor of moral philosophy but still offering the innovative course begun when he held the logic chair. According to analysis by John Bryce, the manuscript notes are chiefly rendered in two hands, with a third hand, perhaps that of a later owner, represented touching up faded letters (*LRBL*, Introduction, 3). One of the two principal writers had a sense of humour, doodling a face which is perhaps that of Smith, and adding: 'This is a picture of uncertainty' (*LRBL*, 113, n. z).

This note-taker also recorded a joke made by Henry Herbert, an English aristocrat who was a boarder in Smith's house during the 1762–63 session, and who was introduced by Smith to David Hume on 22 February 1763 as someone 'very well acquainted with your works' (*Corr.*, 89). On Christmas Eve 1762 Smith discussed in the fifteenth rhetoric lecture La Bruyère's account of the absent-minded man, Menalcas. Herbert adapted a tag from Horace (*Satires*, I.i.69–70) — *Mutato nomine de te fabula* — and wittily equated Menalcas and his professor (*LRBL*, 81). Throughout his career, of course, Smith was often painted as the epitome of absentmindedness. A typical story is recorded by Lady Mary Coke in her journal on Sunday 8 February 1767, as told her by Lady George Lennox:

> [John Damer, son of Lord Milton] made [Adam Smith] a visit the other morning as he was going to breakfast, & falling into discourse, Mr Smith took a piece of bread & butter, which, after he had rolled it round & round, he put into the teapot & pour'd the water upon it; some time after he pourd it into a cup, & when he had tasted it, he said it was the worst tea he had ever mett with. Mr Damer told him he did not in the least doubt of it, for . . . he had made it of the bread & butter he had been rolling about his fingers.[6]

Absentminded or not, Smith could organize and deliver an effective series of lectures on rhetoric. We do not have a version of the first of those heard by Herbert and the anonymous transcribers, but the course represented by the notes fell into the two divisions outlined by Millar: 'an examination of the several ways of communicating our thoughts by speech' (lectures 2–11), and 'an attention to the principles of those literary compositions which contribute to persuasion and entertainment' (lectures 12–30).

The third lecture was a simplified version of the only part of the rhetoric course that Smith allowed to get into print: 'Considerations concerning the First Formation of Languages, and the Different Genius of original and compounded Languages'.[7] It is an example of what Dugald Stewart called '*Theoretical* or *Conjectural History*' (Stewart, 293). Also represented by Smith's 'History of Astronomy' (*EPS*, 31–105), this was a characteristic Enlightenment form of historical inquiry in which naturalistic tendencies in human nature, operating uniformly, are advanced as causes of social and intellectual development and decline, especially in cases or circumstances where contemporary evidence is lacking.[8]

Smith's lecture on the origin of languages offered an answer to a question formulated in Rousseau's *Discours sur l'inégalité* in 1755: how could men create words without generalizing, and how could they generalize without words? Following the lead of Condillac in his *Essai sur l'origine des connoissances humaine* (1746), Smith imagines cave-dwelling savages contriving with relative ease single nouns to communicate about objects connected with their food, drink and shelter; then, with more difficulty, generalizing to apply these nouns to classes of nouns; and finally abstracting to express the qualities and their relations. This process resulted, Smith believed, in the creation of prepositions and adjectives. The savages were also described as requiring another 'master sort of word' to express action, namely, verbs. Smith seems to have been among the first scholars to have distinguished between 'original' languages such as Greek, which he perceived as synthetic — in today's terms, made up of rather few root words, subject to complex inflections to indicate case, number, gender, tense and so on — and 'compounded' or analytic languages, whose prepositions, pronouns and auxiliary verbs are separated from the main stems of words.[9] As the first part of the rhetoric course progressed, students heard on Monday 29 November 1762 that Smith's system for this subject was of a piece with the one he devised for ethics. He made this clear by challenging the standpoint of traditional rhetoric, which held that the expressive force and beauty of language reside in figures of speech. Smith's claim is altogether different:

> When the sentiment of the speaker is expressed in a neat, clear, plain and clever manner, and the passion or affection he is poss<ess>ed of and intends, *by sympathy*, to communicate to his hearer, is plainly and cleverly hit off, then and then only the expression has all the force and beauty that language can give it. It matters not the least whether the figures of speech are introduced or not. . . . [They] contribute or can contribute towards [Beauty] only so far as they happen to be the just and naturall forms of expressing that Sentiment [which] is nobler or more beautifull than such as are commonly met with. (*LRBL*, 25–26)

The 'Grammarians' are confused, in Smith's view, about the role of figures of speech; they do not appreciate the fact that, for example, the beauty of a passage 'flow[s] from the sentiment and the method of expressing it being suitable to the passion'. As a result, they form their systems of rhetoric 'from the consideration of these figures, and the divisions and subdivisions of them'. With some asperity, Smith concludes: 'They are generally a very silly set of Books and not at all instructive' (*LRBL*, 26).

Smith could teach rhetoric as the staple of his 'private' moral philosophy class because his successor as professor of logic, James Clow, had reverted to the traditional approach to the subject. Clow was succeeded, however, by George Jardine, who was one of Smith's favourite pupils in the 1760s. Jardine shared Smith's view about reorganizing the logic course. He described his own scheme most fully in the second edition of *Outlines of Philosophical Education, illustrated by the Method of Teaching the Logic Class in the University of Glasgow* (1825),[10] which incorporates the legacy of Smith's reformulation of rhetoric and its integration into university studies, pedagogical practice still maintained in higher education across North America.[11]   Another student of Smith's, Archibald Arthur (matriculated 1757 or 1758), became in time Thomas Reid's assistant and replacement as professor of moral philosophy (1780–96), then briefly his successor (1796–97). He is described by a contemporary as reverting to Smith's practice of giving in his 'private' class 'those lectures on taste, composition, and the history of philosophy [i.e. science], which before [Smith's] nomination to a professorship at Glasgow, he had delivered as a lecturer on rhetoric in Edinburgh' (Richardson, 'Account', 514). An anonymous source of the same era reveals that Smith's 'History of Astronomy' is mentioned in one of Arthur's 'College exercises', and this information suggests that Smith's concept of the systematic development of philosophy or science was initially formulated in his Edinburgh lectures, then imparted to his Glasgow auditors, and further disseminated by one of them to another generation of Glasgow students.[12]   However seminal and far-reaching the consequences of Smith's innovations in the logic chair, they did not please everyone at the University of Glasgow. A sour note is struck in the correspondence of James Wodrow, library keeper and son of the Presbyterian historian Robert Wodrow. In a letter dated 20 December 1751, he turns down an invitation for the following Saturday because two friends who had planned to accompany him have made up their minds after some delay to attend Smith's rhetoric course, and the professor has been agreeable enough to arrange to give a catch-up lecture that Saturday. Wodrow describes the course to his correspondent, Samuel Kenrick, in these terms:

> You must know that we have got a new sort of Lectures which by their novelty draw all men after them[.] I mean Lectures on Rhetoric by which their heads are stuffed with the Circumstantials adjuncts Heads and tails of Sentences, Nominatives Accusatives and I dont know how much more Grammatical Jargon which you may lay your account to be entertained with at meeting.

Wodrow resumes the topic of Smith's course in another letter to Kenrick, dated 21 January 1752:

Smiths Reputation in his Rhetorical Lectures is sinking every day[.] As I am not a scholar of his I don't pretend to assign the cause. He begins next week to give Lectures on Jurisprudentia which I design to attend. I hear he has thrown out some contemptuous Expressions of Mr Hutchison. Let the young man take care to guard his Censures by the Lines Palisades and counterscarps of his science Rhetoric. For there are some of Mr H[utcheso]ns scholars still about the Coll[ege] who perhaps will try to turn the mouths of the Cannon against himself.[13]

Late in life, Wodrow provided for Lord Buchan a fuller and more favourable account of the rhetoric lectures, as well as some details about Smith briefly seeking to emulate the lecturing style of his master (and Wodrow's), Francis Hutcheson.

As to Smith lecturing on jurisprudence in his first year at Glasgow, this came about because Craigie, Hutcheson's successor as professor of moral philosophy, was too ill by April 1751 to continue teaching, and on 3 September 1751 Smith wrote to Cullen from Edinburgh to say that 'with great pleasure' he would do what he could to relieve Craigie: 'You mention Natural Jurisprudence and Politics as the parts of his lectures, which it would be most agreeable for me to take upon me to teach. I shall willingly undertake both' (*Corr.*, 5). This arrangement was confirmed at a university meeting on 11 September, when it was agreed that William Leechman would teach the 'Theologia Naturalis, and the first book of Mr Hutchesons Ethicks, and Mr Smith the other two books de Jurisprudentia Naturali et Politicis' (quoted in *LJ*, Introduction, 1–2). The textbook alluded to here was Francis Hutcheson's *Philosophiae moralis institutio compendiaria, ethicis & jurisprudentiae naturalis elementa continuens*, published in three volumes at Glasgow in 1742. Even though Smith would be teaching from this source, and it is highly interesting that he bound himself to do so, it is reasonable to suppose that, having little time to prepare new logic lectures for his Glasgow post, he drew on the Edinburgh rhetoric and belles lettres course. Craigie died in Lisbon on 27 November, and there must have been anticipation of this event at the time, also of the eventuality of Smith succeeding him, with a consequent need to find another professor of logic.

These points emerge in another letter to Cullen, written on a Tuesday that same November, when Smith was in Edinburgh. It is of singular interest that Smith mentions Hume as a contender for a prospective vacant post at Glasgow, and he does so in terms that suggest he admired him as a man and as a philosopher. At the same time, Smith reveals the strong streak of prudence in his character, noting that public opinion did not favour Hume, no doubt because of his reputation as a sceptic, and the 'interest' of the university in this respect had to be considered: 'I should prefer David Hume to any man for a colleague; but I am afraid the public would not be of my opinion; and the interest of the society will oblige us to have some regard to the opinion of the public' (*Corr.*, 5).

Perhaps Smith could not easily imagine Hume signing the Confession of Faith before the Presbytery of Glasgow, as was required before admission to a professorship at the university. On the other hand, Smith had good grounds for thinking that Glasgow was not ready for Hume. Wodrow's letter to Kenrick dated 21 January 1752 mentions that the clergy of the city went in a body to Principal Neil Campbell to say that they did not want Hume made a professor. At the same time, Wodrow reports that he is reading Hume's *Political Discourses*, though he does not make much of them. On 10 January of the same year, the Glasgow Literary Society was founded, with Smith as an original member, and on 23 January he read an 'account of some of Mr David Hume's Essays on Commerce' (Duncan, *Notices and Documents*, 132). We may presume that Smith could offer some insights into Hume's work, and that these marked a stage in the development of his own system of economics.[14] Hume's first extant letter to Smith, dated 24 September 1752, mentions earlier correspondence and alludes to discussion between the two friends about the appropriateness of beginning an 'English History' with the reign of Henry VII. Hume asks Smith for hints to improve his *Essays Moral and Political*, then being corrected for the edition of *Essays and Treatises* of 1753; this request suggests that he respected Smith's intellect (*Corr.*, 8). Smith returned Hume's friendship warmly, though he never fell in readily with Hume's schemes to gain his company, and he gave Hume unfailing admiration, perhaps relayed to Glasgow students in the form of the accolade in the *Wealth of Nations*, in which Hume is identified as 'by far the most illustrious philosopher and historian of the present age' (*WN*, 2:790).

II

MEANWHILE, SMITH'S CAREER at Glasgow University progressed. On 22 April 1752 he was unanimously elected by the faculty to the vacant chair of moral philosophy, on the express condition that he content himself with the emoluments of the logic chair until 10 October following (Scott, 140). This measure was taken to cover fair payment for the distribution of Craigie's teaching among a number of colleagues, including Smith. Scottish professors at this period earned an appreciable part of their income from student fees payable to them directly, and therefore had an incentive to teach well, maintain distinction in their disciplines and attract students. Smith noted these features of competition in the academic market and the sad effects of their absence in such universities as Oxford (*WN*, 2:759–61). With eighty to ninety fee-paying students in his 'public' moral philosophy class, and perhaps twenty in the 'private' one — and taking into account other perquisites, such as a rent-free house latterly in Professors' Court on the north side of the attractive college quadrangles — Smith earned in his best years something like £300 per year. This was a respectable professional salary in the Scotland of the day, when a commissioner of customs earned £500 and a judge £700. Smith's income, however, could be cut in half in lean years such as 1753, when he and his successor as professor of logic, James Clow, reported that enrolment was so low that they wished to discontinue their classes (Scott, 67).

As much recent scholarship has demonstrated, the teaching of moral philosophy was at the core of Scottish University education in Smith's time, and of the Scottish Enlightenment as a movement.[15] It should be acknowledged, however, that the Glasgow tradition of a broad approach to that subject went back to the early decades of the sixteenth century, when John Mair taught the *Ethics* of Aristotle, publishing an edition in 1530, as well as taking up economic issues in lectures on the *Sentences* of Peter Lombard. In addition, in the 1570s Andrew Melville and his nephew James Melville taught the moral philosophy of Aristotle (Durkan and Kirk, *University of Glasgow*, 158, 279).

As the distribution of Craigie's duties indicates, the eighteenth-century 'public' moral philosophy course at Glasgow consisted of four parts: natural theology, ethics, jurisprudence and politics. John Millar wrote that in the first part Smith 'considered the proofs of the being and attributes of God, and those principles of the human mind upon which religion is founded' (Stewart, 274). These 'principles' are adduced by Smith in his essay on the history of ancient physics, which argues that 'ignorance, and confusion of thought' in the 'first ages of the world' necessarily gave birth to that 'pusillanimous superstition which ascribes almost every unexpected event, to the arbitrary will of some designing, though invisible human beings, who produced it for some private and particular purpose.' In time, however, philosophers came to regard the universe as a 'complete system, governed by general laws, and directed to general ends, viz. its own preservation and prosperity, and that of all the species that are in it'. The unity of this system suggested the unity of the principle that created it and informed it. Thus, 'as ignorance begot superstition, science gave birth to the first theism that arose among those nations, who were not enlightened by divine Revelation' (*EPS*, 112–14).

Smith's emphasis on perception of a cosmic system accompanying enlightenment in theology is of a piece with his methodology in delivering a system of rhetoric, and he approached ethics, jurisprudence and economics the same way. Such a method gave coherence to the intellectual world he explored for the benefit of his students, and it had its counterpart in the teaching of colleagues such as the scientists William Cullen and Joseph Black. Once again, not everyone relished this approach. That persistent critic of the Glasgow professoriate, Revd. William Thom of Govan, made fun of them falling asleep in their rooms while reading their own systems.[16] Students were impressed, however, as were readers of the books in which these systems were presented. One measure of the endurance of this intellectual tradition was the currency in the new industrial world of the term 'the system', meaning the mechanized production unit in which 'all parts of the plant must operate together'. Thus, in textile production, the spinning mill was organized to accommodate 'the system', so that preparatory machines and spinning frames did not outstrip or fall behind each other, but were balanced in an economic way to produce one weight of yarn or a limited range of weights.[17] In consequence, the architecture and layout of the mills were governed by 'the system', and hence the conditions faced by textile workers.

In the *Wealth of Nations*, Smith drew attention to the mental mutilation that befalls workmen subjected to the process of the division of labour (*WN*, 2:782). His contemporary, Adam Ferguson, had represented this process in the following terms: 'Manufactures . . . prosper most, where the mind is least consulted, and where the workshop may, without any great effort of imagination, be considered as an engine, the parts of which are men.'[18] Smith's antidote to the numbing of the mind consequent on making men cogs in machines, and the political danger inherent in such a state of affairs, was education fostered by the state (*WN*, 2:788). He argued that education would increase the self-esteem of the common people and make them more likely to be esteemed by their superiors, therefore more inclined to hold those superiors in esteem.

The principles appealed to here were traced in the part of Smith's moral philosophy course devoted to ethics. Millar stated that this 'consisted chiefly of the doctrines . . . afterwards published in the *Theory of Moral Sentiments*'. When that book appeared in 1759, the lectures were adjusted accordingly, with ethical doctrines occupying a smaller portion of the course, and greater attention being directed to a fuller illustration of the principles of jurisprudence and political economy (Stewart, 274, 300; *TMS*, Introduction, 4). The doctrines are best summed up in the alternative title to the book bestowed on it in the fourth edition of 1774: 'An Essay towards an Analysis of the Principles by which Men naturally judge concerning the Conduct and Character, first of their Neighbours, and afterwards of themselves'. Smith probably began his lectures by posing two questions: what is virtue, and what drives us to be virtuous? (*TMS*, 265). Thereafter, he would most likely offer a historical survey of answers to these questions provided by philosophers from Plato to Hume, and then present his own system based on a sophisticated exploration of the nature of sympathy as the mechanism by which we judge others. A fragment from the ethics lectures dealing with the topic of justice has survived. It represents an early stage in the development of the course, for the concept of the impartial spectator is missing from it, and it reflects a certain contradiction in Smith's thought between reliance on utility as the ground of justice and insistence on the primacy of natural feelings (*TMS*, 383–401). Perhaps the lectures can be understood as Smith's contribution to a dialogue on moral questions begun by his teacher Francis Hutcheson, continued by his friend David Hume and sustained at the outset of Smith's professorial days by his patron Henry Home of Kames, whose *Essays on the Principles of Morality* (1751) is an important subtext to the *Theory of Moral Sentiments*.

As for the lectures on jurisprudence, which Smith extended to cover political economy, Millar draws attention to their debt to a new source of thought on that subject, in addition to the tradition familiar to Smith from his Glasgow student days, represented by the writings of Grotius, Pufendorf and Hutcheson. The new influence was that of Montesquieu's book, *De l'esprit des lois* (1748):

> Upon this subject [Smith] followed the plan that seems to be suggested by Montesquieu; endeavouring to trace the gradual progress of jurisprudence, both public and private, from the rudest to the most refined ages, and to point out the effects of those arts which contribute to subsistence, and to the accumulation of property, in producing correspondent improvements or alterations in law and government. (Stewart, 274–75)

In his own inquiry into the history of government in England, Millar developed further the approach taken by Smith, making clear its origin and the stimulus it gave him:

> I am happy to acknowledge the obligations I feel myself under to this illustrious philosopher [Adam Smith], by having, at an early period of life, had the benefit of hearing his lectures on the History of Civil Society, and of enjoying his unreserved conversation on the same subject. The great Montesquieu pointed out the road. He was the Lord Bacon in this branch of philosophy. Dr Smith is the Newton.[19]

To be sure, Smith was highly interested in the success of the Newtonian method of analysis and synthesis in astronomy and physics, and like many of his contemporaries, such as Hume, may be seen as responding to the challenge Newton set out at the end of the *Opticks*: 'And if natural Philosophy in all its Parts, by persuing this Method, shall at length be perfected, the Bounds of Moral Philosophy will also be enlarged.' One of Smith's critics, Governor Thomas Pownall, certainly saw the *Wealth of Nations* as a possible *principia* of political economy, and wished that it would become a fundamental textbook in that subject (*Corr.*, 337, 375).

Through good fortune, we have evidence about the presentation of Smith's lectures on jurisprudence during three separate sessions. At some point early in Smith's career at Glasgow, John Anderson, a former student and later a colleague at the university, made notes of what Smith was teaching about jurisprudence and politics. From this source, we learn that Smith had been thinking deeply about one of the factors affecting a country's laws, namely, subsistence, and seems to have developed more completely Montesquieu's idea that there are principally three such modes: those of hunters and fishermen, of shepherds and of farmers. In Smith's account, an additional stage was added, that of the 'establishment of commerce' (Meek, 'New Light', 467, 471).

It was from Hutcheson's concept of natural jurisprudence, however, that Smith's teaching about economics took its origin. In his *Short Introduction to Moral Philosophy* (1747) — as well as in the posthumous *System of Moral Philosophy* (1755), which covered the course he taught about 1737, just before Smith was his student — Hutcheson introduced chapters on price, money and interest, as part of a general discussion of contract (in each work, bk. 2, chaps. 12, 13). Anderson's notes suggest, however, that in dealing in his turn with contract, Smith went considerably beyond Hutcheson, by including such matters as bills of exchange, stocks and paper money. Here we see the birth of Smith's distinctive treatment of economics, perhaps resulting from his awareness that Glasgow had arrived at a comparatively advanced stage of commerce, and that a range of topics connected with contract would therefore be of interest to students. Furthermore, a reference to Hume's essay, 'Of Interest', reveals that Smith was sharing with his students what he had presented to colleagues and citizen members in the GLS about the economic ideas in Hume's *Political Discourses* of 1752 (Meek, 'New Light', 470). Hume certainly was attracting attention in Glasgow at this time, because James Wodrow's previously cited letter of 21 January 1752 mentions that Anderson, the note-taker at these early jurisprudence lectures by Smith, intended 'to become author and publish against Hume', but he apparently abandoned his plan.

When we turn to firmer and fuller evidence about the contents of Smith's *Lectures on Jurisprudence*, in the form of reports of lectures delivered in two concurrent academic sessions — 1762–63 (*LJ* [A]) and 1763–64 (*LJ* [B]) — we find that by this time the economic material had been transferred from the section on contract to that dealing with 'police': the 'policey of civil government', and for Smith's purpose chiefly confined to the 'most proper way of procuring wealth and abundance' (*LJ* [B], 486–87). John Millar gave the following account of this division:

> In the last part of his lectures, [Smith] examined those political regulations which are founded, not upon the principle of *justice*, but upon that of *expediency*, and which are calculated to increase the riches, the power and the prosperity of a State. Under this view, he considered the political institutions relating to commerce, to finances, to ecclesiastical and military establishments. What he delivered on these subjects contained the substance of the work he afterwards published under the title of *An Inquiry into the Nature and Causes of the Wealth of Nations*. (Stewart, 275)

In the Glasgow jurisprudence lectures, Smith attacked the notion that money is the only wealth of a state and presented a theory of economic growth. He argued that this involved division of labour, production and consumption of goods and a money supply adequate to the circulation of goods. Picking up a point made in his Edinburgh jurisprudence course, and repeated in a paper given in 1755—very likely to the Political Economy Club founded by Andrew Cochrane, the lord provost who admitted Smith as a 'Burgess and Gild Brother' of Glasgow (Scott, 82) — Smith stressed the importance of free trade (*LJ* [A], 388–93). From these lectures, an early draft of the *Wealth of Nations*, and two fragments on the topic of the division of labour and land and water carriage (*LJ*, 562–86), we are well informed about the development of Smith's teaching about economics or political economy, as he called the subject, representing it as a 'branch of the science of a statesman or legislator' (*WN*, 1:428). Smith's economic thought is far advanced in these sources, but later encounters with the physiocrats and Turgot, in print and in person, opened up new perspectives on such matters as the circulation of capital and the balance between the productive and unproductive sectors of the economy.[20]

III

SMITH'S LECTURING SCHEDULE was a demanding one, and Hume may well have been correct in fearing that the 'Fatigues of your Class' brought illness to his friend in the spring of 1753 (*Corr.*, 9). From 10 October until 10 June, with only statutory holidays as relief, Smith lectured for an hour every weekday morning at 7:30 to the full moral philosophy class, and then at 11:00 he examined for another hour about a third of those who had attended the first lecture. These were the meetings of his 'public' class. On Mondays, Wednesdays and Fridays he lectured for an hour at noon to his 'private' class.

From *LJ* (A) and *LRBL* it is possible to reconstruct most fully the cycle of his lectures for 1762–63. In his 'public' class he must have lectured on natural theology and ethics from October until Christmas Eve 1762. He seems to have begun the rhetoric course on 17 November and to have completed about half of it by 22 December. On 24 December he began the jurisprudence course; after dealing with private and domestic law by 17 February 1763, when the rhetoric course ended, he opened the topic of justice in his 'public' class on Monday 21 February, and under that heading completed by 24 March his account of the four-stage development of political institutions arising in turn from hunting and fishing, pastoralism, agriculture and commerce as modes of subsistence. When he discussed the rise and decay of feudalism and the growth of Tudor despotism in England, and then the ensuing restoration of civil liberty as a result of Parliament's opposition to James I and Charles I, Smith added his insights to those of Hume and Kames, themselves stimulated by the inquiries of Montesquieu into the spirit of laws. Smith spoke of the power of the nobles declining in England as elsewhere because of the 'introduction of arts, commerce, and luxury' (*LJ* [A], 261), and he took up the theme of opulence created through commerce in the section of his course devoted to 'police', which began on 28 March and must have run through May at least, though we lack the report of the lectures after 13 April (*LJ*, Introduction, 15–27).

According to a letter that James Wodrow wrote to the earl of Buchan in 1808, Smith, in teaching his 'public' class,

> made a laudable attempt at first to follow Hut[cheson]'s animated manner, lecturing on Ethics without Papers walking up & down in his Class room, but not having the same facility in this that Hut[cheso]n had, either naturally, or acquired by continued practise & habit in teaching his academy at Dublin; Dr Smith soon relinquished the Attempt and read, with propriety, all the rest of his valuable Lectures from the Desk. His Theory of Moral Sentiments founded on Sympathy, a very ingenious attempt to account for the principal Phaenomena in the moral world from this one general principle, like that of Gravity in the natural World, did not please Hutcheson's scholars, so well, as that to which they had been accustomed. The rest of his Lectures were admired by them, and by all, especially those on Money & commerce. (Mitchell Library, Buchan MSS, Baillie 3225, no. 47)

This picture of the young Professor Smith seeking to follow the practice of the ebullient Hutcheson, and then prudently retiring to the security of his desk to read his lectures, is complemented by a description of his handling of the opportunity for extempore teaching during the examination hour for the moral philosophy class. Another of his students, William Richardson, found great merit in the oral examination method:

> Such examinations are reckoned of great utility to those who study, as tending to ensure their attention, to ascertain their proficiency, and give the teacher an opportunity of explaining more clearly any part of the lecture which may not have been fully understood. Those who received instruction from Dr Smith, will recollect, with much satisfaction, many of those incidental and digressive illustrations and even discussions, not only on morality, but in criticism, which were delivered by him with animated and extemporaneous eloquence, as they were suggested in the course of question and answer. (Richardson, 'Account', 507–8)

Further evidence of Smith's 'animated and extemporaneous eloquence' comes from John Millar, who wrote that, as a lecturer, his former teacher 'trusted almost entirely to extemporary elocution'. Millar remembered a 'plain and unaffected' rather than 'graceful' manner.[21] He also noted in Smith that crucial interest in his subject which 'never failed to interest his hearers' (Stewart, 275). We might think of Smith expounding his ethical doctrine concerning the objects of reward and punishment in the fashion described by Millar, or dealing with the economic issue of free trade (on 6 April 1763, for example, *LJ* [A], 363), and there could be added to this picture Smith's reliance on signs of the sympathy, or lack of it, of a selected hearer for gauging the effect of what he was saying. Smith described his practice thus to Archibald Alison the elder, a former student who became an Edinburgh magistrate and lord provost:

> During one whole session a certain student with a plain but expressive countenance was of great use to me in judging of my success. He sat conspicuously in front of a pillar: I had him constantly under my eye. If he leant forward to listen all was right, and I knew that I had the ear of my class; but if he leant back in an attitude of listlessness I felt at once that all was wrong, and that I must change either the subject or the style of my address.[22]

Justice cannot be done here to the many notable students who benefited from Smith's teaching, and a brief indication of their range and certain achievements must suffice.[23] Some came from far afield, such as François Tronchin of Geneva, the son of Voltaire's physician, and two Russians, Semyon Efimovich Desnitsky and Ivan Andreyevich Tretyakov, who were sent by Catherine the Great to study in Britain in 1761, and were passed on to Adam Smith by Lord Mansfield, the Scottish-born chief justice of England. They stayed in Glasgow until 1766, receiving much of their instruction from John Millar, and went home to be professors of jurisprudence at Moscow University, where they delivered their lectures in Russian, not Latin, a step like that of Smith teaching his logic class in the vernacular. Desnitsky followed Smithian principles to some degree in his proposals for legal and constitutional reform, some of which were taken up by the empress, and he made speeches about jurisprudence that reflected Smith's standpoint on the four stages of economic development. Tretyakov had a more pronounced interest in economics as a subject, and he sketched a very promising work on the causes of the 'poverty of nations', again based on Smith's principles of social analysis, which a brief career and early death arrested at an early stage.[24]

From native ground there came to Smith's classes such a figure of later eminence in the law as Ilay Campbell, who ended his career as lord president of the Court of Session, and who was reckoned 'greatly superior' to his fellow judges because of his concern for the legal reform and comprehension of 'modern mercantile jurisprudence'.[25] Also destined for the law, but achieving fame as a writer, was James Boswell, who attended Smith's moral philosophy and rhetoric courses in 1759–60 and found in Smith something of a mentor until the powerful personality of Samuel Johnson came to dominate him.[26] A number of future university professors came from Smith's classes: William Trail, the Aberdeen mathematician; John Millar (civil law), William Richardson (humanity), George Jardine (logic), and Archibald Arthur (moral philosophy), all at Glasgow;

and John Robison (natural philosophy) at Edinburgh. In addition, Smith taught, as private pupils, Henry Herbert (later Lord Porchester and first earl of Carnarvon), the Hon. Thomas Petty-Fitzmaurice (brother of the prime minister, Lord Shelburne), and Lord Buchan (founder of the Society of Antiquaries of Scotland).[27] Of lower rank in society were other students who contributed to understanding and advancement of contemporary society: James Gibson, who became a merchant and accountant and wrote a *History of Glasgow* (1777), which paid some attention to the economic development of the city and echoed Professor Smith's sentiments about free trade; and John Stuart, destined to be a parish minister, but also a noted Gaelic scholar, who completed his father's translation of the Old Testament into that language and edited the poems of the greatest Gaelic poet of the eighteenth century, Duncan Bàn Macintyre.[28]

These students carried Smith's ideas, his 'systems' even, into the wide world, apparently in advance of his publications. Thus, there was a 'conspectus' of some sort of the jurisprudence lectures available in Moscow, covering Smith's economic thought, well before the *Wealth of Nations* was published in London on 9 March 1776 (Anikin, *Russian Thinkers*, 48). One obituary of Smith recorded that he was jealous of the 'property of his lectures' and did not want them published, declaring often when he saw somebody taking notes that 'he hated scribblers' (*LRBL*, Introduction, 3). But we have reason to be grateful to those note-takers who defied him. We have even more reason to be grateful to Smith for his interest in publication, begun when he was lecturing in Edinburgh with a preface to an edition of the poetry of William Hamilton of Bangour (*EPS*, 259–62), and continued at Glasgow with his pieces for the first *Edinburgh Review* of 1755–56, which reflected his interest in grammatical studies and in broadening the outlook of the Scottish Enlightenment to take note of recent French thought (*EPS*, 229–56). Distinction as a citizen in the republic of letters, of course, came to Smith with the publication of the *Theory of Moral Sentiments* in April 1759. A captious critic like Revd. George Ridpath might complain that it extended to tedious length because the author was 'used all his life to declaim to boys as auditors',[29] referring to Glasgow students of the period, whose ages in general ranged from fourteen to seventeen, but the book made its mark at home and abroad in Europe, and in the end its fame caused Smith to be drawn away from his Glasgow chair.

As he developed those seminal lecture courses and embarked on a career as a publishing man of letters, Smith was also entrusted at Glasgow University with many administrative duties. Some of these no doubt helped or reinforced his intellectual formation and provided useful experience for his writings, but other responsibilities must have vexed his spirit and drained his energies away from more rewarding work. Despite his reputation for absentmindedness, his colleagues recognized in him a practical bent and entrusted him with the charge of legal and financial matters; fabric and space supervision, including looking after the needs of the Foulis brothers, whose press issued scholarly editions of remarkable quality, and of James Watt, who had embarked on his revolutionary experiments with steam power; negotiation of university interests with government and other agencies; managing the library funds; and various missions of academic diplomacy and governance requiring exceptional skill.

Of great professional interest to Smith was the development of the university library. He served on its committees from his earliest days as a professor and had as special responsibilities bringing into use the new building designed by William Adam, which was at first affected by dampness, looking after accounts and stocking books additional to those secured by the provisions of the Copyright Act of 1709. The titles covered by Smith's 'Quaestor Accounts' from 1758 to 1763 seem to connect with the legal and historical studies that underpinned his work on jurisprudence and political economy (Scott, 178–82). These titles include, on the legal side, four volumes (1739–59) of Mathew Bacon's *New Abridgment of the [English] Law* (later to be completed with a fifth volume in 1766), and the third edition of Stair's *Institutions of the Laws of Scotland* (1759); as well as, on the historical side, de Guignes's *Histoire générale des Huns, des Turcs, et des Mongols* (1756–58), a source for information concerning shepherd societies worked into the analysis of the four stages of socio-economic organization (*LJ* [A], 216); histories of France (le père Daniel), Spain (Ferreras), Naples (Giannone, whose *Civil History* would be attractive to a thinker like Smith), and the state historians of Venice; also Postlethwayt's *History of the Public Revenue*; and seven volumes of a set of seventeen comprising d'Alembert and Diderot's *Encyclopédie*, which Smith had praised in the second volume of the *Edinburgh Review* as an intellectual tour de force (*EPS*, 245–48). Its articles embraced physiocratic reasoning on economic issues and may well have prepared Smith for his discussions in Paris with the leader of the sect, Quesnai, and his independent-minded ally, Turgot.

Smith's record as an enlightened administrator, however, is not entirely without blemish. He was willing to accept a commission to interest the rector of 1761, Lord Erroll, in a scheme to found an 'Academy of dancing, fencing, and riding to be established at Glasgow under the direction of the University' (Scott, 149). He also served on a committee appointed on 25 November 1762 to persuade the magistrates of Glasgow not to allow a playhouse to be established in the city. This body prevailed with the magistrates, appealing to the 'Priviledges of the University of Oxford with regard to preventing any thing of that kind being established within their bounds', a touch which might have come from that former Oxford man, Adam Smith, and the city and university jointly sent a memorial about the matter to the lord advocate, Thomas Miller of Glenlee, who was very likely a former student of Smith's. In the end this law officer encouraged the city and university to prosecute the players if they came to act in Glasgow (Scott, 165–66). There is no record of Smith protesting this matter, though he later expressed the view that the theatre was a valuable moral resource in a community (*WN*, 2:796). It seems a lame excuse to say that the university authorities were afraid of student disturbances connected with playacting (Scott, 163, n. 3).

Smith's greatest challenge as an administrator came after 1761, when William Leechman became principal and set about restoring the power of that office lost through the incapacity of his predecessor, Neil Campbell. A dispute arose between Leechman and his colleagues over the respective powers of principal and lord rector, the latter generally represented by a faculty designate. In the end a committee chaired by Smith, consisting of Joseph Black, John Millar and Alexander Wilson, professor of astronomy and typefounder, drew up a comprehensive document dated 10 August 1762. It bears the mark of Smith's clarity of thought in setting out the supervisory function of meetings chaired by the rector or his designate, the academic nature of the dean of faculty's meetings, and the role of those chaired by the principal in dealing with day-to-day administrative routine, including fiscal matters (Scott, 203–15).

One of the issues between Smith, acting as vice-rector, and Principal Leechman was financial provision for a chemical laboratory. Smith signed on 31 October 1763 a strong defence of this outlay: 'It appeared to the Majority a step highly proper and becomeing the present Reputation of this University to further countenance the study and Teaching of a Science which is one of the most usefull and solid, and which is dayly comeing into greater esteem' (Scott, 218). In his essay on the history of astronomy, Smith had expressed no great esteem for the current state of chemistry (*EPS*, 46–47), but perhaps the researches and teaching ability of Cullen and Black had brought him round to a more positive viewpoint.

By this time, Smith's professorial career was coming to an end. Charles Townshend had written to him on 25 October 1763, inquiring if he was still disposed to travel abroad with his stepson, the third duke of Buccleuch, who would be leaving Eton at Christmas (*Corr.*, 95). This scheme had been promoted by Hume in the spring of 1759, when fame had come to Smith on the appearance of the *Theory of Moral Sentiments* (*Corr.*, 36). Smith advised his colleagues on 8 November that he would probably be leaving Glasgow in the course of the winter, and they unanimously accepted his terms that he would repay the students their fees or pay the university the fees if the students would not accept them. Smith also proposed that his course should be finished by someone appointed by the university, and he would pay the required salary (Scott, 220). Though he had been given three months leave, Smith, after leaving Glasgow in January 1764, sent in his resignation from Paris on 14 February. In his letter, he expresses his anxiety for the 'Good of the College', and his sincere wish that his 'Successor may not only do Credit to the Office by his Abilities but be a comfort to the very excellent Men with whom he is likely to spend his life, by the Probity of his heart and the Goodness of his Temper' (*Corr.*, 101). Perhaps these words are a veiled reference to what was needed to keep in check the stormy academic passions of the 'very excellent Men' revealed in the controversy over the powers of principal and rector. In the event, Thomas Young, who read Smith's lectures to his students (*LJ* [B]), and who was supported for succession to Smith by Black and Millar, did not get the chair of moral philosophy, which went instead to the far more distinguished Thomas Reid of King's College, Aberdeen (*Corr.*, 99–100).

Before Smith left Glasgow, there was an affecting scene in his classroom, when his efforts to return his students' fees were greeted with resistance out of sheer affection for him.[30] As for his own feelings about his professorship, he described them in a letter of 16 November 1787, when he accepted election to the office of lord rector of Glasgow University:

> The period of thirteen years which I spent as a member of that society I remember as by far the most useful, and, therefore, as by far the happiest and most honourable period of my life; and now, after three and twenty years absence, to be remembered in so very agreable a manner by my old friends and Protectors gives me a heartfelt joy which I cannot easily express to you. (*Corr.*, 308–9).

Such is the biographical record of Adam Smith's years as a professor. Though abridged, and therefore imperfect, perhaps it suffices to warrant the claim that he was a useful citizen of Glasgow in this period, as well as of the republic of letters and, in the long run, of the world. According to the standard of his own philosophy, his career in Glasgow certainly seems to have enabled him to live a fulfilling and, therefore, happy life.

Notes

This chapter is a revised version of the Stevenson Lecture that I presented at the ECSSS conference in Glasgow, at the invitation of the University of Glasgow and with the much-appreciated support of that university, the Canada Council, and the University of British Columbia.

References to Smith's writings in this chapter are to the Glasgow Edition published by Oxford University Press, using the following abbreviations: *Corr.*=*The Correspondence of Adam Smith*, ed. Ernest Campbell Mossner and Ian Simpson Ross, 2nd ed. (1987); *EPS*=*Essays on Philosophical Subjects*, ed. W.P.D. Wightman and J. C. Bryce (1980); *LJ*=*Lectures on Jurisprudence*, ed. R. L. Meek, D. D. Raphael, and P. G. Stein (1978); *LRBL*=*Lectures on Rhetoric and*

Belles Lettres, ed. J. C. Bryce (1983); *TMS=The Theory of Moral Sentiments*, ed. D. D. Raphael and A. L. Macfie (1976); *WN=An Inquiry into the Nature and Causes of the Wealth of Nations*, ed. R. H. Campbell, A. S. Skinner, and W. B. Todd, 2 vols. (1976). In addition, Dugald Stewart's 'Account of the Life and Writings of Adam Smith, LL.D.', ed. I. S. Ross, which appears in *EPS*, 265–351, is abbreviated as 'Stewart', and William Robert Scott, *Adam Smith as Student and Professor* (Glasgow, 1937) is abbreviated as 'Scott'.

1. W. J. Duncan, *Notices and Documents illustrative of The Literary Society of Glasgow* (Glasgow, 1831), 16; this list of subjects is corroborated in William Richardson's 'Account' of Archibald Arthur in Arthur, *Discourses on Theological and Literary Subjects* (Glasgow, 1803), 514.

2. John Anderson to Gilbert Lang, 27 Dec. 1750, quoted in R. L. Meek, 'New Light on Adam Smith's Glasgow Lectures on Jurisprudence', *History of Political Economy* 8 (1976): 458.

3. This eighteenth-century medical term has been proposed to cover Smith's mysterious illnesses in Michael Barfoot, 'Dr William Cullen and Mr Adam Smith: A Case of Hypochondriasis', *Proceedings of the Royal College of Physicians of Edinburgh* 21 (1991): 204–14.

4. J. D. Mackie, *The University of Glasgow, 1451 to 1951* (Glasgow, 1954), 177, 181; Ronald G. Cant, *The University of St Andrews: A Short History*, new ed. (Edinburgh, 1970), 91–92; John Durkan and James Kirk, *The University of Glasgow, 1451–1577* (Glasgow, 1977), 85–91, 278–79.

5. GUL, MS Gen. 71 (1714–15), MS Gen. 406 (1712), MS Murray 210 (1729).

6. *The Letters and Journals of Lady Mary Coke*, 4 vols. (Edinburgh, 1889–96), 2:141.

7. It appeared first in a somewhat mysterious periodical: *The Philological Miscellany* 1 (1761): 440–79, and later in the third edition of *TMS* (1767), 437–78. See John Bryce's account of the 'Considerations' in *LRBL*, Introduction, 23–29.

8. Roger L. Emerson, 'Conjectural History and Scottish Philosophers', in *Historical Papers, Communications Historiques*, ed. D. Johnson and L. Ovellette (1984), 63–90.

9. Hans Aarsleff, *From Locke to Saussure: Essays on the Study of Language and Intellectual History* (London, 1982), 147–48, 349, 353, n. 29.

10. Jardine's educational practice is traced by George Davie in *The Democratic Intellect: Scotland and Her Universities in the Nineteenth Century* (Edinburgh, 1961), 10–11, 16–18.

11. For the beginning of the story in America, see William Charvat, *The Origins of American Thought, 1810–1835* (New York, 1961), chap. 3, and Henry E. May, *The Enlightenment in America* (New York, 1978), 342–57. A similar story for Canada has not been investigated, but introductory courses in composition and criticism based on the work of Scottish eighteenth-century writers such as Lord Kames and Hugh Blair, who had affinities with Smith, spread from Dalhousie University in Halifax, Queen's University in Kingston and Knox College in Toronto.

12. See the life of Adam Smith that is prefixed to the twelfth edition of the *Theory of Moral Sentiments* (Glasgow, 1809), xxi. Something of the 'exercise' has survived in the form of 'On the Importance of Natural Philosophy', pt. 2, no. 11 of Archibald Arthur's *Discourses*.

13. Dr Williams' Library, London, MS 24.157 (14), 20 Dec. 1751; MS 24.157 (16), 21 Jan. 1752. Richard Sher generously informed me about these references.

14. See Andrew S. Skinner, 'The Shaping of Political Economy in the Enlightenment', *Scottish Journal of Political Economy* 37 (1990): 145–65, esp. pts. 3 and 4.

15. See, for example, J. C. Stewart-Robertson, 'Cicero Among the Shadows: Scottish Prelections of Virtue and Duty', *Revista Critica di Storia della Filosofia* 1 (1983): 25–49, and three articles in *Studies in the Philosophy of the Scottish Enlightenment*, ed. M. A. Stewart (Oxford, 1990): Roger L. Emerson, 'Science and Moral Philosophy in the Scottish Enlightenment', 11–36; Richard B. Sher, 'Professors of Virtue: The Social History of the Edinburgh Moral Philosophy Chair in the Eighteenth Century', 87–126; and P. B. Wood, 'Science and the Pursuit of Virtue in the Aberdeen Enlightenment', 127–49.

16. J. D. Mackie, 'The Professors and Their Critics', *Proceedings of the Royal Philosophical Society of Glasgow* 72 (1948): 49. For a fuller account of Thom, see chap. 12 below.

17. Mark Watson, *Jute and Flax Mills in Dundee* (Tayport, 1990), 28.

18. Ferguson, *An Essay on the History of Civil Society*, ed. Duncan Forbes (1767; Edinburgh, 1966), 183.

19. John Millar, *An Historical View of the English Government*, ed. John Craig and James Mylne, 3rd ed. 4 vols. (London, 1803), 2:429–30n.

20. See Ian Ross, 'The Physiocrats and Adam Smith', *British Journal for Eighteenth-Century Studies* 7 (1984): 177–89.

21. Another witness, speaking of Smith as a conversationalist, mentioned a 'harsh' voice and 'thick' enunciation, 'approaching to stammering'. *The Autobiography of Dr. Alexander Carlyle of Inveresk, 1722–1805*, new ed., ed. John Hill Burton (London and Edinburgh, 1910), 293.

22. Quoted in John Sinclair, *Sketches of Old Times and Distant Places* (London, 1875), 9.

23. For general background to the students of Smith's time as a professor, see W. M. Mathew, 'The Origins and Occupations of Glasgow Students, 1740–1839', *Past and Present* 33 (1966): 74–94; individuals are identified in W. Innes Addison, *The Matriculation Albums of the University of Glasgow, 1728–1858* (Glasgow, 1913), and Alison Webster, 'Adam Smith's Students', *Scotia* 12: (1988): 13–26 (Mrs Webster kindly provided supplementary details in letters to me).

24. *Speeches Delivered at the Official Meetings of the Imperial Moscow University by the Russian Professors thereof, Containing Their Short Curriculum Vitae* (Moscow, 1819); Norman W. Taylor, 'Adam Smith's First Russian Disciple', *Slavonic Review* 45 (1967): 425–38; A. H. Brown, 'S. E.

Desnitsky, Adam Smith, and the Nakaz of Catherine II', *Oxford Slavonic Papers*, n.s. 7 (1974): 42–59, and 'Adam Smith's First Russian Followers', in *Essays on Adam Smith*, ed. Andrew S. Skinner and Thomas Wilson (Oxford, 1975), 247–73; Andrei Anikin, *Russian Thinkers: Essays on Socio-Economic Thought*, trans. Cynthia Carlile (Moscow, 1988), 40–52. I am grateful to Alpha Demchuk, Vancouver, B.C., for help with Russian sources.

25. Henry Cockburn, *Memorials of His Time* (Edinburgh, 1856), 126.

26. Frederick A. Pottle, 'Boswell's University Education', in *Johnson, Boswell and Their Circle: Essays Presented to L. F. Powell* (Oxford, 1965), 230–53, and *James Boswell: The Earlier Years, 1740–1769* (New York, 1966), 42–54. For a fuller account of Boswell's relationship with Smith, see chap. 8 below.

27. Ronald G. Cant, 'David Steuart Erskine, 11th Earl of Buchan: Founder of the Society of Antiquaries of Scotland', in *The Scottish Antiquarian Tradition*, ed. A. S. Bell (Edinburgh, 1981), 1–30.

28. Derick S. Thomson, *An Introduction to Gaelic Poetry* (London, 1974), 181.

29. *Diary of George Ridpath, Minister of Stichel*, ed. Sir James Balfour Paul (Edinburgh, 1922), 275.

30. Alexander Fraser Tytler, Lord Woodhouselee, *Memoirs of the Life and Writings of the Honourable Henry Home of Kames*, 2 vols. (Edinburgh and London, 1807), 1:194–95n.

5
Thomas Reid in the Glasgow Literary Society

Kathleen Holcomb

The prominence and omnipresence of philosophical societies constituted essential features of the Enlightenment, as contemporaries were well aware. Hutton's *Mathematical Dictionary* (1795–96), for example, lists such societies in cities as distant and diverse as Boston, Philadelphia, Brussels, Bonn, Paris, Manchester, Newcastle, Aberdeen and Edinburgh. In each of them men gathered to grapple with the new intellectual forces that were coming into existence. The members used their societies to develop their ideas and to discover ways to put them into practice. To be sure, not all these societies were quite so dedicated to practical improvement as the Edinburgh Society for the Improvement of Arts and Manufactures, which awarded prizes, but in almost every case the improving spirit permeated their endeavour.

In this international constellation of intellectual organizations, the Glasgow Literary Society shone brightly. Founded in 1752, the GLS was not Glasgow's first Enlightenment society, for Glasgow men were by that time well accustomed to the benefits of such a forum. Indeed, Alexander Carlyle described the Glasgow of his student days, from 1743 to 1745, as bustling with intellectual clubs, including a political economy society dominated by merchants.[1] Unlike that club, the GLS was not specifically oriented towards action, but it did enable its members to clarify their ideas about a wide range of subjects and perhaps encouraged them to act according to the principles they developed in discussions with their colleagues. Members proposed and debated questions covering everything from commercial and artistic matters to Greek grammar and the implications of American independence. The GLS continued its weekly meetings at least until the beginning of the next century, surviving rivalries among its members, university politics and the French Revolution.

Although normally a closed body, the GLS could occasionally be glimpsed by outsiders. The society's earliest surviving regulations, 'The Laws of the Literary Society in Glasgow College' (1764–79), allow the president to invite three visitors with the consent of the week's speaker, and the speaker to invite three visitors without asking anyone. 'But this law concerning six visitors shall extend only to the members of this college and to the Inhabitants of Glasgow it being competent to the Society to admit any number of strangers they shall think proper' (rule 9).[2] Some of the visitors were even asked to speak, though normally they can be presumed to have maintained a respectful silence as great thoughts were expounded in their presence. Alexander Peters, a former student of James Beattie's at Marischal College, Aberdeen, wrote his old professor on 8 December 1778 to describe such an experience:

> There are a great many Literary Societies in Town. The Professors have a meeting of that kind every Friday night; when they deliver discourses, each in his turn, on some Topic of his own choosing, intimated under a penalty, eight days before to all the Members. The speech being made, each gives his opinion, and debates are sometimes carried on with considerable warmth. (AUL, MS 30/2/322)

The warmth of the debates was not always limited to intellectual topics. On 25 December 1778, for example, a majority of eight members voted, over the protests of four, to adjourn the next week's scheduled meeting because 'several of the members are to be out of town during the Holy Days'. When the four protestors held what they claimed was the regular meeting on 1 January 1779, Archibald Arthur read a discourse bearing the title, appropriately enough, 'Remarks on the Dispersion at Babel'. According to the rules, Arthur should have been the president of the next meeting, but when he claimed the chair he was denied it by the majority, upon which a protest was read into the minutes. The adjournment was held to have been pernicious in part because 'it occasioned a dispute in the presence of persons who were visitors to the society'. By that rudeness, it endangered its own future: 'Few it is presumed will choose to be members of a Society where they are to be subjected to the unknown will of the Majority however ready they may be to give obedience to the Laws and Usages that are known'. The protest concludes: 'It is better to dissolve a Society which tramples upon its own Laws and therefore disgraces the name of Literary than for Britons to Subject themselves to a Despotism unknown in Barbarous Countries for even there the law . . . is superior to the will of the greatest Monarchs.'

This episode can be used to illustrate some of the features of the Enlightenment in Glasgow. It was made up of quite heterogeneous materials — the Dispersion at Babel and the resistance to despotism. Its proponents were deeply committed to standards of active civic virtue, to the point of recommending the dissolution of a society that tramples on its own laws. The dissidents and their opponents were equally committed to ethical principles of action, whether that action might entail support or derision for majority decisions. All its members viewed animated debate on formal discourses and controversial questions as the proper way to thrash out differences and, if possible, attain truth.

I

THE CAREER OF THOMAS REID in Glasgow demonstrates just how productive the encouragement of such a group could be. Reid had been invited to Glasgow to assume the chair of moral philosophy vacated by Adam Smith in 1764. Though the offer was not sheer disinterested recognition of merit on the part of the university,[3] it was largely prompted by what was perceived as Reid's successful refutation of David Hume's dangerous scepticism in *An Inquiry into the Human Mind on the Principles of Common Sense* (1764). Reid's refutation rests on the presumption that there are in human nature certain fundamental elements, basic principles, part of our composition, among which are the physical senses. The *Inquiry* establishes the validity of the senses in perceiving reality. But other elements, including 'common sense', make possible not only our individuality but also our social codes, such as language, and our moral perceptions, such as that of moral obligation.[4]

The *Inquiry* was the product of Reid's activity in the Aberdeen Philosophical Society, a group that Reid helped to shape and to which he contributed regularly until his departure for Glasgow. There he read several discourses on the senses that he later revised as the *Inquiry*, presumably in response to discussions with other members.[5] In addition, as the society's bylaws required, he offered supplementary questions on set topics (e.g., an education series) or on topics of personal interest. He continued this pattern in the GLS, which admitted him as a member in November 1764, very soon after his arrival in Glasgow.

The *Inquiry* examined the role of the senses in the phenomena of perception. Reid evidently intended a second volume extending to other mental operations, beginning with memory. Instead of developing the *Inquiry*, however, he finished the investigation by means of discourses read to the GLS.[6] In this way, he continued his practice of submitting his ideas to the criticism of his colleagues before putting them into print. He solicited further comment from his young friends James Gregory and Dugald Stewart in Edinburgh, and discussed the material with Lord Kames in letters and conversation.[7]

In his GLS discourses, Reid patiently unfolds what he declined to call a system, completing the investigation of the human mind begun in the *Inquiry*. A series on memory, imagination, the train of thought in the human mind and abstraction fills out the pattern of perception implied by the treatment of the senses in his first book. Next comes a series investigating common sense, culminating in three essays on the principles of contingent and necessary truths. Beginning in 1777 with a discourse on will, Reid carefully constructed an outline of principles of action — mechanical, animal and rational — which would occupy his attention for the next several years.

Most of the discourses incorporate lecture material from Reid's moral philosophy classes. Many were transformed once more to become *Essays on the Intellectual Powers* (1785); the remainder make up most of *Essays on the Active Powers* (1788). Reid apparently regarded them as two volumes of essays, for he refers to them in this manner in a later discourse (MS 2131/2/II/2). When the first volume was being copied for publication, Reid remarked to James Gregory on 8 June 1783 that 'the materials of what is not yet ready for the copier are partly discourses read in our Literary Society, partly notes of my Lectures' (*Works*, 62). In addition to the *Intellectual Powers* and *Active Powers* discourses, Reid read some extra discourses and considered a few questions on topics of contemporary interest; some papers read after 1788 reconsider problems of constitution, power and volition.

The method of composition implied by Reid's comment to Gregory assumes a coherence of thought which is in fact apparent in any examination of the manuscripts of the lectures and discourses. Such unity is also maintained between the discourses. Read as a series, the discourses on the powers of the mind are remarkably lucid. Although Reid revised them and added material for publication, he had formulated and followed his plan methodically; they required less revision than had some of the material for the *Inquiry*.

Not only discourses, but questions, advanced his exploration of mental science. Some questions were specially designed for this purpose; others were included after the fact,[8] and a few were on separate subjects entirely. One group of questions added to the second book of essays (*Active Powers*) appears to have been less integral than Reid might have wished. Since the discourses on the active powers were not quite large enough to make up a full volume, Reid added some related material. These comprise chapters 4–7 in Essay V: 'Whether an Action Deserving Moral Approbation, must be done with the belief of its being Morally good'; 'Whether Justice be a Natural or Artificial Virtue'; 'Of the Nature and Obligation of a Contract'; and 'That moral Approbation Implies a Real Judgment'. Of these essays Reid commented: 'The substance of the four following chapters was wrote long ago, and read in a literary society, with a view to justify some points of morals from metaphysical objections urged against them in the writings of David Hume, Esq.' (*Works*, 2:645). Reid's editors have assumed uncritically that these four essays date from their author's days in Aberdeen. Reid mentions that they were written in a 'literary society', and Peters's previously quoted letter implies that this was a generic term. However, this term was not used by the Aberdeen Philosophical Society, which is referred to in Reid's letters as 'The Club'. Other external and internal evidence also points to Glasgow as the most likely source of these essays.[9]

Reid's inclusion of the revised material on justice (chap. 5) and contracts (chap. 6) indicates just how inclusive and interrelated his thought had always been. The contract question, for example, inquires into natural language and its relation to the composition of human nature. Some language acts are solitary (like deliberating and forming purposes) and some, such as promises and contracts, are social. Contracts, especially, must depend upon the natural language whose signs are looks and gestures (MS 2131/2/II/14).[10]

From the evidence contained in the fragmentary GLS minutes, it appears that Reid's concentration on the development of his ideas to ready them for publication was not a habit shared by many other members. Lists of their essays indicate that even the most serious intellects in the group tended to be considerably more eclectic in their choices of topics.[11] It was a far commoner practice to articulate a position on a contemporary issue of some importance or an investigation of topics particularly interesting to the discourser. Reid was occasionally willing to deviate from his primary purpose: the continuing examination of the mind. A manuscript set of Reid's Glasgow discourses (MS 3061) shows this variation. Discourses and questions dating from all stages of Reid's association with the GLS look at contemporary issues of some urgency, such as the corn laws, regulation of interest rates, recoinage and trying to find ways to guarantee that the necessities of life will be affordable by the poor. A question from 1768 considers whether there is such a thing as a tacit contract for society; Reid concludes that there is (MS 2131 2/II/10).[12]

Some of these questions are very long and would seem to have left little time for debate by the society, but debate there certainly was. The previously cited letter from Beattie's student Alexander Peters reports on a sharp exchange between Reid and John Anderson at a meeting late in 1778:

> The last point disputed was, Whether the repeal of the penal laws respecting Popery, would be attended with good, or bad consequences, to the kingdom in general? Dr. Reid maintained mildly, that the Repeal would be attended with no bad consequences. Mr. Anderson &c, that it would. — The Nat. Philosopher [Anderson] compared the Papists to a Rattle-Snake, harmless when kept under proper restraint: but dangerous like it, when at full liberty; and ready to diffuse a baleful poison around. (MS 30/2/322)

A lively debate is also likely to have been provoked by Reid's corn law question: 'Whether the Storing or Warehousing of forreign grain or Meal for Reexportation be highly prejudicial to the Interest of this Country, & whether it ought to be prevented if possible?' (MS 3061/3). This topic was introduced as a voluntary or extra question only weeks after one read by John Millar, with whom Reid frequently argued. It is therefore possible that Reid's paper was an answer to Millar's. Presented 30 January 1778, it refers to a provision for warehousing grain in an amendment to the British Corn Law debated in Parliament in the autumn of 1777.[13] One of the measures permitted the tax-free importation of grain in years of scarcity, a controversial issue of long standing. In a letter dated 14 October 1777 to an unnamed correspondent, Sir James Steuart mentions a committee opposing free importation: 'I have had conversations with the Glasgow Theorists. I have even written them on this Subject, to no purpose.' Later in the same letter, Steuart notes that 'Smith has printed in favour of free Importation' and asserts that such a scheme will ruin both manufacture and agriculture.[14]

Reid's counterassessment is expressed in a letter to Lord Kames of 27 February 1778: 'Your Lordship is so kind as to ask what I am doing. I have read three Discourses this Winter in our Society. One upon a Clause of the last Corn Act about Warehousing Grain, a Clause which some meetings of the Landed Gentlemen have resolved to be prejudicial to the Country, I think unjustly' (Ross, 'Unpublished Letters', 31–32). Reid maintains that storing grain will on the whole stabilize its price. He points out that the only parties which stand to lose from such stability are the few landowners whose sole crop is grain produced for the market, and since they are outnumbered by those whose lives would be made easier by smaller fluctuations in price, the fair decision is the one that benefits the majority.

Steuart was clearly the source of most of the technical information in another of Reid's questions: 'What are the bad consequences of the Diminution of our Coin by wearing? and what the means of preventing those Consequences?' (MS 3061/4). Reid's references in this paper and others to Steuart's *Political Oeconomy*, essays first collected in 1767, register his admiration for the author's research, if not all his conclusions. Steuart's recommendation is a version of the 1695 recoinage proposal by Lowndes, which was rejected in favour of Locke's. Reid's proposal does not resemble either Stewart's or Locke's. He had been independently interested in coinage since at least 1762; a letter to Kames of 29 December 1762 anticipates a section of the Glasgow essay:

> I met lately with a manuscript Table of Scotch money, shewing the proportion of a pound scotch to a pound weight of Silver ever since the twelfth Century. By this Table a scotch pound of money was originally a pound of Silver Troy weight. The reigns wherein our money was altered and the particular alterations made are set down and the Authorities quoted in the Margin. By these alterations we now have above 37 pound of our money in a pound of Silver. (Ross, 'Unpublished Letters', 27)

It is difficult to date Reid's recoinage paper. The problem occasioned by the increasing volume of light silver coins prompted frequent calls for reform; but no real reform, or even any substantial new minting of silver coins, occurred until the next century. Reid does not mention proposals to Parliament dating from the early 1770s, which callied for the minting of large quantities of silver coins, or a 1780 proposal for vesting the power of coining with the Bank of England. In 1787 a new issue of shillings and sixpence temporarily relieved the problem, but the new heavy coins, being intrinsically worth much more than the old light ones, were soon melted down, and the problem became even more acute. Such an event would certainly have commanded Reid's attention, and its omission implies an earlier date for this paper.[15]

Reid proposes that the government be responsible only for guaranteeing the fineness of the silver alloy in coins, not for their weight. This would mean that people accepting coins as a medium of exchange would need to weigh them; Reid maintains that people would soon bring their light silver to the mint to be recoined, so that this inconvenience would be only temporary. There would be no advantage to melting down or exporting heavy silver. Although any reform would necessitate some losses to the public or individuals, the effects of the gradual replacement of old by new silver coins would be less than those of the recoinage of 1695.

A second paper on matters of money was proposed as another voluntary question for 20 March 1778: 'Whether it be proper to fix by Law the highest lawfull Rate of Interest, so as to make it Penal in any case, to take a higher Interest for the loan of Money' (MS 3061/5). Ten years later, James Gregory sent Reid Jeremy Bentham's *Defence of Usury* (1788). In a letter of 5 September 1788 thanking Gregory, Reid notes his agreement with Bentham:

> I think the reasoning unanswerable, and have long been of the author's opinion . . . I am least pleased with the 10th letter, wherein he accounts for the infamy of usury. In one of the papers you mention (which I give you liberty to use as you please,) I have attempted an account of that phenomenon, which satisfies me more than his account does. (*Works*, 1:73)

Bentham's account identifies the grounds of the prejudices against usury in anti-Jewish sentiment. Usury is 'acting like a Jew'; it is 'the Jewish way of getting', and has been properly condemned by writers on the subject beginning with Aristotle's statement in the *Politics* that all money is in its nature barren.[16] Although Reid uses many of the same sources, he avoids the specifically anti-Jewish implications by means of a historical overview. His preferred explanation is that there are actually two very different circumstances under which money is lent at interest, but most languages have not evolved terms to describe both. Only in relatively modern times have commercial nations developed mechanisms for financing risky or expensive ventures that necessitate lending money at interest. No generally accepted name has been developed for this circumstance, which is not the same as borrowing upon pledges for small sums in cases of dire necessity. But it is only the latter case for which we have a name; therefore, both the legitimate commercial and the odious greedy actions are called by the same dishonourable name, usury (MS 3061/5, fol. 5).

Though usury was considered so odious, and though such severe penalties for it were still in effect (if rarely enforced), Reid comments that the trade of pawnbroker was temptingly profitable. He mentions a relatively recent scandal:

> A charitable Corporation was established not very many years ago, with a view to prevent the Oppression of the poor by Pawnbrokers. Many Members of the House of Commons and others of Respectable Character were members of this corporation. . . . In a little time this Corporation was corrupted by the trade they carried on; and the publick Cry against their Oppression became so loud that the House of Commons found it necessary to make a parliamentary Enquiry into their Conduct, the Consequence of which was that several Members of the House who were members of that Corporation were expelled and the Corporation was broke.[17]

This kind of usury justly receives the censure of mankind.

Reid's curiosity in matters of finance had its roots in Aberdeen. One discourse (MS 2131/2/II/16) on the subject of paper credit owes its origin to an Aberdeen colleague, David Skene. Reid subsequently proposed a question, 'Whether Paper Credit is beneficial or harmful to a Trading Nation', for debate in the GLS for 1 May 1767. Reid's existing paper of this title is manifestly the one prepared in Aberdeen,[18] but it is always possible that he reused the material.

Another paper, on Euclid, probably had both an Aberdeen and a Glasgow reading. The existing paper (MS 3061/11) was prepared for Glasgow, but it was very likely a revision of the Aberdeen one.[19] Its fundamental purpose is to examine the problem of first principles in geometry. An important argument in the paper is a criticism of some passages in Robert Simson's edition of Euclid; Reid had wrestled with the problem the passage discusses, the definition of a straight line, since at least the 1730s. Reid quite admired the older man and was pleased when they became colleagues at Glasgow University. Parts of the Euclid discourse are extremely flattering to Simson, who had died some years previously. Reid was not particularly pleased with the final version of the paper: 'If the Author had thought this Discourse worthy to be shewn to Mathematicians, he would have transcribed it fair, & put in the proper places the parts that are disjoyned; but as Dr Hope informs him that Mr Playfair desires to see it, he will easily perceive that it is not worth that trouble' (unnumbered last page). Thomas Charles Hope, who had joined the Glasgow faculty in 1787, apparently relayed the request of William Playfair to see the discourse. Playfair was joint professor of mathematics (with Dugald Stewart) at Edinburgh; a note in his 1795 *Elements of Geometry* mentions the discourse with some respect, though he could not quite agree with Reid's suggestion that the definition he had derived was Euclid's own.[20] It would seem, then, that the discourse was read between 1787 and 1795, probably towards the end of this period.

II

THE FACILITY FOR MATHEMATICS exemplified by the Euclid paper was a gift of heredity; Reid was a member of the Gregory family that had produced a number of notable mathematicians for seventeenth- and eighteenth-century English and Scottish universities.[21] Reid's three maternal uncles were mathematics professors. Reid himself had taught mathematics as part of his duties as a regent at King's College, Aberdeen, from 1751 to 1764, and as part of his natural philosophy course he lectured on Newton's *Optics*. As young men, Reid and his friend John Stewart had translated and worked through Newton's *Principia* 'at a time when a knowledge of the Newtonian discourses was only to be acquired in the writings of this illustrious author'. Dugald Stewart reports as well that mathematical pursuits were one of the occupations of Reid's retirement, especially the elements which promoted the study of Newton's works (*Works*, 1:5, 37). In 1780 he sent Kames a careful examination of Newton's design in the *Principia* (*Works*, 1:54–56). This background perhaps sets in context a number of angry discourses directed against the materialism of Joseph Priestley, the one person who ever managed to shake Reid's good nature, which he generally maintained as a matter of policy.

In 1774, Priestley published a polemical attack on Reid, James Beattie and James Oswald. According to Priestley's autobiography, he later regretted his excesses, although a note on a reply by Oswald indicates that he was rather proud of himself for having created such a fuss with so little effort.[22] Reid did not reply to the attack, but he was loyally defended by his Aberdeen colleague George Campbell (*The Philosophy of Rhetoric*, 1776) and his young friend James Gregory (*Philosophical and Literary Essays*, 1792), among others. Later, Reid abstracted *The Doctrine of Philosophical Necessity* (1777) and wrote a separate commentary on it, which is not particularly astringent. In 1775 he was joking with Kames about Priestley's 'mysteries' (*Works*, 1:52). But in due course he prepared 'Observations on the Modern System of Materialism'.

Four drafts are extant, the last of which is fifty-one pages long. George Jardine, Reid's executor, lists 'Observations' as one of the discourses for the GLS. It is not, however, a discourse transformed into a publication, as was true of the *Intellectual Powers* and *Active Powers* discourses. It had always been intended as a separate publication, and Reid derived discourses from *it*.[23]

Three such discourses can be discerned. In the first, Reid shows that Priestley inconsistently adopts portions of Locke's, Berkeley's and Hume's systems which, upon close examination, contradict his. In addition, he considers a matter of far greater importance, an examination of Priestley's claim to have followed Sir Isaac Newton's rules of philosophizing. In the second discourse Reid considers 'what Dr Priestley has said to overturn those two Qualities of Matter, which modern Philosophers since the time of Galileo, & especially since that of Newton, have believed to be inherent in it, to wit Solidity . . . & Inertia.'[24] The third discourse considers Priestley's concept of inherent powers of attraction and repulsion. The fourth discourse, separated from this series by some years, asks whether the soul be material. In addition, two discourses from 1785 and 1786 on liberty and necessity respond to Priestley, and material in an undated manuscript takes up the subject again. The probable total is seven discourses refuting Priestley's materialism, possibly more space than Reid devoted to Hume (MS 3061/20, 22; cf. MS 2131/2/III/13).

It is difficult to imagine Reid offering all this material as discourses. It is very long, for one thing: the first item could not have taken less than two hours to read. The first three 'Observations' are filled with detailed demonstrations and logical refutations and careful quotations, none of which constitute a regular feature of Reid's discourses. It would have made its audience uneasy, not only because of its length but also because in no other public document does Reid subject any person, living or dead, atheistical or pagan, to such unmerciful, reductive attack.

Early in the first discourse, Reid admits into evidence part of Priestley's attack on him. Priestley had included Reid in 'a set of pretended Philosophers, of whom the most conspicuous and assuming is Dr Reid, Professor of moral Philosophy in the University of Glasgow' (MS 3061/24 f2r). This is not the worst of Priestley's insults, but Reid lets them all go and does not refer to any of them again. He generally restrains himself from *ad hominem* attacks, although he does mention that a committed materialist could not, without contradiction, accept Locke's ideas so zealously. *Reductio ad absurdum*, and an innocuous savagery perhaps learned from Martinus Scriblerus, are his chief weapons.

Reid's fundamental contention is that Priestley's claims to Newtonian rigour are false. For example, Priestley's hypothesis that matter is not inert but is capable of initiating motion and thought is depicted as merely a fantasy:

> It is not strange that Dr Priestley should deny that Matter is inert. For it is evident that the Inertia of Matter is inconsistent with its having power to begin Motion & consequently with its being the thinking part in Man. But that he should pretend to build his System of Materialism upon Newtons Rules of Philosophizing, & require that it be tried by that test onely, while it is an essential branch of his System that Matter is not inert, Of this I can make no other Account, but that of Sir Isaac's three Rules, he misunderstood the two first, and overlooked the last. (MS 3061/24 f4v)

In addition, Reid shows that Priestley misrepresents Newton at several crucial points.

A series of *reductio* arguments in the second discourse culminates in an implied attack on Priestley's Protestantism. Priestley claims that solidity is not an essential property of matter. If this is so, Reid demonstrates, if two particles of matter can occupy the same place at the same time, there can be no limit on the number of such particles. Not only unthinking particles are capable of this miracle. Intelligent particles, or even intelligent brains, may occupy the same place at the same time, two or even three of them (MS 3061/2/1, fols. 24–25). Absurd physics leads easily to Papist theology:

> Thus three substances may become one without annihilation, or one substance may become three without creation. Is there not here an Unity in Trinity, & a Trinity in Unity, which I think Dr Priestley holds to be an Absurdity. (3061/2/1, fol. 25)

With ironic generosity, Reid enlists the new hypothetical physics in the cause of unorthodox dogma:

> By the supposition of the penetrability of Matter, I think we might account for Transubstantiation, or at least for Consubstantiation; and I hope those who think themselves obliged to maintain these mysterious doctrines, will be thankfull for a discovery, which affords them an aid that was much wanted. (3061/2/1, fol. 24, marginal note)

In the end, however, what is interesting is not the refutation of Priestley's system, but Reid's clear understanding of what an acceptance of that system would necessarily imply. Reid compares Priestley's system to Newton's, and claims that if the new thinker is correct, the older one is not, and the world will have to be redesigned.

> If Dr Priestleys account of the qualities of matter be true, that System of natural philosophy which was begun by Gallileo, carried on by succeeding experimental philosophers, & conceived to be brought by Sir Isaac Newton, to a degree of perfection very honourable to the human understanding, is overturned to the foundation; and a new one must be raised in its place. Our Mechanicks, our Hydrostaticks & Hydraulicks, our Pneumaticks and Astronomy, are all a delusion. (3061/1/2, fol. 51)

The world is at present without any system of physics, as the experiments for Priestley's new and improved system have not yet been performed. Reid's fear, of course, is not that Newtonian science will suffer but that the Newtonian metaphors, by which modern thinking has been conditioned, and to which it responds, are vulnerable if Newton's method can be so egregiously abused (see especially MS 2131/2/I/5). Priestley may be ingenious, but he is merely showing off, wantonly playing with material he does not understand, careless of the possible consequences.

The collapse of systems was not in itself an object of terror for Reid. He was from the start a supporter of the French Revolution, like some others among his Glasgow colleagues and, like them, encountered animosity for this opinion. One of Reid's last papers for the GLS was read on 28 November 1794.[25] The *Glasgow Courier* for 18 December reported on this discourse, using the title 'On the Dangers of Political Innovation', but it is more and less than that. Some commentators have maintained that this paper marks Reid's conversion to sanity, some that he capitulated to the anti-revolutionary pressures that were applied with increasing force after 1792.[26] It is true that the first seven pages of Reid's manuscript could be read as a condemnation of the French Revolution, though that event is not named. He lists the unlikely circumstances under which a radical change of government might be expected to succeed, and certainly the French Revolution conforms to none of these; but then neither did the American Revolution or the Restoration of Charles II, and perhaps only the Revolution of 1688, which Reid commends, could measure up.

Up to this point, the *Courier*, no friend to political innovation, can be said to have titled the work correctly — and apart from the final paragraph this is the only section that the *Courier* quotes. However, after this rather passionless argument, Reid explores the topic reflected in his own title, 'Some Thoughts on the Utopian System of Government', in a much longer section. The two sections of the discourse have very little relationship to each other. Only in the last paragraph of this extremely long piece does Reid revert to the concept of political innovation, claiming that the 'sacred Tie' between government and governed demands reciprocal duties and energetic preservation: 'It is onely Atrocious Conduct that can dissolve the Sacred Tie.[27]

This conclusion is not after all so different from the resolution of the fracas over the irregularities of the self-governed literary society chronicled at the beginning of this paper. Revolution is not as important as the reexamination of fundamental principles. Accommodation is preferable if at all possible. But when it is not, then atrocious conduct may justify revolution. Reid's attitude towards the French Revolution may well have changed, but he did not necessarily abandon his respect for the rights of man.

The discourse on utopia offers other points of unity with Reid's life. The section which commands most of Reid's interest recommends a life of civic service and sets out a system of intangible rewards for exemplary performance of duties, especially by teachers. It considers problems of politics and property, of finance and commerce, the relation of men to their society. In many ways, it is an appropriate climax to his life's work.

Of course, the GLS was not Reid's only Glasgow activity besides his primary concern with the teaching of moral philosophy. In his early years in the city he attended the lectures of Joseph Black. In 1769 he assisted the astronomer Patrick Wilson in an investigation of the transit of Venus. He was interested in the Clyde-Forth canal. He took his share of university administration, though he did grumble to Kames that one man of business could finish fourteen times the business in one hour of fourteen university professors. He was one of the managers of the Royal Infirmary, which opened in 1794 and repaired the greatest defect of medical study at Glasgow, the lack of a public hospital. He was a supporter of the French Revolution, at some cost to himself. His life and work embody the fusion of intellect, moral integrity and active civic virtue that was the implied ideal of the literary and philosophical societies of Scotland.

Notes

I am grateful to Dorothy Johnston for assistance with manuscript sources and to the AUL librarian for permission to quote from manuscripts in his care.

1. *The Autobiography of Dr. Alexander Carlyle of Inveresk, 1722–1805*, new ed., ed. John Hill Burton (London and Edinburgh, 1910), 81–93.
2. The records of the GLS exist in a partial state in a bound manuscript volume of minutes in the Library of the Royal Faculty of Procurators in Glasgow. The dates of those minutes are: 1 Nov. 1764 (Laws of the Society and list of members); 2 Nov. 1764–25 Jan. 1771; 1 Nov.-22 Nov. 1771; 4 Feb. 1773; 1 Nov. 1776–14 May 1779. (The GLS did not meet between mid-May and November, when the college was not in session.) A typescript of that manuscript volume in the GUL (MS Murray 21.Y.33) is the source of references to GLS records in this essay, unless otherwise noted; another non-contemporary transcript is in the NLS (MS 245/73). Finally, there exists a handwritten book of minutes from the last decade of the century (GUL, MS Gen. 4), which was brought to my attention by Richard Sher.
3. On the patronage of Lord Kames and Lord Deskford, for example, see Ian Ross, 'Unpublished Letters of Thomas Reid to Lord Kames, 1762–1782', *Texas Studies in Literature and Language* 7 (1965): 17–18.
4. On the nature and unity of Reid's philosophy, see especially Knud Haakonssen's Introduction to his edition of Thomas Reid, *Practical Ethics: Being Lectures and Papers on Natural Religion, Self-Government, Natural Jurisprudence, and the Law of Nations* (Princeton, 1990).
5. Transcriptions of some discourses were made by another member, Thomas Gordon. For the history of these papers, see Dorothy Johnston, 'The Papers of Professor Thomas Gordon Relating to the First Aberdeen Philosophical Society, AUL, MS 3107/1–3', *Northern Scotland* 5 (1983): 179–89. See also H. Lewis Ulman, *The Minutes of the Aberdeen Philosophical Society, 1758–1773* (Aberdeen, 1990).
6. Reid's GLS discourses are located in the Birkwood Collection, AUL, mainly in MS 2131, box 2, and MS 3061. All references to Reid's manuscripts are to this collection.
7. Letters to David and Andrew Skene, James Gregory, and Lord Kames were reprinted by Sir William Hamilton as part of the Introduction to Reid's *Philosophical Works*, 2 vols. (1895; rpt. Hildesheim, 1967) (hereafter cited as *Works*). See also Ross, 'Unpublished Letters'.

8. See MS 2131/6/I/10, where, in a note to himself, Reid remarks that the material will do if made a little fuller.

9. *Works*, 2:645n.; Reid, *Practical Ethics*, 20n. Two questions (the originals of chaps. 6 and 7) clearly belong to the GLS, since they were not discussed in Aberdeen at all. The other two topics were discussed in Aberdeen, but they appear to have had a revival in Glasgow. On the whole, if all the material must be assigned to one society or the other, the GLS is the better choice.

10. Reid revised this paper extensively; the printed version does not feature the notion of natural language as prominently as does the paper read for the GLS.

11. W. J. Duncan, *Notices and Documents Illustrative of the Literary History of Glasgow during the Greater Part of the Last Century* (Glasgow, 1831), 134–35 (for Robert and Andrew Foulis's discourses and questions) and 131 (for James Moor's). Archibald Arthur's *Discourses* were edited for publication by William Richardson in 1803.

12. See Melvin T. Dalgarno, 'Taking Upon Oneself a Character: Reid on Political Obligation', in *The Philosophy of Thomas Reid*, ed. Melvin Dalgarno and Eric Matthews (Dordrecht, 1989). The social contract paper is printed in Reid, *Practical Ethics*, 237–44, and discussed in Haakonssen's Introduction, 66–68.

13. It was passed as an Act of 18 Geo. 3. (1778), extending the provisions of the previous Corn Law (13 Geo. 3. c. 43) to Portsmouth, Sandwich, Chichester and Chester, but not to any place in Scotland. However, a severe crop failure in Scotland in 1782 prompted a measure providing relief to certain Scottish counties.

14. Sir James Steuart, *An Inquiry into the Principles of Political Oeconomy*, ed. Andrew S. Skinner, 2 vols. (Edinburgh and London, 1966), 2:736–37. Steuart is referring to Adam Smith's 'Digression Concerning the Corn Trade and Corn Laws', in *An Inquiry into the Nature and Causes of the Wealth of Nations*, ed. R. H. Campbell, A. S. Skinner, and W. B. Todd, 2 vols. (Oxford, 1976), 1:524–43. See Istvan Hont and Michael Ignatieff, 'Needs and Justice in the *Wealth of Nations*: An Introductory Essay', in *Wealth and Virtue: The Shaping of Political Economy in the Scottish Enlightenment*, ed. Hont and Ignatieff (Cambridge, 1983), 20, n. 58.

15. Henry Noel Humphreys, *The Coinage of the British Empire* (London, 1855) records the efforts of the previous century's politicians to rectify the situation.

16. Jeremy Bentham, *Defence of Usury; Shewing the Impolicy of the Present Legal Restraints on the terms of Pecuniary Bargains* (Dublin, 1788), letter 10: 'Grounds of the Prejudices Against Usury'.

17. Aldermen and the lord mayor of London had requested such hearings in the 1730s. In the Parliamentary Reports, they are recorded as having taken place in 1731 and 1732 in the House of Commons, but the bill that followed was not returned from the Lords.

18. The papers of David Skene include a version that resembles Reid's nearly verbatim (AUL, MS 540, fols. 28r-29r).

19. Reid takes issue with some points made by Robert Simson in the fourth edition of his *Euclid* (1756), but in a note he acknowledges that Simson had changed the offending passages in subsequent editions. Had Reid been preparing a new paper for a society whose members remembered Simson very well, he would surely have used the latest edition available. Simson left his library to the University of Glasgow in 1768; all editions of his works would have been available. Reid mentions the edition of 1775 (the fifth) as containing the corrected passages.

20. John Playfair, *Elements of Geometry* (Edinburgh and London, 1795), 351, n.

21. Reid wrote an account of the Gregory family for Hutton's *Mathematical Dictionary* (London, 1795–96). The manuscript of the entry is MS 3061/26. Reid cites the work of his great-uncle David Gregory, the Savilian professor, in the Euclid paper.

22. *Works*, 1:37, note D. For an explanation of Priestley's position, see Jack Fruchtman, 'Reid and Priestley', in *Philosophy of Thomas Reid*, ed. Dalgarno and Matthews, 421–31.

23. One draft is fair copy prepared by a copyist. All the drafts refer to 'chapters' and 'reader', not 'Discourse', though 'Discourse' is written over 'chapter' in one place in the second draft (MS 3061/1/2, fol. 49). Separate addenda (MS 3061/23–24) dovetail with the text in this version, and references in these addenda to 'the Society', 'this Discourse', and a comment, 'On this Subject I have had the honour to read two Discourses to the society, & am now to finish what I intend upon it', indicate that extraction was Reid's method on this occasion.

24. In the draft, this material is found on pages 22–38, but I have not yet identified the separate addenda that turn it into a discourse; marginal notations partially fulfill this function.

25. Minutes of the College Literary Society, 1790–99 (typescript), GUL, MS Gen. 4. In the membership list of November 1794, the elderly Reid is excused from delivering discourses unless he wishes to do so. He appears to have read his last paper to the society on 4 December 1795, 'On the Muscular Motions of the Human Body'.

26. See Henry W. Meikle, *Scotland and the French Revolution* (Glasgow, 1912), 155–56; Alexander Campbell Fraser, *Thomas Reid* (London, 1898). However, William C. Lehmann, *John Millar of Glasgow 1735–1801: His Life and Thought and His Contributions to Sociological Analysis* (Cambridge, 1960), 54n., takes issue with Meikle's contention that in this discourse Reid bowed to the storm. In the biography of Reid's successor Archibald Arthur that was prefixed to Arthur's *Discourses on Theological and Literary Subjects* (Glasgow, 1803), 513, Professor William Richardson, a contemporary of Reid's, uses this piece to support his contention that Reid and Arthur belonged to that class which 'did not augur a great deal of immediate good from the French Revolution; and who believed that whatsoever improvement or reparation might be needful in the government of Britain (and in a government of such long duration, both may no doubt be

occasionally needful), the relief, remedy, or addition, was not to be applied by violent or external agency, but by bringing into proper action the inherent and rectifying principles of our original constitution.'

27. Haakonssen's edition of Reid's *Practical Ethics* prints 'Some Thoughts on the Utopian System' in its entirety (277–99) and includes a discussion of its place in Reid's philosophy (76–85). This quotation is from Reid's conclusion (299).

6

'Jolly Jack Phosphorous' in the Venice of the North; or, Who Was John Anderson?

Paul Wood

The title of this chapter juxtaposes three elements of the problem to be considered. First, since John Anderson (1726–96) is perhaps best known as a teacher of natural philosophy and as the founder of Anderson's Institution (which eventually transmuted into the University of Strathclyde), it is appropriate to include the student sobriquet 'Jolly Jack Phosphorous' in recognition of Anderson's pedagogical achievements. According to Lord Buchan, who attended his course in 1762–63, Anderson was 'by far the ablest Man in his profession of teaching Physics by experiment in Britain' (GUL, MS Murray 502, 201/76, fol. 1). Secondly, John Galt's characterization of Glasgow as the 'northern Venice' is highly suggestive because it evokes canals, commercial power and republicanism. These elements provide an appropriate context for the consideration of the multifaceted career of Anderson, who maintained that institutions of higher learning should be responsive to the needs of commercial societies, and who presented one of his most notable practical inventions, his field cannon, to the French nation in 1792.[1]

Finally, the question 'Who Was John Anderson?' is a deliberate echo of a recent article by Steven Shapin on the seventeenth-century virtuoso Robert Hooke, in which Shapin explores the emerging definition of the role of the experimental philosopher in early modern England.[2] Shapin's essay raises a number of issues pertinent to the study of John Anderson, for even a superficial review of the secondary literature dealing with Anderson's career reveals deep disagreement over his professional identity, stemming from the use of anachronistic conceptions of what constitutes a 'scientist'. By asking this question, moreover, I want to move beyond the stereotype of Anderson as classroom performer and probe little used archival materials in order to discover what these tell us about Anderson's intellectual and practical interests, and his place in the cultural matrix of the Enlightenment. In doing so, I also hope to shed light on the more general issue of the competing definitions of the role of the natural or experimental philosopher in late eighteenth-century Britain.

I

WAS JOHN ANDERSON a man of science? Although an affirmative answer may seem obvious, it was by no means so to one of the great chroniclers of Glasgow University, David Murray, who wrote of Anderson:

> He was an active and intelligent man, and although he was not a student or a scholar or an investigator, he might have been a useful member of the Faculty if he had not allowed vanity, arrogance and a pugnacious disposition to master him . . . . Anderson was a good teacher and a neat experimenter and his classes were well attended, but he made no advance in science . . . . He had no turn for investigation, and . . . took no part in the research work of Professor Black and of James Watt which was carried on beside him. His tastes lay in other directions.[3]

According to Murray, then, Anderson was an effective pedagogue who was primarily interested in pursuits other than natural philosophy.

Prima facie, Anderson's wide-ranging interests would seem to constitute good grounds for scepticism about his scientific pretensions. Before switching to the natural philosophy chair in 1757, Anderson served three years as professor of oriental languages at Glasgow, also teaching French and English and even planning to teach Italian.[4] The sheer diversity of subjects discussed by Anderson in the Glasgow Literary Society attests to the breadth of his interests.[5] Yet Murray's characterization of Anderson's career can be faulted for its lack of empirical detail regarding Anderson's activities as a professor, and for the historically questionable definition of science it assumes. The research and publication ideal that Murray invoked in his description of Anderson was initially constructed in the German universities of the nineteenth century,[6] and it would be wrong to deny Anderson (or his contemporaries) the status of man of science on such a whiggish basis.

Leaving aside the issue of anachronistic criteria, one way of resolving the problem at hand is to adopt a strategy similar to that employed by Shapin when dealing with Hooke, by reconstructing what Anderson did from day to day, identifying his friends and correspondents and cataloging his material possessions. Such a method enables us to trace the pattern of Anderson's life and to arrive at a view of his scholarly identity rooted in the material remains of his career.

What, for instance, does Anderson's library tell us about his interests, aspirations and self-perception? Approximately one half of the titles contained in the library deal with the natural sciences. The remainder encompass a good deal of historical, antiquarian and religious material,[7] a substantial collection of works on military matters, a fair number on moral philosophy, a selection of polite literature, some dictionaries and miscellaneous volumes on music, drama and the visual arts. Of the science books, many are on natural history and chemistry, and only a few on medicine and mathematics. The majority are related to natural philosophy; of these titles, roughly 33 percent are pedagogical texts; 13 percent are on astronomy; 8 percent are on electricity; and the rest are randomly distributed in areas such as optics, magnetism and mechanics.[8] Thus, Anderson's personal library reflects the shifts in his academic career, since it includes a sizable proportion of items on language and polite literature. But it also bespeaks the interests of a serious man of science, well read in both natural history and natural philosophy and familiar with the latest developments in two fields of particular theoretical moment in the second half of the eighteenth century, electricity and pneumatic chemistry. Moreover, if we add to Anderson's books his cabinets of mineral and fossil specimens, his models of water wheels, pumps, windmills and the like, and his instruments, we see that he possessed all the accoutrements of the scientific virtuoso.[9]

Anderson's personal contacts and daily activities are also those of a man of science. Although Anderson remains notorious for his attitudes and behaviour towards his students and colleagues at Glasgow, he was nevertheless on friendly terms with James Watt, John Robison, Thomas Reid and the Wilsons, *père et fils*, who served as the first two professors of practical astronomy at Glasgow.[10] Anderson collaborated with these men in various natural philosophical inquiries. In September 1769, for example, he observed a transit of Venus across the sun along with Reid, mathematics professor James Williamson, the chemist William Irvine and the two Wilsons.[11] Anderson was also moderately clubbable. During the early 1750s he participated in the Considerable Club and, like many of his colleagues, he was active in the GLS, where he discussed, *inter alia*, a variety of scientific questions.[12] Outside Glasgow, Anderson was connected with various learned bodies. He was a fellow of the Royal Society of London and the Royal Society of Edinburgh, a corresponding member of the Society of Antiquaries of Scotland and a member of the Natural History Society of London and of the Society for Agriculture and Economics of the Empress of Russia.[13] He was in touch as well with men of science like Lord Kames, Emanuel Mendes Da Costa, John Hunter, Benjamin Franklin, Richard Price, Revd John Michell and the Venetian naturalist, the Abbé Fortis.

Further evidence concerning Anderson's place in the world of learning comes in the memoranda he jotted into his copy of *The Universal Scots Almanack* for 1765. There he noted that during a visit to Edinburgh on 1 January 1765 he planned to see Patrick Cuming, Matthew Stewart, Revd Robert Dick and William Cullen, among others, and to consult 'Hill's

Book & ye last volume of Transactions [i.e. the *Philosophical Transactions*]'.[14] Anderson thus proposed to combine reading and research with scientific conversation and ecclesiastical politicking during his jaunt to the 'Athens of the North'. A more revealing picture of his daily routine can be formed from the diary he kept from 27 June to 21 October 1782, while he was performing a series of gunnery experiments at Dumbarton Castle. Apart from illustrating the risks of undertaking outdoor activity in the west of Scotland, Anderson's diary records his reading, his writing projects and his social life in this period, and it shows that his daily routine was textured by the culture of the natural sciences. When he was not experimenting with cannon and shot, he was investigating the magnetic quality, and then taking a specimen, of the rock around the castle, as well as measuring 'the Heat of the Loch or Spring, of the Rock, of the River &c:'.[15] The Dumbarton diary also reveals him reading Cronstedt's *Mineralogy*, the third volume of Richard Watson's *Chemical Essays*, Lord Monboddo's *Antient Metaphysics* and unidentified works by Jean-André De Luc, Benjamin Robbins and Joseph Priestley. Anderson was busy writing, too, keeping up his 'Journal of Experiments', correcting a GLS discourse on Buchanan, and penning essays on 'the Advantages of Perforated & Spheroidical Shott', the improvement of artillery and 'on Moisture'.

As for socializing, Anderson received visits at Dumbarton Castle from his Glasgow colleagues Patrick Wilson and William Irvine; William Enfield, who taught natural philosophy at the Warrington Academy; a 'Dr Reimarus from Hamburg' (probably Johann, son of the more famous savant Hermann Reimarus); 'a Party of Botanists from Dr Hope going to Benlomond'; Dugald Stewart, who was then the professor of mathematics at Edinburgh; and Thomas Reid. The entries describing Reid's visit are particularly interesting. When Reid arrived at Dumbarton on 24 October, the weather was especially inclement, and they spent two days together reading 'the Review [probably the *Monthly Review*], McLeod on Patronage, Monboddo's 3d Volumes Priestly &c:'.[16] Anderson and Reid thus conversed about a variety of religious and philosophical topics. Furthermore, at some point in the 1780s Reid was attacking Priestley's *Disquisitions Relating to Matter and Spirit* (1777) in discourses given before the GLS (see Wood, 'Thomas Reid', 324), so it may well be that they were discussing Priestley's reformulation of the materialist system while waiting for the weather to break. Anderson himself remarked that he had had 'much literary Conversation' while at Dumbarton, and his diary confirms that in addition to carrying out various experimental inquiries, a good deal of his time was spent chatting and reading about scientific subjects. The daily routine recorded in the Dumbarton diary and other sources, then, is that of a man of science in late eighteenth-century Britain.

II

IN ORDER TO CHARACTERIZE John Anderson's scientific *persona* with greater precision, it is necessary to consider the natural philosophy course that Anderson taught at the University of Glasgow for almost forty years. Previously, Anderson's champions have celebrated the fact that his biweekly lectures on experimental philosophy were open to non-matriculated (or non-gowned) students, and they have contended that Anderson was an innovator in this regard. Murray and others, however, have rightly insisted that Anderson's practice was no different from that of his predecessors.[17] What made Anderson's course distinctive was not the social composition of his audience but the fact that he followed the precedent of his predecessor, Robert Dick *secundus*, by prelecting on natural historical topics in addition to the cluster of sciences typically covered in courses of natural or experimental philosophy (i.e., mechanics, hydrostatics, pneumatics, optics, electricity and astronomy).[18] Prompted, perhaps, by the formal introduction of natural history into the curricula of the two Aberdeen colleges in 1753,[19]Dick *secundus* first added a natural history component to his syllabus in 1755. This may seem to be a relatively insignificant alteration, but it is arguable that by including lectures on the 'Philosophical History of Nature' Dick helped to institutionalize the constellation of interests in natural philosophy and natural history characteristic of earlier generations of Scottish virtuosi, and thus perpetuate the view of the structure of human knowledge to which they subscribed.[20]

This point is of considerable historiographical moment for two reasons. First, the way in which natural history and natural philosophy were institutionalized at Glasgow further illustrates Roger Emerson's claim that there were important continuities between the aspirations and projects of the virtuosi active at the turn of the eighteenth century and those of the savants usually identified as the creators of the Scottish Enlightenment. The virtuosi engaged in what for them was a set of interrelated inquiries in mathematics, medicine, morals, antiquities, natural history and natural philosophy, and the map of human knowledge they envisaged was embodied in Dick's revised course of natural philosophy. Moreover, these continuities in cognitive structures indicate that we should follow Emerson, Chitnis and others in locating the origins of the Scottish Enlightenment in the late seventeenth century, instead of invoking the Union of 1707 as the primary cause of the intellectual effloresence of eighteenth-century Scotland.[21]

Secondly, John Anderson's *persona* as a man of science comes into sharper focus when we compare his diverse enthusiasms with the set of interests associated with the virtuosi. We have seen that David Murray maintained that Anderson's 'tastes' were not scientific, and to prove his point Murray cited Anderson's writings on antiquities. Similarly, James Muir referred to Anderson's papers on antiquarian subjects, along with a piece 'On the varieties of human kind', as being 'essays of a less scientific character' (*John Anderson*, 15). John Cable has likewise described Anderson's contributions to the GLS on these topics as 'of a peripherally scientific nature', although it is not clear whether Cable thought they were among the 'occasionally odd' subjects Anderson discussed with his fellow members ('Early Scottish Science', 190–91). Yet Murray, Muir and Cable all miss the significance of the range of subjects Anderson canvassed in the GLS and how many of them dovetail with the structure of his natural philosophy course, because they have not placed Anderson in his relevant intellectual and scientific context, namely that of the virtuosi of the late seventeenth and early eighteenth centuries.

Like their European counterparts, the Scottish virtuosi were, among other things, preoccupied with improvement, but the modalities of the improving ethos in Scotland were such that the amelioration they sought was as much cultural and moral as material. Driven by a combination of fierce patriotism and shame at Scotland's perceived backwardness, they sought to advance their nation by promoting useful and polite knowledge. Furthermore, the early Scottish virtuosi combined their patriotism and politeness with a distinctive view of the structure of human knowledge derived from the writings of Francis Bacon, to which I have already alluded. One feature of Bacon's map of learning that was to have important consequences in the eighteenth century was his depiction of the relations between civil and natural history. In his *De Augmentis Scientiarum*, Bacon argued that both were rooted in the faculty of memory, and that there was considerable overlap between them, especially in the sphere of what he called 'mixed histories'.[22] Thus, natural and civil history constituted a continuous field of inquiry, and Bacon's conception of the intimate connections between them informed the practice of Scottish virtuosi from the mid-seventeenth century onwards.[23]

The work of Sir Robert Sibbald, for example, reveals the characteristic virtuoso conjunction of interest in history, antiquities and natural history, reflecting Sibbald's ambition to reconstruct Scotland's past and to discover its potential for future cultural and economic improvement (Emerson, 'Sir Robert Sibbald', 46–47, 53–56). Institutionally, this pattern was subsequently manifest in the Edinburgh Philosophical Society, in the Society of Antiquaries of Scotland and, vestigially, in the Royal Society of Edinburgh.[24] In the educational realm, this conjunction was formally embodied in the restructured curricula of the two Aberdeen colleges, where civil and natural history were taught together in the second-year or 'semi' class; as I have indicated, the moves in Aberdeen may have led Robert Dick *secundus* to revamp his natural philosophy course in 1755. It should come as no surprise, therefore, that John Anderson studied antiquities, history and natural history in the manner of a true virtuoso.

That Anderson shared the virtuoso taste for politeness and patriotism

1. Irish-born Francis Hutcheson (1694–1746), appointed Professor of Moral Philosophy at Glasgow University in 1729, is often considered to be the 'father' of the Scottish Enlightenment.

2. William Leechman, Professor of Divinity (1744–61), and Principal (1761–85) of Glasgow University, advanced the cause of moderate Presbyterianism through the eloquence of his preaching.

ROBERTUS SIMSON

Prof. Matheseos in Coll. Glasg.

3. Robert Simson (1687–1768), Professor of Mathematics at Glasgow University for half a century (1711–61), was a distinguished teacher of geometry and editor of Euclid.

4. William Cullen (1710–1790), the greatest medical name of the Scottish Enlightenment, made important innovations in the teaching of medicine and chemistry at Glasgow University during the late 1740s and early 1750s. He subsequently found fame and fortune as a professor of those subjects in Edinburgh.

5. Joseph Black
(1728–1799),
discoverer of latent
heat, followed
in the footsteps
of his mentor
William Cullen by
teaching chemistry
and medicine
first at Glasgow
University and later at
Edinburgh.

6. William Hunter
(1718–1783), a
student of William
Cullen at Glasgow
who later attained
wealth and eminence
as a physician and
medical educator in
London, bequeathed
to Glasgow University
a magnificent
collection of paintings
and artefacts which
formed the nucleus
of the Hunterian
Museums.

7.   Adam Smith
(1723–1790), world-
renowned philosopher
and author of *The Wealth
of Nations* (1776), was
elected Professor of Logic
at Glasgow University in
1751, transferred to the
chair of Moral Philosophy
in the following year, and
occupied that position
until 1764.

8.   Thomas Reid
(1710–1796), who
succeeded Adam
Smith as Professor of
Moral Philosophy in
Glasgow University in
1764, was the leading
exponent of Scottish
Common Sense
philosophy.

9. John Anderson (1726–1796), a popular if somewhat contentious Professor of Natural Philosophy at Glasgow University from 1757 until his death, developed a rain gauge, an improved cannon and other practical inventions that are depicted here. His will established an institution for the study of 'useful knowledge' that is now the University of Strathclyde.

10. John Millar (1735–1801), author of *Observations concerning the Distinction of Ranks* (1771), transformed Glasgow University into a centre of legal education during his tenure as Professor of Civil Law.

11. James Boswell (1740–1795), biographer of Samuel Johnson, came under the influence of Adam Smith during his attendance at Glasgow University in 1759–60.

12. Following a medical career in Glasgow in the 1740s and '50s, John Moore (1729–1802) achieved fame as a novelist and travel-writer in London.

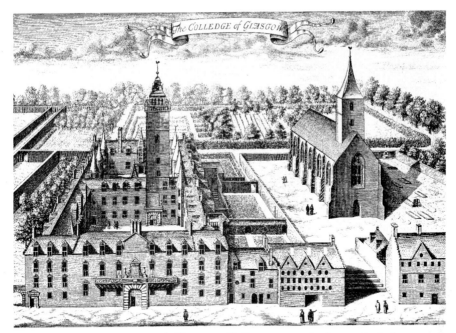

13. John Slezer's view of Glasgow College towards the end of the seven-teenth century contrasts its urban entrance in the High Street (foreground) with its pastoral surroundings.

14. Robert Paul's view of the Middle Walk in Glasgow College garden was a product of the short-lived Glasgow Academy of Fine Arts (1753–1776) established by the booksellers Robert and Andrew Foulis.

15.   The elegant Trongate, as pictured here by Robert Paul, greatly impressed visitors to Glasgow during the eighteenth century.

16.   In the early nineteenth century the High Street entrance to Glasgow College remained much as it had been at the end of the seventeenth century.

can be seen in his discourse 'Of the Propriety of Erecting an Obelisk in Honour of Buchanan' and in his 'Remarks upon a late publication, the title of which is Poetical remains of James the Ist King of Scotland'. Similarly, his efforts in 1761 to establish, under the auspices of the university, an academy for dancing, fencing and riding, his founding of a university essay prize and a prize for elocution in 1770 and his worries about Scotticisms all evince a desire to foster politeness by eradicating the traces of provincialism.[25] Patriotism and the imperatives of practical improvement also sustained Anderson's experiments on artillery and shot, and perhaps his work on military questions generally. Although the French were, in the end, to profit from Anderson's expertise, he did his best to interest Whitehall in his modified gun carriage in the spring and summer of 1789, and he carried on prolonged negotiations with the master general of the ordinance, the duke of Richmond, only to be frustrated by Richmond's scepticism and the machinations of various individuals at Woolwich (MS 7). Anderson's work with rain gauges and barometers, too, should be seen in terms of the virtuosi's fascination with meteorology and its potential for practical application, as well as their desire to compile a natural history of Scotland.[26] Anderson's founding of the university that bore his name can also be seen as a continuation of the efforts of the virtuosi to institutionalize their intellectual ideals. Beginning in the 1670s, men such as Sibbald created new institutional structures and remodelled the Scottish universities in order to achieve their cultural ends. Anderson's statement in his will that the trustees he named were to 'manage an University, or Studium Generale, for the Improvement of Human Nature, of Science, and of the country where they live' (Muir, *John Anderson*, 137) harkens back to the patriotic exhortations of that earlier generation.

From at least the 1760s onwards, Anderson moved in Scottish anti-quarian circles. He remained on friendly terms with his former student Lord Buchan and corresponded with men such as Lord Hailes.[27] While the Forth and Clyde Canal was in its initial stages of construction during the late 1760s and early 1770s, Anderson managed to acquire a number of Roman stones for the college, and his work on the Roman sites located between the Forth and the Clyde places him in the classical and scientific tradition of Scottish antiquarianism that has been delineated by Stuart Piggott. Like Sibbald, Sir John Clerk of Penicuik, Robert Melville and William Roy, Anderson was fascinated by the cultural and military achievements of ancient Rome. But unlike earlier writers on the Antonine wall, such as Alexander Gordon, Anderson seems to have felt no ambivalence about the fact that the Romans had conquered ancient Caledonia.[28] Indeed, Anderson used his review of the known archaeological remains associated with the sites as the basis for a defence of the 'unnatural' style of the sculptures found along the wall, and of the supposed practice of wearing phallic ornaments by 'Roman Ladies of [the] greatest Virtue . . .

in the same manner that our Ladies do a necklace and a Cross' (MS 22, fol. 97).[29] Yet Anderson's discussion of Roman devotional relics dedicated to non-Roman gods demonstrates that he was no uncritical admirer of the civilization of the ancient world. Contrary to those who had contended that these relics proved that the Romans tolerated different religions, Anderson affirmed that the principle of toleration was a creation of the moderns and cited passages from Plato and Cicero to show that both the Greeks and the Romans punished religious dissenters (MS 22, fols. 86–96).

Anderson's appeal to natural historical evidence in his papers on the Antonine wall also points to his affinities with the virtuoso tradition of antiquarianism. When describing one of the pieces of Roman sculpture held by the university, for example, Anderson argued that it was not incongruous to find a boar depicted there even though boars had been extinct 'in this Island for many Centuries' (MS 22, fol. 49), because there were many instances in natural history of species dying out in countries that had progressed from a rude to a cultivated state. In a slightly different vein, Anderson insisted that the general ignorance of natural history in the ancient world contributed to the fantastic imagery found in some Roman art, which was thus excusable even though it was contrary to nature. By contrast, he censured modern artists who created 'Monsters' because great progress had been made in natural history 'since the rivival of Learning' (MS 22, fols. 84–86). Antiquarianism and natural history here overlap in a manner characteristic of the virtuoso tradition.

Moreover, Anderson's papers on antiquarian subjects contain significant traces of the philosophical historian at work. His analysis of the Roman remains discovered between the Forth and the Clyde indicates that antiquarianism and theoretical history were perhaps not so distinct as Piggott has suggested.[30] As one might expect from a man who attended, and took notes at, the lectures of his colleague Adam Smith,[31] Anderson looked at the historical record with an eye to the progress of societies from rudeness to refinement. He also compared the manners of the ancient 'North Britons' with those of contemporary Highlanders, in the manner of a theoretical historian. Anderson wanted to use the antiquarian evidence he surveyed to illuminate the manners of the Romans as well, and his remarks on the role of habit and custom in forming our notions of propriety reflect a decidedly philosophical concern with the workings of human nature (MS 22, fols. 23–24, 49, 97–99). By mixing the preoccupations of the antiquarian and the philosophical historian in his researches on the Roman sites of southern Scotland, Anderson brought together the historical concerns of the earlier virtuosi with those of later figures like David Hume, Adam Smith, William Robertson and John Millar.[32]

Before we turn to Anderson's activities as a natural historian, two preliminary points must be made. First, Anderson maintained that the aims and methods of the civil and the natural historian were largely the same.

In the discourse 'Of Natural and Artificial Systems in Natural History', delivered to the GLS in 1774, he remarks: 'As Civil History is an account of the different Forms of Political Bodies, of the laws by which they are governed, and the Revolutions which they have undergone; so Natural History is an account of the three Kingdoms of Nature, of the different Forms belonging to the Subjects of these Kingdoms, of the laws by which they are governed, and the changes which they have undergone without the interposition of Man' (MS 9, fols. 1–2).[33] Like Bacon and the virtuosi before him, therefore, Anderson believed that there was a smooth transition from the one branch of history to the other because they shared common problems and methods. Secondly, there was a direct link between John Anderson's natural historical pursuits and those of the first generation of virtuosi in Scotland. As Roger Emerson has pointed out, in October 1768 Anderson transcribed a 1703 'List of Materials for a Natural History' by Robert Wodrow, who was in close contact with such English and Scottish virtuosi as Sibbald, John Woodward, Edward Lhwyd, William Nicholson, John Adair and Alexander Edward. Whatever his reasons for copying it, Anderson was apparently conscious of standing in a line of Scottish natural historians that began in Wodrow's generation. In all probability, then, he saw himself as a virtuoso.[34].

One of the most contentious issues dividing natural historians during the eighteenth century concerned the utility of artificial as opposed to natural taxonomic systems.[35] In his GLS discourses for 1774, Anderson endeavoured to steer a middle course between the position of Buffon, who had attacked the use of artificial systems in the 'Premier discours' of his *Histoire Naturelle*, and that of Linnaeus, whom Anderson esteemed as the leading naturalist of the age. Yet his admiration for the great Swedish naturalist was not unqualified, since he faulted Linnaeus for 'a love of System'. He also thought the Swede was prone to pedantry, and he remarked that Linnaeus's classification of primates was 'capricious' (MS 9, fol. 10). However, even though he was critical of specific features of the Linnaean system, Anderson did not question the validity of artificial systems, as Buffon had done.

Buffon's critique of artificial taxonomy was rooted in his conviction that nature is a continuum, and that the taxonomic categories of species, genera, classes and orders are all arbitrary fictions of the human mind. Anderson was sympathetic to the epistemological thrust of Buffon's argument, in so far as he acknowledged that the concepts employed in artificial taxonomies are mental constructs. Nevertheless, he defended the use of such concepts on the grounds that they enable naturalists to classify, and thus to know, the constituents of the mineral, vegetable and animal kingdoms. Anderson also agreed with Buffon regarding the desirability of 'natural' systems of classification, but he insisted that savants could not begin to construct such systems until they had completed the initial task of cataloguing the creation with the help of artificial schemes. Since

Anderson was himself preoccupied with the problem of classifying 'fossils', he used the history of mineralogy to show that it was futile to start with natural systems because they do not isolate permanent properties of bodies that can serve as distinguishing characteristics. Moreover, he indicated that so-called natural systems were implicitly premised on theoretical assumptions about the objects of study and, for him, theories were almost invariably misleading. He was adamant, therefore, that

> if we would be Philosophers, that is accurate in our knowledge, an Artificial System must precede a Natural one, and for this plain reason that the objects of Natural History are numerous, and similar, and till we know them distinctly we are talking and writing of we know not what. We are like those pretenders to Science in other Subjects who will not give accurate definitions, and who therefore may write and dispute forever, and forever will be wide of the truth. (MS 9, fol. 6)

Anderson, then, rejected the basic thesis of Buffon's 'Premier discours' regarding the uselessness of the Linnaean system, and stoutly defended the utility of artificial taxonomic schemes.[36] Furthermore, there are hints in his discourses that his defence was at least partly tied to his pedagogical role, for Anderson remarked to his colleagues that 'the use of a System is for a Student to become acquainted with Bodies in the easiest manner, and to learn such marks as will distinguish them forever' (MS 9, fol. 15ᵛ).

Having discussed the respective merits of natural and artificial systems, Anderson turned to a consideration of the topical issue of the racial differences observable in mankind. In the *Histoire Naturelle*, Buffon had attributed such differences to the influence of climate, but Lord Kames had challenged this account in the 'Preliminary Discourse' to his *Sketches of the History of Man*, which first appeared in 1774, the year of Anderson's discourses.[37] Whereas Buffon had claimed that all of humankind constituted a single species, Kames contended that the different races of men were in fact distinct species, having (in the case of Amerindians) their own separate origins. Although Kames's polygenism was compatible with the idea of God's omnipotence, it was difficult to reconcile it with the letter of the scriptures, and in responding to Kames's position Anderson set out to discover 'whether there is reason to believe, independent of Revelation, that all the Human kind are descended from one Pair, or that different Pairs, with different qualities, were created in different parts of the Earth' (MS 9, fol. 16).

According to Anderson, all the relevant evidence suggested that mankind had descended from the same parents. Anderson appealed first to the 'analogy of nature', arguing that because plants and animals could flourish in very different climatic conditions there was 'no reason from Analogy for believing that different Races of Men were created for different Climates'. He alleged as well that Kames's theory was incompatible with the evident perfectibility of man. He maintained that Kames's polygenism entailed that 'Men would be prisoners in particular latitudes', which was manifestly not the case, since they were able to 'range from Zone to Zone' and thus become 'both the Lords and the Philosophers of the whole creation' (MS 9, fols. 22–23).

Secondly, after reviewing the various characteristics of the six races or 'varieties' of humankind observable around the globe, Anderson concluded that variations in hair, stature and appearance could all be accounted for in terms of such physical and moral causes as climate, food, manners and modes of life. However he did recognize the force of Kames's argument that climatic differences alone were insufficient to bring about variations in skin colour, and he invoked the occurrence of disease to explain how the races of mankind might have come to have such diverse colours and complexions. Citing instances of inexplicable changes in coloration, he affirmed that there existed a power of nature capable of producing the different colours of the six races, even if the laws governing this power were essentially unknown (MS 9, fols. 24–38). As for the anatomical differences between the races that had been alleged by various natural historians (including Kames), Anderson denied that they had been sufficiently well established to be credible, and consequently believed that they could not be used to support a theory like Kames's (MS 9, fols. 38–41).[38]

Buffon's criterion for identifying the members of a given species provided Anderson with his third argument against Kames. Following Buffon, Anderson insisted that two animals were from the same species if they could mate and have fruitful progeny. Since individuals from different races could do so, he inferred that the six human races were not distinct species, but varieties having common ancestral parents. Elaborating on this theme, he cited the example of the numerous varieties of cows, sheep and dogs. He pointed out that interbreeding among the varieties within each species seemed to eliminate distinguishing characteristics, which implied a reversion to the common ancestral type. Moreover, Anderson was able to show that the variations observable in these three species were the direct result of climate, diet and the intervention of man. Thus, he concluded that if the pronounced differences between the varieties of species in the animal kingdom could be attributed to such causes, it was reasonable to assume that the variations among men were the product of similar factors (MS 9, fols. 41–46).

Finally, Anderson turned to the moral and intellectual differences among humankind. According to him, three variable characteristics had been used as evidence for the view that the races of man had not descended from the same original parents: the 'aversion or liking to strangers', cowardice and courage, and the capacity for cultivating the arts and sciences. Regarding these characteristics, he affirmed first that 'it seems certain from the concurring testimony of all Historians' that man is a gregarious animal who has kindly affections towards his kind when there is no occasion to feel threatened and, secondly, that cowardice and courage, as well as the propensity for improvement, 'depend entirely upon habit and political institutions' (MS 9, fol. 46). Anderson, then, agreed with Kames that intellectual and moral attributes are not determined primarily by the environment (as Montesquieu and a host of other authors had claimed), but are shaped by social institutions, education and culture. Yet at the same time Anderson attacked Kames's contention that variations in courage or other such qualities proved that the individual races of humankind were distinct creations. For Anderson, the falsity of Kames's position was manifest, because the differences between nations, or even between the members of the various professions in one country, were just as significant as those adduced by Kames to demonstrate the existence of separate races. This point suggested to Anderson that the variations in moral qualities discussed by his friend resulted from the same causes that produced divergent national and professional characters.[39]

On the basis of his review of the relevant evidence, therefore, Anderson was convinced that the scriptural account of the creation of man was corroborated by the findings of natural history, and that Kames's polygenism was profoundly mistaken. To explain why Kames had been misled, Anderson ended his discourses with a philosophical fable about the opinions of a 'free-thinking Arabian groom', and in drawing the moral of his tale he sketched a highly perceptive pen portrait of Kames:

> He is an honest man. He searches with avidity for truth. But with these excellent qualities he is misled by the same causes which have misled many philosophers of great name. An inattention to the Analogy of Nature. The love of a new Theory. A partial view of facts. And the disbelief of the existence of a fact unless we can tell for what reason it did exist, and by what immediate cause it was produced. (MS 9, fol. 60)

Whatever their theoretical and methodological differences, however, the two Scots were engaged in a common enterprise, namely the reconstruction of the natural history of man. Like Kames, Anderson looked to the writings of Buffon and other natural historians, to travel accounts and to the works of civil historians in order to compile his 'facts' about the different states and progress of humankind. Indeed, both Kames's *Sketches* and Anderson's discourses illustrate clearly the fluid boundaries of natural and civil history and the continued influence of the Baconian map of human knowledge on the cultivation of learning in eighteenth-century Scotland.[40]

Bacon's chart of the sciences also provides a key to understanding the relationship between natural history and natural philosophy in Anderson's writings and researches. Quite apart from the obvious point that Bacon insisted that a truly inductive philosophy had to be founded on a comprehensive history of the creation, his description of what he called the 'history of arts' is highly significant, since for Bacon this branch of natural history recorded the phenomena produced by the experimental and mechanical manipulation of nature (*Philosophical Works*, 403, 405–6, 427–30). In the late seventeenth and eighteenth centuries, what came to be known as the 'experimental philosophy' was closely related to such a history of arts, in so far as this new type of philosophical practice sought to establish facts and laws through experiment and to exclude speculations about efficient causes. Moreover, the works of Hume and Reid provided a sophisticated epistemological justification for this shift away from the Baconian search for efficient causes. Following the lead of Malebranche, Berkeley and some of the early Newtonians, they redefined the notion of natural laws, such that Reid could write that 'the laws of nature are nothing else but the most general facts relating to the operations of nature, which include a great many particular facts under them'. Consequently, their view arguably helped to collapse experimental philosophy into a form of natural history dedicated to discovering and describing the laws governing matter.[41]

These trends are clearly reflected in Anderson's natural philosophy teaching at Glasgow, where he gave two distinct (though related) courses. His 'physics' or natural philosophy lectures on Mondays, Wednesdays, Fridays and Saturdays dealt with 'the Tenets, and History of the different Sects of Natural Philosophers . . . together with Mathematical Reasonings upon *Facts*, which are taken for granted', whereas on Tuesdays and Thursdays he gave prelections on experimental philosophy, in which 'no Mathematical reasonings are used; but the *Facts* are exhibited, upon which the Mathematical Reasonings are founded; and these Facts, or Experiments . . . are accompanied with short Explanations'.[42] His experimental philosophy classes were, therefore, taken up primarily with the description of the 'facts', and in his lectures he espoused the methodological ethos of the experimentalists. He taught his students that 'the proper office and the highest Boast of true Philosophy is to ascertain facts, to explain their Connections and so to bring us still nearer to the Fountain of all knowledge', and that we must be content to ascertain such connections without discovering what the efficient causes are which bring them about.[43] Hence Anderson presented experimental philosophy as a largely descriptive enterprise which, in effect, differed little from natural history, so that his inclusion of prelections on the three kingdoms of nature was less intrusive than it might otherwise have been. Furthermore, one of the functions of his natural philosophy course was to provide a classification of material bodies on the basis of their different experimentally established qualities, such as their electrical or magnetic properties. Consequently, natural and experimental philosophy were for Anderson partly classificatory enterprises like natural history; he apparently thought that the primary difference between them was that natural philosophy studied nature experimentally, whereas natural history considered the natural order 'without the operations of Art', although this distinction was by no means a firm one.[44] Natural philosophy and natural history were thus closely related in Anderson's mind, because both aimed at the description and classification of the creation.

III

I HAVE ARGUED THAT Anderson can best be understood as a virtuoso in the tradition of Sir Robert Sibbald. By way of conclusion, I want to explore briefly the broader ramifications of my argument. In local terms, it is significant that the first professor of natural philosophy at Anderson's Institution, Thomas Garnett, followed Anderson's example and included lectures on mineralogy (and geology) in his natural philosophy class.[45] More importantly, Garnett proposed to offer a course 'on the philosophy of natural history', which was to feature prelections on the theory of the earth and the natural history of man. Regarding the latter topic, Garnett said he would 'trace [man's] progress from infancy to old age, the unfolding of reason, the faculty called instinct, &c. Next will follow a view of the philosophy of living matter, with a general outline of physiology; the effects of different climates on the colour of the human species; [and] the progress of man in society, from rudeness to refinement' (*Observations*, 2:200–1). Garnett's projected course, therefore, contains the same combination of the natural and civil histories of man that was to be found in Anderson's writings and in those of the Scottish virtuosi generally. Yet the fact that Garnett planned to discuss the 'philosophy of natural history' in a series of lectures separate from those on natural philosophy signals the fact that the virtuoso ideal of combining the two spheres of knowledge was beginning to crumble. Consequently, while Garnett may have perpetuated aspects of the virtuoso tradition during his brief career at Anderson's Institution, the structure of his prelections reflects the advent of increasing specialization and fragmentation in the world of learning, and a redrawing of the map of the human sciences.

Garnett was an Englishman (albeit educated at Edinburgh), and one must understand the English roots of his scientific outlook in order to elucidate more fully the background to his proposals. Although the presence in England of the virtuoso as an identifiable social type has not gone unremarked by historians, the English virtuosi have often been typecast as dilettantes and amateurs, and their supposed dominance in the proceedings of the Royal Society of London has been taken as a symptom of that august body's institutional decline following the resignation of Sir Hans Sloane as president in 1741.[46] From the Restoration onwards, however, men with natural historical and antiquarian interests, such as Walter Charleton, Robert Plot, Edward Lhwyd, John Woodward, William Stukeley and Sloane, were key figures in the institutionalization of natural knowledge; even though their intellectual achievements do not rival those of their contemporary, Sir Isaac Newton, they cannot be dismissed out of hand as historically insignificant simply because they do not conform to present-day stereotypes of 'real' scientists. Rather, we must see the virtuoso as representing the typical man of science in England for much of the eighteenth century. The Baconian map of knowledge was institutionalized not only in the Royal Society but also in a host of provincial groupings, where men conversed about antiquities, natural history, natural philosophy and improvement in the same way that their counterparts did north of the Tweed.[47]

With the founding of the Linnean Society in 1788, however, new specialist societies emerged, and the growing division of intellectual labour in the natural sciences destroyed the connections between antiquarianism and the study of nature that the virtuosi had hitherto so assiduously cultivated.[48] At the close of the Enlightenment, therefore, the virtuosi in both England and Scotland were being replaced by men of science whose cognitive horizons and technical competences were increasingly specialized, and who redefined their scientific roles accordingly.[49] John Anderson's career and the early years of his Institution tell us much about the aspirations of the virtuosi in the Enlightenment, as well as about the genesis of a new role for men of science at the turn of the nineteenth century.

Notes

I wish to thank Roger Emerson and Richard Sher for comments on earlier drafts of this essay; Carol Gibson-Wood for transcriptions of the Anderson-DaCosta correspondence and for her superior sense of style; J. Malcolm Allan for help with the Anderson Collection; and the Social Sciences and Humanities Research Council of Canada and the Advisory Research Committee of Queen's University for financial support. I am also grateful to the trustees of the National Library of Scotland, as well as the librarians of the British Library, Glasgow University Library, Strathclyde University Archives and the Andersonian Library, University of Strathclyde, for permission to quote from manuscripts in their care.

1. John Galt, *The Last of the Lairds*, ed. Ian A. Gordon (Edinburgh, 1976), 64. In 1793 Anderson was pilloried in the press for his 'democratic' principles and for having sent his gun to Paris; see *Asmodeus; or, Strictures on the Glasgow Democrats* (Glasgow, 1793), 24.

2. Steven Shapin, 'Who Was Robert Hooke?', in *Robert Hooke: New Studies*, ed. Michael Hunter and Simon Schaffer (Woodbridge, U.K., 1989), 253–85. Unlike Shapin, however, I am not concerned here with the possible contradictions between an actor's social status and his or her social role. Cf. Michael Hunter and Paul B. Wood, 'Towards Solomon's House: Rival Strategies for Reforming the Early Royal Society', *History of Science* 24 (1986): 49–108, which is reprinted in Michael Hunter, *Establishing the*

New Science: The Experience of the Early Royal Society (Woodbridge, U.K., 1989), 185–244.

3. David Murray, *Memories of the Old College of Glasgow: Some Chapters in the History of the University* (Glasgow, 1927), 379–80 (also 117, for a less temperate assessment). Cf. James Coutts, *A History of the University of Glasgow: From Its Foundation in 1451 to 1909* (Glasgow, 1909), 227: 'Though neither a great man nor a great scientist, [Anderson] was a capable and energetic teacher, and for many years the most notable member of the academic society.'

4. James Muir, *John Anderson: Pioneer of Technical Education and the College He Founded*, ed. James M. Macaulay (Glasgow, 1950), 2–3.; Coutts, *University of Glasgow*, 213, 227–28. In fact, Anderson wanted the humanity chair but lost out in the politicking surrounding the appointment; see Anderson to Gilbert Lang, 16 Jan. 1755, John Anderson Papers, Strathclyde University Archives [cited hereafter as SUA], MS A/2/2, fol. 1r.

5. John A. Cable, 'Early Scottish Science: The Vocational Provision', *Annals of Science* 30 (1973): 190–91.

6. Charles E. McClelland, *State, Society, and University in Germany, 1700–1914* (Cambridge, 1980), 122–23, 162–89.

7. Anderson appears to have inherited the religious library of his grandfather of the same name, a Presbyterian minister and controversialist active early in the century. This implies that works on religion did not figure significantly in his own acquisitions (this point courtesy of Richard Sher).

8. 'An alphabetical catalogue of books; belonging to John Anderson, Professor of Natural Philosophy in the University of Glasgow', Andersonian Library, University of Strathclyde, MS 48 (unless otherwise noted, all subsequent references to manuscripts are from this collection). Of the 206 titles on natural philosophy, natural history and chemistry that I have noted, 114 are on natural philosophy (55%), 59 on natural history (29%) and 33 on chemistry (16%). I should emphasize that these figures are only approximate. The library catalogue found in MS 46 dates from c. 1799 and includes titles published after Anderson's death. The account of Anderson's library in Muir, *John Anderson*, 70–79, is based on the printed catalogue of 1832 and therefore not entirely reliable.

9. The instruments owned by Anderson at an early stage of his career are catalogued in the 'Copy of a list of instruments in the physical apparatus room of Glasgow College and subscribed by Mr. Anderson P.N.P. June the twentieth and sixth day one thousand seven hundred and sixty years', MS 7.2. His collection of natural history specimens is also listed in 'Catalogue of fossils July 1767', AL MS 27; see also the 'Catalogue of a collection of fossils arranged according to Crostedt's Mineralogy, in English, London printed by Dilly, 1770', AL MS 36. Anderson bequeathed his equipment and natural history collections to Anderson's Institution, and these were quickly augmented by the trustees and by the first professor of natural philosophy, Thomas Garnett; see AL MS 46 for lists drawn up in 1799 of the apparatus and cabinet of 'fossils', and Garnett, *Observations on a*

Tour through the Highlands and Part of the Western Isles of Scotland, new ed., 2 vols. (London, 1811), 2:195–96.

10. On Anderson and Watt, see Murray, *Memories*, 388–89, and Muir, *John Anderson*, 9. Robison's letter to Watt of 25 February 1800, in *Partners in Science: Letters of James Watt and Joseph Black*, ed. Eric Robinson and Douglas McKie (London, 1970), 337, shows that Robison did some substitute teaching for Anderson, though in the end he did not have a high opinion of Anderson's abilities (Murray, *Memories*, 112). On Anderson and Reid, see P. B. Wood, 'Thomas Reid, Natural Philosopher: A Study of Science and Philosophy in the Scottish Enlightenment' (Ph.D. thesis, University of Leeds, 1984), 143–44.

11. Alexander Wilson, 'Observations of the Transit of Venus over the Sun, contained in a Letter to the Reverend Nevil Maskeleyne, Astronomer Royal, from Dr. Alexander Wilson, Professor of Astronomy in the University of Glasgow', *Philosophical Transactions of the Royal Society of London* 59 (1769): 333–38.

12. On the Considerable Club, which also included the natural philosopher Thomas Melvill among its members, see Anderson to Gilbert Lang, 13 Feb. 1750, SUA, MS A/2/1. Anderson was elected a member of the GLS in 1753; see W. J. Duncan, *Notices and Documents Illustrative of the Literary History of Glasgow, During the Greater Part of Last Century* (1831; rpt Glasgow, 1886), 133.

13. See 'Memoir of Professor Anderson', *The Glasgow Mechanics' Magazine; and Annals of Philosophy* 3 (1825): vi.

14. Roger Emerson has pointed out to me that the reference to 'Hill's Book' probably refers to the initial volumes of Sir John Hill's *The Vegetable System*, 26 vols. (London, 1759–75), which had been given to the Royal College of Physicians of Edinburgh by Lord Bute. See Emerson, 'Lord Bute and the Scottish Universities 1760–1792', in *Lord Bute: Essays in Re-interpretation*, ed. Karl W. Schweizer (Leicester, 1988), 153. Anderson's contacts with Cuming and Dick suggest that he did not move within the orbit of William Robertson's Moderates in the kirk, and it is significant that in 1765 Cuming mounted a serious challenge to the supremacy of the Moderates, discussed in Richard B. Sher, *Church and University in the Scottish Enlightenment: The Moderate Literati of Edinburgh* (Princeton, 1985), 130–34.

15. 'Dumbarton Castle', MS 33. Anderson described his measurements of temperature in his 1782 discourse, 'Of the Moisture in Houses that Are Situated on Prominent Rocks', MS 40, fols. 8–9. For his gunnery experiments, see the 'Journal of Experiments', MS 8.

16. Anderson's reference to Monboddo is frustratingly ambiguous because the third volume of Monboddo's *Antient Metaphysics* did not appear until 1784.

17. Anderson is portrayed as a hero of adult education in the 'Memoir of Professor Anderson' and in D. C. M'Vail, *Anderson's College: Its Founder and Its Medical School* (Glasgow, 1879). For criticisms of the heroic view,

see Murray, *Memories*, 113–14, 387–93; Cable, 'Early Scottish Science', 181–94. The practice of having an open experimental philosophy course at Glasgow dates from around 1710; see sect. 5 of the *Proposals by the Faculty of the University of Glasgow for Buying Instruments Necessary for Experiments and Observations in Natural Philosophy* [Glasgow, 1710], reproduced in Peter Swinbank, 'Experimental Science in the University of Glasgow at the Time of Joseph Black', in *Joseph Black 1728–1799: A Commemorative Symposium*, ed. A. D. C. Simpson (Edinburgh, 1982), 31. But to give Anderson his due, he was far more successful in attracting pupils than his predecessors had been.

18. E.g., Robert Dick, *A Course of Experiments and Lectures on Mechanics, Hydrostatics, Pneumatics and Optics; to be begun on Tuesday the sixth of November, and continued during the Session of the College* (Glasgow, 1753). For the structure of Anderson's course, see his *A Compend of Experimental Philosophy* (Glasgow, 1760), which lists the natural historical topics covered at 5–7, 53–56.

19. P. B. Wood, *The Aberdeen Enlightenment: The Arts Curriculum in the Eighteenth Century* (Aberdeen, 1993).

20. For Dick, the philosophical history of nature consisted of 'a methodical arrangement of Animals, Vegetables and Minerals, and an enquiry into their nature, properties and uses in Philosophy, Medicine and Arts' (quoted in Murray, *Memories*, 111).

21. Roger L. Emerson, 'Sir Robert Sibbald, Kt, the Royal Society of Scotland and the Origins of the Scottish Enlightenment', *Annals of Science* 45 (1988): 60–67, and 'Science and the Origins and Concerns of the Scottish Enlightenment', *History of Science* 26 (1988): 333–66; Anand C. Chitnis, 'Agricultural Improvement, Political Management and Civic Virtue in Enlightened Scotland: An Historiographical Critique', *Studies on Voltaire and the Eighteenth Century* 245 (1986): 475–88, and 'The Eighteenth-Century Scottish Intellectual Inquiry: Context and Continuities versus Civic Virtue', in *Aberdeen and the Enlightenment*, ed. Jennifer J. Carter and Joan H. Pittock (Aberdeen, 1987), 77–92.

22. *The Philosophical Works of Francis Bacon*, ed. John M. Robertson (London, 1905), 437.

23. See Barbara Shapiro, *Probability and Certainty in Seventeenth-Century England: A Study of the Relationships between Natural Science, Religion, History, Law, and Literature* (Princeton, 1983), chap. 4; Joseph M. Levine, *Dr. Woodward's Shield: History, Science and Satire in Augustan England* (Berkeley, 1977); Stuart Piggott, 'The Ancestors of Jonathan Oldbuck', in Piggott, *Ruins in a Landscape: Essays in Antiquarianism* (Edinburgh, 1976), 133–59, and *William Stukeley: An Eighteenth-Century Antiquarian*, rev. ed. (London, 1985); Iain Gordon Brown, *The Hobby-Horsical Antiquary: A Scottish Character 1640–1830* (Edinburgh, 1980). See also P. B. Wood, 'The Natural History of Man in the Scottish Enlightenment', *History of Science* 27 (1989): 89–123.

24. See Roger L. Emerson, 'The Philosophical Society of Edinburgh, 1737–

1747', and 'The Scottish Enlightenment and the End of the Philosophical
Society of Edinburgh', both in *British Journal for the History of Science*
12 (1979): 168, and 21 (1988): 57–59, 61–63. See also Steven Arthur
Shapin, 'The Royal Society of Edinburgh: A Study of the Social Context
of Hanoverian Science' (Ph.D. thesis, University of Pennsylvania, 1971),
143–46, 218–19, 227–35. As Shapin and Emerson indicate, the history of the
RSE in its early decades illustrates the disintegration of the virtuoso ideal.
For example, the split between antiquities and natural history embedded
in the distinction between the Literary and Physical Classes suggests that
specialization was beginning to take place.

25. MSS 5, 12, 25; Muir, *John Anderson*, 13, 15; William Robert Scott, *Adam
Smith as Student and Professor* (1937; rpt. New York, 1965), 149–50;
*Regulations concerning the Premiums given to the Masters of Arts by Mr.
Anderson Professor of Natural Philosophy in the University of Glasgow*
(Glasgow, 1770); Murray, *Memories*, 115.

26. On Sibbald's circle and meteorology, see Emerson, 'Sir Robert Sibbald',
55–56. Meteorological questions were also discussed in the Edinburgh
Philosophical Society and in the Royal Society of London. See Emerson,
'Philosophical Society', 177, and C. R. Weld, *A History of the Royal Society*,
2 vols. (1848; rpt. New York, 1975), 1:434–35. Significantly, Major-general
William Roy, whom Anderson nominated as one of the three impartial
referees for the demonstration of his modified gun carriage in London,
published an essay on barometers in the *Philosophical Transactions* in 1778.
For Anderson's papers on relevant subjects, see his measurements of annual
rainfall in Glasgow for the years 1784–95 and his 1780 discourse 'Of Rain
Gauges', MSS 15 and 15²; 'Experiments upon the Mensuration of Heights
by yᵉ Barometer', MS 26; and, in a related vein, Anderson's 1782 discourse
'Of the Moisture in Houses', referred to above. See also C. G. Wood, 'John
Anderson's Rain Gauge', *The Philosophical Journal: Transactions of the
Royal Philosophical Society of Glasgow* 5 (1968): 138–50.

27. In his Dumbarton Castle diary, Anderson mentions writing to Hailes on 3
July 1782, and that letter survives in the NLS, MS 722,824. For his relations
with Buchan, see GUL, MS Murray 502, 201/76.

28. Piggott, 'Ancestors', 135–45; Coutts, *University of Glasgow*, 332–33. The
collection of stones in the college was noted in Thomas Pennant, *A Tour
in Scotland 1769*, 3rd ed. (Warrington, 1774; rpt. Perth, 1979), 232–33.
In so far as James Watt was involved in the construction of the canal, it
may be that he and Anderson had occasion to work together surveying
the Roman remains. For Anderson on the Roman sites, see MS 22, which
apparently brings together the texts of various discourses Anderson gave in
the GLS. In this manuscript, Anderson makes critical use of the standard
eighteenth-century sources on the sites, Alexander Gordon, *Itinerarium
Septentrionale* (1726) and John Horsley, *Britannia Romana* (1732).

29. One wonders what Anderson would have made of Richard Payne Knight's
collection, *An Account of the Remains of the Worship of Priapus* (London,
1786).

30. Piggott, 'Ancestors', 150–55. See also Stuart Piggott, *Ancient Britons and the Antiquarian Imagination: Ideas from the Renaissance to the Regency* (London, 1989), chap. 5, though even Piggott cites an example of an antiquarian employing the four-stages theory.

31. For a transcription and discussion of Anderson's notes of Smith's lectures, see Ronald L. Meek, 'New Light on Adam Smith's Glasgow Lectures on Jurisprudence', in *Smith, Marx, and After: Ten Essays in the Development of Economic Thought* (London, 1977), 57–91. As noted in chap. 4 above, Anderson's notes contain materials on the four-stages theory of social development. In the introductory lecture to his natural philosophy course, Anderson used the example of spectacles made in Nuremberg to discuss the division of labour involved in their production (MS 24, fol. 13).

32. Anderson, however, would probably not have thought of himself as a philosophical historian when writing about the Roman remains, as he remarked at one point: 'In the former dissertations I wrote as an Antiquary, as a Critic, and as an observer of manners, and therefore I had no occasion to have recours to first principles' (MS 22, fols. 109–10). Anderson seems to have had a clear idea of the antiquary's role, for he was highly critical of those who did not live up to his ideal of the 'true Antiquarian' (MS 22, fols. 64–65).

33. Cf. MS 'Institutes of Physics', 5^r–6^r

34. Emerson, 'Science and Scottish Enlightenment', 361, n. 63; 'Copy of a Small Tattered Book Lent to Me by the Reverend Mr Peter Woodrow Minister at Turbowtoun, which he says is a catalogue of the curiosities collected by his father the minister of Eastwood', MS 10. The list is dated 'Glasgow College Octr. 1st. 1768'. This manuscript has been identified as a copy of a list of 'shotles' that Wodrow refers to in a letter to the advocate Alexander Stevenson, 15 Aug. 1700, in *Early Letters of Robert Wodrow, 1698–1709*, ed. L. W. Sharp (Edinburgh, 1937), 108. A list of shottles compiled by Wodrow survives in NLS, MS 13.2.8.

35. Among the Scottish naturalists who grappled with this question were David Skene, Charles Alston and John Hope. See Skene, 'Discourses on Natural History', AUL, MS 480/1/1–7; A. G. Morton, *John Hope 1725–1786: Scottish Botanist* (Edinburgh, 1986), 22, 24–25, 30; Emerson, 'Philosophical Society', 177.

36. Anderson was equally critical of the Frenchman's practice as a naturalist in the *Histoire*, for he noted that Buffon's descriptions were often imprecise, and that he resorted to the use of systematic characters when confronted with the sheer variety of the animal kingdom (MS 9, fol. 5). Anderson notes in the text that he had earlier delivered to the GLS a discourse on the distinctions between the three kingdoms of nature (MS 9, fols. 2–3), but the manuscript of this discourse no longer exists among his papers.

37. Anderson was thus one of Kames's earliest critics. For another early response, see David Doig, *Two Letters on the Savage State, addressed to the Late Lord Kames* (London, 1792). Doig's first letter was begun in December 1774 and was passed on to Kames by an intermediary.

The Scottish context of Anderson's discourses is discussed in Robert Wokler, 'Apes and Races in the Scottish Enlightenment: Monboddo and Kames on the Nature of Man', in *Philosophy and Science in the Scottish Enlightenment*, ed. Peter Jones (Edinburgh, 1988), 145–68.

38. Significantly, Anderson indicated (MS 9, fol. 38ᵛ.) that Monboddo's cases of humans with vestigial tails were likewise suspect.

39. Anderson did suggest that climatic conditions inhibited blacks from making progress in the arts and sciences (MS 9, fols. 52–53) but, like many of his contemporaries, he claimed that despotism was the major obstacle to moral and intellectual progress. See Anderson, 'Lecture First at the Experiments', MS 24, fol. 27.

40. Bacon's influence was complemented in various ways during the eighteenth century by the writings of Locke, Buffon and Rousseau; see Wood, 'Natural History'. Anderson apparently remained interested in the problems raised by Kames's *Sketches*, for his 1796 library catalogue (MS 48) includes a copy of J. F. Blumenbach's *De Generis Humani Varietate Nativa* (1775).

41. David Hume, *Enquiries concerning Human Understanding and concerning the Principles of Morals*, ed. L. A. Selby-Bigge and P. H. Nidditch, 3rd ed. (Oxford, 1978), 164–65; Thomas Reid, *An Inquiry into the Human Mind, on the Principles of Common Sense* (Edinburgh, 1764), 315.

42. 'Lecture First at the Experiments', MS 24, fols. [1]-2. Anderson's historical interests are reflected in the fact that his lectures contained far more historical information than was typical for a natural philosophy course. Usually such courses began with an introductory prelection which included a survey of the development of natural philosophy from the ancients to the eighteenth century. Anderson, however, incorporated historical surveys into his discussion of such topics as gravitation and magnetism, partly to inculcate the appropriate methodological morals.

43. The quotation comes from the section on electricity in the unpaginated manuscript version of the third volume of Anderson's *Institutes of Physics*.

44. See the unpaginated manuscript version of Anderson's Introduction to his *Institutes of Physics*. As his lectures demonstrate, Anderson's concern with classification was related to his pedagogical role, in so far as the clarity of his lectures depended on his arrangement of his materials.

45. On Garnett, see S.G.E. Lythe, *Thomas Garnett (1766–1802): Highland Tourist, Scientist and Professor, Medical Doctor* (Glasgow, 1984).

46. See, for example, Dorothy Stimson, *Scientists and Amateurs: A History of the Royal Society* (New York, 1948), 139–40. Stimson restates in a more blatant form the view of C. R. Weld, *History of the Royal Society*, 1:483.

47. See, *inter alia*, John Nicols, *Literary Anecdotes of the Eighteenth Century*, 6 vols. (1812; rpt. New York, 1966), 6:6–8, on the Spalding Gentleman's Society; A. E. Musson and Eric Robinson, *Science and Technology in the Industrial Revolution* (Toronto, 1969), 190–99, on the Derby Philosophical Society; A. J. Turner et al., *Science and Music in Eighteenth-Century Bath* (Bath, 1977), 82–83, 95, on the Bath Philosophical Society; Derek Orange, 'Rational Dissent and Provincial Science: William Turner and the Newcastle

Literary and Philosophical Society', in *Metropolis and Province: Science in British Culture 1780–1850*, ed. Ian Inkster and Jack Morrell (London, 1983), 205–30. The case of Newcastle is instructive, for a Society of Antiquaries and a Natural History Society were formed by members of the Literary and Philosophical Society in 1813 and 1829, respectively. The process of specialization was thus taking place.

48. J. N. Hays, 'Science in the City: The London Institution, 1819–40', *British Journal for the History of Science* 7 (1974): 158, and 'The London Lecturing Empire, 1800–50, in *Metropolis and Province*, ed. Inkster and Morrell, 101–5, argue that specialization occurred most dramatically in the London public lecturing circuit in the 1820s and 1830s.

49. This is not to say, however, that men of science were increasingly *professionalized*; for a helpful discussion of this point, see Roy Porter, 'Gentlemen and Geology: The Emergence of a Scientific Career, 1660–1920', *The Historical Journal* 4 (1978): 823–25.

7

'Famous as a School for Law, as Edinburgh . . . for medicine': Legal Education in Glasgow, 1761–1801

John W. Cairns

On 9 January 1827 a special sub-commission of the Royal Commission for Visiting the Universities and Colleges in Scotland questioned the current regius professor of civil law at Glasgow University, Robert Davidson. Davidson described his professorship as being in civil or Roman law, adding that he lectured on Scots law in a course lasting one year. He revealed, however, that the course on Roman law was not always taught, because often fewer than five students appeared to take it, and he was no longer willing to lecture to such a small number. He had not taught it now for four or five years. When the commissioners asked him if, before that, it had been regularly taught, Davidson replied: 'Mr. Millar, my predecessor, was a man of great eminence; he was quite a speculative man; I consider myself rather a practical man. This was a very famous school of Roman Law in Mr. Millar's time.'[1]

Davidson explained that the bulk of his pupils were writers' clerks and apprentices in Glasgow, who afterwards regularly went to writers' offices in Edinburgh and often took a course of lectures from the Edinburgh professor of Scots law before returning to practice in Glasgow. Very few joined the Faculty of Advocates. Statistics provided to the commissioners also showed that enrolments in law were relatively low. Davidson only attracted students to his lectures in Scots law, which the Faculty of Procurators in Glasgow, the local society of lawyers, required future members to attend (*Evidence*, 2:145–46). Almost all of his students were from Glasgow and its immediate neighbourhood (University Register of Law Students 1818–1843, GUA 26,798).

The location of the University of Glasgow is one possible reason for Davidson's failure to attract students. 'Glasgow lies under many obvious disadvantages, as a school of law', wrote John Craig in 1806.[2] Proximity to the courts was recognized as a major asset in attracting students and eminent professors to the University of Edinburgh.[3] Nor was Davidson alone among Glasgow professors of law in having difficulty attracting significant numbers of students. John Craig reported that law students 'seldom exceeded four or five, and sometimes fell short even of that number' before the appointment of John Millar in 1761, although this has proved impossible to verify (Craig, xi). Yet Millar's extraordinary success during a tenure of forty years shows that Glasgow's distance from the courts is not an entirely adequate explanation for Davidson's problems.

That John Millar was outstandingly successful is clear from all accounts. Arthur Browne, professor of civil law in Dublin, wrote in 1797 that 'above all, the learned Professor of Glasgow . . . has acquired most deserved celebrity, and has attracted many of the youth of this country, as well as of England within the sphere of his instruction.'[4] Thomas Newte remarked in 1791 that the income from 'the Professorship of Law, owing to the reputation of the present incumbent, Dr. Millar, is generally about 900l. per annum.' He expressed surprise that Millar had 'not been removed to Edinburgh!'[5] Robert Heron stated in 1793 that 'although Glasgow be the seat of no Supreme Court of Justice; yet has it become famous, above almost every other place in Britain as a school for Law.' To hear Millar's lectures, 'students resort hither from all quarters of Britain. Glasgow is, in short, famous as a school for Law, as Edinburgh as a school for medicine.'[6] It is another kind of testimony to Millar's influence that so many of the royal commissioners who visited Glasgow University in 1827 were former students who had risen to positions of eminence in law and government, including the earl of Lauderdale, Sir William Rae, Lord Justice-Clerk Boyle, George Cranstoun (Lord Corehouse) and James Moncrieff.[7]

The reasons for Millar's success were complex, but they seem to lie in his expansion of the Glasgow law curriculum, in the content of his courses and in his abilities as a teacher, as well as in the weakness of legal education in contemporary Edinburgh during crucial periods of his tenure. Millar taught law as a polite, enlightened discipline; Davidson did not, and so lost what Millar had gained.

I

THE REGIUS PROFESSORSHIP of civil law at Glasgow University was founded late in 1713 and first filled in 1714.[8] There had been three professors prior to Millar: William Forbes, William Crosse and Hercules Lindesay. Forbes taught courses on Roman law and Scots law, but at some point he seems to have given up teaching the latter. Born around 1670, he stopped teaching in the later 1730s, possibly in 1739, because of increasing age, leaving Lindesay to teach classes on Justinian's *Institutes* and *Digest*. Lindesay had hoped to succeed Forbes, but after the latter's death in 1745 the chair was given to Crosse, who attempted to treat it as a sinecure. Lindesay taught in his stead, either privately or as his substitute. Crosse resigned in

October 1749 and was replaced early in 1750 by Lindesay, who continued to teach only courses on the *Institutes* and *Digest*, at some time starting to teach the former in English rather than the customary Latin.

The creation of the chair in civil law was part of the general expansion of the Scottish universities during the early eighteenth century. The faculty at Glasgow were probably influenced in their decision to establish it by the success of the private teachers of law in Edinburgh, and almost certainly by the creation of a chair of civil law in the University of Edinburgh in 1710. They wished to develop legal education in Glasgow on the model provided by the faculties of law in the Netherlands, which had built on the work of humanist scholars in sixteenth-century France. The focus was primarily on civil law, though collateral studies in universal history, Roman antiquities and philology were also emphasized. By the time of the creation of the regius chair, natural law had come into prominence as an integral part of legal education, and municipal law was also increasingly seen as a desirable university discipline.

Legal education did not live up to this ideal under the first three professors in Glasgow. After Forbes stopped lecturing on Scots law, the practice was not resumed — a serious deficiency after 1750, when the Faculty of Advocates started to examine all candidates in that subject. Collateral studies in history and classics had been available at one time; whether they remained so is unknown. On the other hand, natural law was always taught by successive professors of moral philosophy. The main problem faced by legal education in Glasgow, however, was the difficulty of attracting significant numbers of students. This difficulty would have made the chair unattractive to men of ambition, who would have been unable to supplement their low earnings from student fees by practising at the bar. Nevertheless, the faculty at Glasgow were determined that legal education should succeed, and for that reason they drove the sinecurist Crosse from the chair. They learned from their experience of the first three professors that what was needed was a young, energetic man of ability as a teacher, who would be committed to building up the law classes in competition with those offered by the professors in Edinburgh.

Believing that John Millar was such a man, the faculty moved remarkably quickly to secure his appointment by the Crown. Lindesay died on 2 June 1761; the king signed a warrant for Millar's presentation to the chair on 15 June, and he was duly admitted on 15 July.[9] Just twenty-six years of age, Millar was younger on appointment than any of his predecessors. Unlike Crosse, who at thirty-two had also been relatively young, Millar had not had time to build up connections at the bar, and the faculty must have hoped he would devote his youthful energies and full attention to developing law classes in Glasgow. As a highly regarded protégé of Adam Smith and Lord Kames, and the first occupant of the civil law chair to have been educated entirely in Scotland rather than at least partly in the

Netherlands, Millar would have been expected to introduce the polite education in law that the faculty desired.[10]

On the basis of a ruling that the university gave to Crosse, Craig described the classes on the *Institutes* and *Digest* that Millar taught five days each week as 'the proper business of the Professorship'.[11] Craig suggested that Millar found he still had some leisure, and consequently taught a class on government three days a week and, in alternate years, a class on Scots law on the other two days.[12] He added that 'a few years before his death, Mr Millar was led . . . to prepare and deliver a course of Lectures on English Law' (Craig, xxi), though there is some uncertainty about just when he began to give that class.[13] However this may be, in years when Millar taught either English or Scots law, he would usually have lectured for three hours each day, five days per week.[14] But Craig's remarks raise the general question of whether Millar taught all the other courses from his first appointment to the chair or introduced them gradually, as Craig implied. The rest of this section will be devoted to teasing out the sequence of Millar's development of the law curriculum, and to considering what may have been his reasons for acting as he did.

We can assume that Millar taught both his statutory, 'public' classes on the *Institutes* and *Digest* in every academic session from his appointment until his death in 1801, with the possible exception that in 1761–62 he taught only that on the *Institutes*, as was common for professors first undertaking their duties. Lehmann claimed that 'in his first years, Millar tells us, he tried also to cover, or at least deal with, the Pandects in his basic year-course on civil law'.[15] It is implausible that Millar would have taught only one of the two traditional courses on Roman law for more than his first year, or have had a novel, 'combined' course, and Lehmann's remark is unsupported by any evidence and probably rests on a misunderstanding of a remark reported in a set of student notes of lectures on the *Institutes*.[16] Craig commented that Millar considered 'the employment of a whole winter in tracing . . . the exact line of Roman Law . . . a mere waste of time and study. Whatever it was useful to know of the Institutes, he thought might be sufficiently taught in the half of the session, or term; and he wished to devote the rest of it to a course of Lectures on Jurisprudence.' Millar accordingly divided his course on the *Institutes* into two parts, covering, first, the *Institutes* itself and, secondly, jurisprudence (Craig, xx). Craig implied that before Millar's appointment the whole of one academic year was taken to teach the *Institutes* in Glasgow. The traditional practice in Scotland, however, had been to teach the same course on the *Institutes* twice in one year, as Lindesay did.[17] It is therefore likely that Millar replaced a second, identical class on the *Institutes* with the lectures on jurisprudence.[18]

If, as Craig implied, these lectures on jurisprudence were added some years after Millar's occupancy of the chair in 1761, there is some circumstantial evidence pointing to when and why Millar carried out this innovation. First, it is most unlikely that he would have introduced his lectures on jurisprudence before Smith's resignation as professor of moral philosophy at Glasgow in 1764, as otherwise he would to some extent have duplicated what his teacher taught from that chair.[19] Secondly, it is possible that Millar developed the jurisprudence lectures to counteract the influence of Thomas Reid, who replaced Adam Smith as professor of moral philosophy at Glasgow in 1764.[20] Millar had actively opposed Reid's appointment in a letter of 2 February 1764 that urged Smith to do the same,[21] and Reid and Millar were to become noted for their philosophical disagreements at meetings of the Glasgow Literary Society (Craig, lxi-lxii). Since Reid, like Smith, included jurisprudence in his moral philosophy classes, which were commonly attended by law students because of the complementary nature of the subject matter,[22] Millar may have wished to teach jurisprudence in a manner more like that of his teacher Smith than Reid could be expected to do. Thirdly, there was by this time a definite demand for classes in jurisprudence. Robert Bruce, the Edinburgh professor of public law and the law of nature and nations, had forty students in session 1763–64, the last that he taught.[23] Bruce's resignation from this chair in 1764, to be replaced by the sinecurist James Balfour, might mean that Millar started teaching jurisprudence in order to fill a gap in the market. This market demand was created in part by the Faculty of Advocates' exhortations, in 1760 and 1762, that young men proposing to become advocates attend the classes of the professor of public law and the law of nature and nations in Edinburgh, as well as by the advocates' proposals that intrants be asked questions on the law of nature and nations in their examinations.[24] These factors, then, point to Millar beginning to lecture on jurisprudence as his second course on the *Institutes* some time after 1764.

Much can be learned about the range of Millar's teaching from an examination of newspaper advertisements for his classes. Millar does not appear to have started specially advertising his individual classes until the *Glasgow Journal* for 3/10 October 1765 advertised that he would begin prelections on the *Institutes* and *Digest* on 4 November, and lectures on the law of Scotland on 11 November. An advertisement to the same effect appeared in the same paper on 2/9 October 1766. An advertisement on 15/22 January 1767, however, stated that Millar's lectures on 'the Private Law of Scotland' would begin on 3 February. Either Millar was giving the same course of lectures on Scots law twice in 1766–67, or else his lectures in the first half of the session were on Scots *public* law. Since there was no January advertisement in the session 1765–66, we do not know which, if either, of these two possibilities applied then. In the *Glasgow Journal* for 15/22 October 1767 Millar advertised prelections on Justinian's *Institutes* and *Digest* and lectures on the public law of Scotland that would begin in November. The same three classes were advertised in October 1768 and 1769, whereas in November 1770 he only advertised lectures on the public law of Scotland. In none of these academic years were there advertisements in January for a class on Scots private law.[25]

On 10/17 October 1771 Millar advertised in the *Glasgow Journal* prelections on Justinian's *Institutes* and *Digest* and 'Lectures on Government' (the first time that term is used). In January 1772 he advertised 'Lectures on the Law of Scotland' as beginning on the twenty-first of the month (*GJ*, 26 Dec. 1771/2 Jan. 1772, 9/16 Jan. 1772). The following academic year, for session 1772–73, Millar advertised prelections on the *Institutes* and *Digest* and lectures on government (*GJ*, 8/15 Oct. 1772). There was no advertisement in January 1773 for lectures on Scots law. On 7/14 October 1773, however, the *Glasgow Journal* advertised that Millar would begin in November lectures on government and Scots law, as well as his prelections on the *Institutes* and *Digest*. Thereafter, with occasional insignificant gaps, due to either missing issues of newspapers or a failure to advertise, the newspaper advertisements reveal the pattern described by Craig of annual prelections on the *Institutes* and *Digest* and lectures on government (sometimes described as public law), and lectures every second year on Scots law (once described, in the *Glasgow Chronicle* for 12/19 October 1775, as Scots private law).[26] This pattern breaks down in the 1790s, apparently because of a change in Millar's practice of advertising rather than a change in his teaching: in 1791, 1793 and 1795 he advertised only lectures on Scots law (these are years when he would have taught this class according to his regular pattern), and in 1799 he once again advertised classes on the *Institutes*, *Digest*, government and Scots law, thus conforming to his earlier established practice.[27]

The start of Millar's almost continuous practice of special advertising in 1765 suggests that the session 1765–66 marked a change in his teaching, and this change must have been the introduction of classes on Scots law. Before this date it had been sufficient to advertise generally, so that the *Glasgow Journal* of 21/28 October 1762 merely stated that 'the Professors of Medicine and Law will begin their Lectures upon Monday the first of November'. This wording implies that Millar then gave only his statutory, 'public' classes on civil law, and that interpretation is supported by the allocation to Millar by a university meeting on 11 May 1762 of a classroom for lectures on civil law, making no mention of other classes (GUA 26,642: 147). This dating of the introduction of Millar's Scots law lectures is further supported by the fact that his account of criminal law is strongly influenced by that in the third edition of John Erskine's *Principles of the Law of Scotland*, which appeared in 1764.[28] Since Millar appears to have done little in the way of radical re-thinking of any of his lectures in later years, this suggests that he introduced those on Scots law after 1764, that is, in academic year 1765–66. The lectures on government or public law seem to have grown out of his classes on Scots law which, at least from 1767, if not earlier, he divided into the public law of Scotland and the private law of Scotland, possibly not teaching the latter every year, and teaching it from January to May. From 1771–72 he described the former course as being on government or public law generally, and from 1773 he described the latter class, which he now taught every second year beginning in November, as being on Scots law (only once described as Scots private law). Finally, Millar added a class on English law in the 1790s, probably in the sessions 1798–99 and 1800–1801, in academic years when he would not normally have taught Scots law.

II

WHATEVER THE EXACT STAGES of development, it is clear that by around 1770 Millar had greatly expanded the curriculum of legal studies in the University of Glasgow. Although this achievement in itself is insufficient to explain his success, it clearly suggests that he was attracting enough students to make it worthwhile to develop new courses. Millar's curriculum might seem to reflect a traditional, humanist ideal in legal studies of history and natural law, combined with study of civil and municipal law, but he had transformed it into something new and exciting. This section will suggest that the content of his courses and his methods of teaching did much to make him such an outstanding success, especially when legal education was weak in Edinburgh between 1765 and 1786.[29]

Millar grounded all his courses on law in a philosophy derived from Adam Smith's *Theory of Moral Sentiments*. Millar strongly identified himself as Smith's pupil, even using Smith's image as his seal (see GUL, MS Gen. 1035/178). It is unnecessary to discuss Millar's legal theory at length, as it has recently been the subject of an important article by Knud Haakonssen,[30] but some general remarks will be useful. Millar's starting point in discussing law is his notion of rights. Laws are based on 'the various rights acknowledged and protected by society' (Craig, xxxii). These rights are derived from the moral sentiments, according to which actions are approved on the basis of their utility and propriety. When individuals are wronged, they feel resentment, and spectators feel indignation. Rules of justice arise in this way, spontaneously, from concrete situations. Individuals, then, have a right not to be wronged. Spectators interfere in disputes in order to assist individuals with whose motives they sympathize. They do so not only disinterestedly, in order to prevent an injustice, but also out of self-interest, since they realize that they themselves might someday be in a similar predicament (Craig, xxvi-xxxv). Rights so established vary from place to place and time to time, according to the character, history and manners of different societies, though Millar also stresses that long-established customs are not readily abandoned and can continue to exist even if defective for a changed society (Craig, xxxv-xxxix).

The historical elaboration of rights is of great importance in Millar's theory, because once societies have developed beyond a primitive stage, governments provide the means of enforcing rights in the courts and possess the authority to legislate them into law. In his first course on the *Institutes*, Craig says, Millar expounded Johann Gottlieb Heineccius's *Elementa juris civilis secundum ordinem institutionum* (1725) (Craig, xx).[31] This was the most popular textbook of the day.[32] He started, however, with some lectures discussing vice and virtue and distinguishing law from ethics.[33] He then raised the question of whether or not legal studies should start with the law of one's own country. He pointed out that in most European countries other than England the practice was to begin with the laws of other nations before concluding with the national law. If this practice were adopted, he commented, then 'the Roman law must attract particular notice. The Romans were a great people, possessed extensive territories and therefore must have had much experience as of necessity many private quarrels and disputes would come to be decided in their wide empire' (12). There followed a survey of the history of Roman law and its reception in Europe (12–19).

Then Millar moved on to the text of Heineccius, going through it paragraph by paragraph, though not lecturing on each, and occasionally departing from the sequence for reasons of clarity and ease of exposition (98). He finished with obligations arising *quasi ex delicto*, leaving aside the account of actions. It appears that at one time he had continued to follow Heineccius to the end of the *Institutes*, but gave that up because the account of actions was so cursory that students could not readily follow it. He explained that in the second class, however, he would pay more attention to the courts and forms of procedure of the Romans (165–66). This first course was at a relatively elementary level, though Millar did allude to the social and political causes underlying the law on, for example, *patria potestas* (31–32); it seems normally to have run to around seventy lectures, delivered between early November and early to mid-February (e.g., 163–66, lecture 73).[34]

The second course on the *Institutes*, that dealing with jurisprudence, opened with advice on reading and then presented a discussion of moral theory, leading to an account of rights and the progress of law (e.g., NLS, Adv. MS 20.4.7, fols. 2+–23+). Millar analysed law as concerning rights and actions, with rights, in turn, concerning either persons or things. The rights of persons arose from the relationships of husband and wife, parent and child, master and servant, guardian and ward. The rights of things were divided into real and personal. Real rights concerned property, servitude, pledge and exclusive privilege. Personal rights arose by contract, delinquency or crime. Actions were the means of asserting these rights.[35]

This analysis is familiar from Smith's *Lectures on Jurisprudence*.[36] In fact, Millar's lectures strongly resemble Smith's, except for Millar's sharper focus on Roman law.[37] The division of law in this way was fundamental for Millar. Thus, in discussing persons in the first course, he told his class that 'the method used by our Author is a little faulty beginning with Master and Servant It would have been more natural to begin with the Rights of Husband and wife than of Parent and child, Master and Servant Guardian and Pupil' (25). He thus ignored or failed to appreciate the historical and legal significance of the divisions of the law of persons in the *Institutes*.

A student reported Millar as characterizing the second course thus:

> In the first course I endeavoured to explain the fact of the Roman law which seems to have been the chief thing intended in the publication of the Institutes — In doing this I have avoided reasoning on the principles whereon their decisions are founded. In going over the subject a second time I think these principles ought to be the chief consideration and in the course of this Investigation we shall be led to compare the Roman law with that of other Nations. (1; second pagination sequence)

In another set of notes, he is recorded as stating:

> It shall now be our cheif employment to enquire into the principles of the Roman Law, and to compare them with those of other countries. The aim of Students of Roman Law at this period, ought to be not merely to know what was the Roman System. That would be of little consequence of itself. It has properly no authority by the Law of this country, or of most of the other modern nations in Europe. It has however a regard paid to it as the system of Lawiers and Judges of great experience, and of a country which subsisted for such a long tract of time, and where we may consequently expect to find the rules of Jurisprudence of the most perfect kind. As however in the most perfect of all human Systems, there are numberless imperfections and Blemishes, it will certainly be proper in those who study the Roman Law at this period, to enquire into the justice or propriety of these regulations. This can only be done by comparing it with the Laws of other countries, and with our own natural feelings of right and wrong. This is certainly a very usefull exercise, as it enlarges our experience. (NLS, MS 20.4.7, fols. 1r-2r)

Craig aptly characterized this second class as one 'in which [Millar] treated of such general principles of Law as pervade the codes of all nations, and have their origin in those sentiments of justice which are imprinted on the human heart' (Craig, xx). This course usually consisted of forty-six lectures, given between mid-February and the start of May (e.g., 1 and 399; second pagination sequence: 46 lectures, 21 Feb.-1 May 1778).

Millar's course of approximately 116 lectures on the *Digest* started at the beginning of November and ran to around the beginning of May.[38] The notes that survive seem to be schematic outlines rather than full reports of what was said.[39] Paragraph references in these notes demonstrate that Millar used as his textbook Heineccius's compend of the *Digest*, *Elementa juris secundum ordinem pandectarum* (1727), which was, like his compend of the *Institutes*, the popular student textbook of the day. Craig commented on this course:

> The multifarious doctrines to be explained in the Pandects prevented him from shortening the time alloted for that branch of legal study; but, aware that the ordinary arrangement is confused, and almost unintelligible, he soon published a new syllabus, following very nearly the order of the Institutes, according to which he discussed the various and sometimes discordant laws of Rome, and the still more discordant opinions of Roman lawyers. (Craig, xx)

Although printed syllabuses survive for other courses, none has yet been discovered for Millar's lectures on the *Digest*. One set of student notes states: 'The order observed in the Institutes has been formerly explained — But no regard is had to this order, either in the Pandects or Codex and it is difficult to say what has been the view of arrangement in these compilations.' Millar accordingly discussed the deficiency of the structure of the *Digest*, and he seems to have referred to his published outline for the order to be observed in the course (GUL, MSS Murray 93, fols. [1]r-[3]r). Study of the notes shows that, as in the second course on the *Institutes*, he expounded the *Digest* according to the Smithian analysis of law into rights and actions, an approach that involved a complete rearrangement of the sequence of the *Digest* (see Cairns, 'John Millar's Lectures', 378, n. 70). Given that the surviving manuscripts contain only a detailed scheme, rather than a full report of what Millar actually said in his class, it is difficult to give a full assessment of this course. As Lehmann notes ('Observations on the Law Lectures', 68–70), he obviously dealt with the *Digest* in considerable detail and raised the type of historical issues that interested him. He seems also to have made at least occasional references to modern Scots law (e.g., GUL, MS Murray 94, fol. [60]r, lect. 59). The lectures assumed that students had already attended the course on the *Institutes* (GUL, MSS Murray 93, fol. [1]r, and 94, fol. 48v, lect. 54).

From 1773 onward, Millar usually started his lectures on Scots law a week after those on the *Institutes* and *Digest* (e.g., *GJ*, 7/14 Oct. 1773; *Glasgow Chronicle*, 12/19 Oct. 1775; *GJ*, 4/11 Oct. 1781), though in the late 1780s and 1790s he tended to start them in the same week (e.g., *GM*, 20/27 Oct. 1785; *GM*, 13/20 Oct. 1789; *GC*, 15 Oct. 1799). The syllabus that Millar published for this course under the title *Heads of the Lectures on the Law of Scotland, in the University of Glasgow* (Glasgow, 1777 and 1789) indicates that he aimed to deliver fifty lectures, and surviving class notes confirm this pattern.[40] He finished the course about the beginning of May (e.g., GUL, MS 347:477 has the date 4 May 1776 at the end of lect. 52). One set of student notes reports Millar as describing this course in these words:

> The Law of any Country comprehends a Set of Rules which the Inhabitants are bound to obey and wherever there is a Rule for performing an obligation

there must be a corresponding right to inforce the performance — To every Rule therefore there is a corresponding Right — The enumeration of these Rights will be the same thing as the enumeration of the Rules. — To enumerate the Rights then is the first object of Law

But as it is necessary that every Rule of conduct be promulgated to the people that they may know how to observe them, So it is necessary that some provision be made for enforcing these Rules and compelling the people to observe them — For this purpose Courts of Justice are established — The knowledge of the different Courts — The Causes to which they are competent — and the legal methods of obtaining redress of grievances before these Courts, constitute the second great object of Law — But as the different Courts of Justice and the Jurisdiction of Judges fall properly to be considered in a political point of view though no doubt connected with the Law of a Country — We have therefore reserved these for part of a Course of Lectures on Government

The Lectures therefore proposed to be given on the Law of Scotland naturally divide themselves into the consideration of

1st Rights and 2d Actions.

Rights may be divided into two Grand divisions. vizt. such as arise from the distinctions of persons and their Ranks in society — and such as are independent of this distinction which is understood to comprehend every other Right — These Rights are therefore distinguished into

1st. Rights of Persons.

2nd. Rights of Things.

Millar next described the various rights of persons and things, before concluding his analysis of his course with this comment: 'Actions depend upon the Nature of the Right they are intended to vindicate, for as every Right may be violated, so there must of course be an action corresponding to every Right' (GUL, MS Gen. 178:2–5, second pagination sequence).

Thus, the starting point for Millar's account of Scots law was once more his version of Smithian analytical jurisprudence. Millar did not explain here the philosophy underlying it, but rather used it as a scheme of exposition and classification. But just as he referred students to the lectures on government for an account of the Scottish courts,[41] so he probably assumed that students had already taken the lectures on the *Institutes* or were taking them concurrently. Although presented as an assumed classification, it was nonetheless so central to his account of Scots law that it determined his attitude to it (see Cairns, 'John Millar's Lectures'). Millar himself described the course as following, with a few exceptions, the structure of Justinian's *Institutes*, 'chiefly because the order observed therein is best in itself' and 'because students of the Law of Scotland are generally supposed to be acquainted with the Civil Law of which the Institutes of Justinian make a part' (GUL, MS Gen. 178: 1–2).

Given that the lectures on English law were slotted, in alternate years, into the time occupied by those on Scots law, they had to be roughly the same length, and this is confirmed by the one set of surviving notes, consisting of forty-eight lectures from session 1800–1801 (GUL, MS Gen. 243). Whereas the lectures on Scots law, after a short historical survey of sources and some introductory remarks on literature, started with an analysis of the law into rights and actions before dealing straight away with the substantive law in terms of that analysis, those on English law commenced with a relatively lengthy history of the law, a discussion of its peculiarities, and an account of its sources, before explaining the 'method' to be followed (GUL, MS Gen. 243:1–27). Millar told his class:

> To find out a sort of method corresponding with the divisions observed by the English Lawyers, and at [the] same time to enable us to form a distinct idea of the whole system, is one of the most difficult parts of the English Law; and this arises from the want of method in the writings of the English Lawyers. All systems of law ancient as well as modern are subject to this defect, but the English, in a particular manner, from the circumstances already taken notice of, and which it is needless for us here to repeat [suffer from it particularly]. (GUL, MS Gen. 243:27)[42]

He went on to explain:

> In the first place then, the method followed by the Roman Civilians, and in imitation of them, by the later writers upon Roman jurisprudence, is the radical method we wish to follow. In the next place, we shall with a small degree of accommodation, give the outlines of the English method, reduced to that of the Roman. According to the method adopted by the Roman Civilians, law is divided into two great classes, the doctrine of rights and the doctrine of actions. (GUL, MS Gen. 243:27)

Millar in fact treated English law according to his Smithian analysis, influenced slightly by the structure of Blackstone's *Commentaries* (GUL, MS Gen. 243:31–32). For one following a Smithian theory of justice, English law was of particular interest, as Haakonssen explains (*Science of a Legislator*, 151–53). Millar stated:

> Though considered as a practical system of laws, the English is perhaps as compleat as any system can be; yet it has in it this peculiarity, that it has not like all other systems, been introduced by the speculations of philosophers and legislators; but has arisen to its present state of perfection, slowly and gradually, assisted in its progess by certain accidents, and completed by long experience and observation. (GUL, MS Gen. 243:1)[43]

Millar's lectures on government or public law attracted the most attention among his contemporaries, and allegedly the most students. The topic was inevitably controversial, and Millar felt obliged, in a letter of 16 August 1784 to Edmund Burke, then rector of the university, to defend himself from the charge of using the lectures on government to inculcate republican principles (GUL, MS Gen. 502/36).[44] A comparison of the 1778 and 1783 editions of Millar's published syllabus, *A Course of Lectures on Government; Given Annually in the University* (the first is bound into NLS, MS 3931), reveals that Millar originally intended to devote forty-four lectures to the subject, but sometime between 1781 and 1783 he increased the planned lectures to forty-eight by introducing a new preliminary lecture and another four on the government of Ireland, the national debt, the constitution of Parliament with regard to its division into three branches and the period of its duration, and the state of the royal prerogative, while at the same time reducing three lectures on the English courts to two.[45] This expanded version was thereafter substantially maintained, although Millar did add new matter, such as on the French Revolution, without altering the overall structure of the course.[46]

As actually delivered, the number of lectures could greatly exceed that mentioned in the published syllabus. Thus, in 1780–81, when following the earlier syllabus of forty-four lectures, Millar in fact delivered fifty-eight (NLS, MS 3931:299). Newspaper advertisements reveal that sometimes he started the lectures on government during the same week as those on the *Institutes* and *Digest*, sometimes the week after, but always on the same week as that in which he started to lecture on Scots law, should it be a year in which he was doing so.[47] In 1781 the course finished on 6 April (NLS, MS 3931:299), whereas subsequently it ran a few weeks longer (e.g., GUL, MS Gen. 180/3, fol. 665, ending on 29 Apr. 1789; GUL, MS Hamilton:116[530], 1 May 1798). This change in timing most probably reflects the expansion of the course.

In 1798 Millar is reported telling his students:

In studying the Science of Government, the most important object is that of our own Country — but the Governments of other Countries must also be taken into consideration —

The Governments of all Countries discover a great analogy and resemblance from the great uniformity in the faculties, the desires, the wants, the circumstances of mankind —

There must also be, in the government of different nations, a great diversity of regulations —

Thus by comparing the Systems in different Countries we may judge concerning the expediency of different institutions and enlarge our views concerning the principles of Government.

For similar reasons we ought to examine each particular system historically, tracing each regulation from the origins through all the subsequent changes. (GUL, MS Hamilton 116:1–2)

These considerations led Millar to cover three broad topics in the lectures on government: the origin and progress of government in society; illustrations of this topic from particular governments, namely Athens, Sparta, Rome, France, Germany, England, Scotland, Ireland (after 1781) and ecclesiastical jurisdiction; and the present state of government in Great Britain, including discussions of Parliament, the royal prerogative and English and Scottish courts.[48] The lectures again show Millar's indebtedness to basic tenets of Smith's thought and demonstrate his historical and comparative approach. He thus based the origins of authority either on personal qualities or superior wealth, strengthened by custom which created a habit of obedience (e.g., Mitchell Library, MS 99, fol. i; GUL, MS 289:15–29; GUL, MS Gen. 180/1, fols. 7–16). The progress of government was explained according to Smith's stadial analysis (e.g., GUL, MS Gen. 289:31–33). Whereas the other four courses all concerned the rights of individuals and the method of their enforcement, that on government dealt with legislative power, national defence and securing public tranquillity by the appointment of magistrates and the establishment of courts of justice (GUL, MS Gen. 289:1). It thus dealt with the framework within which private rights arose, were recognized and could be enforced.

Millar's five classes were all interrelated and to some extent built on one another. The courses on the *Digest*, Scots law and English law presupposed that students had taken the course on the *Institutes*. The course on government dealt with Roman government at some length, while also dealing with the courts of Scotland and England; the lectures on Scots law referred to those on government in this respect. Within Millar's curriculum, the accounts of legal theory and government were of particular importance, and they obviously indicated where his main intellectual interests lay. His lectures were calculated to promote critical reflection on law by placing it within a historical and political context. His stress on law as recognizing the rights of individuals was an aspect of this perspective: government ought to be aimed at preserving and enforcing these rights and inscribing them in law.

Craig rightly summed up Millar's course in jurisprudence in these terms:

> By proving that no institutions, however just in themselves, can be either expedient or permanent, if inconsistent with established ranks, manners, and opinions, a system of Jurisprudence checks inconsiderate innovation, and indiscriminate reform; while, on the other hand, it points out, to the enlightened Legislator, such parts of the municipal code, as, introduced during ruder times, have remained in force, long after the circumstances from which they arose have ceased to exist, and directs him in the noble, but arduous, attempt, to purify and improve the laws of his country. (Craig, xl-xli)

The course in government instructed the 'young Lawyer . . . in the spirit and real intention of the Laws' and opened up 'to the future statesman . . . views of human society, of the nature and ends of Government, and of the influence of Public Institutions on the prosperity, morals, and happiness of states' (Craig, lvii). The type of questions Millar wished his students to consider is indicated by the prizes offered to the law class for essays in 1786 and 1787, on such topics as 'Is it expedient that the National Representatives in Parliament should be obliged to follow the instruction of their constituents?' and 'Whether is a popular Government favourable or unfavourable to the Fine Arts?' (*GM*, 27 Apr./4 May 1786 and 25 Apr./2 May 1787).[49]

The traditional way of teaching law had been for the professor to adopt a particular textbook on which to dictate notes, section by section.[50] Professors would also quiz or 'examine' students on the topics of previous lectures. The focus was on students' memorization of what had been dictated to them. Whereas Scots law was always taught in English, dictates and examinations in civil law were traditionally given in Latin (see Cairns, 'Rhetoric, Language, and Roman Law', 35–37). Though he followed examples established elsewhere, Millar was very much an innovator as a teacher of law. He extended to the course on the *Digest* Lindesay's innovation of teaching the *Institutes* in English — thus earning the disapproval of the Faculty of Advocates in 1768 (NLS, FR 2: 255; Cairns, 'Rhetoric, Language, and Roman Law', 39–40, 54–55, n. 76). In his classes on civil law, he examined his students daily on the topics of previous lectures, using Latin because that language was used in the trials in civil law for admission as an advocate (Craig, xiii–xiv).[51] Only his first course on the *Institutes* and his course on the *Digest* were closely connected with textbooks, and these were the standard ones of the day.

Millar nonetheless routinely recommended various works to his students. In the second course on the *Institutes*, he continued to examine the class on Heineccius's textbook (1, second pagination sequence), but he also recommended Vinnius's commentary on the *Institutes*, though 'both large and often dry', and he generally preferred Vinnius's view to that of Heineccius (2, second pagination sequence; NLS, Adv. MS 20.4.7, fol. 2r). Whereas students with little time were advised to stick to Heineccius, Millar also suggested that they should read 'some good author on general Jurisprudence'. In words reminiscent of the opening of one set of Smith's *Lectures on Jurisprudence*, Millar recommended Grotius, 'the first who wrote on this subject and . . . still one of the best' (2, second pagination sequence; cf. Smith, *Lectures on Jurisprudence*, 397–98). Of commentaries on Grotius, he recommended as by far the best that of Cocceius the younger, presumably *Samuelis de Cocceii introductio ad Henrici de Coceii Grotium illustratum* (1748). The advice to read Grotius was intended for all students, not just those short of time; but he added that 'upon disputed points [he] wou[l]d advise [the class] to turn up the Corpus and exercise [their] own Judgment on it' (2, second pagination sequence; NLS, Adv. MS 20.4.7, fol. 2r).

In Scots law, Millar recommended John Erskine's *Principles of the Law of Scotland* (1754) both as the 'most distinct book on this Subject', and because 'his method is much the same with that we intend to follow'. He undertook to refer students to parts relevant to his lectures. He also referred them to Erskine's *Institute of the Law of Scotland* (1773). These two works were the ones he chiefly recommended to students. After Erskine, he recommended *The Institutions of the Law of Scotland* by Lord Stair because 'he makes many Comparisons with the Roman law, and reasons much upon the principles'. Students were warned, however, that Stair's account of the law was obsolete, and that the work was 'ill arranged' (presumably because it did not follow the Smithian division of the law into rights and actions). Millar next described Lord Bankton's *Institute of the Laws of Scotland in Civil Rights* (1751–53) as gathering together 'a most laborious Collection of Facts' and containing many things not found in Erskine or Stair, but 'Collected with little Judgement'. He also recommended that the class read a complete collection of decisions, and pointed out that Sir George Mackenzie's *Laws and Customes of Scotland, In Matters Criminal* (1678) was inaccurate and obsolete on criminal law (GUL, MS Gen. 347:6–8). The collection of decisions that Millar wished his students to read would have been an alphabetical one such as Lord Kames's two compilations, *Remarkable Decisions in the Court of Session,* 1716–52 (1728, 1766) and *Decisions of the Court of Session; abridged in form of a Dictionary* (1741).

Besides not using a textbook as the basis of instruction in most classes, Millar also departed from the tradition of dictating set notes to students. He preferred to speak extemporaneously from headings. The notes surviving from his lectures seem to be of two types: notes taken by students in class, even if written into a fair copy, and schematic but relatively full and detailed outlines of the lectures. Since two of the latter type (GUL, MS Gen. 1078 and MSS Gen. 289–91) are in the hand of Millar's son James, the mathematician, they probably indicate what the professor had in front of him when he spoke.[52] Other sets of outlines may be copies of the notes from which Millar was accustomed to lecture extemporarily.[53] Millar's aim in adopting a freer, more extemporaneous style of lecturing was to engage the students intellectually by making the presentation livelier. In this he is said to have succeeded. He was reputed to be a compelling teacher, who could kindle his pupils' enthusiasm for whatever he taught, and to whom they felt able to turn for advice about their examinations for admission to the Faculty of Advocates.[54]

It is unfortunate that no precise information is available about the size of Millar's classes. On 11 May 1762 a chamber within the college was assigned as a classroom for civil law (GUA 26,642:147), possibly because Millar's classes had grown too large for their old quarters. It is certain that Millar attracted increasing numbers of students, for on 10 and 18 October 1775 the faculty authorized alterations in the law classroom in order to increase the number of seats (GUA 26,690:324; see also the faculty minutes for 24 Jan. 1777, GUA 26,691:90). Anecdotal evidence is unanimous about the large size of his classes. Craig stated that 'he had, frequently, about forty students of Civil Law; while those who attended his Lectures on Government, often amounted to a greater number' (Craig, xi). Craig's claim gains some collateral support from a pamphlet published early in 1785, in connection with one of Professor John Anderson's many disputes with his colleagues. Hostile to most of the faculty, including Millar, it claims that, as a result of the disputes among the faculty, 'the students in the first Law Class are 12 or 14, in the second 4, and in the Government Class about 15; which numbers do not make the half of what were in these classes a few years ago.'[55] In the academic session 1784–85 Scots law was not taught, so it is easy to identify the first class as that on the *Institutes* and the second as that on the *Digest*. Thus, the pamphlet leads to the conclusion that Millar could normally have expected about thirty to forty students in civil law and over thirty in government. In the next academic year, in fact, Millar claimed in a letter to Burke dated 13 November 1785 that his enrolments were the highest they had been in some years, despite the continuing dispute in the university (GUL, MS Gen. 502/40).

Matriculations in law at Edinburgh University provide indirect evidence that throughout the 1770s and 1780s Millar's classes grew significantly in size.[56] Between 1763 and 1770 Robert Dick, the professor of civil law, had between twenty and twenty-eight students each year. During the next twenty years, Dick's students numbered between two and nineteen a year, and matriculations showed a generally downward trend, with no students listed in some years. Between 1763 and 1765 John Erskine, the professor of Scots law, had class sizes ranging from thirty-one to forty-six. His successor, William Wallace, had a peak of fifty-two students in 1766–67, but thereafter his largest class was forty and his smallest ten, with a generally downward trend from around 1770. These figures probably underestimate the total size of the classes, but they suggest that enrolments in law at Edinburgh were dropping over these years. Since it was becoming much less common for Scots to study civil law in the Netherlands during this period,[57] the students must have been going to Glasgow.

Millar attracted students not only because he was a skilful teacher but also because Dick and Wallace were not especially distinguished professors. When Millar's pupil David Hume was appointed to the Edinburgh chair of Scots law late in 1786, enrolments there virtually doubled; and when John Wilde replaced Dick in 1792, the listed students of civil law jumped in number from five to twenty-four, though they dropped dramatically in the later 1790s, as Wilde became mentally ill. Millar may well have exploited the weakness in Edinburgh legal education between 1765 and 1786 in order to build up his own classes. He probably started to teach Scots law in the year Erskine resigned, just as he may have started teaching jurisprudence in his second class on the *Institutes* when the Edinburgh chair of public law passed to a sinecurist in 1764. The fortunes of Edinburgh as a centre of legal education revived with the appointment of Allan Maconochie to the public law chair in 1779, and especially with the appointments of Hume and Wilde in 1786 and 1792, respectively. By then, however, Millar's reputation was well established. The relatively poor state of legal education at Oxford, Cambridge and Trinity College, Dublin no doubt increased Millar's attractiveness among English and Irish students;[58] but his main rivals for students must always have been the professors in Edinburgh, and the statistics drawn from Edinburgh classes suggest that he was very successful in building up his own classes at their expense. Nor do we need to assume that increases in matriculations in law at Edinburgh after the appointments of Hume and Wilde necessarily caused a decrease, or, at any rate, a significant decrease, in the size of Millar's classes because, since students not uncommonly moved between Glasgow and Edinburgh, some who enrolled in law at Edinburgh could also have attended Millar's lectures, while, from the 1780s, the total number of law students in Scotland was increasing.[59]

III

IN 1777 MILLAR'S MENTOR, Lord Kames, said of current legal education in Scotland:

> Our law-students, trained to rely upon authority, seldom think of questioning what they read: they husband their reasoning faculty, as if it would rust by exercise.
> Nor is the exercise of reasoning promoted in any degree by public professors . . . . [N]othing is presented to the young gentlemen but naked facts.[60]

The only professor exempted from these criticisms was Millar. 'Were law taught as a rational science', Kames added, 'its principles unfolded, and its connection with manners and politics, it would prove an enticing study to every person who has an appetite for knowledge. We might hope to see our lawyers soaring above their predecessors; and giving splendor to their country, by purifying and improving its laws' (xiii).

The success enjoyed by Millar in his forty years in the Glasgow chair of civil law was due in large measure to his offering students a full and interesting curriculum intended to foster the type of critical thinking about law that Kames recommended. A key factor in this process was the comprehensive, integrated character of Millar's courses. Millar provided a complete legal education of the polite and philosophical type deemed desirable in the age of the Scottish Enlightenment, covering government and politics, jurisprudence, civil law and municipal law. Although some scholars have perceived a tension or contradiction in Millar's thought between his politics and his 'scientific' natural jurisprudence,[61] the exposition of politics in his lectures on government was apparently developed from his lectures on the public law of Scotland and was clearly considered by Millar himself to be part of his general curriculum. Rights might emerge historically, but in polite societies, or societies advancing in civilization, it is the task of government, through the political process, to inscribe rights in legislation and to provide courts to recognize and enforce them. Millar's personal qualities as an energetic and stimulating teacher enhanced the presentation of this new legal curriculum. Although Glasgow's situation may not have been advantageous for a school of law, Millar's ability and energy overcame this limitation. This was especially true during the crucial period from the mid-1760s to the mid-1780s, when Millar was making his reputation and had little serious rivalry as a law teacher. The type of complete education in law envisaged by the Glasgow University faculty in 1714 was thus finally achieved by Millar, who succeeded in turning Glasgow into the pre-eminent university for legal study in Britain during the second half of the eighteenth century.

The Glasgow faculty made a brilliant decision in 1761 when they resolved to secure the appointment of Millar; he more than justified their expectations. By teaching law as 'a liberal and enlightened science', Millar attracted future statesmen and leaders of the bar to classes that were designed to educate 'an accomplished liberal and enlightened Advocate'.[62] By contrast, under his successor Robert Davidson, the son of Principal Archibald Davidson, the Glasgow University law school was reduced to providing courses for the apprentices and clerks of provincial lawyers. Davidson made no attempt to perpetuate the broad, intellectually innovative curriculum that had enabled Millar to overcome the problems Glasgow faced as a law school. He had neither the ability nor the will to offer the range of legal education that Millar had developed. It is true that Davidson was competing, very unequally, for students of Scots law against David Hume in Edinburgh, but so, at times, had Millar; and Davidson in his first years offered only courses in civil law, where he did not face such strong rivalry. It is difficult to escape the conclusion that, had not the Faculty of Procurators in Glasgow from July 1796 required apprentices being examined for admission to produce evidence of attendance at a class on Scots law,[63] Davidson would have had virtually no students at all.

Six days after Millar's death on 30 May 1801, Henry Brougham wrote to his friend James Loch, complaining that 'they mean to give poor J. Millar's class to that stupidest of all brutes Robt. Davidson'.[64] Whatever the justice of Brougham's characterization, which no doubt owes much to political differences, it is plain that Davidson's personal limitations contributed to the decline of the Glasgow law school from the enlightened eminence to which it had risen under Millar. In the summer of 1827, a few months after his interview with the royal commissioners, Davidson was rather coolly described in the pages of the *Caledonian Mercury* as 'fully adequate' in his academic position, whereas the same article in marked contrast waxed enthusiastic when discussing his more illustrious predecessor: 'Celebrated as an author at a time when our country was singularly fertile in great writers, this eminent person acquired a still more enviable reputation as a teacher of law, and by the united force of genius, talents and indefatigable perseverence, raised himself to the very highest place amongst modern *Antecessores*.'[65] Small wonder that the royal commission's general report of October 1830, without mentioning names, by implication severely criticized the narrowly 'practical' and 'technical' programme of the Glasgow law school under Davidson and voiced approval for the broadly 'speculative' approach to the training of lawyers that Millar had done so much to develop. 'It will be in vain to hope that the independence and character of the Bar can be maintained, if the study of Law is not conducted on an enlightened and philosophical plan', the report asserted.[66] Millar's educational programme was thus endorsed and vindicated.

Notes

I have benefited much from the enthusiastic help of Michael Moss and his staff in Glasgow University Archives and David Weston in Glasgow University Library. To my advantage, earlier drafts were read by Roger Emerson, Andrew Hook, Hector MacQueen, Richard Sher and Alan Watson.

1. *Evidence, Oral and Documentary, taken and received by the Commissioners appointed by his Majesty George IV. July 23d, 1826; and re-appointed by his Majesty William IV., October 12th, 1830; for visiting the Universities of Scotland. Volume II.* University of Glasgow, 1837 Parliamentary Papers 36:146 (cited hereafter as *Evidence*).
2. John Craig, 'Account of the Life and Writings of John Millar, Esq.', prefixed to John Millar, *The Origin of the Distinction of Ranks: or, an Inquiry into the Circumstances which give rise to Influence and Authority, in the different Members of Society*, 4th ed. (Edinburgh, 1806), xi (cited hereafter as 'Craig').
3. *The Edinburgh University Journal, and Critical Review* (1 January *1823*): 8–13, excerpted in *The Tounis College: An Anthology of Edinburgh University Student Journals 1823–1923*, ed. J.T.D. Hall (Edinburgh, 1985), 13.
4. Arthur Browne, *A Compendious View of the Civil Law, being the Substance*

of a Course of Lectures read in the University of Dublin, 2 vols. (Dublin, 1797), 1:17.

5. Thomas Newte, *Prospects and Observations; on a Tour in England and Scotland: Natural, Oeconomical, and Literary* (London, 1791), 65.

6. Robert Heron, *Observations Made in a Journey through the Western Counties of Scotland; in the Autumn of 1792*, 2 vols. (Perth, 1793), 2:418.

7. On these men as Millar's pupils, see William C. Lehmann, *John Millar of Glasgow, 1735–1801: His Life and Thought and his Contributions to Sociological Analysis* (Cambridge, 1960), 36–37n. (cited hereafter as 'Lehmann'); for their membership of the sub-commission, see *Evidence*, 2:1.

8. The following discussion of the early years of the Glasgow chair is drawn from John W. Cairns, 'The Origins of the Glasgow Law School: The Professors of Civil Law, 1714–61', in *The Life of the Law: Proceedings of the Tenth British Legal History Conference*, ed. Peter Birks (London, 1993), 151–94, and 'William Crosse, Regius Professor of Civil Law in the University of Glasgow, 1746–1749: A Failure of Enlightened Patronage', *History of Universities* 12 (1993):159–96.

9. See Cairns, 'William Crosse'182–83; Roger L. Emerson, 'Lord Bute and the Scottish Universities 1760–1792', in *Lord Bute: Essays in Re-interpretation*, ed. Karl W. Schweizer (Leicester, 1988), 147–79, esp. 153–54.

10. Lehmann, 16–18; Ian Simpson Ross, *Lord Kames and the Scotland of his Day* (Oxford, 1972), 95–97; Alexander Fraser Tytler, *Memoirs of the Life and Writings of the Honourable Henry Home of Kames*, 2 vols. (Edinburgh, 1807), 1:198–201.

11. Craig, xix; Cairns, 'William Crosse', 177–78. NLS, MS 3930 (Lectures on the *Institutes*, 1779–80) shows that he lectured daily, giving in total 123 lectures; GUL, MSS Murray 93–95 (Lectures on the *Digest*, 1790–91) shows that he gave 116 lectures and also indicates daily lecturing.

12. NLS, MS 3931 (Lectures on Government, 1780–81) shows that Millar taught government on Mondays, Wednesdays and Fridays.

13. Heron's *Observations* of 1793, 2:418, mentions lectures on English law along with those on jurisprudence, government, civil law and Scots law that attracted students to Millar's classes 'from all quarters of Britain', but Heron may have attributed to John Millar the lecture course on English law that his son James, then assistant professor of mathematics, was given permission to teach by the faculty on 7 December 1792 (GUA 26,694:269). William C. Lehmann, 'Some Observations on the Law Lectures of Professor Millar at the University of Glasgow (1761–1801)', *Juridical Review* (1970): 74, points to a letter that John Millar wrote to William Adam on 4 August 1798, which suggests that the lectures on English law were first given by him in 1798–99 (see also GUL, MS Gen. 243).

14. 'Statistical Account of the University of Glasgow' (1794), in Thomas Reid, *Philosophical Works*, 2 vols. (1895; rpt. Hildesheim, 1967), 2:734, states that 'in his public department' Millar lectured daily for two hours: that is, two hours daily on Roman law, which was what the Act of 1727 was

interpreted as requiring him to teach, one hour on the *Institutes*, one on the *Digest*. The third hour of lectures was devoted to government, Scots law, or English law. See *Evidence*, 2:277.

15. Lehmann, 'Observations on the Law Lectures', 67.
16. NLS, Adv. MS 28.6.8:165–66, first pagination sequence. In so far as newspaper advertisements survive for Millar's lectures, they confirm the teaching of both courses from 1765 onward.
17. See Lockhart Gordon and David Ross to George Bogle, rector, 17 Nov. 1748, GUA 30,222. For Professor Dick's similar practice in Edinburgh, see Hugo Arnot, *The History of Edinburgh* (Edinburgh, 1779), 398.
18. John Erskine's letter to Lord Cardross, 24 Nov. 1762, EUL, MS La.II.238, confirms that Millar gave two courses on the *Institutes* in 1762–63. It also implies that they were identical or nearly identical, but Erskine was probably not well informed about Millar's practice in this respect.
19. The strong Smithian foundation of Millar's legal teaching is discussed below. If there is any truth to the speculation I am putting forward here, Millar's lectures on government may also have been started as a Smithian response to Reid's very different way of teaching that subject.
20. This speculation was suggested to me by Nicholas Phillipson.
21. *The Correspondence of Adam Smith*, ed. Ernest Campbell Mossner and Ian Simpson Ross, 2nd ed. (Oxford, 1987), 99–100. Millar wished Thomas Young to succeed Smith. It is unknown what Smith's views were on his potential successors, and there is no reason to believe he agreed with Millar. See *Selections from the Family Papers preserved at Caldwell*, 2 vols. in 3 (Glasgow, 1854), 2, pt. i:232–33.
22. On the natural jurisprudence component of Reid's moral philosophy course, see Thomas Reid, *Practical Ethics: Being Lectures and Papers on Natural Religion, Self-Government, Natural Jurisprudence, and the Law of Nations*, ed. Knud Haakonssen (Princeton, 1990). (Reid's assistant and successor, Archibald Arthur, also taught natural jurisprudence; see 'Notes, Taken by James Neilson, from Mr. Arthur's Lectures on Natural Jurisprudence, given in the University of Glasgow. Glasgow. From 10 March 1788 to [blank] 1788', GUL, MS Gen. 832.) On Millar's students attending Reid's classes, see Reid to Andrew Skene, 14 Nov. 1764, in Reid's *Works*, 1:40. On the general relationship of law and moral philosophy, see John Erskine to Lord Cardross, 24 Nov. 1762, EUL, MS La.II.238, where Erskine, obviously anxious that Cardross know Pufendorf, agrees that Cardross should take Smith's class on moral philosophy along with Millar's on the *Institutes*.
23. See 'Matriculation Roll of the University of Edinburgh. Arts-Law-Divinity' (transcribed by Alexander Morgan), EUL, 3 vols., 1:262.
24. Minutes of the Faculty of Advocates, 1751–1783, NLS, F.R. 2, 127 (8 Jan. 1760) and 147 (5 Jan. 1762). I am grateful to the Faculty of Advocates for permission to examine and cite their records. For a discussion of this development, see John W. Cairns, 'The Influence of Smith's Jurisprudence on Legal Education in Scotland', in *Adam Smith Reviewed*, ed. Peter Jones

and Andrew Skinner (Edinburgh, 1992), 168–89, and 'The Formation of the Scottish Legal Mind in the Eighteenth Century: Themes of Humanism and Enlightenment in the Admission of Advocates', in *The Legal Mind: Essays for Tony Honoré*, ed. Neil MacCormick and Peter Birks (Oxford, 1986), 253–77, esp. 265–66.

25. *Glasgow Journal* (cited hereafter as *GJ*), 20/27 Oct. 1768, 26 Oct./2 Nov. 1769, 1/8 Nov. 1770. The last of these advertisements does not mention the classes on the *Digest* and the *Institutes*, probably because they had already begun on 4 November; those on public law were due to begin on 11 November and, at this period, normally started a week later.

26. *GJ*, 27 Oct./3 Nov. 1774 (*Institutes*, *Digest*, government); *Glasgow Chronicle: or, Weekly Intelligencer*, 12/19 Oct. 1775 (*Institutes*, *Digest*, government, private law of Scotland); no advertisements traced in 1776, 1777, 1778 (probably due to missing issues in surviving runs of newspapers); *Glasgow Mercury* (cited hereafter as *GM*), 21/28 Oct. 1779 (*Institutes*, *Digest*, public law, law of Scotland); *GM*, 5/12 Oct. 1780 (*Institutes*, *Digest*, public law); *GM*, 4/11 Oct. 1781 (*Institutes*, *Digest*, public law, law of Scotland) (see also *GJ*, 4/11 Oct. 1781); *GM*, 10/17 Oct. 1782 (*Institutes*, *Digest*, public law); *GM*, 16/23 Oct. 1783 (*Institutes*, *Digest*, public law, law of Scotland); *GM*, 14/21 Oct. 1784 (*Institutes*, *Digest*, government); *GM*, 20/27 Oct. 1785 (*Institutes*, *Digest*, public law, law of Scotland); no advertisements traced in 1786 and 1787; *GM*, 7/14 Oct. 1788 (*Institutes*, *Digest*, public law); *GM*, 13/20 Oct. 1789, and *Glasgow Advertiser and Evening Intelligencer*, 16/19 Oct. 1789 (*Institutes*, *Digest*, law of Scotland, public law); *GM*, 21/28 Sept. 1790 (*Institutes*, *Digest*, public law).

27. *GM*, 18/25 Oct. 1791; *Glasgow Courier* (cited hereafter as *GC*), 20 Oct. 1791, 24 Oct. 1795 and 15 Oct. 1799; *Glasgow Advertiser*, 21/25 Oct. 1793.

28. See John W. Cairns, 'John Millar's Lectures on Scots Criminal Law', *Oxford Journal of Legal Studies* 8 (1988): 364–400, esp. 388–91.

29. See John W. Cairns, 'Rhetoric, Language, and Roman Law: Legal Education and Improvement in Eighteenth-Century Scotland', *Law and History Review* 9 (1991): 31–58, and 'John Millar's Lectures'. Lehmann, 'Observations on the Law Lectures', gives a very useful survey of Millar's classes; see also Lehmann, 'John Millar, Professor of Civil Law at Glasgow (1761–1801)', *Juridical Review* (1961): 218–33.

30. Haakonnssen, 'John Millar and the Science of a Legislator', *Juridical Review* (1985): 41–68. For a fuller account of what follows, see also Cairns, 'Rhetoric, Language, and Roman Law', 41–43, and 'John Millar's Lectures', 374–80.

31. Craig's claim is readily verified from surviving student notes, e.g., NLS, MS 2743, fol. 18v. As well as this (incomplete) manuscript of the first course on the *Institutes*, so far the following notes have been discovered as surviving: NLS, Adv. MS 28.6.8 (first and second course on the *Institutes*, 1777–78); NLS, Adv. MSS 20.4.7–8 (second course, 1778);

NLS, MS 3930 (first and second course, 1779–80); GUL, MSS Murray 78–82 (first and second course, 1788–89); GUL, MSS Murray 96–98 (first and second course, 1789–90); GUL, MSS Gen. 812–14 (first and second course, ascribed to 1789); GUL, MS Murray 77 (first course incomplete, copied from GUL, MSS Murray 96–98 in 1794); GUL, MS Murray 332 (second course, incomplete, 1793); EUL, MSS Dc.2.45–46 (second course, 1794); GUL, MS Hamilton 117 (second course, 1798).

32. An edition of this work aimed at Scottish law students was published at Edinburgh in 1780.

33. E.g., NLS, Adv. MS 28.6.8:1–11, first pagination sequence; lects. 1–3. Parenthetical references in the discussion that follows refer to Adv. MS 28.6.8, using (unless otherwise noted) the first pagination sequence.

34. See also, e.g., NLS, MS 3930:155–56 (lecture 72, 15 Feb. 1780); GUL, MS Murray 96, fol. 111v (lecture 65, 8 Feb. 1790).

35. For a useful analytical breakdown of the second course, see NLS, MS 3930: 299–301. All surviving manuscripts of the second course follow this structure.

36. On Smith's analytical jurisprudence, see above all Knud Haakonssen, *The Science of a Legislator: The Natural Jurisprudence of David Hume and Adam Smith* (Cambridge, 1981), 99–134.

37. Adam Smith, *Lectures on Jurisprudence*, ed. R. L. Meek, D. D. Raphael, and P. G. Stein (Oxford, 1978), 397–554.

38. E.g., *GJ*, 3/10 Oct. 1765, starting 4 Nov.; *GM*, 13/20 Oct. 1789, starting 3 Nov.; *GC*, 15 Oct. 1799, starting 5 Nov. GUL, MS Murray 92, fol. 55v shows he finished on 29 Apr. 1791, which fits with having started that year on 1 Nov. 1790 (*GM*, 21/28 Sept. 1790), generally lecturing five days per week and delivering 116 lectures in all.

39. GUL, MSS Murray 91–92; GUL, MSS Murray 93–95. The first of these consists of two volumes from an originally four-volume set of notes. The second is possibly a copy of the complete version of the first; if so, both date from 1790–91.

40. GUL, MS Gen. 347, 52 lectures from 1775–76; MS Gen. 178, 51 lectures (MS dating from 1783); MSS Murray 83–87, 50 lectures from 1789–90; MS Gen. 1078, 50 lectures (MS dated 1792); and (incomplete) MSS Gen. 181/1–3 (originally) 50 lectures dating from 1789–90. Special circumstances apply to the last three sets, since they are schematic outlines rather than student transcripts of what Millar actually said in class. An incomplete set of lectures on Scots law dating from 1778–79 is still in the possession of Meyer Boswell Books of San Francisco: J. H. Baker, 'Migrations of Manuscripts', *Journal of Legal History* 6 (1985): 236.

41. In GUL, MS Gen. 347, the student who wrote up the fair copy of the notes on Scots law added after them the lectures on the Scottish courts from Millar's course on government.

42. The bracketed words are a conjectural resconstruction, as the manuscript ends at 'repeat'.

43. For further discussion of Millar's lectures on English law, see John W.

Cairns, 'Eighteenth-Century Professorial Classification of English Common Law', *McGill Law Journal* 33 (1987): 225–44, esp. 233–35, and Lehmann, 'Observations on the Law Lectures', 73–76.

44. This letter shows that the allegations of Millar's supposed republicanism (discussed in Lehmann, *John Millar*, 67–71) predated the era of the French Revolution, when attention was drawn to them by hostile contemporaries.

45. That this change occurred after 1780–81 is clear from the fact that lectures from that date (NLS, MS 3931) conform to the 1778 edition of the *Course of Lectures on Government*. AUL, MS 133 is dated 1782 and conforms to the earlier syllabus; since it is a fair copy, however, it is impossible to be certain of the date of the lectures it contains.

46. See *A Course of Lectures on Government; Given Annually in the University of Glasgow* (Glasgow, 1787) (bound into GUL, MS Gen. 180/1); GUL, MS Hamilton 116 (1798); GUL, MS Gen. 290:34–44.

47. E.g., *GJ* 10/17 Oct. 1771, 8/15 Oct. 1772, 7/14 Oct. 1773, 27 Oct./3 Nov. 1774; *GM* 4/11 Oct. 1781, 10/17 Oct. 1782, 16/23 Oct. 1783; *GC* 15 Oct. 1799.

48. For a good account of these lectures, see Craig, xli–lvii. Among the surviving sets of notes on these lectures are the following: Mitchell Library, MS 99; GUL, MS Gen. 203; NLS, MS 3931; AUL, MS 133; GUL, MS Gen. 179; GUL, MSS Gen. 289–91; GUL, MSS Gen. 180/1–3; GUL, MSS Murray 88–90; GUL, MS Hamilton 116. Other sets are privately owned. These sets are listed in chronological order, although the first two are undated. Not all are complete.

49. No other law prizes are ever mentioned in the prize lists published every year at the beginning of May.

50. The method is explained by Alexander Bayne, the first professor of Scots law at Edinburgh University, in *A Discourse on the Rise and Progress of the Law of Scotland, and the Method of Studying it*, in Sir Thomas Hope, *Minor Practicks: or Treatise of the Scottish Law*, ed. Alexander Bayne (Edinburgh, 1726).

51. See further George Jardine, *Outlines of Philosophical Education, Illustrated by the Method of Teaching the Logic Class in the University of Glasgow*, 2nd ed. (Glasgow, 1825), 463–64.

52. For the argument about the connection with Millar of GUL, MS Gen. 1078 and MSS Gen. 289–91, see Cairns, 'John Millar's Lectures', 369–71, n. 33.

53. In GUL, MSS 88–90, on what was originally the title page of each of the first two volumes (now pasted to the end boards), is written: 'These Notes contain nothing additional to what are used in the class, unless some very few particulars marked on the left hand page.' See also GUL, MS Murray 91, fol. [i]r: 'Copy of the Notes used by Mr. Millar upon the Pandects in the University of Glasgow'.

54. See Millar to A. Campbell, SRO, GD 170/1990. For a fuller account of Millar's style of teaching, see Cairns, 'Rhetoric, Language, and Roman Law', 39–43, 47–49.

55. *A Letter by Students of Divinity, Law, Medicine, and Philosophy, in Glasgow College, to the Reverend William Taylor, D.D.* (Glasgow, 1785), sig. Cr. For the background, see J. D. Mackie, *The University of Glasgow 1451–1951: A Short History* (Glasgow, 1954), 206–9.

56. What follows is based on data in 'Matriculation Roll in the University of Edinburgh', vols. 1 and 2.

57. Robert Feenstra, 'Scottish-Dutch Legal Relations in the Seventeenth and Eighteenth Centuries', in *Scotland and Europe 1200–1850*, ed. T. C. Smout (Edinburgh, 1986), 128–42; Paul Nève, 'Disputations of Scots Students Attending Universities in the Northern Netherlands', in *Legal History in the Making*, ed. W. M. Gordon and T. D. Fergus (London, 1991), 95–108.

58. See J. L. Barton, 'Legal Studies', in *The History of the University of Oxford. Volume 5. The Eighteenth Century*, ed. L. S. Sutherland and L. G. Mitchell (Oxford, 1986), 593–605; D. A. Winstanley, *Unreformed Cambridge: A Study of Certain Aspects of the University in the Eighteenth Century* (Cambridge, 1935), 57–60, 122–26; and R. B. McDowell and D. A. Webb, *Trinity College Dublin 1592–1952: An Academic History* (Cambridge, 1982), 65–66, 81, 138–39.

59. For the increase in the total number of law students, see the statistics on admission to the Faculty of Advocates in the following works by Nicholas Phillipson: *The Scottish Whigs and the Reform of the Court of Session 1785–1830* (Edinburgh, 1990), 189; 'Lawyers, Landowners, and the Civic Leadership of Post-Union Scotland', in *Lawyers in their Social Setting*, ed. D. N. MacCormick (Edinburgh, 1976), 171–94, esp. 175; 'The Social Structure of the Faculty of Advocates in Scotland 1661–1840', in *Law Making and Law Makers in British History*, ed. Alan Harding (London, 1980), 146–56, esp. 148–50. If the Faculty of Advocates was increasing in size, so probably were all bodies of lawyers.

60. Henry Home, Lord Kames, *Elucidations Respecting the Common and Statute Law of Scotland* (Edinburgh, 1777), viii-ix. For a discussion of Kames's views on legal education, see Cairns, 'Rhetoric, Language, and Roman Law', 37–38.

61. On this point, see Michael Ignatieff, 'John Millar and Individualism', in *Wealth and Virtue: The Shaping of Political Economy in the Scottish Enlightenment*, ed. Istvan Hont and Michael Ignatieff (Cambridge, 1983), 317–43. Cf. Haakonssen, 'John Millar', which I find convincing.

62. These words are drawn from *Report Made to His Majesty by a Royal Commission of Inquiry into the State of the Universities of Scotland*, in 1831 Parliamentary Papers 12:54.

63. This regulation was introduced by the royal charter granted to the Faculty of Procurators on 1 July 1796. See the Sederunt Books of the Faculty of Procurators, 1761–1796 (esp. 4 March 1796) and 1796–1832 (esp. 15 July 1796, pages 1, 8, 15, 47), Library of the Royal Faculty of Procurators, Glasgow. I am grateful for permission to examine and cite these records.

64. In *Brougham and his Early Friends: Letters to James Loch, 1798–1809*,

ed. R.H.M. Buddle Atkinson and G. A. Jackson, 3 vols. (London, 1908), 1:275.

65. James Browne, *Remarks on the Study of the Civil Law; occasioned by Mr Brougham's Late Attack on the Scottish Bar* (Edinburgh, 1828), 34–35 (containing Browne's articles from the *Caledonian Mercury*).

66. *Report Made to His Majesty*, in 1831 Parliamentary Papers 12:53–54.

PART II

Beyond the Academic
Enlightenment

8

Boswell in Glasgow: Adam Smith, Moral Sentiments and the Sympathy of Biography

Gordon Turnbull

'Boswell was a student at the University of Glasgow from the autumn of 1759 to the end of February 1760, when he unceremoniously terminated his course by running away to London.'[1] So begins Frederick A. Pottle's account of James Boswell's abbreviated year as a Glasgow University student. The impact of this experience on Boswell's mind and subsequent career has been little discussed by scholars — probably because the consequences of that unceremonious termination (Boswell's adventures in London, especially during his second visit, which resulted in his *London Journal* of 1762–63) attract attention more readily. Moreover, on the specific point of his intellectual development, the period in Glasgow is bracketed by his livelier and admittedly more formative years at the University of Edinburgh and his more arduous and exacting studies in law, again at Edinburgh and then at Utrecht.[2] Lord Auchinleck had, as is now well known, abruptly removed his scribbling son from Edinburgh and its literary and theatrical distractions and frivolities. In the more culturally constricted atmosphere of Glasgow, young Boswell rapidly tired of his academic confinement and eloped, as he said, to London, for a curious mixture of short-lived fervour to become a Roman Catholic and, under the improbable moral care of Lord Eglinton, dissipation.

Yet during that abbreviated academic year, Boswell found himself a privileged witness of one of the intellectual pinnacles of the Enlightenment in Glasgow, Adam Smith's course of lectures in moral philosophy, out of which the *Theory of Moral Sentiments* and, much later, the *Wealth of Nations* would grow. I propose to argue that the general content of these lectures, as much as Smith's character and social manner, deeply impressed Boswell, with consequences for his public and private writings, the biographical theory underlying his accounts of Paoli and especially Johnson and (my focus later in this chapter) his practice as an advocate and his records of his legal career. Though explicit references to Smith's thought in Boswell's writings are in fact few, intellectual and conceptual echoes are many, and the journals hint at a complex life-long relationship with what Boswell heard in his Scottish university education. It is most gratifying for modern professional academics to detect such residues, since Boswell at first glance seems to be one of those annoying undergraduates — we have all met some — lively and intelligent, but upon whom not much of what we have to say really sticks. Signs remain in Boswell's copious writings of a troubled engagement with, amounting to an incomplete resistance to, Smith's epistemology — specifically his theory of social spectatorship as a moral monitor, an idea for which Boswell seeks, with only variable success, to substitute a proto-Romantic faith in an autonomous or self-generating ethics.

Perhaps the importance of Boswell's encounter with Smith at the height of his effectiveness as a teacher has been lost because of the later souring of the relationship. Frank Brady's account of the second half of Boswell's life contains only a handful of isolated references to Smith, illustrating the relationship as it stood in later life.[3] Memories of Smith's civility, and a compliment from Smith (that Boswell possessed a happy facility of manners) appear from time to time in Boswell's journals and letters, but the passing years brought changes, the broader reasons for which are not difficult to trace. Whereas Boswell over the course of his erratic life would cling to a troubled but heartfelt faith in Christianity, Smith would produce what Boswell saw as an 'absurd eulogium' on that recurring source of Boswellian anxiety, the infidel sceptic David Hume (14 Sept. 1779).[4] Later, at a meeting of the Club in London, in a light-hearted discussion about which members ought to pay for wine, Gibbon ('a disagreeable dog') alone 'stickled for Smith', because, says Boswell, 'he is a brother infidel' (28 March 1781; *Laird*, 297–98). In Brady's terse summary of Boswell's social life while an advocate in Edinburgh, Boswell 'avoided deists and Whigs like Adam Smith' (Brady, *Later Years*, 194).

The decline in Boswell's estimate of Smith (whom he in certain other moods treasured as an acquaintance of real eminence) runs parallel to the deepening of his affinities with the Episcopal Tory Englishman, Samuel Johnson. The process had early beginnings, as we know from Boswell's 'Harvest' journal (Sept.-Nov. 1762). The young Boswell, as Pottle notes, 'had for years been reading Johnson with delight', showing independence from his 'critical Mentors, Kames, Adam Smith, and Hugh Blair', all of whom 'disparaged Johnson's writing as heavy and pedantic' (Pottle, *Earlier Years*, 112). In his lectures on rhetoric, Smith's exemplars of bad style were Shaftesbury and Johnson. Johnson himself, for his part, candidly remarked to Boswell in 1763 that he and Smith when they met 'did not take to each other'.[5] Smith told Boswell (in what seems to have been a cordial enough conversation in London) that he thought Johnson was suffering from 'a certain degree of insanity' (2 Apr. 1775).[6] On Easter Sunday 1783 (Easter being one of Boswell's regular high points of religious solemnity and new moral resolve), Boswell urged himself to ask Johnson's advice on whether it was right for him to 'associate with

Adam Smith as formerly friendly to' him (20 April 1783).[7] Whether the question was actually asked is not recorded.

In Glasgow the next year, on 10 April 1784, breakfasting with Smith, Edmund Burke, Dugald Stewart, John Millar and others, upon Burke's appointment as lord rector of the University of Glasgow, Boswell confessed himself 'a little flurried from the consciousness of . . . being in the midst of opposition'. But he conducted himself 'very well', and fell into thoughts of what the years had done: his admiration for Burke (of whom he first heard in Smith's lectures twenty-four years earlier, and whom he then regarded as 'a planet in the heavens') holds firm, and is indeed heightened by reviving thoughts 'which I had *then* [referring to his year in Glasgow] in company with Adam Smith, and those I had *now*' (*Applause of the Jury*, 203–4). Burke has remained in the Boswellian firmament; Smith's star has faded. Smith makes one of his last and most memorably revealing appearances in Boswell's writing in a footnote in the *Life* to some Johnsoniana provided by Bennet Langton. After quoting Garrick's opinion that Smith's conversation is 'flabby', Boswell accuses Smith of professional academic conversational stinginess:

> Smith was a man of extraordinary application, and had his mind crowded with all manner of subjects; but the force, acuteness and vivacity of Johnson were not to be found there. He had book-making so much in his thoughts, and was so chary of what might be turned to account in that way, that he once said to Sir Joshua Reynolds, that he made it a rule, when in company, never to talk of what he understood. (*Life*, 1082–83, n. 2.)

Boswell here accuses his former teacher of a self-serving academician's careerist conversational hoarding, the reason for the footnote being a pointed contrast with Johnson, everywhere in the *Life* a figure of spectacular articulacy and copiously dispensed conversational prowess. Boswell applies to Smith in this footnote a kind of social equivalent of the prudentially accumulationist values that surround capital in the *Wealth of Nations*.

I

IMPORTANT FEATURES OF Smith's thought persist, nonetheless, in Boswell's records — most notably, Smith's concern with the social dimensions of sympathy, and a sceptical sense of the moral stability of masculine social identity. Both writers in their different mediums (Smith in a systematic ethical treatise, Boswell in the scattered, fluctuating medium of a daily journal) concern themselves with fellow-feeling and an internalized social monitor — public masculine conduct under, and as a function of, the social gaze. Both writers, products of the Enlightenment in Scotland, reflect a post-Union ethics of compromise: Smith's theory of sympathy and Boswell's careers in legal representation and biography turn on the self's adjustments to, and incorporations of, the pressures of the other, a micropolitical correlative of what was happening at the national level, with Scotland no longer a self-contained or self-determining polity. The journals, in which Boswell habitually turned his encounters with others into striking biographical vignettes, show at all points what a twentieth-century Johnsonian biographer attributes to the *Life*: '[Boswell's] gift for empathy and dramatic imitation'.[8] In an often-quoted moment of self-commentary in the *Life*, Boswell says his mind in time became *'strongly impregnated with the Johnsonian aether'* (*Life*, 1 July 1763, 297). Elsewhere in his journal Boswell comments on his capacity to tune himself to the needs of any company — a characteristic which provided him alternately with satisfaction and distress. In the course of his passionate defence in 1774 (a crucial chapter in Boswell's legal career) of an important criminal client, the sheepstealer John Reid, Boswell notes: 'I had *by sympathy* sucked the dismal ideas of John Reid's situation . . . so I suffered much more than John did' (30 Aug. 1774; emphasis added).[9]

Examples of many kinds can be cited to illustrate Boswell's aptitudes for imaginative plasticity, for profound sympathetic identification, for adopting the characterological style of figures from high life and low. To quote Alastair Fowler's summary of the important innovations of the *Life*, Boswell 'moves decisively away from the tradition of idealized panegyric'. Fowler properly locates Boswell in the new regions of sensibility: his biography is the expression of 'a new sensibility, an intuitive sympathy (however inadequate) for his subject's inner life'.[10] Similarly, Peter Conrad sees the Boswellian Johnson as a herald of romanticism, and Boswell as an heir of Richardson, with character seen from within, even though the *Life* is in part 'modelled on the classic biographies written by Johnson himself — verdicts on moral character, legalistic distributions of praise and blame.'[11] (Boswell experimented with classical biography in the Plutarchan lineaments of Paoli, but even there the hero of action shares space with the hero of contemplation, the meditative or self-reflexive self, and in the long run, Paoli's later appearances in Boswell's records mark him as a heroically failed man of action — a variant of the Prince Charles Edward figure of the Hebridean journal). 'Classical biography studies the probity of public character', says Conrad (383); 'Boswell's concern is the private man' — and the *Life* is positioned halfway between those 'epics of anarchic, organic consciousness', *Tristram Shandy* and 'The Prelude'.

Such observations illuminate the private diaries, too. Boswell's life-long experimentations with the constitutively theatrical properties of character reflect and are the issue of Scottish Enlightenment interrogations of the structure and continuity of, as well as the fluid boundaries between, individual and social identity. Young Boswell's move from Edinburgh — with its lively theatre life, opportunities for 'scribbling' and infatuations with actresses — to a sober and untheatrical Glasgow exposed him, paradoxically, to a deeper engagement with ideas of theatricality and spectatorship. Smith's theory of sympathy, which reinscribes in a theatre/spectator paradigm Humean arguments about the instability of the boundaries of human identity, offered Boswell an effective theoretical channel for the keen attractions to theatre he had felt earlier in Edinburgh, and the later theatre of Johnsonian performance. In Smith's thinking, Boswell encountered the idea that theatricality profoundly informs social ethics: theatricality is not mere show, but a central property of moral conduct.[12] The *London Journal* of 1762–63 records a continuing engagement with questions of theatricality and morals, spectatorship and sympathy;[13]and decades later the *Life of Johnson*, moving famously in 'scenes', would hold its subject forever in a grand spectacle of articulacy.

At first, in the days 'then' recalled on the occasion of Burke's appointment as rector of the university, Boswell's admiration for Smith knew no bounds. Indeed, he told John Johnston of Grange that his 'greatest inducement' for coming to Glasgow (apart, evidently, from his father's wishes) had been 'to hear Mr. Smith's lectures', which he pronounced (what follows is the editorial reconstruction of a letter defective in some places) '[tr]uly excellent': Smith's 'Sentiments [are striking, profound] and beautifull, the method in [which they] are arranged clear, accurate and [orderly, his lan]guage correct perspicuous and elegan[tly phrased]'. Smith's 'private character' is, moreover, 'realy amiable' (Glasgow, 11 Jan. 1760).[14] In this letter, as Pottle remarks, Boswell 'spoke of Smith more highly than of any other teacher he had ever had' (Pottle, *Earlier Years*, 42) — although Pottle stresses that it was Smith's lectures on rhetoric and belles lettres, rather than ethics and political economy, that made the greatest impact on Boswell's mind.

We learn from Boswell's correspondence elsewhere that he included the *Theory of Moral Sentiments* among the books he sent Margaret Montgomerie, the future Mrs Boswell, as part of his efforts to instruct her mind.[15] The recommended reading put Smith's treatise in some notably good company: it includes also portions of scripture and Johnson's *Rambler* essays — important to keep in mind because Boswell's direct references to the *Theory of Moral Sentiments* before this date suggest disagreement with Smith's major arguments. At a particularly gloomy moment in his largely bleak Utrecht period, in March 1764, some five years after its first publication, Boswell undertook a serious and careful reading of Smith's treatise. There survives in Boswell's writing unluckily only a bare outline, tantalizingly brief, of his complete response, since his fully written Dutch journal was later lost, and what remain are his memoranda, journal notes and letters to and from friends.

During his stay in Holland, Boswell made his most heroically strenuous and sustained efforts, somewhat against the grain of his natural temperament, at laboriously systematic academic study. As part of this programme, he undertook his serious and careful reading of Smith's book — about which, he reports on 5 March 1764, he had been speaking with Rose, his Scots acquaintance in Utrecht. Boswell's report, because it survives only in notes, is condensed and thus not a little cryptic:

> Yesterday you was gloomy but better. Rose drank coffee with you, and you related to him your having shaved [Boswellian slang for having spoken and behaved foolishly]. This was wrong. Never repeat past follies but to very intimate friends. You talked of Smith's Sympathy, and said that when passion rose high, you had a faculty in your own mind called Reason; you appeal to that. You find he disapproves; you dare not act. This is all within yourself. If you act, he condemns you. There is no occasion for a far-fetched appeal to others, which at best is but vague; and if others are bad, must be bad. Envy cannot be accounted for on Smith's principles. Think on this.[16]

The passage appears to reject Smith's notion of moral conduct as a function of social observation. But, addressing himself in the second person, as he frequently does in his notes and memoranda, Boswell's text implicitly challenges its own claim that ethical self-appraisal is 'within yourself', and it virtually enacts Smith's moral division of the self — the self as agent and the self as that which has internalized the social and morally monitoring gaze of the 'impartial spectator'. Who describes himself as 'gloomy', and who admonishes himself 'never to repeat past follies'? 'Reason', that other standby of Enlightenment epistemology, stands in here for a secular version of conscience. But Boswell's memorandum rapidly personifies Reason, from 'that' ('You appeal to that') to 'he' ('you find he disapproves') — a stern, forbidding preceptor (possibly rooted in his father Lord Auchinleck, or the Calvinist God, and more crucially the legal and judicial proscriptions they both warrant). Moral scrutiny from within an autonomous subject, a personal creed, yields (at least pronominally) to the external. What Boswell thinks of as 'within' the self plainly stands as an internalization of social assessments, producing such emotions as shame at 'past follies'. And that second person pronoun itself moves imperceptibly from the particularity of the Boswellian recording voice to the social 'you' — meaning all people, everyone, the social community.

Boswell's exertions to resist Smith, through a belief in an individuated and self-determining moral identity, show up more clearly two days later (7 March 1764).

> Yesterday you did very well. You thought that Smith's system was running mankind, melting them, into one mass in the crucible of Sympathy. Whereas they are separate beings, and 'tis their duty as rational beings to approach near to each other. You are to give an analysis of Smith's book. (*Holland*, 174)

The analysis, if written, has not survived — appearing if anywhere in the lost Dutch journal. But even here in these brief notes, Boswell's attempt to reject Smith's thinking bumps into implicit concessions to it. His fear that Smith's theories of sympathy obliterate individual human distinction finds curious solace in the idea that our 'duty as rational beings' impels 'separate beings' to approach near to each other. The 'rational' being here, like the 'duty' it undergirds, invites the same remarks as Reason (and conscience) in the earlier entry — an internalized moral monitor.

Later in his continental experiences, Boswell would continue to struggle to shake off his youthful need to absorb the identities of other admired, stable, eminent men, and take pride in himself as an 'original' — but in terms that repeatedly acknowledge his status as moral spectacle in a social theatre. (These Utrecht memoranda themselves, in fact, mark the very act of asserting independence from his former teacher, whose teachings nonetheless still engage him, and mark a local instance of his larger drift in affinities away from his Scottish youth, towards literary ambitions based in London and Johnson). 'I am in reality an original character. Let me moderate and cultivate my originality', he exclaims in Berlin. 'God would not have formed such a diversity of men if he had intended that they should all come up to a certain standard . . . . Let me then be Boswell and render him as fine a fellow as possible' (20 July 1764).[17] This is certainly to say that 'himself' will be a 'rendering' — a theatrical representation. Some weeks later he openly acknowledges that his renderings of himself result from a fear of censure: 'Why seek to please all? Why fear the censure of those whom I despise? Let me boldly pursue my own plan" (6 Aug. 1764; *Grand Tour, Germany*, 51–52); 'I saw my error in suffering so much from the contemplation of others . . . . I must be Mr Boswell of Auchinleck, and no other' (9 Aug. 1764; 53). Smith in the third part of his treatise ('Of the Sense of Duty') writes: 'We can never survey our own sentiments and motives, we can never form any judgment concerning them; unless we remove ourselves, as it were, from our own natural station, and endeavour to view them as at a distance from us.'[18] 'Mr Boswell of Auchinleck' remains ever circumscribed by his occupation of a social theatre, or he could not so denominate himself. As his entries in Utrecht and later in Germany show, Boswell fears loss of individual distinction, melted in a crucible of 'sympathy', but is impelled nonetheless by anxieties of spectatorial assessment it has been Smith's purpose to analyse.

Earlier, in his *London Journal*, Boswell had been more inclined to model his sense of spectatorship on Addison and Steele, a voice of genial, urbane, comprehensively generous distance. Although far from being without sentiment and certain capacities for sympathy, the spectator of Addison and Steele depended more upon a capacity for distanced observation. As Steele wrote in *Spectator* no. 266: 'I have . . . so frequently said that I am wholly unconcerned in any Scene I am in, but merely as a spectator.' Boswell uses the *persona* of the *Spectator* to deflect various kinds of serious emotions, as he uses, most significantly, his fantasy identity of Macheath to deflect moral guilt. Watching himself play Macheath with women of the town allows him to turn transgression into pleasurable theatrical fiction. But the execution of the Macheath-like Paul Lewis provides only the most jarring of several instances that destroy Boswell's illusions of spectatorial distance. When Lewis hangs, powerful senses of guilty fellow-feeling with a dashing, attractive young rebel against moral orthodoxy come into play. The Lewis incident shocks Boswell out of spectatorship as moral detachment; the genial, urbane tone of the *Spectator* essays evaporates, as Boswell freely confesses to his reader, Grange, his terror, horror and inability to sleep alone (*London Journal*, 3–6 May 1763; 250–54).

Spectatorship becomes moral involvement, turning on complex emotional and theatrical substitutions of spectator and sufferer. The execution of Lewis arouses a fellow-feeling that far outstrips the sentimental catharsis Boswell experiences and reports in this journal as a playgoer at Drury Lane and Covent Garden, where his identifications with those Shakespearean son/heroes, princes Hamlet and Hal, engaged like Boswell with powerful fathers and usurpers, can bring tears to his eyes (e.g., 10 Jan. 1763; 134). Such moments mark Boswell's trajectory in this journal away from the Irish actor and elocutionist Thomas Sheridan, whom he had earlier installed as another mentor in Edinburgh (see Pottle, *Earlier Years*, 65), towards Johnson (the two had been separated irreparably over Sheridan's resentment at Johnson's remarks, maliciously reported out of context, on Sheridan's receipt of a royal pension.) Sheridan (though I cannot argue fully for this trajectory here) represents theatre as mere show (voice, elocution); Johnson, ill-disposed towards actors and the theatre, appears at the end of the journal as a figure of the Word as morally weighty, a spectacle of articulacy not as mere voice but as moral monitor. We are reminded that Boswell was first attracted to Johnson as the sturdy moralist of the *Rambler* essays. From mere spectator (Addison and Steele) through theatre (Sheridan) to the *Rambler*: that is Smith's lecture sequence, from rhetoric to ethics.

<h1 style="text-align:center">II</h1>

ALL THE EMOTIONS SHOCKED into agitation by the death of the Macheath-like Paul Lewis —guilt, anxiety about complicity (through fantasy identification with a criminal hero), the internalization of social suppresion, sympathy (or fellow-feeling), fear of ghosts (those phantom representations of an only ambiguously surviving disembodied essence of a self) — strikingly characterize many of the records of Boswell's later legal career, especially his capital criminal cases. Boswell's legal career remains undeservedly neglected. Boswell was a better advocate than popular misapprehension has it, and the cases I am about to mention, while immensely revealing, are emphatically not typical of the routine of his twenty years of practice. Capital criminal trials tended to invade his private records in a way that civil causes usually did not. In his sequence of capital criminal clients, from the luckless receiver of a stolen watch, Robert Hay, to the forger John Raybould, to the sheepstealer John Reid, Boswell records an extraordinary chronicle of Smithian sympathy, not in theoretical abstraction, but lived.

Boswell thought, by the time he went to visit the condemned Robert Hay in prison, that he had won his way to a resistance to sympathy. He hears a sermon and 'doleful' psalms on Sunday in the Tolbooth, and remarks: 'Your mind now so strong' that the scene left 'no impression' (*Wife*, 28). But an earlier entry (11 Feb. 1767) reveals more of Boswell's actual compassion (and introduces, by the by, the question — worthy of separate pursuit — of sympathy and social class): 'Why it is, I know not, but we compassionate less a genteel man' (*Wife*, 26), which means that Boswell feels more sympathy for his social inferiors. And a later entry (2 Apr. 1767), written after Hay's execution, shows Boswell shocked out of his hard-won resistance into a night like those he spent after the demise of Paul Lewis: 'At night had fear of ghosts [thinking of] . . . poor Robert Hay' (*Wife*, 52).

Boswell regularly feared the ghosts of the clients he lost to the gallows — those ghostly demarcations, phantom displacements of the spectatorial self. Boswell absorbs the emotions of the client and therefore, in Smith's sense, sympathizes with him. Smith writes in section 2 of the *Theory of Moral Sentiments*, 'Of Merit and Demerit':

When the guilty is about to suffer that just retaliation, which the natural indignation of mankind tells them is due to his crimes; when the insolence of his injustice is broken and humbled by the terror of his approaching punishment [Smith is carefully unspecific about whether this humbling and this terror is the malefactor's or the spectator's]; when he ceases to be an object of fear, with the generous and humane he begins to be an object of pity. (88)

But in the Hay trial and elsewhere, fear continues to coexist with Boswellian pity: Boswell's moral perplexities stem from senses of complicity both in his client's criminal/heroic defiance of Scots religious/legal authority and in that authority's lethal power over him.

With Boswell's next client to be lost to the scaffold, the forger John Raybould, the degree of imaginative invasion intensfies. With Raybould, Pottle remarks, Boswell 'now begins the macabre practice of exhorting the condemned man and quizzing him as to how he expects to feel in the moment of dissolution' (Pottle, *Earlier Years*, 355). More pointedly, Raybould appears in Boswell's nocturnal disturbances well before his execution (21 Feb. 1768): 'I had dreamt of Raybould under sentence of death. I was gloomy . . . . Tea home, then visited Raybould, that my gloomy imagination might be cured by seeing the reality' (*Wife*,

130). Boswell speaks to Raybould of religion, reads from the Epistle of St John, and marvels at the ease with which Raybould confronts his fate. The conversation between victim and spectator finally resolves itself in a curious exchange of shared sentiment, written up as tactfully as possible:

> He told me when he first came to Scotland he did not know the difference between an agent and an advocate. I saw him beginning to smile at his own ignorance. I considered how amazing it would be if a man under sentence of death should really laugh, and, with the nicest care of a diligent student of human nature, I as decently as possible first smiled as he did, and gradually cherished the risible exertion, till he and I together fairly laughed. (*Wife*, 131)

The tensions of fellow-feeling release themselves in a grimly comic but real-life theatre of contagious shared response.

Three days later, Boswell watches his client's execution, and works hard at emotional resolve: 'I tried to be quite firm and philosophical . . .', but he admits to 'uneasy sensations' as Raybould 'stood long on the ladder' (*Wife*, 131). What dispels Boswell's gloom on this occasion ('When I came home I was a little dreary, but it went off and I slept well') is, significantly, theatre itself (he watches, of all things, *The Beggar's Opera*, far and away the most important fictional work in Boswell's self-conception) and human sociability.

> At night I was with Lady Crawford at *The Beggar's Opera*, which quite relieved any gloom. The songs revived London ideas, and my old intrigues with actresses who used to play in this opera [mainly Mrs Love, who used to play Polly opposite West Digges's Macheath] . . . . The farce was *The Vintner Tricked*. It was curious that after seeing a real hanging I should meet with two mock ones on the stage. (*Wife*, 131–32)

As noted earlier, one of the emotional functions that playgoing performed for Boswell was an innocuous emotional release, a sentimental cartharsis, which produced none of the fear of guilty complicity that executions did. At first he went to see Raybould after his upsetting dream so that, as he said, his 'gloomy imagination might be cured by seeing the reality'; now theatrical executions work cathartically to drive away the image of the real one. In the playhouse, sentimental sociability relieves Boswell of the moral burden of Smithian fellow-feeling.

But that remedy was not to be a permanent one. The most damaging loss for Boswell's legal career came in the cause of the sheepstealer John Reid — well known not just to readers of Boswell's published journals but also to viewers of the televised version of this episode that was co-produced by BBC Scotland and Yale University Films, *Boswell for the Defence* (1983). Though Boswell worked at the law for many years more, this loss, in Brady's words, 'crystallized his distaste for the Scottish bar' and 'destroyed his momentum as a lawyer' (Brady, *Later Years*, 105). His record of the trial summarizes, and is the culmination of, tendencies adumbrated in cases like those of Hay and Raybould. 'I drank tea with Grange,' Boswell reports on 30 August 1774,

> but was gloomy. I had by sympathy sucked the dismal ideas of John Reid's situation, and as spirits or strong substance of any kind, when transferred to another body of a more delicate nature, will have much more influence than on the body from which it is transferred, so I suffered much more than John did. (*Defence*, 288)

To move back in time a little: in three essays for the *London Magazine* in 1770, 'On the Profession of a Player', Boswell explicitly links theatricality and the profession of law, and puzzles over the theatrical quality of the barrister's adoption of a client's part in court. He ponders the 'mysterious power' by which a player 'really is the character which he represents', and explains it as 'a kind of double feeling'; and that feeling 'is experienced in some measure' also 'by the barrister who enters warmly into the cause of his client, while at the same time, when he examines himself coolly, he knows that he is much in the wrong, and does not even wish to prevail'. For Smith, in a very careful paragraph added to the draft revision of the 1759 edition of the *Theory of Moral Sentiments*, the courtroom appears as a metaphoric site of moral spectatorship of the self, and the criminal trial is a figure for ethical self-appraisal:

> When I endeavour to examine my own conduct, when I endeavour to pass sentence upon it, and either to approve or condemn it, it is evident that in all such cases, I divide myself into two persons; and that I, the examiner and judge, represent a different character from that other I, the person whose conduct is examined into and judged of. (113)

In bouts of fellow-feeling for criminal clients — the guilty anti-heroes who populate the remarkable biographical underworld of Boswell's diaries, and are the moral opposites of high-minded figures like Paoli and Johnson — Boswell internalizes the legalistic distributions of praise and blame that structure both classical biography and the workings of criminal justice. As I have suggested, Boswell, in his Dutch journal notes, literalizes Smith's metaphor of the courtroom as a figurative locus of moral self-appraisal: the self that acts and the self that is acted upon by societal assessments become the 'I' who speaks in the journal and the 'you' of the self-admonitory notes and memoranda.

Subtle intellectual nuances inform, then, Boswell's swerve from Edinburgh to London, from a career in law in which language has the capacity to incarcerate and destroy, to a career in biography, in which language has the capacity to confer a kind of immortality. The swerve was made via Glasgow. It would be to the *Life of Johnson* that Boswell would turn most effectively what W. Jackson Bate terms his 'gift for empathy and dramatic imitation'. Although Boswell's journal is the output of the endlessly self-generating textual self, Boswell remained always inscribed within systems of social arbitration, with an acute consciousness of how each utterance and gesture would look to a spectatorial gaze. When, more than twenty years after his first meeting with Johnson, recorded memorably in the *London Journal*, Boswell came to rewrite the scene for inclusion in the *Life*, he added some remarkable details. As if in obedience to the dead King Hamlet's injunction to 'remember!', Boswell's memory retrieves the wit of Tom Davies, who Horatio-like announces to Boswell/Hamlet Johnson's unexpected arrival with: 'Look, my Lord, it comes' (*Life*, 16 May 1763; 277). This is no longer the ghost of guilty criminal complicity, but a playful theatrical fiction from the sympathetic Davies: Johnson appears as the admonishing father, when the expectations of the public were prodding the guiltily procrastinating Boswell into the arduous and in the end heroic task of assembling his biography. It is the benign spectre of Johnson, not the lost souls of the criminal clients, that is permanently alive in the *Life*, and Boswell's long wrestling with the moral demands of the sympathetic absorption of character would find its fullest expression in his innovative biography — impregnated as he was by the Johnsonian ether. An instability at the boundaries of his identity is usually used to castigate Boswell, in the personality-bashing tradition from Macaulay to Donald Greene; yet that instability is one of the conditions Smith's theory presupposes for the very possibility of social harmony, and one of the conditions that made possible the most influential contribution to literary biography ever written.

Notes

1. Frederick A. Pottle, 'Boswell's University Education', in *Johnson, Boswell and Their Circle: Essays Presented to L. F. Powell* (Oxford, 1965), 245.
2. Frederick A. Pottle discusses Boswell's course in arts at the University of Edinburgh in *James Boswell: The Earlier Years, 1740–1769*, esp. 23ff. He notes the impact on Boswell's mind of John Stevenson's class in logic, which 'had a lasting effect on Boswell . . . both for good and for evil'. The metaphysics in Stevenson's course proved to be 'unsettling', but Stevenson also 'opened and enriched his mind' by introducing him to great works of ancient and modern literature, and a 'more coherent and comprehensive foundation for criticism than he is commonly supposed to have had' (25).
3. Frank Brady, *James Boswell: The Later Years, 1769–1795* (New York, 1984).
4. *Boswell: Laird of Auchinleck, 1778–1782*, ed. Joseph W. Reed and Frederick A. Pottle (New York, 1979), 135. The journal entry, in which Boswell records his conversation with Smith (who had been appointed commissioner of customs two years earlier) at the Edinburgh customs house, expresses Boswell's annoyance also at Smith's attack on English university education,

in *An Inquiry into the Nature and Causes of the Wealth of Nations*, ed. R. H. Campbell, A. S. Skinner and W. B. Todd, 2 vols. (Oxford, 1976), bk. 5. 'Since his absurd eulogium on Hume and his ignorant, ungrateful attack on the English university education, I have had no desire to be much with him. Yet I do not forget that he was very civil to me at Glasgow.' See also the entry for 29 Sept. 1780 (*Laird*, 255, and n. 4a).

5. James Boswell, *Life of Johnson*, ed. R. W. Chapman, rev. J. D. Fleeman (Oxford, 1980), 14 July 1763, 303.

6. *Boswell: The Ominous Years, 1774–1776*, ed. Charles Ryskamp and Frederick A. Pottle (New York, 1963), 115.

7. *Boswell: The Applause of the Jury, 1782–1785*, ed. Irma S. Lustig and Frederick A. Pottle (New York, 1981), 107–8.

8. W. Jackson Bate, *Samuel Johnson* (New York, 1975), 364.

9. *Boswell for the Defence, 1769–1774*, ed. William K. Wimsatt and Frederick A. Pottle (New York, 1959), 288. For a fuller discussion of the Reid trial, see Gordon Turnbull, 'Boswell and Sympathy: The Trial and Execution of John Reid', in *New Light on Boswell*, ed. Greg Clingham (Cambridge, 1991), chap. 7. See below, 173.

10. Alastair Fowler, *A History of English Literature* (Oxford, 1987, rev. paperback ed., 1989), 177.

11. Peter Conrad, *The Everyman History of English Literature* (London, 1985), 382.

12. For a full discussion of the idea of theatricality in the *Theory of Moral Sentiments*, see David Marshall, *The Figure of Theater: Shaftesbury, Defoe, Adam Smith, and George Eliot* (New York, 1986). ·

13. *Boswell's London Journal, 1762–1763*, ed. Frederick A. Pottle (New York, 1950).

14. *The Correspondence of James Boswell and John Johnston of Grange*, ed. Ralph S. Walker (New York, 1966), 7.

15. Margaret Montgomerie to Boswell, received 4 July 1769, in *Boswell in Search of a Wife, 1766–1769*, ed. Frank Brady and Frederick A. Pottle (New York, 1956), 218; and 17 Oct. 1769, *Wife*, 336.

16. *Boswell in Holland, 1763–1764*, ed. Frederick A. Pottle (New York, 1952), 174.

17. *Boswell on the Grand Tour: Germany and Switzerland, 1764*, ed. Frederick A. Pottle (New York, 1953), 29.

18. *The Theory of Moral Sentiments*, ed. D. D. Raphael and A. L. Macfie (Oxford, 1976), 110.

9

John Moore, the Medical Profession
and the Glasgow Enlightenment

H. L. Fulton

D r John Moore (1729–1802), the father of Sir John Moore of
Corunna, lived in Glasgow from 1736 to 1777. Trained in medicine, apprenticed in the city and educated there and abroad, he
practised his profession until 1772, when he accepted the position as tutor
and travelling physician to the young duke of Hamilton, with whom he
lived in Europe for nearly five years. A year after his return to Glasgow,
Moore gave up practice, moved to London (as his cousin Tobias Smollett
had done thirty years earlier) and remained in England until his death
in 1802. There he earned a reputation for his contributions to popular
literature and his liberal political views.

This chapter is chiefly concerned not with Moore's London years or his
close connections with Smollett, whose life he not only wrote but to some
extent emulated,[1] but rather with Moore as a representative figure of the
Enlightenment in Glasgow. The Scottish Enlightenment is sometimes
depicted as an urban intellectual phenomenon based in Edinburgh. There
is a danger, however, in evaluating the Glasgow Enlightenment in those
terms. Because Glasgow was a different city, governed by merchant life,
commercial development, foreign trade and 'popular' preaching, any
criteria evaluating Glasgow's contribution to this urban intellectual and
social phenomenon must take the city's particular history into account.
Whereas Nicholas Phillipson stated in 1973 that 'there is an important
sense in which the history of the Scottish enlightenment *is* the history
of Edinburgh', an influential essay published by Roger Emerson in that
same year implied that Glasgow's Enlightenment should be evaluated
according to different criteria and emphases from its eastern neighbour.[2]

Emerson's message must be taken seriously. Recent commentators on
the Enlightenment in Edinburgh have noted some conservative political
tendencies, which aimed to justify the social *status quo* and protect
the interests of the political and intellectual establishment.[3] But one
cannot equate the career and intellectual interests of John Moore with
the conservative Edinburgh Enlightenment because Moore grew up in

a different city and followed a different professional path. If the essential aspect of the Enlightenment in Edinburgh is 'order', as Thomas Markus seems to believe,[4] then perhaps the essential aspect of the Enlightenment in Glasgow is 'improvement' and civic development. The chief manifestations of Enlightenment that characterize John Moore and the city he hailed from are a concern for education, a receptivity to foreign influences, a desire to modernize one's profession and a wish to improve the urban environment. All these interests are progressive and consistent with the aims of a city concerned largely with foreign trade and economic development, as well as with an applied science curriculum of the kind that was promulgated in Anderson's Institution.

I

FOLLOWING THESE CRITERIA, I shall focus on certain aspects of Moore's career and make the case that he was one of eighteenth-century Glasgow's most 'enlightened' figures. Moore was initially a child of the Glasgow Enlightenment, in the sense that Glasgow trained him in medicine, and what we know of his profession suggests that he kept himself at the forefront of his trade. But in more general, cosmopolitan ways he deserves our attention because of his lifelong interest in comparative culture and political ideas. I am interested specifically in the impact of Montesquieu on his work, his sympathy for natural law theories and his enthusiasm for the French Revolution.

A good place to begin this inquiry is in 1742, when Moore, at the age of twelve, matriculated at Glasgow University under the professor of humanity, George Rosse.[5] Rosse's class reinforced the rigorous preparation in Latin that Moore had received at the Glasgow Grammar School. Even in his last years, Moore was able to quote his favourite Latin authors — Horace, Juvenal and Tacitus — from memory and with affection. Besides Rosse's humanity class, Moore attended Glasgow University at a most propitious time. Among its twelve professors were Alexander Dunlop, perhaps the most distinguished professor of Greek in Scotland and the leader of the progressive party in the faculty;[6] the eminent geometrician Robert Simson; and most outstanding of all, Francis Hutcheson, who taught moral philosophy, and has often been called 'the father of the Scottish Enlightenment'.[7] In 1743 the faculty would be enriched with the addition of William Leechman in divinity, and the following year William Cullen would come up from Hamilton to lecture on medical and chemical subjects.

The physical setting was equally becoming. Compared to the college buildings in Edinburgh, which have been characterized as 'makeshift and mean', the buildings below Glasgow Cathedral on the High Street were 'handsome . . . commodious . . . and comfortable', consisting of several quadrangles of two storeys and courtyards, containing classrooms, reception halls, a library and an adjoining plaza for professors' lodgings.[8] The students seemed as promising as the faculty and buildings. Alexander Carlyle observed that at this time 'there appeared to be a marked superiority in the best scholars and most diligent students in Edinburgh, yet in Glasgow, learning seemed to be an object of more importance, and the habit of application was much more general.'[9]

The hunger for learning and 'improvement' may have been due to the composition of the student body. W. M. Mathew suggests that Glasgow was less a 'professional' university (i.e., preparing boys for vocations in medicine, law and the church) than the other three Scottish universities and was more oriented towards a general and practical curriculum. Its student body resembled that of a modern North American municipal university more than a 'private' school. Of the estimated 580 students enrolled between 1740 and 1749, sixteen percent of their fathers were ministers of the kirk, but fully twenty-six percent of the boys had fathers in commerce. Of the more than one hundred students whose later occupations are known, almost a quarter went on to some career in commerce or government, rather than the liberal professions.[10]

Other than Rosse and Dunlop, one cannot be sure which professors Moore studied with. Very likely he took Hutcheson's moral philosophy class in the third year of his arts course, but soon after matriculating he was persuaded by a fellow student to follow medicine, training for which was undertaken by the Faculty of Physicians and Surgeons of the city, separate from the university. Candidates in medicine were booked apprentices for five years, though the actual term in nearly every case was only three.[11] If ever there were an aspect of city life where attempts were made to 'improve' the general welfare of Glasgow, it could be found in medicine — specifically from the time when the university hired William Cullen for the purpose of establishing a medical curriculum.[12]

Moore's masters, William Stirling and John Gordon, comprised the most distinguished medical copartnership in Glasgow. Stirling, licensed to practice since 1712, came from a prominent family in western Scotland.[13] In Smollett's *Humphry Clinker*, Matthew Bramble calls Gordon a 'patriot of a truly Roman spirit . . . the great promoter of the city workhouse, infirmary and other works of public utility. Had he lived in ancient Rome, he would have been honoured with a statue at the public expence.'[14] Perhaps more than any other member of the medical establishment, Gordon had a strong interest in public health, which he passed on to Moore. Coutts cites him as the first to offer lectures in anatomy at the university, some time before the establishment of a chair in that subject. Frequent references to Gordon in the burgh minutes attest to his collaboration with Stirling in seeing to the city's indigent. The great teacher of midwifery in the early half of the century, William Smellie of Greenock, said that he learned the obstetrical use of the blunt hook from Gordon (Coutts, *University of Glasgow*, 484). Gordon was one of the most 'enlightened' physicians in the west of Scotland during the early eighteenth century, and his work was seminal in the medical improvement of the city. Until Cullen arrived to inaugurate a formal curriculum of lectures at the university, however, there was no programme of academic study in medicine comparable to that at Edinburgh.

Medical instruction commenced the year before Moore matriculated, and by the time of his apprenticeship, Robert Hamilton, a student of Herman Boerhaave at Leiden University and the first of several Hamiltons to teach at Glasgow, began lecturing in anatomy with the permission of the incumbent, Thomas Brisbane, while John Crawfurd lectured in surgery.[15] We know that Moore studied with Hamilton. When Cullen arrived in 1744, he came without a chair, but his political connections secured him the next best thing, a university lectureship apparently created just for him. That autumn Cullen began to lecture extramurally on the theory and practice of 'physick', and after a suspension of a year while the Pretender was active in the neighbourhood, he resumed lecturing, along with Hamilton and George Montgomerie (*Glasgow Journal*, 27 Sept. 1742 and 15 Sept. 1746). He offered his course in English — still something of an innovation, though Hutcheson and Andrew Rosse had done this in Glasgow before him.

After the death of Boerhaave, Cullen and his Scottish colleagues took the lead in medical instruction in Europe. Before he left Glasgow for Edinburgh in 1756, Cullen was known as the most popular lecturer in medical subjects in the United Kingdom. Arthur Donovan states that as a teacher Cullen was 'no mere conformist; he was a daring and innovative teacher and a lecturer whose instruction sparkled with a vitalizing purposiveness that looked beyond the confines of the specific subjects he taught.'[16] In addition to the manner in which he organized his lectures, he was known for his critical, sceptical approach to his material, which may explain why he waited so long to place his work in print. We can be certain that Moore attended Montgomerie's and Cullen's lectures on the theory and practice of medicine.

The greater amount of practical, clinical instruction that Moore received was at the hands of Stirling and Gordon, and one of the best opportunities came through their long-standing association with the Touns Hospital. Established in 1733 with the special encouragement of Gordon,[17] to provide for the health and education of the poor and to be a kind of workhouse, the Touns Hospital enlisted the services of the medical corporation of Glasgow at first gratuitously, but eventually paying a small salary. Its directors recognized the need to isolate the sick from the merely indigent, and in 1739 they created a separate infirmary, staffed with its own nurses and keeper — a development that signifies the first step in the gradual process of converting the

European hospital into a clinic for modern medical instruction.[18] This new building accommodated thirty-six beds with room for expansion, cells for the mad and a large anatomical chamber, 'well illuminated where it is intended that the Physician who attends the Hospital shall give lectures to the Apprentices of Chirugeons or other Students, upon the diseases which may prevail in the Infirmary.' In this addition were treated 'many Rhumatick Fevers, Pleuritick Disorders, Inveterate Scurvies, scropulous Distempers, Jaundice, Dropsies', etc.[19] This hospital and infirmary was located on the Old Green along the Clyde, at the foot of the Saltmercat, where Moore lived with his mother and sisters.

In John Gordon, Moore was fortunate to have an enlightened master who was interested in the problems of midwives and difficult deliveries. Since the 1720s, before Gordon first came to know Smellie, he had been concerned in the practical aspects of deliveries and the training of midwives, and in 1739 the Faculty of Physicians and Surgeons, in lieu of a chair of midwifery at the university, took steps to train and license midwives in the greater Glasgow area, including Lanark, Ayrshire, Renfrew and Dumbartonshire. Although licensing midwives was permitted under the royal charter of 1599, the faculty had never asserted this prerogative, preferring to allow women to handle such matters according to traditional practice. However, Smellie was lecturing on midwifery in London, and Edinburgh University had had a chair in this subject since 1726. Under these circumstances, Glasgow decided to upgrade the work of the local women by instruction and examination, with no other object than to prohibit the ignorant from practice. Between 1741 and 1743, more than thirty candidates were examined, and twenty-eight approved.[20] As apprentice to Gordon, Moore was in a good position to learn midwifery firsthand, and in subsequent years he continued his interest in this area.

After three years as an apprentice, Moore received permission to seek further training abroad and signed on as a surgeon's assistant with the North British Fusiliers, on campaign during the War of Austrian Secession. In 1747 this move was not considered unusual. The need to broaden one's medical training, even in service outside the kingdom, was generally acknowledged; Smollett had done so eight years earlier. Moore was stationed at the hospital at Maestricht for the better part of a year.[21] After that he went to London to study with William Hunter, another of Scotland's great physicians.[22] Hunter, unlike his competitors, advertised that 'Gentlemen may have the opportunity of learning the Art of Dissecting . . . in the same manner as at Paris', which meant that, however he managed it, every student would have his own cadaver.[23] It is thought that Moore also studied with William Smellie, with whom Hunter had boarded when he first came to London in 1739. Moore became something of an authority on midwifery in Glasgow in the 1760s and probably learned its secrets from both Hunter and Smellie. Moore may have met Smollett at this time as well — perhaps through Hunter.

In the late spring of 1749, when the preliminaries of the peace had been signed, Hunter, Moore and other Scots left for the Continent. Moore was to serve as family surgeon to the duke of Albemarle in Paris, attend lectures in medicine with the famous Jean Astruc and study dissection at the municipal hospitals. A detailed account of his activities was submitted to Cullen.[24] Moore remained in France for two years, giving rise to his life-long enthusiasm for that country. In the spring of 1750 he received an offer from Gordon to join the partnership in Glasgow, since Stirling was leaving to go into business. Having planned a career in military medicine, Moore was initially reluctant to accept, even though Glasgow offered the prospect of a secure future. But after stopping in London for a refresher course with Hunter, he finally returned to his native city.

The point of this narrative is to show that Moore was a physician who studied widely with different masters and sat at the feet of some of the most famous physicians and medical teachers of his day. His training exemplifies two developments in medical instruction in Scotland in the mid-eighteenth century. One can simply be called 'pragmatic' because it emphasized direct observation of symptoms and a practical response to them. His apprenticeship with Gordon would have conveyed that. Similarly, in the training of male-midwives, study with William Smellie, Gordon's former student, would have concentrated on 'problem' deliveries.

The other development could be termed 'polite', a concept of critical importance in the study of the Enlightenment in Scotland. In medicine this concept was conveyed by William Cullen, who always taught his medical students to be respectable physicians,[25] and by Cullen's former pupil William Hunter, who taught his pupils in male-midwifery to develop their reputations beyond difficult deliveries by becoming fashionable and popular *accoucheurs*.[26] When Moore was approached by Gordon, he was fairly young — only twenty-one — but he was obviously mature and competent. And he had been very well prepared.

Upon returning to Glasgow, Moore distinguished himself as a participant in the public health and improvement of the city. In the eighteenth century this meant epidemics. If the bills of mortality in Glasgow can be admitted as evidence of his medical concerns, Moore spent more time in pediatrics than with adult diseases. Much to which his patients were exposed was mortal and beyond cure. By far the most fatal child-killer was smallpox, even though the eighteenth century saw the discovery and development of the technique that ultimately eradicated it. Although a recent medical historian supposes that variolation did not take hold in the Scottish Lowlands until later (Hamilton, *Healers*, 96), the Glasgow Faculty of Physicians and Surgeons became involved in this practice early in the 1750s, with Gordon and Moore leading the way. The *Glasgow Courant* reported on 13 June 1756 that out of 651 persons innoculated since 1752, only one had died. Later in that decade Moore assumed the chief care of the ill in the Touns Hospital.

But Moore soon wearied of the daily routine of general practice and looked for ways to alter his employment while augmenting his income. When in 1762 the newly crowned George III made available £1000 'for the Encouragement of Arts and Sciences in Scotland' — doubtless a concession to Lord Bute — Moore approached his kinsman, William Mure of Caldwell, who had succeeded Lord Milton as manager for Scottish affairs, about being appointed to a new chair of midwifery at Glasgow. His petition was ably seconded by another close friend, the Glasgow University professor of natural philosophy, John Anderson, who was always zealous about proposals of practical benefit to the city.[27] The chair was not established at that time, and Moore advertised extramural instruction in midwifery in the *Glasgow Courant* for 10 March 1763.

Although Moore made several other attempts to join the ranks of the university, he was never destined to become part of it. The closest he ever came to the faculty was through friendships and marriage ties. Soon after returning to Glasgow, Moore married Jean, elder daughter of the late John Simson, the Glasgow divinity professor who had been relieved of his teaching duties in 1729 on charges of heresy. Moore did not gain membership in the Glasgow Literary Society, which was principally composed of university faculty from the time of its foundation in 1752, but with several merchants of his own age he established in the same year a debating and social society, the Hodge-Podge Club, which included one professor from the university, Alexander Stevenson. This group started with lofty aspirations, as the manuscript records show, but after about two years the members settled into a more prosaic routine of fellowship, toasts and card games.[28] During this period, when he was otherwise busy building up his clientele and raising a numerous family, his closest friend was the professor of civil law, John Millar.[29]

II

MOORE CONTINUED IN MEDICAL PRACTICE until 1772, when a series of circumstances resulted in the opportunity to travel abroad with the duke of Hamilton. According to the generous terms of this arrangement, Moore was able to retire from medical practice to pursue a writing career. In an 'autobiographical letter' to his children, he confessed that 'I had no great taste for the Manners of the inhabitants of Glasgow', and that while abroad with the duke had 'taken a great dislike to return to the Profession of Medicine — I preferred a Moderate income in any Other respectable way to the greatest that could be acquired by visiting Sick people . . . . I had uneasiness & disgust in that of rolling thro' the Streets from Morning [sic] from One disease to another.'[30] What chiefly attracted Moore abroad was the chance to change careers. His only published work on medicine, *Medical Sketches* (1786), summarizes his disenchantment with actual medical practice. He had come to feel strongly that, with few exceptions, no medicines he dispensed did much good:

> It is astonishing how exceedingly apt medical practitioners of every denomination are to impute to drugs that salutary effect which proceeds from the universal influence of another cause. . . . This *vis medicatrix naturae*, this constant tendency in nature to overcome disease . . . is acknowledged by all candid and discerning practitioners to have a powerful influence in the cure of diseases.[31]

In reaching this conclusion, Moore remained sceptical that anything else would work.

Yet one wonders what other personal feelings lay behind his decision to quit the city of his childhood and adult years. Had the affected manners of the wealthier and more successful tobacco lords proved more than he could stomach?[32] He could not have felt sympathetic to the 'popular' vein of preaching in the Glasgow pulpits, or to the clerical resistance to theatre in the city, led by his neighbour, Revd John Gillies. Excluded from the university, did he find himself increasingly grouped with the wrong party in town-gown relations? Whatever disgusted him about life in Glasgow, Moore became part of the 'brain drain' that eroded the intellectual life of that city around mid-century and included such luminaries as Smollett, Smellie, the Hunter brothers, Cullen, Adam Smith and Joseph Black.

As soon as Moore returned from his tour of duty with the duke and moved his family to London, he began to revise his travel journals with an eye towards publication. *A View of Society and Manners in France, Switzerland, and Germany* appeared in 1779; *A View of Society and Manners in Italy* came two years later. Both were very successful.[33] The titles imply an interest in drawing general conclusions from particular observations. Throughout both books Moore was predominantly interested in describing the governments and customs of the countries he visited, and he frequently attempted to summarize the *'esprit général'*, the *'caractère commun'* of the natives. Occasional references to Montesquieu reveal Moore's acquaintance with *De l'esprit des lois* (1748), which he may have read as early as 1750, when he was in Paris with Smollett, and perhaps discussed with John Millar sometime later. When Moore settled with the duke of Hamilton outside Geneva in 1773, Montesquieu was the French author they spent the most time studying.[34] Like so many other Scottish intellectuals, Moore was fascinated with the ideas of the French thinker.

Montesquieu was just one of many French authors Moore absorbed during his Glasgow years. Citations in his works reveal an acquaintance with La Bruyère, Boileau and Rousseau. Epigrams of La Rochefoucauld are cited twelve times in his most famous novel, *Zeluco* (1798), and his travel books cite *La Nouvelle Eloise* (1762). Yet Moore in his observations seems always to have in mind the principal tenets of *De l'esprit des lois*. As he recounts the customs of a continental city or small principality, he is always wondering whether there is a dominant trait of character peculiar to the people of a particular nation; whether this character is determined by climate or any other physical or moral cause; and whether the laws of the people are the necessary result of the other factors that Montesquieu claimed directly influenced (or should influence) them, such as religion, customs and manners. Moore discovered a number of instances where Montesquieu's principles seem to have been borne out, but his predominant reaction tends to be sceptical. The prevailing factor Moore found to shape laws, governance and custom was simple habit or precedent, however irrational, often carried to unreasonable lengths.

I can offer no more than a cursory look at the way some of Montesquieu's ideas are reflected in Moore's travel writing. While travelling in Italy, after several years in northern Europe, Moore's attention was caught by contrasts. In the Italian states he witnessed the interaction of Catholicism, post-feudal governance, commerce, poverty and happiness. Although Moore tended to be cynical towards governments that employed religion, superstition and ceremony to subdue their subjects, he was able to appreciate, much in the pragmatic spirit of Montesquieu, the benefits of the peasants living around Naples, blessed with several natural advantages. Nor did he, like some Edinburgh moralists, presume a necessary connection between political liberty and happiness:

> I have seen far more poverty than misery. Even the extremity of indigence is accompanied with less wretchedness here than in many other countries. This is partly owing to the climate and fertility of the soil, and partly to the peaceable, religious, and contented disposition of the people. (*Manners in Italy*, letter 73)

By contrast, the common people of the German states must work; their alternative is indeed misery. Peasants of southern Italy can be happy while idle; moreover,

> they discover a species of sedate sensibility to every sense of enjoyment, from which, perhaps, they derive a greater degree of happiness than any of the other [peoples]. The frequent processions and religious ceremonies, amusing and comforting them, serve to fill up their time, and prevent that ennui, and those immoral practices, which are apt to accompany poverty and idleness.

Moore does not mean to sound condescending here: better there were industry, which would augment the riches of everyone, 'yet the general happiness, which is a more important object, will be promoted by blending the occupation of industry with a considerable proportion of such superstitious ceremonies as awaken the future hopes without lulling the present benevolence of the multitude', that is, adapting commerce to the traditional mores of the area. Wherever there is poverty, there will be a greater degree of religious credulity. But of greater consequence is the general welfare, and these peasants in southern Italy were in his opinion 'unquestionably in a more comfortable state than a benevolent mind could wish them' (*Manners in Italy*, letter 73).

Moore's strong partiality towards the liberties guaranteed by the British constitution made him seek them everywhere, and the longest section of *Manners in Italy*, on Venice, narrates how this proud republic, 'founded on the first law of human nature, and the undoubted rights of men' (letter 7), came to sacrifice its ancient liberty of the subjects for the sake of political security. In his time it functioned as little more than a small despotism, completely at the mercy of the Council of Ten and the State Inquisitors. Why did Venice continue to tolerate the unlimited power of these institutions when it lay wholly in the nobles' power to revoke it? In this as elsewhere among the peoples of Italy, Moore found the force of custom and precedent to be stronger than any scientific circumstance that Montesquieu could have identified. In other words, they would endure the terror of their own evil rather than suffer political change. 'The prejudices which each particular nation acquires in favour of its own are difficult to be removed', even though they support an intolerable political system (letter 22). Similarly, the landlords in Naples could improve the general welfare if only they would grant leases to their tenant farmers, but 'the love of domineering is so predominent in the breasts of men who have been accustomed to it from their infancy, that . . . many of them would rather submit to be themselves slaves . . . than become perfectly independent [if it meant] giving independence to their vassals' (letter 58).

In one of the most strikingly radical passages in *Manners on Italy*, Moore declares:

Let the princes be distinguished by splendour and magnificence; let the great and the rich have their luxuries; but in the name of humanity, let the poor, who are willing to labour, have food in abundance to satisfy the cravings of nature, and raiment to defend them from the inclemencies of the weather!

If their governors, whether from weakness or neglect, do not supply them with these, they certainly have a right to help themselves. — Every law of equity and common sense will justify them, in revolting against such governors, and in satisfying their own wants from the superfluities of lazy luxury. (letter 59)

This passage provides a suitable transition to the subject of Moore's radicalism. When Moore moved to London in 1777, he quickly associated himself with the Foxite Whigs; at the outbreak of the French Revolution his closest friends in London were dissenting members of Parliament like William Smith, as well as radical writers like Helen Maria Williams, Samuel Rogers, Henry Fuseli, Mrs Barbauld and John Millar's most notorious student, the earl of Lauderdale. He even become a close friend of one of London's most infamous radicals, Tom Paine. When the revolution broke out in 1789, Moore was overjoyed, and the next six or seven years were completely given over to the contemplation of events across the Channel. Closer to political developments than if he had remained in the North, Moore entertained the most partial enthusiasm for the proceedings of the various elected assemblies in France, which filled him and many other radical Whigs in England with hope that the nation he loved would soon experience the liberties and privileges the British had enjoyed since 1689. After one evening with Paine in 1791, he remarked:

> This [man] has an inveterate [aversion] to Monarchy & is Zealous to have it over thrown all the World over . . . . He is convinced that Mankind would be happier by the Republican form of Government. . . . For my part I Suppose that the Republican form may be the best on the whole which is not quite proved, Still I imagine we ought not to push thro' bloodshed & a Civil war to attain it, if a Mild limited Monarchy is in our power without bloodshed — [However,] the difference between a free Government & a Dogmatic one is so Great that the former can hardly be purchased by Mankind at too high a price.[35]

What ultimately became of Moore's ardent enthusiasm for developments in France is the subject of another study. Suffice it to say that he found subsequent events in both France and England disillusioning, although he held out to the last for a cessation to the war.[36]

III

THIS ACCOUNT OF MOORE'S LIFE is a study of enlightened influences, medical and literary, shaped in part by the city that nurtured him in his younger years, but which he ultimately abandoned. As a representative of the Scottish Enlightenment, he is a singular figure. As a lover of liberty, he resembles to some extent the 'popular' clergy in the Glasgow pulpits during the 1760s; but on account of his rejection of his mother's Calvinism and his sympathy for his wife's beleaguered father, he cannot stand with them. Moore is a complex example, a Glasgow example, of an enlightened Scottish writer who carried his liberal sentiments out of his native land and displayed them in Europe and London. We see in the cases of James Thomson, Smollett and others what can happen to a Scottish literary figure who flees his native hills for richer pasturage: he becomes a writer to a larger audience. Although he ultimately seems to have had more in common with French thinkers and Thomas Paine, Moore as an émigré remained a prototypical Scot.

Notes

1. Both Smollett and Moore were apprenticed to the same surgeons in Glasgow, augmented their training with military experience and travel and quit their

intended careers in order to pursue a literary life in London. They kept up a fairly regular correspondence, and Moore became one of Smollett's first biographers.

2. Phillipson, 'Towards a Definition of the Scottish Enlightenment', and Emerson, 'The Enlightenment and Social Structures', both in *City and Society in the Eighteenth Century*, ed. Paul Fritz and David Williams (Toronto, 1973), 99–143, quoting Phillipson at 125.

3. Among these are Thomas A. Markus's study of the political function of classical architecture in Edinburgh, 'Buildings for the Sad, the Bad and the Mad in Urban Scotland 1780–1830', in *Order in Space and Society: Architectural Form and Its Context in the Scottish Enlightenment*, ed. Thomas A. Markus (Edinburgh, 1982), 25–114; Richard B. Sher's study of the conservative thinking of the William Robertson circle of Moderate Edinburgh churchmen, *Church and University in the Scottish Enlightenment: The Moderate Literati of Edinburgh* (Princeton, 1985), esp. 175–212; and T. M. Devine's essay on the failure of radical reform in the 1790s, 'The Failure of Radical Reform in Scotland in the Late Eighteenth Century: The Social and Economic Context', in *Conflict and Stability in Scottish Society 1700–1850*, ed. T. M. Devine (Edinburgh, 1990), 51–64.

4. Markus, 'Buildings and the Ordering of Minds and Bodies', in *Philosophy and Science in the Scottish Enlightenment*, ed. Peter Jones (Edinburgh, 1988), 169.

5. *The Matriculation Albums of the University of Glasgow from 1728 to 1858*, ed. W. Innes Addison (Glasgow, 1913), 29a.

6. William Robert Scott, *Francis Hutcheson: His Life, Teaching and Position in the History of Philosophy* (1900; rpt. New York, 1966), 82.

7. Gladys Bryson, *Man and Society: The Scottish Inquiry of the Eighteenth Century* (Princeton, 1945), 8; T. D. Campbell, 'Francis Hutcheson: "Father" of the Scottish Enlightenment', in *The Origins and Nature of the Scottish Enlightenment*, ed. R. H. Campbell and Andrew S. Skinner (Edinburgh, 1982), 167.

8. Frederick A. Pottle, *James Boswell: The Earlier Years, 1740–1769* (New York, 1966), 42.

9. *The Autobiography of Dr. Alexander Carlyle of Inveresk, 1722–1805*, new ed., ed. John Hill Burton (London and Edinburgh, 1910), 79.

10. W. M. Mathew, 'The Origins and Occupations of Glasgow Students, 1740–1839', *Past and Present* 33 (1966):90. Nine percent of the Glasgow students followed a career in medicine.

11. H. L. Fulton, 'Smollett's Apprenticeship, 1736–1739', *Studies in Scottish Literature* 15 (1980):175–86.

12. On the establishment of the medical programme at Glasgow in the 1740s, including Cullen's role, see James Coutts, *A History of the University of Glasgow* (Glasgow, 1909), 476–511; John D. Comrie, *A History of Scottish Medicine*, 2nd ed., 2 vols. (London, 1932), 343–62; John Thomson, *An Account of the Life, Lectures and Writings of William Cullen, M.D.*, 2 vols. (Edinburgh and London, 1859); John Glaister, *Dr. William Smellie and*

his Contemporaries (Glasgow, 1894); A. Freeland Fergus, *The Origin and Development of the Glasgow School of Medicine* (Glasgow, 1911); and David Hamilton, *The Healers: A History of Medicine in Scotland* (Edinburgh, 1981), 124–26.

13. His family endowed the Stirling Library in the city. See Andrew Duncan, *Memorials of the Faculty of Physicians and Surgeons of Glasgow, 1599–1850* (Glasgow, 1896), 250, and T. M. Devine, *The Tobacco Lords: A Study of the Tobacco Merchants of Glasgow and their Trading Activities, c. 1740–90* (Edinburgh, 1975), 39.

14. Tobias Smollett, *The Expedition of Humphry Clinker*, ed. Thomas R. Preston (Athens, Ga., 1990), 239.

15. According to Coutts, *University of Glasgow*, 485, Brisbane 'had a rooted aversion to Anatomy and would not face the work of dissection'.

16. A. L. Donovan, *Philosophical Chemistry in the Scottish Enlightenment: The Doctrines and Discoveries of William Cullen and Joseph Black* (Edinburgh, 1975), 3.

17. Andrew Brown, *History of Glasgow*, 3 vols. (Glasgow, 1795), 2:47.

18. E. Ackerknecht, *Medicine at the Paris Hospital, 1794–1848* (Baltimore, 1979), 17; Othmar Keel, 'The Politics of Health and the Institutionalization of Clinical Practice in Europe in the Second Half of the Eighteenth Century', in *William Hunter and the Eighteenth-Century Medical World*, ed. W. F. Bynum and Roy Porter (Cambridge, 1985), 220.

19. *Regulations for the Touns Hospital of Glasgow, with an Introduction Containing a View of the Hospital and the Management of the Poor* (Glasgow, 1830), 6, and *A Short Account of the Touns Hospital in Glasgow, with the Regulations and Abstracts of the Expenses for the First Eight Years*, 3rd ed. (Glasgow, 1743), 23. The arrangement in this institution was a slightly expanded reproduction of what Toby Gelfand calls the 'ideal' Boerhaavian clinic — beds for six males and six females — a limited selection of patients for more focused examination. See Gelfand, 'The Hospice of the Paris College of Surgery (1774–1793), a Unique and Invaluable Institution', *Bulletin of the History of Medicine* 47 (1973): 375, and Keel, 'Politics of Health', 235.

20. MS Minutes of the Faculty of Physicians and Surgeons, Royal College of Physicians and Surgeons, Glasgow.

21. A medical account of this campaign can be found in Sir John Pringle, *Observations on the Diseases of the Army* (London, 1752).

22. *The Works of John Moore, M.D. with Memoirs of his Life and Writings*, ed. Robert Anderson, 7 vols. (Edinburgh, 1820), 1:iv-vi. Anderson's memoir provides the general outline of Moore's medical training.

23. George C. Peachey, *A Memoir of William and John Hunter* (Plymouth, 1924), 80.

24. GUL, Cullen Papers; Thomson, *Life of Cullen*, 1:585–87.

25. 'Both Cullen and [John] Gregory were cultured men and aimed to impress on their students that medicine was a learned and genteel occupation', writes Christopher Lawrence in 'Ornate Physicians and Learned Artisans:

Edinburgh Medical Men, 1726–1776', in *William Hunter*, ed. Bynum and Porter, 170.

26. See Roy Porter's summation of Hunter's career, 'William Hunter, a Surgeon and a Gentleman', in *William Hunter*, ed. Bynum & Porter, 7–34.

27. John Anderson to William Mure, 8 Jan. 1763, and John Graham of Dugaldston to William Mure, 10 Jan. 1763, in *Selections from the Papers Preserved at Caldwell Castle*, 3 vols. (Edinburgh, 1845), 2:ii, 165–66.

28. MS minutes in the possession of C. D. Donald of Stirling. See also John Strang, *Glasgow and its Clubs* (London and Glasgow, 1859), 34–66.

29. William C. Lehmann, *John Millar of Glasgow, 1735–1801: His Life and Thought and his Contributions to Sociological Analysis* (Cambridge, 1960), 28. I am grateful to Michel Faure for pointing out that Millar was given the tutelage of Moore's younger sons when Moore and his eldest son accompanied the duke of Hamilton abroad in 1772. See John Craig, 'An Account of the Life and Writings of John Millar, Esq.', in Millar's *Observations concerning the Distinction of Ranks in Society*, 4th ed. (Edinburgh, 1806), xcii.

30. 'Sketches of my Own Birth & Certain Circumstances', a manuscript in the possession of Sir Mark Heath of Bath, cited with his permission.

31. *Medical Sketches* (Providence, R. I., 1794), 11.

32. Strang, *Glasgow and its Clubs*, 40–41, described some of the more successful as having

a hauteur and bearing; . . . they kept themselves separate from the other classes of the town; assuming the air and deportment of persons immeasurably superior to all around them; and treating those on whom they looked down, but on whom they depended, with no little superciliousness . . . . They were the princes on the Plainstaines, and strutted about there every day as the Rulers of the destinies of Glasgow. Like the princely merchants . . . who formerly paced the Piazetta in Venice, or occupied the gorgeous palaces in the Strada Balbi of Genoa, the tobacco lords distinguished themselves by a particular garb, being attired, like their Venetian and Genovese predecessors, in scarlet cloaks, curled wigs, cocked hats, and bearing gold-headed canes.

33. H. L. Fulton, 'An Eighteenth-Century Best-Seller', *Publications of the Bibliographical Society of America* 66 (1972): 428–33. *Manners in Italy* went through fourteen printings in twenty-two years.

34. Duke of Hamilton to William Mure, 18 June 1773, NLS, MS 4946, fol. 73.

35. Manuscript journal of the political events of 1790–92, cited with permission of its owner, Sir Mark Heath.

36. On Moore's reaction to the events of 1792 and the years following, see his *Journal of a Residence in France*, 2 vols. (London, 1793–94). See also H. L. Fulton, 'Disillusionment with the French Revolution: The Case of the Scottish Physician John Moore', *Studies in Scottish Literature* 23 (1985): 46–65, and Alain Morvan, 'Peur de la France et peur de la Revolution dans les romans de John Moore', in *La Peur*, ed. Alain Morvan (Villeneuve d'Ascq, 1985), 113–25.

10

Images of Glasgow in Late Eighteenth-Century Popular Poetry

Richard B. Sher

In 1773, with the spirit of the Edinburgh New Town very much in the air, Robert Fergusson looks forward to the day when the beauty of his city will be compared favourably with that of rival Glasgow:

> Nae mair shall Glasgow striplings threap
> Their city's beauty and its shape,
> While our new city spreads around
> Her bonny wings on fairy ground.[1]

It is interesting that these verses appeared in a separately published poem bearing the title *Auld Reikie, A Poem*, reflecting perhaps a certain ambivalence within Fergusson between his love of the smoky, smelly old town he knew so well and his hopes for urban improvement through modernization. His words also reflect a tension that was widely perceived between Edinburgh and Glasgow. One city was depicted as cramped and polluted yet highly cultured, while the other was wealthy and beautiful but smaller and less refined. Accustomed to associating urban economic growth with industrialization and environmental destruction, we may find these pairings somewhat strange. But that is how matters appeared to eighteenth-century visitors to these cities. And just as enlightened Edinburgh could never quite shake the stigma of its smoke and stench, so clean, beautiful Glasgow could not easily escape the charge that, though increasingly urban, it was not truly urbane. This chapter will consider the images of Glasgow found in several poems written about the city during the last three decades of the eighteenth century, when Glasgow, like Edinburgh, was struggling to define its modern identity.

I

AT THE SAME TIME THAT Robert Fergusson was vividly depicting Edinburgh life in poems published, for the most part, in Walter and Thomas Ruddiman's *Weekly Magazine, or Edinburgh Amusement*,[2] an anonymous

'Epigram' on Glasgow appeared in the 12 June 1773 number of *The Glasgow Museum, or, Weekly Instructor* (see Appendix I). This was one of the first poems about Glasgow to appear in print in the eighteenth century,[3] and I do not know of it ever being noticed since that time. The fact that it appeared just when Fergusson was publishing his poems about Edinburgh is surely no accident. In the 1770s both cities were experiencing greater civic awareness as they prepared to undergo urban development projects on an unprecedented scale: Edinburgh somewhat abruptly and dramatically, through the creation of a completely 'new town', Glasgow more gradually but almost as impressively, through the steady westward expansion of the city.[4] Both towns were also growing more populous and more literate, as shown by the emergence of local, weekly magazines like the ones just mentioned. Midway between newspapers appearing two or three times per week and national monthlies like the *Scots Magazine*, and bearing the names of their cities of publication right in their titles, these local weeklies were specialized enough to print poems dealing with local matters; and sometimes the poems were in Scots, as were many of Fergusson's contributions to the *Weekly Magazine*.

Though the anonymous author of the 'Epigram' in the *Glasgow Museum* is no great poet, this poem provides a fascinating and witty view of Glasgow at a particular moment in its history, a moment of hesitation and uncertainty in the midst of a long-term forward thrust. Along with the rest of Scotland, the city was then suffering an economic and financial crisis symbolized by the recent failure of the Ayr Bank. The Forth and Clyde Canal, which was to connect trade between the East and West, had made great progress since construction began in 1768, but it was no longer clear that existing funds would be sufficient to finish the job (in fact, work would be temporarily halted in 1775). As Glasgow grew steadily wealthier, sending its sons to the corners of the British Empire for profit and glory, there were doubts not only about how the city's progress would be affected by the financial crisis, which reduced the amount of credit available for tobacco merchants and other entrepreneurs, but also about whether it was providing adequately for its less fortunate residents. Finally, there was the question of just how refined Glasgow should try to be, especially in light of the town's traditional role as a centre of evangelical Presbyterianism. Since 1764 serious attempts had been made to sustain a theatre, that great symbol of enlightenment and gentility that Calvinists deplored, but evangelical ire and apparent arson had rendered the undertaking less than secure. More recently, a company of players that included the well-known actor West Digges had left the city after three consecutive seasons (1768–71), leaving Glasgow without theatre until the latter part of 1773.[5]

All these points of tension are explored in the anonymous 'Epigram'. The poem is divided into two parts: twenty lines on the complex interplay

of commerce, culture and religion, followed by another twenty-four lines
titled *'Extempore, on Reading the above Verses'*. The opening stanza
takes note of Glasgow's familiar commercial identity, but in a manner
that suggests an ugly old woman who originally rose to prominence when
she 'rear'd her commercial head'. In an effort to 'ape her betters'

> She dress'd — learn'd to read — and — (tho' strange is the fact!)
> She got her a Playhouse — and people to act!

Since the financial crisis of 1772–73, however, Glasgow's drive towards
refinement had come under scrutiny. There occurred a symbolic shift in
the drink of choice from claret to port, which was cheaper, in part because
Portuguese goods had lower import duties than those from France. And
the poet makes an ironic recommendation that the theatre be transformed
into a house of the Lord:

> First, shut up the playhouse – that court of the Devil!
> Dame Fortune, depend on't, again will be civil;
> And, lest love of pleasure your thoughts should be reaching,
> Suppose twice-a-week you should open't for preaching:
> How happy a thought! – for, as needy your state is,
> You may company have, and hypocrisy gratis.

With their mockery of the religious argument that the nation's misfor-
tunes can be traced to hedonistic backsliding, and their supposed appeal
to the merchant class because religious 'hypocrisy' is free, these lines
bring the first part of the poem to a biting conclusion, reminiscent of
Fergusson's satirical barbs at religious hypocrisy in Edinburgh.

The second part of the poem seems at first to be a serious answer to the
first. The commercial foundations of Glasgow's greatness are admitted
but now presented as worthy, even 'noble':

> That Glasgow on the base of commerce rose
> A noble fabric, all the world knows.

It is pointed out that this commercial foundation has brought the city
foreign 'arts and treasures' and enabled 'her sons to fly from pole to pole'.
In the course of this boasting, however, the supposed responder seems to
go too far, and lets it slip that all this wealth does not necessarily help
those who are less fortunate or who lie outside the city's privileged élite:

> Rich in her industry, she sits secure
> Nor heeds the clamour of the vain and poor,
> If Scotland suffers she must have her share,
> And trust to trade her loses to repair.

After a passing shot at the role of 'Scribes and Lawyers' in bringing about
the banking crisis, the author tries to emphasize, in the closing lines of

the poem, Glasgow's friendly, mutually beneficial relationship with her 'sister' town: Glasgow supports the economic development of Edinburgh through the building of the Forth and Clyde Canal, while Edinburgh provides Glasgow with cultural improvement in the form of theatrical entertainment.

> And far from grudging to her sister town,
> The pedlar, petty fogging, great renown.
> She charitably hopes the best for all,
> And wishes success to the great canal;
> Hopes that no error in her calcule lurks
> To send her begging for her public works.
> Glasgow, mean time, sues to her sister kind,
> Thither to send that sense and taste refin'd,
> That can for hours with great indifference feel
> Nature and Shakespeare broke upon the wheel.
> Poor Digge's fate is here most justly mourn'd
> Bad goods are sent, bad goods, must be return'd.

Though the meaning of the concluding lines is somewhat obscure, perhaps the poet regrets the departure of Digges's theatre company while accepting, in commercial idiom, its necessity.

We do not know the name of the *Glasgow Museum* poet, but in the next decade poems on Glasgow were published by two men who can be identified with certainty: John Mayne (sometimes spelled Main or Mein) and Robert Galloway. Interestingly enough, neither was a native Glaswegian, though each lived in the city at least for a time. The remainder of this chapter will be concerned with their contrasting visions of Glasgow in the 1780s, which seem to reflect popular attitudes at a time of rapid urban change.

II

JOHN MAYNE, BY FAR THE better known of the two poets, was born in Dumfries in 1759 and educated at the grammar school there.[6] After completing a local apprenticeship as a printer, he went to Glasgow and worked for the famous Foulis printing firm. While still in his teens he began publishing Scots poetry, notably 'Siller Gun' (1777), which according to Walter Scott 'surpasses the efforts of Fergusson, and comes near to those of Burns' (quoted in Reid, *Glasgow Past and Present*, 1:443). Robert Fergusson was certainly a great influence. It is said that they met in Dumfries in 1773, when Mayne was just fourteen years old and Fergusson at most twenty-three — though just a year away from his early death.[7] 'Siller Gun' not only mentions Fergusson but also contains explanatory notes that identify him as a man 'well known for his ingenious compositions in the Scots dialect', including his description of Edinburgh in 'Hallow-Fair'. Like Fergusson before him, Mayne became associated with the *Weekly Magazine*, and the connection was not by chance; the number for [14] April 1779 contains a Scots poem entitled 'To the Publisher of the Weekly Magazine' that Walter Ruddiman's introduction declares 'not a despicable imitation of Fergusson, whose genius we wish to see revived'. It is in fact a tribute to Fergusson as much as to the magazine (a word that the poet manages to rhyme in the closing stanza with a version of his own name, 'Jockie Mein'). Two of the poem's twelve 'habbie' stanzas illustrate this point:

> At ony time whan ane has leisure,
> Your Magazine affords great pleasure;
> They'll fin't a braw poetic treasure,
>   Let wha will pree't:
> But fair we miss our ain braid measure
>   Sin Robie die't.
>
> To tell the truth — he was a callan,
> That Scotlan' now has nae sic saul in,
> An' than he gart his nummers fall in
>   Wi sicken skill,
> That nowther Hamilton nor Allan
>   Cou'd match his quill.

Mayne's preference for 'Robie' Fergusson over William 'Hamilton' of Bangour and 'Allan' Ramsay seems to have been rooted in Fergusson's stature as a beloved older associate, or 'callan', whom the poet plainly tried to emulate in a variety of ways.[8] During the course of 1780 Mayne's 'Hallowe'en' and an expanded version of 'Siller Gun' both appeared in the *Weekly*, and these two poems were reissued together at Glasgow in 1783, along with 'Epistle to Mr Walter Ruddiman'.[9] In that year Mayne also published 'Glasgow. A Poem', with which this section will be chiefly concerned (see Appendix II). Celebrating his adopted city in verse may be seen as an attempt by Mayne to do for Glasgow what his hero Fergusson had done for Edinburgh.

In 1787 Mayne went to London, where he spent the rest of his life as a moderately successful figure in the printing and periodical publishing trade. In 1789 he became printer, and the following year joint proprietor, of *The Star and Evening Advertiser*, with which he remained closely affiliated until late in life. Mayne's fame as a poet, however, rested mainly on his youthful Scottish poems, which he continued to revise and reprint while living in London. After his death in 1836, the *Gentleman's Magazine* praised Mayne as second only to Burns among the poets of Scotland.

Few modern critics would be likely to accept this judgement. Yet if Mayne was no Burns or Fergusson, he was a good Scots poet who deserves to be better known today, in large part for his 'Glasgow. A Poem'. The poem's somewhat confusing publishing history is of considerable interest. At the time of its initial appearance in the December 1783 issue of the *Glasgow Magazine and Review*, it was a modest piece of seventeen 'habbie' stanzas signed 'J. Main'. In the 1790s James Brash and William Reid republished it twice, with one additional stanza and other revisions: once with a slightly revised title, 'Glasgow: A Poem, in Scots Verse', in the second volume of their *Poetry: Original and Selected* (Glasgow, [1797]),[10] and once in an eight-page pamphlet entitled *Glasgow. A Poem. To which is added, Prince Robert. An Old Scottish Ballad* (Glasgow, n.d.). Meanwhile, Mayne was in the process of expanding the poem into a work of sixty stanzas, which was separately published at London in 1803 and later reprinted in its entirety in Robert Reid's *Glasgow Past and Present*, as well as in George Eyre-Todd's 1903 anthology of Glasgow poets.[11] In the 1980s both the original 1783 version and a portion of the expanded 1803 version were reprinted in anthologies of Scottish poetry,[12] but to the best of my knowledge nothing has ever been published on the differences between the versions, or on the poem's significance as a vision of eighteenth-century Glasgow.

In sharp contrast to the *Glasgow Museum* 'Epigram' of 1773, Mayne's 'Glasgow. A Poem' is in all its versions a civic booster poem.

> HAIL, GLASGOW! fam'd for ilka thing
>   That heart can wish or siller bring;

From this opening couplet (further emphasized in the 1803 version by the substitution of an exclamation point for a semicolon after 'bring'), it is clear that Mayne's image of Glasgow is that of an urban utopia. If the original version of the poem succeeds, as I think it does, it is largely because Mayne's use of Scots language conveys the sense of amazement of a semi-worldly country lad seeing the town for the first time. In the second stanza, for example, the poet expresses his astonishment at the multitudes of people living in the town and their ability to find enough food and money to appear so well fed, well dressed and 'fair':

> Within the tinkling o' thy bells,
> Wow, Sirs, how mony a thousand dwells!
> — Where they get bread they ken themsels,
>   But I'll declare,
> They're ay weil clad in gude bein shells,
>   And fat and fair.

By using common language and words of wonder like 'wow', and by raising questions he cannot fully answer, the poet is saved from the appearance of crude civic chauvinism.

So it goes throughout the original version of the poem. Two stanzas praising Glasgow University are introduced by lines so friendly and disarming that they banish all hint of academic snobbery:

> If ye've a knacky son or twa,
> To Glasgow College send them a';

The next stanza makes the claim that there is no unemployment in Glasgow, but does so from a popular perspective, as if the astonished visitor is telling working class friends back home about the abundant opportunities the town offers. The same impression is given by the poet's observation that 'the houses here / Like royal palaces appear!' There is the inevitable description of the thriving commercial city, made interesting by the picture of merchants gathering at the Cross between one and two o'clock each day to 'shine like Nabobs' and 'chat' about trade. The religious character of the city is quickly disposed of in a line or two, while several stanzas are devoted to the beauty of the women on Glasgow Green. The last stanza is not smug about all the city has achieved; rather, it is a prayer for continued prosperity, phrased not in the language of commerce but in that of family love.

Though clearly not in a class with Robert Fergusson's 'Auld Reikie', the 1783 version of John Mayne's 'Glasgow' has an innocent charm that entitles it to consideration as the first important poem about eighteenth-century Glasgow. Like the *Glasgow Museum* 'Epigram' of 1773, it captures a particular moment in the town's history: not, however, the moment of uncertainty that accompanied the financial collapse of the early 1770s but the moment of elation that marked the end of the American war and the beginning of Glasgow's economic resurgence. The *Glasgow Magazine and Review* had been founded to celebrate that very feeling; as the publisher, John Mennons, observed in the dedication to the first issue in October 1783: 'To Commerce we owe our present happy state of civilization, and our emerging from that profound ignorance and barbarism, which, like a thick-cloud, for many ages, overspread the western part of the world.'[13]

How unfortunate that Mayne, in an effort to improve the poem, made it so much worse. The 1803 version of 'Glasgow. A Poem' is almost four times longer than the original, but it loses the sense of naive wonder that gives the 1783 version its charm. In referring to the vastness of Glasgow's population, for example, the line 'Wow, Sirs, how many a thousand dwells!' is changed to the more pedestrian 'How mony a happy body dwells;' (2/447).[14] When the poet tries to rekindle the old sense of wonder, as in the following tribute to the age of commerce,

> Wow, Sirs! it's wonderful to trace
> How Commerce has improved the place! (36/451)

the attempt fails, in part because the act of tracing historical improvements implies a degree of knowledge and historical perspective that is incompatible with genuine awe. The new tone is more self-consciously celebratory and didactic:

> Hail, Industry, thou richest gem
> That shines in virtue's diadem; (29/451)

Supplementing the original two stanzas on Glasgow University are five new ones (nos. 5–9) that laud particular professors active at the university during the age of the Enlightenment — William Leechman, Francis Hutcheson, William Wight, Thomas Reid, Robert Simson, William Cullen and Adam Smith[15]— as well as the sixteenth-century humanist George Buchanan, the Glasgow-educated London physician William Hunter and the Scots poet and antiquary Alexander Geddes, whose praise of 'Glasgow. A Poem' before the Society of Antiquaries of Scotland in 1792 had supposedly induced Mayne to produce an expanded version.[16] These stanzas are of interest as a poetic expression of pride in Glasgow's intellectual life.

> Nor is it students, and nae mair,
> That climb, in crowds, our College stair:
> Thither the learn'd, far-fam'd, repair,
>   To clear their notions;
> And pay to ALMA MATER there,
>   Their warm devotions.

> Led by a lustre sae divine,
> Ev'n GEDDES visited this shrine!
> GEDDES! sweet fav'rite o' the Nine!
>   Shall live in story;
> And, like yon constellation, shine
>   In rays o' glory!

> O! LEECHMAN, HUTCHESON, and
> REID fu' of intellectual light!
> WIGHT and SIMPSON, as the morning bright!
>   Your mem'ries here,
> Tho' gane to regions o' delight,
>   Will aye be dear!

> 'Mang ither names, that consecrate
> And stamp a country guid or great,
> We boast o' some that might compete
>   Or claim alliance,
> Wi' a' that's grand in Kirk or State —
>   In Art or Science!

> Here great BUCHANAN learnt to scan
> The verse that makes him mair than man!
> CULLEN and HUNTER here began
>   Their first probations;

And SMITH, frae Glasgow, form'd his plan,
   'The Wealth o' Nations!' (5–9/447–48)

Long, dense footnotes identify these men of letters.[17] The figures in stanza 7 are characterized thus:

The Rev. Principal Leechman, and Dr. Wight, Professor of Divinity, were great ornaments of this University. The merits of Dr. Hutcheson, as a moral philosopher, are well known. Those of Dr. Reid, who filled after him the chair of Moral Philosophy, author of *An Inquiry into the Human Mind*, and of two *Essays on the Active and Intellectual Powers of Man*, can never be sufficiently admired. Dr. Robert Simpson, F.R.S., Professor of Mathematics, author of a new *Translation of Euclid*, and other mathematical writings, is justly ranked as the first mathematician of the age in which he lived. Mr. Burke was once a candidate for the Professorship of Logic, but did not succeed. He was afterwards elected Lord Rector — an honour of which he always spoke as one of the greatest he had ever received. (448, n. 1)

And those in stanza 9 are described at the bottom of the page in the following manner:

The elegant Latin poet and historian, Buchanan; Drs. Cullen and Hunter, the former the first physician of his day, the latter surpassed by none for his knowledge in anatomy; Dr. Adam Smith, famed throughout Europe for his *Inquiry into the Causes of the Wealth of Nations*; together with other illustrious names, a particular enumeration of which would far exceed the limits of this publication, received here the rudiments of that learning by which they soared in the most elevated heights of fame. (448, n. 2)

Other footnotes inform English readers about the great buildings, institutions and engineering feats mentioned in the poem, such as the Forth and Clyde Canal (which 'displays, in a striking view, what can be effected by the art and perseverance of man' [450, n. 3]), Crookstone Castle and the Kelvin Aqueduct Bridge.[18] The pedantic aspect of these footnotes is painfully obvious, as when the line 'Or clip, wi' care, the silken soy' gets this treatment in a note: 'The words *silken soy* are in reality a tautology, they being the English and French terms for silk, connected together; but are employed in Scotland to denote, simply, silk' (448, n. 3).

Many of the new stanzas have less to do with Glasgow than with Mayne's sentimental perceptions of Scottish history and culture. Tears are shed for Mary Queen of Scots,

The angel-form o' SCOTLAND'S QUEEN,
   In deep despair! (44/453)

as well as for 'patriot WALLACE' (45/453). And wandering through Glasgow's streets, the poet yearns for the abilities of a much greater predecessor to describe the scene:

> O! for the muse o' BURNS sae rare,
> To paint the groups that gather there!
> The wives on We'n'sdays wi' their ware —
>   The lads and lasses,
> In serlying crouds, at Glasgow Fair;
>   And a' that passes!
>
> But, oh! his muse that warm'd ilk clod,
> And rais'd up flow'rs where'er he trod!
> Will ne'er revisit this abode!
>   And mine, poor lassie,
> In tears for him, dow hardly plod
>   Thro' Glasgow causae! (14–15/449)

These stanzas reveal how much the poet reveres Burns, whose characteristically suggestive way of depicting such scenes is clearly evoked in the line 'And a' that passes!'. But in reminding the reader how well Burns might have brought to life the bustle of Glasgow Fair, Mayne inadvertently draws attention to his own shortcomings.

The effect of the added stanzas and footnotes is to break the flow of the poem and to transform the poet from an astonished young visitor into an experienced and knowledgable insider. Geared primarily for an English audience, the 1803 version of Mayne's 'Glasgow' contains an element of self-conscious civic and national boasting that is far less subtle and genuine than the naive boosterism found in the Scottish original of 1783. What had been entertaining quickly becomes cloying. The poet now seems to be writing Scots verses for the amusement of English readers looking for something quaint, or for Glaswegian exiles in London hungry for nostalgic, chauvinistic fare.

III

IF MAYNE CORRUPTED HIS POEM on Glasgow by removing it from its Scottish context, no such danger existed for our second Glasgow poet. Robert Galloway wrote only for Scottish audiences. Galloway was born in 1752 in Stirling, where he learned the trade of shoemaker. After moving to Glasgow he worked in bookselling and supposedly ran a circulating library.[19] Despite his obscurity, he did well enough to have his *Poems, Epistles and Songs, Chiefly in the Scottish Dialect* printed at his own expense by William Bell in 1788. Four years later he published, again at his own expense, a second edition that added some fifteen new poems and announced his double role as both 'bard and bookseller'.[20]

Since he trained as a shoemaker, there may be some truth to Galloway's claim, in the Preface to the *Poems*, that he was 'an entire stranger' to the learned languages and sciences. Whatever the extent of his formal

learning, however, Galloway probably minimized it intentionally in order
to authenticate his stature as a popular Scots poet in the tradition of
Ramsay, Fergusson and above all Burns, who sometimes played the
same game. Their poetry incorporated folk elements, popular sentiments
and Scots vocabulary that were sometimes considered incompatible with
formal learning. Galloway himself makes the connection with these poets
in the immodest conclusion to his 'Epistle to the Author':

> Ramsay and Fergusson, by turns,
> Play'd sweetly baith, — now in their urns:
>   For them nae mair auld Scotia mourns,
>   Or says alas!
> Now she has Galloway and Burns,
>   To fill their place.[21]

In the more modest sequel, 'The Author's Answer', Galloway affects surprise and uneasiness at being placed in such illustrious company by the
author of the preceding poem (155–58). Modern critics are likely to feel
the same way. Even Galloway's premature death in 1794, shortly before his
forty-second birthday (though not quite so premature a death as those of
Fergusson or Burns), did not help to establish his reputation as a Scots poet.

No matter how inferior he may seem when compared to the three
greatest Scots poets of the eighteenth century, Galloway deserves to be
rescued from the total oblivion into which he has fallen. The power of his
vision alone entitles him to that consideration. Galloway's is a strong voice
for Whig cultural nationalism and the common man. His 'On Recovery
of the Highland Dress' is a fascinating celebration of Highland culture;
his 'Address to the Convention of Royal Boroughs of Scotland, met for
a Reform' is one tradesman's sincere plea to his brethren for honest
government; his 'The Laird and the Cotter' tells of the awakening of
a good but absentee laird who learns, upon his return to Scotland, that
a cotter with more than forty years on the land was driven off when his
own factor raised rents in hard times. When the cotter lectures the laird
on the responsibilites of his class, no punches are pulled:

> Thus Scotland groans with English laws
> And few at home to hear the cause,
>   A' sneak up to the court:
> Your money's spent in London town,
> Supporting ev'ry gaiming loun,
>   That makes of you their sport.
> The factor treasures riches up,
>   And leaves the laird to sell;
> And when they land them on their dowp,
>   Gude morning, fare ye well.
> Then stay at hame, or y're to blame,
>   And spend your money here;

> The nation then will bless your name,
> And wish you better cheer. (38–39)

The addition in the second edition of a poem praising the medieval Scottish patriot William Wallace (whose picture graces the frontispiece) reinforces Galloway's identity as a Scottish poet.

Among Galloway's poems are several that commemorate his native Stirlingshire and four that deal with his adopted city of Glasgow. The latter may not be among his best work poetically, but they are of some importance as early expressions of working class visions of Glasgow in the late eighteenth century. Two recount the spectacle of Lunardi's first and second balloon flights, when all Glasgow turned out to witness history in the making. Another describes in twenty-six stanzas the annual event known as 'Glasgow Fair', which has maintained a continuous existence for more than eight hundred years.

Galloway was at his best when using the traditional 'habbie' stanza that we encountered in 'The Laird and the Cotter', as well as in Mayne's 'Glasgow. A Poem'. In 'Glasgow Fair', however, he turned to another traditional mode of Scots poetry, that of the 'Christis Kirk'. The reason behind this choice seems plain enough: Galloway was copying Robert Fergusson's 'Hallow-Fair' (1772). Though Galloway's poem is twice as long as Fergusson's, the similarities between the two works are striking. Like Fergusson, Galloway is describing an early modern urban fair, and particularly the adventures of common people there; he uses not only the 'Christis Kirk' stanza but the particular variation on it that Fergusson had introduced in 'Hallow-Fair', featuring a more varied rhyme scheme (A B A B / C D C D E) than was traditional;[22] he even concludes each bobwheel with the word 'day', as in 'Hallow-Fair'. What a pity that the comparison does not extend to the poetical talents of the two poets!

Still, 'Glasgow Fair' has its charm. The first eight stanzas set the stage, as we follow a group of young people dressing for the fair and then walking the six miles to town. At stanza 9 they catch sight of Glasgow's steeples and hand round snuff in anticipation. In stanza 10 they arrive at the 'Brig-end', where 'weavers, wrights and smiths' are just quitting for the day in order to go to the fair. And then it's into the heart of the town and the fair, where one of the lads is identified as Jonny Galt, 'Head-servant to the laird'. At the end of the first part (stanza 16), the action moves to Jonny's attempts to woo Nell, with whom he dances 'twa reels a' round' and then goes walking among the vast crowds. Part II begins with images of street scenes, including venders who grab the arms of passers-by and ask 'What will ye buy?', and pickpockets who 'try your purse to catch'.

In pt. 2, stanza 4, the poet surveys the scene and points out the variety of reasons that have brought so many people to the fair:

> Let but a man, o' hearing short,
> Look round him at a fair;

And view the fo'k, o' ilka sort,
  That are assembl'd there;
Some for spulzie, some for sport,
  And some to gather lear',
And some wi' knaves, for to resort,
  The booty for to share
    Some ither day. (95)

As in Fergusson's 'Hallow-Fair', which finishes with an unfortunate confrontation.between the town guard and a helpless drunk, 'Glasgow Fair' concludes with a scene of violence, for Jonny and his friends engage in a fight with some 'rogues' who insult their 'lasses'. The poem — and the fair — are brought to an end in a full-scale riot:

Then dogs and cats and dirt were flung,
  Enough to fyle the air;
And ev'ry wand'ring gillet dung,
  To finish Glasgow Fair. (97)

We are reminded that in spite of its reputation as a clean, quiet, beautiful city, eighteenth-century Glasgow, like other early modern towns, also had its share of crime and disorder.

Galloway's best Glasgow poem, 'Glasgow Reviewed and Contrasted', is written in English rhymed couplets (see Appendix III). It experiments with three voices that reveal different aspects of the city. In the first three stanzas the poet himself, writing in the first person, takes a stroll through the town on a clear, still winter night. As he walks he considers the vanity of man, who so often misuses the talents that nature bestows. This meditative state is shattered by the poem's second voice, that of a 'drunken blunderer' who trumpets a tribute to the city for five stanzas, which the poet hears while hiding close by. The drunk praises Glasgow's most notable features: its spacious, regular streets; its fine buildings; its five crosses; its great cathedral, with its fine bell; Montrose's lodging, with its significance in seventeenth-century Scottish history; its college; its eleven parishes and its chapels, representing a variety of religious denominations; and its town plan, which requires only one more step in order to be complete:

And that is taking down the lump of stone
That formerly did bear the name of Glasgow Tron. (180)

At this point the poet and the drunk are both startled by the sound of the third voice, 'a spectre . . . of antient form' that finishes the poem with a long speech. For two hundred years the spectre has 'sat by this bell' and watched the town. It has seen great changes, as Glasgow went from being 'sma', below the hill' to large and built up. 'Streets, and wynds, and lanes, and noble structures' have appeared, and 'thatch houses' have been transformed into 'palaces'. Unlike the drunk, however, the spectre does not present these changes in a positive light. On the contrary, change has brought a new sense of dissatisfcation with good, plain things. The 'frugal honesty' and thrift of the old days have given way to a desire to get rich quick. The spectre's speech concludes with a comparison of the new Glasgow to 'rich Babylon', whose wealth did not protect it from a descent into oblivion.

One of the more interesting aspects of 'Glasgow Reviewed and Con-trasted' is its use of English and Scots. The poet himself uses English, interspersed with one or two insignificant Scots usages like 'su' for 'so' and 'frae' for 'from'. The drunk who praises the development of Glasgow uses pure English, without so much as a single Scots word or expression. The spectre's speech, however, is laced with Scots words that convey a sense of folksy contentment with the good old ways. For example, in Glasgow of old:

> A buffin on a woman's head then was
> Thought far superior to the best of gauze,
> A mankie gown, of our ain kintra growth,
> Did mak them very braw, and unco couth,
> A tartan plaid, pinn'd round their shoulders tight,
> Did mak them ay su' trim, and perfect right; . . .
> As for the man, he wore a gude kelt coat,
> Which wind, nor rain, nor sun, could scarcely blot;
> The plaiding hose he wore, and bannet blue,
> When they grew auld, he then gat others new; (181–82)

Note that in these lines every approved item of apparel is given a Scottish association, either by its obvious connection with Scottish culture ('a tartan plaid' and 'plaiding hose') or by the use of Scots or archaic words to identify or modify it ('a buffin', 'a mankie gown, of our ain kintra growth', 'a gude kelt coat', 'bannet blue'). The one modern form of clothing is described in English: 'the best of gauze'. A conspicuously large number of Scots words and spellings are used in these ten lines, including verbs such as 'mak' for 'make' and 'gat' for 'got', and adjectives such as 'auld' for 'old'. Scots is used to recreate an urban folk past that has been demolished in the name of progress. The 'auld' articles of clothing are inextricably connected with the old language and the old way of life.

Though 'Glasgow Reviewed and Contrasted' is not a great poem, it does express a strong point of view about the city and its development. The speech of the drunk prepares the reader for a booster poem like John Mayne's 'Glasgow', but what the drunk has to say is contradicted, indeed utterly obliterated, by the speech of the spectre, who confirms the poet's initial fears about human vanity. The drunk conveys the positive, vaguely Anglicised viewpoint of short-term improvers, the spectre the critical, long-range perspective of one who has seen the city transformed from Defoe's 'cleanest and beautifullest and best built' little town into a large, spiritually ugly place, where any 'booby' 'with fifty pounds or so' can 'in less than seven years . . build a street'. This is not the witty cynicism of the anonymous *Glasgow Museum* poet of 1773 or the naive civic boosterism of the young John Mayne; rather, it is very close to Robert Fergusson's vision of old Edinburgh on the eve of modernization.

The contrast between John Mayne and Robert Galloway is instructive. Both were originally apprenticed to trades; both approached Glasgow as outsiders; and both drew poetic inspiration from the city. Mayne, however, was educated at grammar school and was able to climb the social ladder that led to economic prosperity in London. From a printer's apprentice in Dumfries he rose to prominence as a London printer and publisher, and when he died, after a long life, the *Gentleman's Magazine* paid tribute to his achievement as a man and poet. Mayne's vision of Glasgow during the period 1783–1803, when his 'Glasgow. A Poem' was expanded on a scale that paralleled the economic and demographic development of the city itself, was thoroughly positive. For him, late eighteenth-century Glasgow constituted a miraculous phenomenon of economic opportunity and visionary civic enterprise — a phenomenon from which he had personally benefited.

For the Stirlingshire shoemaker turned bookseller-poet Robert Galloway, on the other hand, the rapid development of late eighteenth-century Glasgow was a matter for concern. It seemed to him that the good old values of the city, symbolized by simple, virtuous attire and the rock-solid stability of the Glasgow Tron, were being corrupted and destroyed by the new spirit of acquisition and growth. Just as Mayne's personal success reflected the affirmative nature of his vision of the town, so Galloway died at age forty-one almost unknown and unnoticed. Like most of the old Scots ways that he so fervently endorsed in his best Glasgow poem, Galloway was destined to be dead and virtually forgotten before the eighteenth century reached its end.

Notes

I wish to thank David Daiches, Andrew Hook and Alan McKenzie for their helpful comments on an earlier draft of this chapter, and Carl MacDougall for his splendid readings of Mayne's and Galloway's poems at the Glasgow conference.

1. Robert Fergusson, 'Auld Reikie', in *Poems by Allan Ramsay and Robert Fergusson*, ed. Alexander Manson Kinghorn and Alexander Law (Edinburgh, 1985), 150. See also David Daiches, *Robert Fergusson* (Edinburgh, 1982), 117, and Tony MacManus, 'Robert Ferguson: The Cheil Amang Us', *Edinburgh History Magazine*, no. 2 (1989), 4–8.
2. One of Fergusson's most famous depictions of 'Auld Reikie' appears in his

poem 'The Daft Days', which was published in the *Weekly Magazine* on 2 Jan. 1772. See Daiches, *Robert Fergusson*, 1–6.

3. An earlier poem, Dougal Graham's 'John Highlandman's Remarks on the City of Glasgow', is reprinted in the pamphlet *Four Glasgow Poems*, ed. Hamish Whyte (Glasgow, 1981), 6–9. A fuller collection of Glasgow poems has not yet appeared as this book goes to press: *Mungo's Tongues: Glasgow Poems 1630–1990*, ed. Hamish Whyte (Edinburgh, 1993).

4. A. J. Youngson, *The Making of Classical Edinburgh* (Edinburgh, 1966); Andrew Gibb, *Glasgow: The Making of a City* (London, 1983).

5. Walter Baynham, *A Brief History of the Glasgow Stage* (Glasgow, 1892), 12–25.

6. Unless otherwise noted, information on Mayne's life is drawn from the obituary in the *Gentleman's Magazine*, 1836, which is reprinted in Robert Reid, *Glasgow Past and Present*, 3 vols. (Glasgow, 1884), 1:443–47.

7. Fergusson visited Dumfries in 1773 and published in the *Dumfries Weekly Magazine* for 28 September a celebratory poem entitled 'Dumfries' (see Daiches, *Robert Fergusson*, 119). According to G. W. Shirley, *Dumfries Printers in the Eighteenth Century* (Dumfries, 1934), Mayne was the apprentice who copied this poem for the press within twenty-four hours of its composition.

8. In the poem, a footnote identifies 'Robie' as 'Mr Roger Fergusson, a young man whose abilities are too well known to need any further mention.'

9. John Main, *Two Scots Poems. The Silver Gun, in Three Cantos. and Hallow-e'en* (Glasgow, 1783) (the line on Fergusson quoted above occurs at p. 7 in this edition). The most recent version of 'Siller Gun' is the one in *Longer Scottish Poems*, ed. Thomas Crawford et al., 2 vols. (Edinburgh, 1987), 2:174–75.

10. See J. C. Erving, 'Brash and Reid Booksellers in Glasgow and Their Collection of *Poetry Original and Selected*', *Records of the Glasgow Bibliographical Society* 12 (1936): 1–21, and Hamish Whyte's remarks in *Four Glasgow Poems*, 10.

11. Reid, *Glasgow Past and Present*, 1:442–54; George Eyre-Todd, *The Glasgow Poets: Their Lives and Poems* (Glasgow and Edinburgh, 1903), 64–89.

12. *A Book of Scottish Verse*, ed. Maurice Lindsay and R. L. Mackie (London, 1783) reproduces twenty-three stanzas of the 1803 version. The original 1783 version is reproduced with a short introduction and bibliography in Whyte, *Four Glasgow Poems*.

13. Quoted more extensively in Richard B. Sher, 'Commerce, Religion and the Enlightenment in Eighteenth-Century Glasgow', in *The History of Glasgow*, vol. 1, ed. T. M. Devine and Gordon Jackson (Manchester, 1994). See also David Daiches, *Glasgow* (London, 1977), 102–3.

14. Parenthetical references are to stanza/page in the version of the poem that appears in volume 1 of Reid, *Glasgow Past and Present*, where it is entitled simply 'Glasgow'.

15. Alan McKenzie has suggested to me that in these stanzas Mayne may have

been copying Fergusson, who made something of a speciality of celebrating his professors in verse. It is not known, however, if Mayne ever attended any lectures at the university.

16. Eyre-Todd, *Glasgow Poets*, 64. On Geddes and vernacular poetry generally, see F. W. Freeman, *Robert Fergusson and the Scots Humanist Compromise* (Edinburgh, 1984), 5–6.

17. The original, 1783 version contained only one footnote identifying the 'Merchant's House' as a charitable institution for 'decayed citizens and their families'.

18. The last of these structures inspired an anonymous poem in Brash and Reid's first volume of *Poetry: Original and Selected* [1796], 'Verses Viewing the Aqueduct Bridge'.

19. Besides a reference in William Anderson, *The Scottish Nation*, 3 vols. (Edinburgh, 1863), I have discovered only brief paragraphs on Galloway in Joseph Irving's *Book of Scotsmen Eminent for Achievements . . .* (Paisley, 1882) and in the supplement to Joseph Robertson's *Lives of the Scottish Poets*, 3 vols. (London, 1821–22), 3:128. He is not included in Eyre-Todd's *Glasgow Poets*.

20. The only evidence of his bookselling that I have been able to discover is in the imprint of *The Trial of the Rev. Thomas Fyshe Palmer, before the Circuit Court of Justiciary, held at Perth, on the 12th and 13th September, 1793, on an Indictment for Seditious Practices* (Edinburgh, 1793), where 'R. Galloway' is listed among those selling the book in Glasgow. To the extent that an association of this kind indicates an ideological preference, Galloway may perhaps be linked to the radical Friends of the People in Scotland, an organization congratulated in the Preface by one of its Edinburgh leaders, William Skirving, who was also the book's publisher.

21. Robert Galloway, *Poems, Epistles and Songs, Chiefly in the Scottish Dialect. To Which Are Added, A Brief Account of the Revolution in 1688, and a Narrative of the Rebellion in 1745–46, continued to the Death of Prince Charles in 1788* (Glasgow, 1788), 154. All poems referred to in the following discussion are from this edition.

22. Allan H. MacLaine, *Robert Fergusson* (Boston, 1965), 64–70.

Appendix I

'Epigram' from the *The Glasgow Museum, or, Weekly Instructor* 2 (12 June 1773): 215.

> When Glasgow first rear'd her commercial head
> And set cockahoop on the shoulders of trade
> The aukward old Besom, grown bold with their feeding,
> Must needs ape her betters, — To shew 'em her breeding,
> She dress'd — learn'd to read — and — (tho' strange is the fact!)
> She got her a Playhouse — and people to act!
> But lately alarm'd at the lose of her store,
> This crazy old hag is grown dull as before;

Her sons swear they ne'er will be able to bear it,
And in penance are drinking plain Port 'stead of Claret:
Not a smile can Appollo extract with his lyre,
For the loss of their coal has extinguish'd their fire!
   But courage, my lads! be consistent throughout,
And œconomy soon shall bring matters about;
First, shut up the playhouse — that court of the Devil!
Dame Fortune, depend on't, again will be civil;
And, lest love of pleasure your thoughts should be reaching,
Suppose twice a-week you should open't for preaching:
How happy a thought! — for, as needy your state is,
You may company have, and hypocrisy gratis.

Extempore, on Reading the above Verses

That Glasgow on the base of commerce rose
A noble fabric, all the world knows.
She bids her sons to fly from pole to pole.
Where Sol enlightens or where ocean roll,
And in her fleets bring to their native strand,
The arts and treasures of each foreign land;
Rich in her industry, she sits secure,
Nor heeds the clamour of the vain and poor,
If Scotland suffers she must have her share,
And trust to trade her loses to repair.
Unhurt, she sees the Scribes and Lawyers pranks,
But wishes they would cease directing Banks:
And far from grudging to her sister town,
The pedlar, petty fogging, great renown.
She charitably hopes the best for all,
And wishes success to the great canal;
Hopes that no error in her calcule lurks
To send her begging for her public works.
Glasgow, mean time, sues to her sister kind,
Thither to send that sense and taste refin'd,
That can for hours with great indifference feel
Nature and Shakespeare broke upon the wheel.
Poor Digge's fate is here most justly mourn'd
Bad goods are sent, bad goods, must be return'd.

Appendix II

John Mayne, 'Glasgow. A Poem' (original version), *The Glasgow Magazine and Review* (December 1783): 153.

HAIL, GLASGOW! fam'd for ilka thing
That heart can wish or siller bring;
Lang may thy canty *musics* ring,
   Our sauls to chear;
And Plenty gar thy childer sing,
   Frae year to year:

Within the tinkling o' thy bells,
Wow, Sirs, how mony a thousand dwells!
— Where they get bread they ken themsels,
   But I'll declare,
They're ay weil clad in gude bein shells,
   And fat and fair.

If ye've a knacky son or twa,
To Glasgow College send them a';
Whare, for the gospel, or the law,
   Or classic lair,
Ye'll find few places hereawa'
   That can compare:

There they may learn, for sma' propine,
Physician, Lawyer, or Divine:
— The gem that's buried in the mine
   Is polish'd here,
Till a' its hidden beauties shine,
   and sparkle clear. —

In ilka house, frae man to boy,
A' hands in GLASGOW find employ:
E'en maidens mild, wi' meikle joy,
   Flow'r lawn and gauze,
Or clip wi' care the silken-soy,
   For Lady's braws.

Look thro' the town; — the houses here
Like royal palaces appear!
A' things the face o' gladness wear, —
   The markets thrang, —
Bus'ness is brisk, — and a's asteer
   The streets alang.

'Tween ane and twa, wi' gawsy air,
The MERCHANTS to the Cross repair;
And tho' they shine like Nabobs there,
   Yet, weil I wat,
Commerce engages a' their care,
   And a' their chat:

Thir wylie birkies trade to a'
The Indies and America;

Whate'er can mak' ae penny twa,
　　Or raise their pride,
Is wafted to the Broomielaw,
　　On bony Clyde.

Yet, after a', shou'd burghers fail,
And fickle Fortune turn the scale;
Tho' a' be lost in some hard gale,
　　Or rocky shore,
The Merchant's House maks a' things hale
　　As heretofore.

　— O Sirs! within but little space,
This GLASGOW's turn'd an unko place!
Here Piety, in native grace,
　　Abounds in store;
And Beauty's saft enchanting face,
　　Wi' gowd galore.

Whae'er has daner'd out at e'en,
And seen the sights that I hae seen!
For strappan Ladies, tight and clean,
　　May safely tell
That, search the kintry, *Glasgow green*
　　Will bear the *belle*:

There ye may find, beyond compare,
The bluiming rose, and lily fair;
The killing smile, bewitching air,
　　The virt'ous mind,
And a' that Bards hae fancy'd rare
　　In woman kind.

But what avails't to you or me
How bony, gude, or rich they be?
　— Shou'd ane attempt, wi' langing eie,
　　To mak' his maen,
They'd, scornfu', thraw their heads a-jee,
　　Nor ease his pain. —

If ony simple Lover chuse
In humble verse his joe to ruise,
The eident *Porters* ne'er refuse,
　　For little siller,
To bear the firstlings o' his muse,
　　Wi' caution, till her.

But waesuck for the *Chairmen* now,
Wha ne'er to a day's wark dught bow;
Sair will her lazy *nainsel* rue,

Wi' heavy granes,
That e'er our streets were lin'd anew
   Wi' gude plane stanes:

Whan Writer lads, or Poets bare,
Frae Ball or Play set hame their Fair,
Their lugs'll no be deav'd nae mair
   (When pursie's tuim)
Wi *'Bony Lady, shuse a shair!*
   Ye'll fyle ye're shuin.'

— O GLASGOW! may thy bairns ay nap
In smiling Plenty's gowden lap;
And tho' their daddies kiss the cap,
   And bend the bicker,
On their auld pows may blessings drap,
   Ay thick and thicker.

Appendix III

Robert Galloway, 'Glasgow Reviewed and Contrasted', in *Poems, Epistles and Songs, Chiefly in the Scottish Dialect* (Glasgow, 1788), 176–83.

Ae winter night, impell'd by strong desire,
I took my wauking stick, and left my fire,
With nae design to enter house or hauld,
Until again I landed in my fauld.

Up Glasgow streets I gaed, and they were clean,
For neither man nor beast was to be seen;
The shops were shut, and ev'ry thing was still;
For it was wearing near the hour of twel'.
The moon shone clear, the stars all seem'd to vie
Whig cou'd excel in so serene a sky.
My thoughts recoil'd, by viewing such a plan;
I then thought on the vanity of man.

What then is man! no more nor less than dust;
He laughs a while, and then return he must,
And give account, how he his time has us'd,
To mend his talent, or his part abus'd:
An awful reck'ning this, to those who spoil
The best of talents, and the precious oil
That lavish Nature does on them bestow,
To worst of purposes do often throw.

Thus meditating, still I wander'd on,
Until I came just hard by Glasgow Tron.

I heard a drunken blunderer afar,
And to escape his din, I step'd ajar
Below the pillars, then I stood su' snug,
Till he advanc'd, not ten years frae my lug.
With bacchanalian stride, he took his stand,
And, with a voice like trumpet, gave command.

Fair Glasgow, now, step forth and make your claim,
For, 'mongst the first of cities stands your name;
Sing forth your beauties, hitherto untold,
Your outside painted, and your inside gold.
Your spacious streets, so regular in form,
Your stately fabrics, fit to stand a storm:
Your state to paint, night hardly gives me time,
But for to try't will scarce be deem'd a crime:
Her form is oval, spreading with her wings;
Or, as a balance, when it equal hings.
Five crosses she contains, which make her vie
With most of modern towns beneath the sky:
Saint Mungo's kirk stands high, from East to West,
And of a' Scotland's choirs it looks the best;
Two stately spires it bears, in one a bell,
For bulk and costly wark it does excel;
Three places here for worship, in repair,
And many a decent prelate has been there:
A mile it measures round, in ev'ry square;
So this must be a decent house of pray'r.

Montrose's lodging does our notice claim,
And shows a taste, still worthy of the name.
Its situation does command a view,
Envy'd by all, and but excell'd by few.
Here gallant Graham did rest himself a while,
When he set free the king o' Britain's Isle:
When Cromwell and his corps push'd all before him,
He, at Kilsyth, did push about the jorum;
He then, at Glasgow, set the pris'ners free,
Likewise to Edinburgh granted liberty.

The College next, I think, commands respect,
The place of learning we must ne'er neglect:
Two stately squares it shows, with halls all round;
Where youths are taught in learning most profound,
To fill the Pulpit, or the Bench, or Bar,
To make them councils for or peace or war.
Here come the Nation's hopes from ev'ry quarter,
And do their cash and time for education barter.

Eleven parishes this city does contain,
And full as many chapels here remain
Of different opinions; and, what is odd,
The same communion, and most holy God
Is worshipped, seemingly with fervent zeal;
And no man speaks against the public weal:
All this is gain'd by act of toleration,
Which certainly is good, if kept in moderation.
Three miles the city measures, square and square,
And many a handsome fabric sure is there.
The plan is near compleat, but only one,
And that is taking down the lump of stone
That formerly did bear the name of Glasgow Tron.

The story ended, then we heard a voice,
The Bacchanal and I both trembl'd at the noise.
A spectre then we saw, of antient form,
Its body huge, its countenance a storm;
Upon the nether battlements it stood,
And thus address'd its brother craft aloud.

Stay, blund'ring mortal, stay until I tell
What I have seen, since I sat by this bell:
Twa hunder year and mair I've kept this ground,
And great's the alteration all around;
For then the town was sma', below the hill,
Tho' now, you ev'ry creek and corner fill
With streets, and wynds, and lanes, and noble structures,
That show a taste, just like their wise conductors:
What now are palaces, were only then
Just warm thatch houses, fit for honest men,
Who with their frugal wives cou'd rear a breed;
Bot what they spun themselves they nought did need:
A buffin on a woman's head then was
Thought far superior to the best of gauze,
A mankie gown, of our ain kintra growth,
Did mak them very braw, and unco couth,
A tartan plaid, pinn'd round their shoulders tight,
Did mak them ay fu' trim, and perfect right;
A leather shoe they wore, with silver pin,
Of hameward make, and digg'd at Menstra Green.
As for the man, he wore a gude kelt coat,
Which wind, nor rain, nor sun, could scarcely blot;
The plaiding hose he wore, and bannet blue,
When they grew auld, he then gat others new;
But yet this homely race, they minded trade,
In frugal honesty they fortunes made,
That did not dwindle thro' amang their hands,

But to their heirs left houses, cash, and lands;
They squar'd by conscience, and by hands did strive;
This was the best, and surest way to thrive;
But now these honest men have fill'd their urn,
And things, in course, have ta'en another turn;
For riches then were got by slow degrees,
Now handsome fortunes are procur'd with ease:
Send but a speaking booby into town,
With fifty pounds or so, to set him down;
In less than seven years he'll build a street,
Wou'd hurt an Irish lord for to repeat;
But be not proud of all these buildings fair,
And stately lands, that do ly here and there:
Where is rich Babylon, so fam'd of old,
With gates of brass, and bars of massy gold?
The place, unnotic'd now, can scarce be told.

Liberty, Piety and Patronage: The Social Context of Contested Clerical Calls in Eighteenth-Century Glasgow

Ned C. Landsman

I n 1762 the public peace of the city of Glasgow was disturbed by a series of protests in the town's churches, kirk sessions and town council over the town council's plan to alter the established procedure or 'Model' for appointing ministers to the city's churches. For more than four decades, vacancies in those churches had been filled through a process requiring the joint consent of the council, the local congregation and a 'general session' comprising the ministers and elders of all the city's churches. Now, with the Wynd Church about to fall vacant, the town council, under the leadership of the powerful lord provost Andrew Cochrane, announced its intention of abandoning the Model and assuming the principal voice in the process for themselves. This action provoked protests from 'Modellers' within the town council, the general session and the citizenry in a pamphlet war that lasted nearly two years.[1]

The ruckus that ensued will sound familiar to readers of Richard B. Sher's striking analysis of the 'Drysdale Bustle' that erupted in Edinburgh in the very same year.[2] The two controversies represented similar responses to what were parallel and probably connected attempts by the town councils of those cities to wrest the power of clerical presentation away from generally orthodox and doctrinaire ministers and elders. Still, Glasgow is not Edinburgh, and explanations of events in the one do not necessarily offer the most illuminating perspective upon the other. If Sher's depiction of the controversy in the ecclesiastical capital tells us much about the ethos of the Moderates and their connections with those known as 'the people above', the dispute over the Glasgow Model is just as revealing of the values of the evangelical or 'Popular' party in the church and their relationship to the commercial sector of that commercial city. As in Edinburgh, the town council would succeed in its attempt to claim the patronage of the city's kirks. As in the Drysdale affair also, the victory proved ephemeral; indeed, it was a good deal more so in Glasgow. Whereas Edinburgh would subsequently divide its pulpits between Moderates and Popular men (much to the disgust of the Moderate leadership), the Glasgow ministry would continue to be vigorously Popular. The town council's initiative in Glasgow represented not so much an attempt to swing that city towards a Moderate ministry as to provide a foothold for Moderates in a city that was predominantly Popular at all levels. The result illustrates the very different religious climate that existed in Glasgow and much of western Scotland.

The existence of such a climate, not just in Scotland's backwaters but within the commercial city of Glasgow, belies the common division of Presbyterianism in eighteenth-century Scotland into a party of Moderates and a party of fanatics, an enlightened few and a credulous many. It calls into question as well the charge, levelled initially by the Moderates, that popular opposition to patronage derived principally from a steadfast resistance to the forces of innovation and enlightenment. In the middle years of the century, Glasgow was both the most rapidly developing commercial city in Scotland and the most evangelical, and defenders of piety and orthodoxy there derived from some of its most innovative groups, including merchants active in the American trade and some powerful artisans. These groups would involve themselves in a multitude of new enterprises in diverse products such as sugar and linen. They would create extensive and meticulously organized transatlantic trading networks. And, with their commercial partners in America, they would develop some novel perspectives on both civil and ecclesiastical affairs.

The ethos these groups would articulate was at once commercial and evangelical. It contained aspects that were surprisingly liberal, cosmopolitan and transatlantic, extending their outlook beyond the traditional confines of sect and nation to the larger British Protestant world. Some of these features are more often associated with the Enlightenment; all contributed substantially to the commercial development and cultural transformation of western Scotland. I would like to suggest, in other words, that there was a good deal more to the enlightening of Glasgow than the polite Enlightenment of the literati.

The nature of that ethos is captured especially well in Popular party conceptions of liberty, a term replete not only with political connotations but with social and cultural ramifications as well. Those included a culture of participation, practical education and self-improvement. The Popular understanding of liberty, though it did not wholly replace older and narrower conceptions, was at the heart of the resurgence of opposition to patronage in Glasgow and the West of Scotland in the second half of the eighteenth century.[3]

I

THE ONSET OF THE CONTEST in Glasgow had been signalled eight years earlier by the death of John MacLaurin, a Popular party leader, opponent of patronage and long-time evangelical minister at the Ramshorn Church. Upon his death, the kirk session at his church recommended as his successor Revd John Erskine, then of Culross, another prominent evangelical who was among the most respected ministers in the church. The town council, then led by Andrew Cochrane's ally, Provost George Murdoch, demurred from simply ratifying the session's choice, announcing instead their intention of abandoning the Model. In the event, they waived that right in order to facilitate the calling of a minister as esteemed as Erskine. When he declined the post, deadlock again appeared imminent, until the provost proposed that all agree to call Paisley's Robert Findlay, an evangelical clergyman highly respected by all concerned parties. The issue was safely concluded for the time being.

No such accommodation could be worked out in 1762. In that year, the town completed the construction of its seventh church, St Andrews, to which William Craig of the Wynd Church removed with his congregation. Immediately, the council announced that it would not be bound by the Model in calling a new minister to the Wynd. For months the two sides engaged in negotiations for a New Model, while a pamphlet war raged between supporters and opponents of the town council. Finally, the town council unilaterally adopted its own plan and presented a Moderate, George Bannatyne, to the post. That move drew protests from the general session and from several councillors, including the prominent merchant Archibald Ingram, who had been elected lord provost of Glasgow since the controversy began.

Who was Archibald Ingram? We know little of his early life. By all accounts he was a self-made man, supposedly of rather niggardly disposition. Highly successful as a tobacco trader, Ingram was the brother-in-law of the town's leading merchant, John Glassford. He was also among the founders of the Glasgow Arms Bank and the principal developer of the Pollokshaws Printfield Company, one of the innovators in calico printing in the city. Despite his notorious thriftiness, Ingram was not unwilling to donate money to causes he considered worthy, which were usually connected with industry and evangelical religion. During the 1730s he had taken the lead in organizing a group of merchant investors, including Glassford, in sponsoring a series of evangelical publications, an effort that began what turned out to be a substantial surge in religious publishing in Glasgow. Ingram was also a major sponsor of the art academy developed by the brothers Robert and Andrew Foulis.[4]

The protest Ingram offered in the town council in 1762 appears, at first glance, a rather surprising document. It lists six different objections to the town council's decision to abandon the old Model, which can be grouped into three broad categories. One is, of course, religious: the town council's actions would introduce 'a very improper set of ministers into this city', to the detriment of both piety and morals. Yet in spite of Ingram's longstanding evangelical commitments, he did not mention his religious concerns until almost the end of this rather long document, and then only briefly.[5]

Ingram devoted far more space in his dissent to a second category of objections: that the town council's actions would be inconsistent with liberty, broadly defined. In fact, Ingram incorporated several different conceptions of liberty into his argument, ranging from the republican to the civic to the contractual. He denied that the council possessed any sovereign authority over the people. The 'fundamentall reason of committing power to the rulers in any society', Ingram asserted, was nothing more than the difficulty of arranging for the whole public to take part. 'All the priveleges which the individualls can without inconvenience exercise in a body, every lover of liberty should wish them to continue in possession of.' Therefore, 'what an apparently absurd and self contradictory measure is it to carry a process . . . in the name of the community when the very partys opposing them are the members, nay almost every inferior society of which that community is composed.'

For the council to exert such a power would have evil consequences. It risked 'the intrigues of faction' and the corruption of the ministerial office, leading to a 'slavery of the worst and most dishonourable kind'. Ingram's commercial background was evident as well. It was, he wrote, 'indecent . . . (to say no more) for the magistrates and council, who were but one of the partys' to the Model, to 'break through the agreement by an act of their own, in opposition to the other body concerned . . . . What security, after this example, can the session or inhabitants have?'

That Ingram would employ the rhetoric of liberty in opposing the town council's action is hardly surprising, given its near ubiquity in eighteenth-century British discourse. Moreover, orthodox Presbyterians had used claims of liberty in opposing patronage since the seventeenth century. But those earlier arguments had employed a concept of liberty that was severely restricted. Theirs was essentially a sectarian understanding, one that granted Presbyterians the freedom to establish what they perceived to be divinely mandated religious forms without interference from civil or ecclesiastical authorities. It lacked connotations of universality or reciprocity. Such a concept certainly accords with traditional understandings of a Popular party that promoted sanctions against supposed infidels such as David Hume and Lord Kames and would vigorously oppose repeal of the penal laws against Roman Catholics. What is surprising is that during the second half of the eighteenth century the Modellers and opponents of patronage within the Church of Scotland began to develop conceptions of liberty which, though far from universal, had substantially wider ramifications.

The extent to which Popular Party conceptions of liberty in the second half of the eighteenth century differed from traditional notions can be illustrated by comparing their arguments against the patronage policies of the Moderates at the ascendancy of William Robertson and his party in 1752 with those of another orthodox group, the seceders, who had abandoned the Church of Scotland in a protest over its patronage policies several decades earlier. The seceders were an avowedly traditionalist group. To them, the tolerance of patronage had represented but one in a series of grievances they had with an establishment that had in their view repeatedly fallen away from the beliefs and practices of Scotland's first reformers. Compare that with the answer prepared by Popular party spokesmen to the so-called 'manifesto' of the Moderates, the 'Reasons of Dissent' lodged in the General Assembly in 1752 by William Robertson and his circle. In their answer, the Popular party writers defended their actions not on the basis of scripture and church tradition, as had the seceders, but rather on the grounds of a liberty of conscience that was the birthright of all Protestants. Ironically, in that debate it was the Moderates who invoked longstanding Scottish and Presbyterian tradition against the libertarian claims of their opponents. Henceforth Popular party leaders, including the Modellers, would almost always phrase their opposition to patronage with reference to a liberty of conscience or 'Christian liberty' that applied not only to Presbyterians but to all Protestants.[6]

The Popular party clergy's support for liberty of conscience was far from unlimited, of course; during the 1770s they would strenuously oppose the repeal of the penal laws against Roman Catholics, as Robert Kent Donovan has shown in detail.[7] But to classify that opposition simply as bigotry, as Donovan does, while not wholly wrong, tends to discount some important changes in the grounds of opposition among a prominent segment of the Popular party. Such Popular party spokesmen as John Erskine, William Porteous and John McFarlane, in their particular and somewhat peculiar understanding, believed they were not abandoning liberty but protecting it. The opposite of liberty, as they understood it, was arbitrary authority, which, to their way of thinking, was the essence of 'Popery' and a threat to liberty. Most, though not all, disavowed interference with the private practices of Roman Catholics and objected only to public efforts and proselytizing. Such distinctions were of little immediate benefit to British Catholics, of course, but they would provide the basis for the rapid abandonment of Popular Party opposition to repeal during the 1790s, when French infidels and revolutionaries replaced Roman Catholics as the primary threat to British liberty.[8]

A second way in which Popular party conceptions of liberty differed from those of their orthodox predecessors was that they rejected narrowly national as well as sectarian definitions; their universe was British rather than simply Scottish, and they viewed liberty as the product of both Scottish and English traditions. Popular party spokesmen began to employ a rhetoric of British liberty rather consistently after the Jacobite rebellion of 1745, which they perceived as a real threat both to Protestantism and Parliament. Thus, in a thanksgiving sermon preached in 1746, Alexander Webster offered thanks for the recent glorious deliverance, 'when all seemed well nigh lost'.[9] He equated this event with Mordecai's rescue of the Jews and with the more recent successions of William and Mary and the Hanoverians, both of which were British and Protestant rather than just Scottish or Presbyterian deliveries. Glasgow's Modellers defined themselves in similarly British terms. One pamphleteer expressed his indignation at the council's action, 'as a free Briton, and an inhabitant of a country of liberty'.[10]And in appealing against the town council decision before the bar of the General Assembly of the Church of Scotland, the appellants declared that 'while we glory in liberty as British subjects', the inhabitants of the Royal burghs continued under 'the most deplorable slavery'.[11] References of that sort became commonplace in Popular party disputation.

A third point about Popular party conceptions of liberty is their willingness to defend religion and religious liberty on the basis of their secular ramifications. That was very much in keeping with the general trend among Scottish evangelicals, who increasingly defended 'religious truth' for 'its moral influence' and detailed 'the influence of religion on national prosperity'. Not only did Archibald Ingram devote scant attention to religious concerns in his town council dissent; even where he discussed religion he emphasized not the fact of impiety but its results, such as indolence and poverty. The same point is apparent in the far more eloquent *Seasonable Address to the Citizens of Glasgow* by the Modeller Patrick Nisbet, who outlined just how broad the consequences of liberty could be. In countries 'groaning under the yoke of civil and ecclesiastical tyranny', wrote Nisbet, 'Observe the fruitful fields turned into a howling wilderness, and the cultivation of the finer arts unknown, or banished.' By contrast, in a land of liberty, 'opulent trade bustles in every city, and cheerful commence spreads her sails through every quarter of the globe; there the elegant arts are cherished . . . peace and harmony reign in every family, and render every society flourishing.'[12]

II

AS NISBET'S DESCRIPTION SUGGESTS, liberty, piety and prosperity were all connected in Popular party conceptions. All were considered matters not simply of institutions or forms of government but of spirit. It was the job of the ministry to inculcate proper values and a proper spirit. One of the Modellers' main arguments was that those appointed under the Model had done this so successfully that, as one declared, the 'genius of civil and ecclesiastical liberty' was now the 'distinguishing characteristic of the city',[13]a situation that was unlikely to continue under council patronage.

It is often supposed that evangelicals shunned moral preaching. In fact, they lectured extensively on such topics as 'Christian Benevolence' and 'The Education of Poor Children'.[14] Their principal objection was not to the preaching of morals *per se*, but rather to the methods that some of their opponents used. Morals, in the Popular party view, required a spiritual rather than simply a rational foundation for the bulk of the population. That perspective underlay one of their main arguments against patronage. However knowledgeable a presentee might be in matters of theology and ethics — and by no means did they consider all to be sufficiently knowledgeable — that qualification would be of no use unless the candidate also possessed the ability to convey not only the *matter* of piety and morals but also their *spirit*, and convey them to the whole congregation rather than just the privileged few.

Popular conceptions of liberty were also markedly participatory. Richard Sher and Alexander Murdoch have questioned the accuracy of the label 'Popular' for the opponents of patronage within the national church, contending that the Popular party did not support truly popular or congregational calls to the ministry but rather promoted the rights of heritors and elders.[15] In regard to the *selection* of ministers, they are surely correct, but to leave matters there is to measure eighteenth-century evangelicals against a rather modern conception of participation that is inextricably linked to election. In a more fundamental sense, the Popular party clergy, while not democratic, certainly were popular in that they unequivocally supported the right of congregations to participate in the process of choosing their minister and to obtain the kind of ministry they sought, by rejecting candidates they deemed unsuitable, whether on the basis of doctrine, behaviour or style.

Popular party writers identified congregational calls as a means of instilling the spirit of liberty in the congregation, an opportunity ordinarily denied to the bulk of the population in the exclusive world of Scottish politics. Popular calls, along with popular resistance to undesirable presentees, helped to disseminate both the spirit and habits of liberty. During the 1770s such ministers as Glasgow's John Gillies and Paisley's John Snodgrass began a concerted campaign to mobilize a Popular party majority within the ecclesiastical electorate, aiming to overturn the pro-patronage policies of the General Assembly in something very much like democratic, interest politics.[16]

If the Popular party clergy were indeed concerned with the inculcation of values, the ones emphasized were not the polite values of the Moderates but those of tradesmen, such as industry, thrift, education, self-improvement and self-worth. Archibald Ingram worried that patronage would lead not only to impiety among the labouring classes but also to indolence and poverty. The Paisley town council, involved in a dispute of its own, recounted how the town had purchased the patronage of its churches from Lord Dundonald so that 'piety and industry might go hand in hand'.[17] Ingram also expressed concern about the impact of the Model controversy upon burgh finances, 'for which they [the town council] are trustees and committed to manage with frugality'.

His fellow councillor John Pagan expressed this concern even better, remarking without a bit of self-consciousness that the town council's actions risked 'wreathing the yoke of patronage around the necks of the inhabitants', which 'at any rate ought not to be done at the expense of the funds of the corporation' (*Extracts*, 7:125–28). These were just the sort of values that were promoted by the many artisan societies that sprang up among the various trade groups in the city,[18] and by the praying societies that developed in conjunction with the spread of evangelical revivalism from the 1740s onwards.

The Modellers, and patronage opponents in general, identified strongly with the aspirations of the trading classes. The Popular party minister Patrick Bannerman, writing on the subject of ecclesiastical and civil liberty, complained that in the burghs 'the great body of the people, those of most respect and usefulness in the commonwealth', had neither representation nor liberty.[19] Govan's William Thom remarked that the very study of history involved too much attention to the deeds of the great and was silent about the bulk of the people, who were, nonetheless, of 'infinitely more importance'.[20] And a tradesman, writing about the Model, levelled equally strong criticism at the town council and the general session, neither of which had the authority to represent the people. He recommended instead a new model that would divide power among *three* segments of the community — the merchants and the elders, as in the old Model, and the trades — so that so 'numerous and important a body' could obtain the influence to which it was entitled.[21]

Patronage was thought to undermine all those values. Instead of personal achievement, it promoted social connections; instead of autonomy, dependence; instead of practical education, polite conversation; instead of an inner-felt system of ethics, a reasoned moral code. As Bannerman asked, how could commerce ever be secure unless ministers instructed their parishioners in piety and sound morals? How could parishes obtain 'faithful and zealous ministers' when interest attached youths not to improving their moral and intellectual qualities but to seeking out presentations? The culture of patronage, in Bannerman's view, exalted rank, polite education and aristocracy. By contrast, popular calls encouraged 'good sense, piety' and the 'free and virtuous principles' of the middle ranks (Bannerman, *Address to the People of Scotland*, 4ff.). To Councillor Pagan, the principal virtues of the Model were its promotion of the zeal for public liberty within the town and the avoidance of dependence upon the favour of great men (*Extracts*, 7:125–28).

The emphasis upon such values as industry and achievement leads us back to the third category of objections that Archibald Ingram raised against the town council's abandonment of the old Model, reflected in his very first reason for dissent: that the actions would detract from the 'dignity' (he used the word twice) of the town council, of which he had the 'honour' to be a member. To abandon the Model without the consent of the kirk sessions would represent a breach of contract, of law, and of faith, and would harm the reputation of the town council. In Ingram's world, contract and reputation were essential values, as important to the merchant as industry and self-worth to the artisan and, like them, closely related to self-improvement and personal achievement. In such a view, piety, industry and dignity were integrally related. One can almost hear the voice of Nicol Jarvie, the proud and pompous merchant in Sir Walter Scott's *Rob Roy*, and in this instance Scott got the attributes exactly right: the exaggerated self-assurance and the self-conscious promotion of personal dignity, rooted in a supreme confidence in the ultimate superiority of tradesmen's values.

The whole point of Ingram's earlier venture into evangelical publishing had been to emphasize the connection between piety and industry, reflected in tracts such as Thomas Watson's *Body of Practical Divinity* and in the works of John Flavel, which explicitly linked work and spirituality.[22] Ingram's had been a non-sectarian effort to promote a very practical divinity, by publishing works that were English as well as Scottish, and Congregational as well as Presbyterian. Over the next several decades, that effort would be continued in Glasgow and Paisley by weavers and other artisans who subsidized a dramatic expansion in evangelical publishing of works of marked diversity in origin and doctrine but heavily weighted towards practical religion. Their contributions to evangelical publishing can be traced in the many subscription lists contained in evangelical works found within the collection of eighteenth-century Glasgow publications in the Mitchell Library, especially works published by John Bryce.[23]

Among the Glasgow protesters, one finds suggestive features in the identities of the most evangelically inclined merchants. They were, on the whole, self-made men who had risen from the ranks of tradesmen or lesser merchants. That characteristic, of course, hardly distinguished them from their fellows in the rapidly growing commercial city, but that is precisely the point: merchants were still connected to tradesmen in a number of ways. At the same time, they were increasingly linked to growing transatlantic commercial and evangelical networks. Ingram is a case in point. His ventures in calico printing, designed to service a transatlantic market, also helped to boost the position of tradesmen in a flourishing textile industry. His publications in practical divinity were designed to appeal to those very same tradesmen.

Ingram's most prominent supporter on the council was the merchant John Pagan. Like Ingram, Pagan was an American trader whose interests would extend well beyond tobacco. By the 1770s, Pagan would invest rather heavily in American lands in several colonies and in the emigrant trade, employing as his partner John Witherspoon, the Popular party minister from Paisley who had gone on to serve as president of the College of New Jersey at Princeton. Witherspoon would become a major promoter of Scottish emigration to America and would articulate a sophisticated concept of provincial liberty that was as much liberal and commercial as religious and political.[24]

Protests against the threat to the Model were not confined to the ranks of the Glasgow town council. The general session also objected to the town council's action. At the top of the list in the session's dissent were several merchants, most of whom were connected to the Glassford group, including Archibald Smellie, Arthur Connell and, at their head, Lawrence Dinwiddie. Dinwiddie also had important American and evangelical connections: his brother Robert was governor of Virginia and the man who first allowed the evangelical minister Samuel Davies (one of Witherspoon's predecessors at the College of New Jersey) to preach in that colony. Three of Dinwiddie's sisters married prominent evangelical clergymen. There would be many other family ties between those merchants and the Popular clergy: Arthur Connell, for example, was the son of the orthodox clergyman Matthew Connell of East Kilbride. The sons of Glasgow evangelicals Robert Findlay and John Hamilton also would be prominent in the city's commercial community.[25]

Opposition extended beyond the council and general session to concerned citizens about whom little is now known. Two objectors whom we do know something about were David Dale, the renowned New Lanark entrepreneur, and his business partner, the candlemaker Archibald Paterson, who led a withdrawal from the Wynd Church during the dispute over the Model and established a new meeting house of their own called the 'Chapel of the Scotch Presbyterian Society'. The career of Dale, who eventually became an Independent, exemplifies in exaggerated form the link among evangelicalism, entrepreneurship and industry.[26]

In the years after the dispute over the Model, evangelical merchants apparently strengthened their position within the burgh. Archibald Ingram was chosen as provost even as the controversy raged, as part of what one Modeller described as an attempted revolution in the 'sett' for the town council. In future years, evangelical councillors would be even more successful. When George Bannatyne died just five years after his appointment to the Wynd Church, the town council chose as his successor the Popular party minister William Porteous. The next vacancy was filled by the equally evangelical Thomas Randall, chosen under the guidance of Provost Arthur Connell, a business partner of Ingram. Those men would connect Glasgow's evangelical community to a wider transatlantic network of merchants and evangelicals (*Extracts*, 7:316–17, 402).

Within the commercial city, the principal opposition to their leadership would come not so much from Moderates and patrons as from more radical groups of tradesman and sectarians, many in the seceder and Independent communions. In 1762 some members of those groups published statements that objected not only to the town council's plans but also to the claim of a general session composed only of ministers and elders to represent the public interest without expressed popular authority for that task. Such groups within the Glasgow community would continue to espouse radical causes for the remainder of the century.[27]

In the statements of Archibald Ingram and others, and in the more radical protests of some of the tradesmen, we find expressions of a set of cultural trends far removed from those of Scotland's celebrated literati. Yet in their concerns for improvement, autonomy and practical education, in their transatlantic perspective and in their vision of popular liberty, Glasgow's merchants and tradesmen developed their own version of enlightenment — what might be called an evangelical or tradesmen's enlightenment — that contributed at least as much as the Enlightenment of the literati to the growth, development and modernization of the commercial city of Glasgow. And through the transatlantic networks of merchants, ministers and tradesmen in which they participated, Scottish evangelicals would play a significant role in disseminating those values throughout the British provincial world.

Notes

1. Most of the pamphlets in this controversy can be found in two bound volumes in the GUL, entitled 'Patronage Debates-Scotland' and 'Form of Calling Ministers to the City of Glasgow 1762–64'; in two bound volumes in the Mitchell Library entitled 'Pamphlets on the Wynd Church, Glasgow' and 'A Collection of Pamphlets Published in the Years 1762 and 1763'; and in a volume of patronage pamphlets in the NLS.

2. Sher, 'Moderates, Managers and Popular Politics in Mid-Eighteenth Century Edinburgh: The Drysdale "Bustle" of the 1760s', in *New Perspectives on the Politics and Culture of Early Modern Scotland*, ed. John Dwyer et al. (Edinburgh, 1982), 179–209.

3. This is not to suggest that some of the western populace did not continue to offer more traditional Presbyterian objections to patronage, especially in rural areas and within the seceder communions. But even some of the seceders adopted a more libertarian stance. The best summary of this material is still Gavin Struthers, *A History of the Rise, Progress and Principles of the Relief Church* (Edinburgh, 1843). A good modern treatment of the secession churches is badly needed.

4. On Ingram's career, see the correspondence of 'Kippen, Glassford and Company' in the Strathclyde Regional Archives, Mitchell Library, Glasgow; T. M. Devine, *The Tobacco Lords: A Study of the Tobacco Merchants of Glasgow and their Trading Activities, c. 1740–90* (Edinburgh, 1975), 181; the third volume of Robert Reid, *Glasgow Past and Present*, 3 vols. (Glasgow, 1884); *The Provosts of Glasgow from 1609 to 1832*, ed. James Gourlay (Glasgow, 1942), 78–79; and John Oswald Mitchell, *Old Glasgow Essays* (Glasgow, 1905), 122–25.

5. Ingram's dissent is printed in full in *Extracts from the Records of the Burgh*

of Glasgow, 1760–1780 (Glasgow, 1912), 7:119–24, from which the following discussion is drawn.

6. See Nathaniel Morren, ed., *Annals of the General Assembly of the Church of Scotland, 1739–1766*, 2 vols. (Edinburgh, 1838–40), 1:243–60; Michael Boston, *The Nature of Christian Liberty Explained, the Violations of it Marked, and the Weapons by which it ought to be Defended Pointed Out* (Edinburgh, 1777).

7. Donovan, *No Popery and Radicalism: Opposition to Roman Catholic Relief in Scotland, 1778–1782* (New York, 1987).

8. See especially William Porteous, *The Doctrine of Toleration, Applied to the Present Times* (Glasgow, 1778).

9. Alexander Webster, *Heathens Professing Judaism, When the Fear of the Jews Fell upon Them* (Edinburgh, 1746), 30, 44–45.

10. *A Letter from W. M., Gentleman, to J. C., Citizen of Glasgow*, 24 March, 1762, 2, 5.

11. *Memorial . . . by the Appellants*, April, 1764, 8.

12. Nisbet, *A Seasonable Address to the Citizens of Glasgow, upon the Present Important Question, Whether the Churches of that City Shall Continue Free, or Be Enslaved to Patronage?* ([Glasgow], 1762), 12–13. See also John Witherspoon, *The Trial of Religious Truth by its Moral Influence* (Glasgow, 1759) and John Erskine, *The Influence of Religion on National Prosperity* (Edinburgh, 1757).

13. *A Continuation of the Historical Account of the Debates which Happened in the Years 1755, 1761, and 1762, concerning the Model, or Form, for Calling Ministers to the City of Glasgow* ([Glasgow], 1762), 25–28.

14. Thomas Randall, *Christian Benevolence: A Sermon Preached Before the Society in Scotland for Propagating Christian Knowledge* (Edinburgh, 1763); John Erskine, *The Education of Poor Children Recommended: A Sermon, Preached . . . before the Managers of the Orphan-hospital, and Published at their Desire* (Edinburgh, 1774).

15. Sher and Murdoch, 'Patronage and Party in the Church of Scotland, 1750–1800', in *Church, Politics and Society: Scotland 1408–1929*, ed. Norman Macdougall (Edinburgh, 1983), 197–220.

16. *Copy of a Printed Letter, Signed John Gillies. Addressed to the Elders of the Synod of Glasgow and Air* (Edinburgh, 1784); John Snodgrass, *An Effectual Remedy for Preserving Our Ecclesiastical Liberties Addressed to the Elders of the Church of Scotland* (Glasgow 1770). See also Andrew Crosbie, *Thoughts of a Layman Concerning Patronage and Presentations* (Edinburgh, 1769).

17. *Case of the Magistrates and Town-Council of Paisley, the Minister and Session of the Laigh Church, and the Minister of the High Church at that Town, Appellants* [Edinburgh, 1758].

18. See Ned C. Landsman, 'Evangelists and their Hearers: Popular Interpretation of Revivalist Preaching in Eighteenth-Century Scotland', *Journal of British Studies* 28 (1989): 120–49.

19. Bannerman, *An Address to the People of Scotland, on Ecclesiastical and Civil Liberty* (Edinburgh, 1782), 20.

20. Thom, *A Candid Enquiry into the Causes of the Late and the Intended Migrations From Scotland* (Glasgow, n.d.), 28–29.

21. *A Letter to the Inhabitants of Glasgow in the Present Disputes about a Model for Calling Ministers to the City* (n.p., 1761). See also *A Brief and Simple Narrative of the Rise, Progress, and Effects of Patronage . . . By A Linen Manufacturor* (Glasgow, 1782).

22. Thomas Watson, *A Body of Practical Divinity*, 3rd ed. (Glasgow, 1734); John Flavel, *The Whole Works of the Reverend Mr. John Flavel. Late Minister of the Gospel at Dartmouth in Devon*, 3rd, ed., 2 vols. (Edinburgh, 1731). Watson's book was 'printed for Archibald Ingram, merchant in Glasgow', and Ingram was among a number of individuals for whom Flavel's *Works* was printed, including two other Glasgow merchants, John Rowand and John Neulands.

23. See Ned C. Landsman, 'Presbyterians and Provincial Society: The Evangelical Enlightenment in the West of Scotland, 1740–1775', in *Sociability and Society in Eighteenth-Century Scotland*, ed. John Dwyer and Richard B. Sher (Edinburgh, 1993): 194–209, esp. 199.

24. Landsman, 'Presbyterians and Provincial Society', and 'Witherspoon and the Problem of Provincial Identity in Scottish Evangelical Culture', in *Scotland and America in the Age of the Enlightenment*, ed. Richard B. Sher and Jeffrey R. Smitten (Princeton, 1990), 29–45.

25. *Petition of the General Sessions of Glasgow, 1763*, in GUL, 'Patronage Debates-Scotland'. On Dinwiddie, see *Provosts of Glasgow*, ed. Gourlay, 65–66.

26. George Stewart, *Curiosities of Glasgow Citizenship* (Glasgow, 1881), 56–59; David J. McLaren, *David Dale of New Lanark: A Bright Luminary to Scotland* (Milngavie, 1983), chap. 6.

27. *Letter to the Inhabitants of Glasgow*; and *A New Year's Gift to the Inhabitants of the City of Glasgow, Queries Proposed Concerning the Power and Management of the Town Council of the City of Glasgow, For Some Years Past* (n.p., 1762). Still standard on late eighteenth-century political disputes is Henry W. Meikle, *Scotland and the French Revolution* (Glasgow, 1912).

Evangelical Civic Humanism in Glasgow: The American War Sermons of William Thom

Robert Kent Donovan

After 1763, when the American colonists began to criticize British policies, some Scottish observers responded sympathetically to the Americans' plight. Identification readily appeared because of parallels between Scottish and American society, which were both 'caught up by a process of fairly rapid and fundamental change, while at the same time remaining deeply conservative'.[1] As the colonists debated taxation and trade regulations, the Scots debated their country's economics, its military defence and the policies of its church, and they quarrelled on occasion about the colonies. The American conflict divided opinion in Scotland and sharpened Scottish debate over domestic issues. Although many Scots supported imperial policies, others defended America in public meetings, the press and, most important for our immediate purpose, the pulpit.[2]

At Glasgow, the foremost supporter of the colonists was William Thom, minister of Govan on the south bank of the River Clyde. Other Glasgow clergy may have preached for the colonists, but Thom alone published sermons on the need for conciliation: *The Revolt of the Ten Tribes* (hereafter *RTT*), preached 12 December 1776 and published 1778; *Achan's Trespass in the Accursed Thing Considered* (hereafter *ATAT*), preached 26 February 1778 and published 1779; and *From Whence Come Wars?* (hereafter *FWCW*), preached 9 February 1779 and published 1782.[3] When Thom preached the first of these war sermons, he was sixty-six years old and no stranger to discussion of America, or to debate over an array of other problems.

Thom's comments on America give us the opinions of a locally celebrated, indeed notorious, citizen who lived in sight of one of the empire's leading commercial centres. His ideas are of interest today for their unusual mixture of traditional, orthodox Calvinism and civic humanism. In his writings, the thoroughgoing evangelicalism of the Popular party in the established church — a loosely organized connection with which Thom developed ties as his career advanced — unites easily with the progressive, sometimes radical, doctrines of the 'true' or 'old' Whigs.

Evangelical Calvinism may appear to predominate, and so will claim our attention first, but we shall see that civic humanist influences are no less present.

I

THE CAREER OF WILLIAM THOM was characterized by highly eclectic thinking and bold, some said reckless, fault-finding, making him difficult to place in church politics. Like other radical Scotsmen of his day, he was long dismissed as a colourful eccentric. Alexander Carlyle, who associated with him at a Glasgow literary club in the mid-1740s, considered him 'a learned man, of a very particular but ingenious turn of mind'.[4] Sir Walter Scott knew him by reputation as an overstrenuous advocate of temperance.[5] In the nineteenth century, the annalist Nathaniel Morren remarked that he was remembered more 'for eccentricity and sarcasm, than for prudence and piety'.[6] Only recently has Thom become the object of serious interest. In the late 1940s J. D. Mackie judged his sermons 'of surprising quality' and his satires worthy of Swift, and within the last decade several commentators have pointed to him as a notable publicist and reformer.[7]

Although not a Glasgow native, Thom was born within the boundaries of the Synod of Glasgow and Ayr, at New Monklands. He received his M. A. degree from Glasgow University in 1732 but waited years for a parish of his own, until in 1746 the university, which he would later criticize so often, presented him to nearby Govan.[8] Wrangling with his patrons over a dilapidated manse, a meagre stipend and what he saw as university mismanagement occupied him for years and doubtless made him alive to other injustices at home and overseas.[9]

As a seasoned cleric, Thom had a pronounced evangelical outlook and impeccable Popular party credentials. The fact that his evangelical rhetoric is not always as marked as that of some of his colleagues may explain why observers found him difficult to label. But evangelical he was, and his writings reveal his loyalty to the agenda of the Popular or, as he said, the 'Strict' party. The foremost sign of his allegiance was his opposition to church patronage, the process by which authorities such as the Crown, the lairds, the burgh councils or, as in Thom's case, the universities appointed the clergy to parish charges. Against the pro-patronage Moderate party, the Popular party persistently argued not, in most instances, for democracy or congregationalism but for the right of local heritors (landowners) and church elders to participate in a representative and, hence, 'popular' selection process.[10] Ironically, Thom himself had faced local opposition to his ordination at Govan, for reasons that remain obscure.[11] Once settled there, however, he took up his pen against patronage, defending Scottish heritors and elders who considered it an autocratic and erastian procedure.[12]

Thom's opposition to church patronage alone would mark him as a Popular party man, but his friendships, his views on church and state politics, and his ethical and spiritual beliefs also reveal that allegiance. He shared the outlook of friends such as John Gillies of Blackfriar's Church, Glasgow, whom he defended for 'insisting on the depravity of human nature, and the necessity of revelation', and John Witherspoon, minister at Paisley, and later president of the College of New Jersey (Princeton).[13] Like some of his Popular party colleagues, Thom regretted British government interference in the kirk and had ambivalent feelings about the Union of Scotland and England (*RTT*, 44; *ATAT*, 39–40). Like them, too, he was of two minds about Scottish Presbyterian seceders from the established church, admiring their strict doctrine but deploring the schism they caused. He also shared party suspicion of Roman Catholicism, a well-known evangelical prejudice.[14]

Such attitudes were informed by Popular party ideas about ethics and spirituality. Thom held that deportment should avoid 'the looks of carelessness, indifference, or levity' (*Enquiry*, 7). He condemned card parties, balls and the theatre, as well as the use of pipe-organs and sung anthems in the church.[15] He insisted on strict Sabbath observance, family prayers, regular parish visiting by the clergy and the evangelical tradition of outspoken or 'painful' address that would 'pierce . . . to the heart'.[16] This conviction encouraged him to preach as boldly as he did during the American War. Behind such attitudes was an 'experimental' or experiential spirituality, which made him deplore both 'hidebound' formalism and fashionable scepticism (*Enquiry*, 20; *Scheme*, 26). He urged ministers to 'preach oftenest in those subjects which are mentioned oftenest in the Bible' and to use 'the style and language of holy scripture' (*Sober Conference*, 45; *Task-Masters*, 161). He embellished his own sermons, including those on America, with biblical quotes, although his style, as we shall see, did not always cleave to that of the Good Book.

Thom's Popular party allegiance helps to explain his abiding interest in America. Early ties between Scottish Presbyterians and American Calvinists multiplied and strengthened in the revivals of the 1740s: the Great Awakening and the Cambuslang Wark near Glasgow. Those relationships, though perhaps less intense in later years, remained sturdy, especially in the Popular party. Thus, when the Revolution occurred, the Church of Scotland clergy who defended the colonists were all Popular party men. Perceptive Scots increasingly recognized similarities with Americans in language, in consciousness of provincial status in an English-dominated empire, and in awareness of change in a still largely preindustrial society. Many clergy who would later join the Popular as well as the Moderate parties also had come under broader, more generous tutelage as university reforms occurred, encouraging them to look beyond a strictly national culture and church (Landsman, 'Witherspoon', 33–34). Furthermore, Scottish-American trade and Scottish service in the Seven Years War heightened identification with the colonists, as Thom himself commented.[17]

America concerned the Popular party first and foremost, however, because of religion. Calvinists like Thom eschewed individualism for a far-reaching, indeed, transcendent communalism. Evangelical community-mindedness, seen in emphasis on family prayers and parish visiting, reached beyond the parish to a vast congregation at home and abroad — a communion of saints, with no spatial or temporal bounds, including 'all nations and tongues'.[18] Thus, the party prized American Calvinist churches, preaching, as Thom did, for their welfare and for the conversion of Native American tribes (*Task-Masters*, 206). For some, moreover, the colonies figured in an apocalyptic millenialist eschatology, a final fulfilment of history in which, more and more, America loomed large. This eschatology was dynamic, with successes and reverses arriving in a 'sacred scenario' to culminate in the future.[19] In this plan, the saints would actively assist the unfolding of the divine will. Although history's last moments — the Second Coming and the Last Judgement — might invite a gloomy interpretation, Calvinists who were confident of their election contemplated them optimistically. At the same time, unpredictability as to the future's exact course contributed uncertainty and tension to the faith: though the millennium was inevitable, the saints had to strive for it anyway.[20] Uncertainty hovered over the locus of the final unfolding, too, but in the 1740s Americans had reflected upon their continent as providentially chosen. Some British commentators had agreed that America might be the promontory on which the thousand years associated with the Second Coming would unfold.[21]

America as a providentially appointed plantation for distressed Scots had attracted William Thom's interest before the Revolution began. In a 1770 sermon, moreover, his optimism attained apocalyptic heights. God had founded America for needy Scots and would safeguard and speed their voyage. Once there, they would know 'joy and wonder' in practising 'the true faith' and would 'enlarge the boundaries of the Mediator's kingdom' by converting 'the poor Indians'. Within this scheme America's future was dazzling; it would be as a garden of Eden, where all things would be new. Matrimony, freed of old-world conventions and poverty, would be purified; the population would multiply; and industry flourish: 'How joyful the thought! It may be that which is intended by the sounding of the seventh angel: "There were great voices in heaven saying, the kingdoms of this world are become the kingdom of our Lord and of his Christ; and he shall reign for evermore. Sing then, o barren, thou that didst not bear; break forth into singing, and cry aloud."'[22]

II

WILLIAM THOM'S APOCALYPTIC CALVINISM helps to explain his apprehensions when disagreements surfaced between the American colonists and the British, as well as his mounting anxiety when warfare broke out. Action is an antidote to anxiety, and Thom's fears led him to preach for America. In doing so, he had several advantages. Govan, Glasgow and southwestern Scotland constituted Popular party strongholds, where he was sure of a receptive audience. He also preached at opportune times, on national fast days set aside for reflection on the conflict, when the congregation was primed for intense concentration on political themes.[23] In these fast day sermons, Thom often mediated between evangelical truth as he perceived it and the political crisis he was witnessing. He often used an exalted evangelical rhetoric, a widely accredited phraseology that would have lent plausibility and, for some listeners, verity to his remarks (Pocock, *Virtue, Commerce and History*, 8; Tillich, *Protestant Era*, xiii-xiv). Although the government appointed fast days to promote conquest, not conciliation, Thom inverted that aim. Instead of crying up victory in war, he warned against the folly, duplicity and corruption of its prosecutors.

Thom may have relished the irony of preaching for the colonists rather than against them, but he did not invest his sermons with the irony and sarcasm that he typically used in regard to other problems. He viewed the war with an earnestness that banished levity. Although these sermons defy easy intellectual and stylistic classification, they exhibit a religious seriousness. They also display other traits of Popular party homiletics: they are cautious and conciliatory politically, despite their outspoken language; they are penitential and providentialist in spirituality; they have a unique Protestant historical outlook; and they draw widely on biblical paradigms.

The Popular party clergy sometimes had to bear the epithet 'wild' or 'enthusiastic', and sometimes they deserved it. More often, however, they adopted a cautious, conciliatory programme and tone, considered appropriate for members of a state church. Consequently, Thom chides government neglect of compromise: 'One would think that princes, rather than drench the nations in blood, should meet and finish their senseless differences by friendly conference — or compromise them by arbitration' (*FWCW*, 33). This sentiment echoes his earlier hopes that 'God grant that the parent and child may soon return to live in friendship' (*ATAT*, 36). All three sermons blame the British government entirely for the rupture of understanding, the outbreak of war and the continuation of hostilities. They also place responsibility for peace with the Crown. Thom views peace so urgently, however, that the last of the sermons, despite its focus on government failings, suggests that the colonists should accept the terms offered by the earl of Carlisle's peace commission in 1778. He hints at the same time that the colonists may win the war, but he does not contemplate independence (*FWCW*, 28). In this regard, apocalyptic expectations, while not explicit, may have influenced his conviction that the colonies must continue within Britain's domain.

Caution also influences other comments. Thom preaches on warfare in general, not on the particular events of the American Revolution. He refers to British atrocities, but in rhetorical queries, not pointed accusations, asking: 'Have no villages, no towns, no cities been wantonly burned?' He suggests that British troops have engaged in 'theft, or pillage, or plunder, or robbery', but once again does so in questions or hints (*FWCW*, 35; *ATAT*, 31). In treating the war itself, he stresses the length of the conflict, not the details of its conduct. He objects repeatedly to 'this lasting American war' and asks 'if this kingdom doth not contribute to its depopulation and ruin, by its fond pursuit of this tedious American war . . . ?' (*ATAT*, 15, 24, 35–37). By the time of his last sermon in February 1779, however, Thom is phrasing his questions more boldly, asking if the ministry has not prolonged the war purposely, 'so that they may get more gold and silver to consume in luxury, high living, drunkenness and gluttony, or in gaming, lewdness and expensive debauchery, grown up to a scandalous height, unheard of till this age' (*FWCW*, 37–38). Yet he remains cautious, criticizing the administration, not the king, and holding to the traditional fiction of the wise monarch misled by his creatures.

Although Thom spares George III, he does not hesitate to condemn the nation. The war is in his view divine judgement on the participants, particularly on the British government. The sermons are Calvinist jeremiads in which the preacher censures the nation for its sins, warns it to repent and admonishes it to reform. For Thom, divine purpose moves through history, in this case through the events of war. That purpose, though sometimes obscure, can often be ascertained by the elect. Even before the outbreak of hostilities, Thom tells his audience that 'God speaks to you by facts, by the visible course of his providential wisdom'. During the war itself, he again asserts that 'of the dispensations of Providence, we are able to perceive many of the wise reasons, though we are too blind to see them all'. The sermons assume that God has a covenant with his people and will not abandon them, but rather will purge and tutor them to discern events and act accordingly. The saints can turn from sin and also convert others to justice. Faced with a colonial war that is difficult to win, Thom issues the classic challenge of the jeremiad: 'Whilst we fast and pray for success in this tedious and lamentable war, let us, let our rulers and commanders, examine whether there be not some unjustifiable steps we have taken' (*FWCW*, 35). This admonition was legally mandated, for the fast day proclamation of 26 February 1778, quoted in *Achan's Trespass*, recommends that 'we and our people may humble ourselves before Almighty God, in order to obtain the pardon for our sins . . . for averting those heavy judgments which our manifold sins and provocations have most justly deserved' (*ATAT*, 14).

This belief in salutary judgements on nations owes much to the doctrine of the suffering church, which still appealed to eighteenth-century evangelicals. It explained why 'wrongs' such as patronage and the ascendancy of the Crown and aristocracy were inflicted on the kirk as warnings and possible purgatives. Thus, Thom's first fast day sermon interprets Britain's losses as divine punishment: 'Most certainly, we deserve a stroke.' Later, as success continues to elude the government, Thom repeats the theme: 'The church and people of God may sometimes be long in adversity . . . . God leaves his people long in trouble to alarm their consciences, to check them in their wild career, and force them to think of the eternal world' (*RTT*, 44; *FWCW*, 32).

Not surprisingly, the foremost sin of that 'wild career' is pride. Just as the Israelites experienced defeat for boasting of their might, so the British might suffer the same fate for their arrogance (*ATAT*, 23–24). Their sins exceed pride and boasting, however. In all three fast day sermons, Thom condemns the British ruling classes for opulence, venality, injustice and oppression. 'In all ages, they were the rich who were the most covetous, as well as the most oppressive' (*RTT*, 38, 41). They 'lay a grievous yoke on the poor' without fear of reproof, for 'respect will be shown to the man with the gold ring and the gay clothing, the man who hath riches, who hath a liberality of soul to furnish out a copious and splendid entertainment to the judges' (*ATAT*, 32, 39–40). Again: 'Have not only a few been enriched, and the rest been borne down and oppressed?' (*FWCW*, 2–3). In criticizing the great as luxury-loving and haughty, Thom follows a well-established evangelical custom, but he goes beyond it in condemning their political activities. These sins have prolonged the war, which must be devoutly pondered.

The preacher who launches jeremiads over the heads of his people does so not to dishearten them but to encourage them to seek God's guidance and conform to his will.[24] Fasting, prayer and hearing sermons reveal that will, but history offers counsel of great value. Thom places the American conflict within a sacred history viewed from a traditional Protestant perspective, stressing the age-old struggle of the saints with evil. He considers as relevant, for example, the wars that a corrupt monarch like Charles II, allied with Louis XIV, waged against the Dutch Calvinist brethren of the Scots (*ATAT*, 14–15; *FWCW*, 14–15). He praises Britain's righteous conduct during the Seven Years War, where victory 'came from God', against forces aiming 'to bring us under Popery and arbitrary power' (*ATAT*, 30, 42). In this historiography, the Reformation and the Glorious Revolution figure monumentally in religion and politics alike, bringing about greater freedom as well as a purer faith (*RTT*, 32).

This historical perspective extends directly into the American War. In *Achan's Trespass*, preached amid rumours of a Franco-American alliance,

Thom warns that Great Britain may be invaded by the French, 'a Popish Pretender along with them' (*ATAT*, 47). Fear of French intervention offers yet another reason for seeking peace. In the *Revolt of the Ten Tribes*, Thom remarks that if government conciliates the colonists, 'a grateful people will more readily come forward to defend against foreign invasion' (*RTT*, 16). As French involvement becomes more likely, he cautions the Scots to pray that they be spared 'the violent hostilities of France' at home, and that the combatants come to terms, lest the Americans 'being seduced by the fallacious promise of assistance . . . should fling themselves into the arms of France' (*FWCW*, 6). Roman Catholic domination over America seems to play a role in averting him from contemplating the colonies' independence.

For Thom, the usable past extended into the most ancient times, and he quoted scripture to make political, rather than exclusively theological, points. As was the custom, he preached at length, sometimes citing biblical passages a full page long. His sermon-texts emphasize scriptural parallels for the American War, and particularly instances of resistance to corruption and dictatorship. The text of *Revolt of the Ten Tribes*, 1 Kings 12:1–30, recounts how Solomon's idolatrous son, King Rehoboam, continued his father's harsh rule, ignored the advice of the elders for better government, and listened only to his self-seeking new advisors. As a result, Jehovah 'rends his kingdom', leaving Rehoboam monarch only of the tribe of Judah. The analogy with a stubborn British king, a self-seeking cabinet and a division of empire is so clear that the preacher does not have to comment on it in detail. The text of *Achan's Trespass*, Joshua 7:1–26, censures one of Joshua's soldiers who had stolen spoils of war dedicated to God, bringing down divine wrath on Jericho. This sermon was the first to suggest that British politicians and generals had prolonged hostilities against America in order 'to enjoy the emoluments and honours of command' (*ATAT*, 38), though Thom did not push the analogy to the point of recommending that they should suffer the same punishment as the thief Achan, who was stoned and burned along with his children. The last sermon comes from the Epistle of James, 4:1–3, a text that requires no commentary:

> From whence come wars and fighting among you? Come they not hence, even of your lusts that war in your members? Ye lust, and have not: ye kill, and desire to have, and cannot obtain: ye fight and war, yet ye have not, because ye ask not. Ye ask and receive not, because ye ask amiss, that ye may consume it upon your lusts.

Evangelicals recognized a close resemblance between the people of Israel and themselves, between their history and contemporary experiences (Sher, 'Witherspoon's *Dominion*', 50). In William Thom's sermons, however, the resemblance amounts to a common identity. The modern faithful are not simply analogous to the Israelites but identical to them in a transcendent sense. The saints and the ancient chosen people are types of the same community mystically conceived. *Achan's Trespass*, therefore, refers to its culprit's crime as against 'the church', not against the Jews or the Temple, just as elsewhere Thom describes the deliverance of 'the Jewish church' from captivity in Babylon (*Sober and Religious Conference*, 24; *ATAT*, 19). Thus, while his historical sense sweeps back over centuries (and forward to the end of all centuries), it also telescopes historical time, pressing past events into current ones so that history acquires a startling, alarming relevance.

Thom used scripture not only to point out injustice and sin but also to recommend reforms. He suggests that the British should follow the example of the Israelites when they detected Achan's theft, recovered the spoils and punished him. The just everywhere should expose robbery and resist tyranny (*ATAT*, 29–30). Just as the ten tribes retaliated against Rehoboam, so the British may retaliate when 'the senators and those assembled to take care of the rights and liberties of the common people' are negligent in the face of misgovernment (*RTT*, 38).

The Bible fortified Thom's appeal in yet another way. Its ancient sacred language, translated into the ornate English of the King James version and combined with the preacher's plain eighteenth-century style, created what J.G.A. Pocock might call a rich polyglot rhetoric of considerable dimension, texture and force (Pocock, *Virtue, Commerce and History*, 8–12). The liturgical circumstances of Thom's preaching are once again relevant. The Word is central to Calvinism, and it is no exaggeration to say that reading it, expounding it and preaching upon its embodiment in scripture occupied virtually every moment of divine service in the eighteenth-century kirk, except when the minister's voice rose in extempore prayer (a petition itself biblically embellished). There were no hymns or anthems in Thom's church, and the authoritative *Westminster Directory* enjoined not only preaching sermons with biblical texts but also expounding an additional two chapters from each Testament on Sundays. In assessing the impact of Thom's sermons, one must keep in mind how receptive his listeners and readers would have been to the biblical dimension of contemporary events .

III

WILLIAM THOM'S USE OF terms like despotism, arbitrary power and 'the rights and liberties of the common people', along with his evangelical utterances, alerts us to the complexity of his thought as well as the idiosyncracies of his rhetoric. The sermons we have mined for orthodox Calvinism just as readily yield civic humanist or True Whig rhetoric and concepts. One example occurs when Thom asks why God allows his people, the church, to suffer setbacks and defeats. Why has Islam gained over Christianity, or Popery checked the Reformation? In the same passage, remarkably, he also asks why in the secular realm 'those who contend for the interest of liberty, of virtue, of the public good' sometimes fail. He ponders the plight of Christian martyrs for freedom and justice but also of pagan opponents of despotism like Cassius and Brutus (*FWCW*, 31). He moves easily from evangelical concerns to classical ones and seems to be equally at home in both traditions.

The same juncture of thought and expression occurs everywhere in Thom's works. Ned Landsman has commented on Thom's criticism of the Scottish economy and society, to which he posed emigration as a solution. But as we have seen, apocalyptic hopes also coloured his views on emigration, and in the very same sermon. Although his writings may be considered evangelical constructs, his Whig humanism also appears in his rhetorical style, in his use of classical intellectual sources, in his values and moral judgements, in his attitude towards reforms and in his programmes for bringing those reforms about. Before examining this aspect of his American war sermons, a general survey of his civic humanist or Real Whig opinions may be useful.

Modern readers of William Thom's sermons, accustomed to regarding evangelicals as enthusiasts, will find his homiletic style surprisingly rational, dispassionate and cool. Although some of his works — his emigration-tract paean to America and his anti-university lampoons, for example — have a vibrant or heated tone, the sermons on the American war seldom rise to that pitch. He confronts the subject seriously, in a grave, if often detached, manner. Alan Heimert has noted that American 'Liberals' of the day preached to inform, whereas 'Calvinists' preached to arouse (Heimert, *Religion and the American Mind*, 18), but William Thom sought at least as much to instruct as to stir people. One cannot hear the preacher of these sermons thundering at his congregation. Despite frequent scriptural quotations, his remarks do not have the impacted, 'crabbed' style of some other orthodox evangelicals.

In addressing the war, Thom relies on reason, not emotion. He is the sort of evangelical who can declare, even in a non-political sermon, that 'reason and speech are the two principal faculties by which mankind are distinguished from the animal creation; by the use of reason we find out truth, and by speech we communicate it to others' (*Task-Masters*, 206). He confidently seeks the conversion of Native Americans because they, 'like all men, possess reason' and are open to persuasion (*Sober and Religious Conference*, 23). Rational intent, not simply prudence, explains why Thom relies on generalizations, a device that also contributes to his often lofty, considered tone. He criticizes government misdeeds, but never in specific terms. He decries wars in general, as if he were searching for 'laws' to promote 'a habitual dislike of war, and a strong aversion to begin any particular war' (*RTT*, 32; *FWCW*, 32). His evangelical dread of losing the colonies undoubtedly influences his appeals for conciliation, but those appeals also arise from a deep commitment to reasoned settlements.

In polemics on a wide range of issues, Thom sets almost as high a value on secular knowledge, especially classical knowledge, as on scripture. He prizes history, both ancient and modern, and with characteristic irony declares that it can teach 'people such notions of liberty as are incompatible with the dutiful submission which subjects owe to their magistrates' (*Scheme*, 37). In his religious writings, too, he recommends secular learning as 'both pleasing and profitable' (*Sober and Religious Conference*, 39), advice he himself followed in his war sermons. Despite his rationalism, however, Thom rejects the 'metaphysical Jargon' of speculative philosophy. This aversion to philosophy, which marks his attacks on higher education, leads him to shun philosophizing in his works, all of which aim at a practical moral result (*Defects*, 3–6; *Trial*, 27–29). He comments in his war sermons on ideals like liberty and mercy but never speculates about the ideological concerns that may lie behind the colonial protest. His interest lies in behaviour and morality, not metaphysics. Thom shows admiration for humanist literary forms like the dialogue or colloquy and uses humanist vehicles like the essay, tract or letter and the oration or sermon, which are designed to persuade in brief compass rather than speculate at length (*Sober and Religious Conference*, 38).

Thom's debt to civic humanism was not limited to literary style and historical sources. His writings also display the full range of civic humanist concepts subscribed to by radical Whigs. His knowledge of classical authors underlies his use of the classical republic as an ideal polity in his observations on the state, the empire and even the church. One of his satires on Glasgow University is situated in the mythical state of Clutha (Clyde), a model republic. Clutha's ideal citizens are propertied men with the economic autonomy to resist corruption and tyranny by cultivating the ruling temperament known to civic humanists as *virtù*. Thom argues that schooling should aim 'to enlarge the capacity, to encrease the powers and improve the virtue of mankind'. The definition of virtue as capacity, fortitude or talent was not a Christian concept in origin, of course, but he adapts it to a Christian context (*Candid Enquiry*, 64). He idealizes the lesser lairds or gentry and substantial farmers of his day as having the actual or potential virtue needed to balance or limit the ambition and power of the greater nobles and the Crown. Although the commercial classes who own no land awake his civic misgivings, he nonetheless includes them in his model republic (*Candid Enquiry*, 13–15, 21; *Trial*, 19).[25]

Whereas the ideal citizenry in civic humanist thought governed a state of limited territory, for Thom, an imperial-minded Whig, the virtuous republic included the colonies. He admired Chatham for extending Britain's sway and endorsed the view that 'the seat of empire' would move to North America (*Task-Masters*, 207–8), a secular expectation complementing his apocalyptic eschatology. Thus, in promoting emigration he viewed the colonies not only as havens of pure religion but also as plantations governed by laws 'esteemed to be the perfection of human reason'. The empire, in turn, would profit from Thom's emigrants, for they were farmers, the virtuous class *par excellence* (*Task-Masters*, 202–4, 215). Thom also conceived the ideal kirk as a virtuous republic, where propertied men of middle rank (i.e. the elders and heritors), and the clergy they chose, might balance the interest of a noble or royal patron. In this he differed from some Popular party clerics, whose ecclesiology proceeded from a religiously, not a humanistically, conceived paradigm (*Letter*, 13–14).

For civic humanists, the republic — whether a state, an empire or a church — always faced the threat of corruption and despotism, since *fortuna* dictates degradation. For Thom, a particular menace to church and state in Scotland and America came from Popery, especially when the war invited French interference. Although he sometimes derided Roman Catholicism as an 'absurdity', he usually viewed it as a species of despotism (*Enquiry*, 21–22; *RTT*, 37; *FWCW*, 38). Another threat to the ideal church came from church patronage, which tended to destroy 'the democratical power' in the church and to enhance the monarchical power in church and state alike (*Short History*, 47–49). When Thom turned to menaces faced by civil government, he decried corrupt, undue influence not simply as unjust but as 'a disturbance of the political conditions necessary to human virtue and freedom'. He held that 'human society, after a long progress in civilization and refinement, verges back to corruption' with something like inevitability (*Trial*, 16).[26]

In 1766 Thom had observed that 'the government of Great Britain must, in the way of natural operation, approach nearer and nearer to absolute monarchy, as all other limited monarchies that ever existed in the world have done' (*Short History*, 46–47). In 1783 he repeated the resolution of the Whig member of Parliament John Dunning that 'the influence of the Crown has grown great, and is daily increasing' (*Letter to the Author*, 10). Like other radical Whigs, he viewed the Whig oligarchy as the agents in Great Britain and the empire of tyranny, blaming them for depredations in the church, overexactions as landlords and extravagance in raising the national debt through corrupt government and a protracted, unnecessary war.[27] His objections to their 'luxury, dissipation, and extravagance' were rooted as much in his radical Whig ideology as in his evangelical Calvinist doctrine, and he held up against those vices the virtues of frugality and austerity, deemed essential to good government (*Information to Emigrants*, 12, 14; *Information Concerning North Carolina*, 4). That these were also the fruits of an awakened Christian life made them all the more compelling.

True Whig or civic humanist values also appear in Thom's many proposals for reform. The improving agents are always 'the people', identified as farmers, honest burgesses, landed gentlemen and aristocrats (presumably uncorrupted) (*Trial*, 40–41). To augment their influence, Thom recommends extending the militia to Scotland, armed citizens being indispensable to the republic of virtue. To the same end he speculates about extending the franchise to include more Scottish landed proprietors of middling rank (*Scheme*, 25; *Candid Enquiry*, 22). Thom's reform agenda, however, avoided root-and-branch alterations. Rather than eliminate unjust institutions, he proposed reforming or restraining them with a balancing agency or make-weight. He did not want to abolish Glasgow University, much as he despised it, but envisioned instead an academy to compete with it (*Defects*). In the kirk, patrons could remain, but with the ruling elders, landed heritors and emancipated ministers 'mitigating' their influence (*Short History*, 30; *Letter*, 33–34). For impoverished farmers and craftsmen, he recommended not agitation but emigration to America, where plentiful land, 'almost without taxation', might enable them to cultivate virtue and strengthen the virtuous estate within the imperial republic (*Task-Masters*, 198–201). The Native Americans, for their part, appealed to him as 'a people plain, and uncorrupted by luxury or false refinement', who could presumably fortify good government as well as the true church (*Task-Masters*, 206).

The most progressive feature in Thom's rather sedate reform programme was his recommendation of organized action for the oppressed. At a time when commerce and industry would soon promote individualism, he still conceived of society as an amalgamation of communities such as the church, the university and the farming class. But when he urged farmers to organize against the competitive 'roups' or auctions of leases that served to push up rents, the proposal seems daring and 'modern'.[28] With similar advice he encouraged emigrating Scots to strengthen their resolve and protect their interest with organized companies (*Task-Masters*, 195–96; *Candid Enquiry*, 5). When the American war drew to a close and other issues began to claim more of his attention, he defended the novel anti-patronage associations that the Popular party organized in an effort to reform the kirk (*Letter to the Author*, 7).

When William Thom examined the abuses that lay behind the American war and proposed solutions for them, he used the same civic humanist approach that he employed for abuses at home. In his view, imperial disasters arose from the arrogance of a government that ignored the colonists' complaints before 1775 and subsequently prolonged hostilities to its own profit. Such pride distressed Thom as a Christian, of course, but also as a True Whig. He believed that British rulers had departed from the polity of the republic of virtue in two particulars: ever greater corruption, especially in finance, and ever harsher injustices, which arose from corruption. Such abuses might damn the nation spiritually, but they would also enmesh it in tyranny. As for corruption, Thom alludes obliquely to government pensioners, bribe-takers and flatterers encouraging the prosecution of the war (*RTT*, 10).

As the war goes on, these allusions become sharper and more secular, in attacks on those who 'purloin or embezzle . . . the national revenue' and 'misapply public money . . . in foreign, or unnecessary wars', using pensions, bribes and places 'to subvert the public liberty' at home and abroad (*ATAT*, 26–27). Thom's last sermon on America specifically criticizes the judicial system, familiar to its author from litigation he brought against Glasgow University: 'Society is corrupted, and courts of justice are corrupted in proportion . . . . Great and wonderful is the influence of the opulent.' His boldest invective is directed against the war ministers: 'Sometimes wicked ministers of state engage their master in a war merely to screen themselves from condign punishment; to divert or stifle the clamour of an injured people against their covetous and bungling administration, they willfully involve the nation in all the miseries of war' (*FWCW*, 2–3, 8–9). They aim, as always, to enhance the monarch and aggrandize themselves, thus unsettling the republic of virtue's political balance: 'Almost every minister of state strives, with all his might, to increase the prerogative of the crown, and to abridge the privileges of the subject' (*RTT*, 38).

The corruption that Thom deplores inevitably creates injustice. Although an admirer of colonial legal systems, he warned his countrymen before the war that 'we have indeed, for some time past, been hearing a voice or cry from North America, that its liberties, solemnly secured by charter, are like to be infringed; that some wrong-headed statesmen have been pursuing measures detrimental to the mother-country.' Few could have foretold 'such ruinous laws with respect to America as in fact they have lately enacted' (*Task-Masters*, 204). After the war began, Thom added criticisms of government's rejection of the colonists' petitions for redress. When aggrieved subjects meet with 'a contemptuous defiance', he states, the empire must endure 'the flame and expense of a dangerous war' (*RTT*, 20). Furthermore, a prolonged war may lead to the establishment of a standing army, anathema to civic humanists. British success abroad can come only after long, costly hostilities and the imposition of such a force. This fearful spectre moved him, just as his evangelicalism did, to plead for peace. A permanent army large enough to garrison America can only burden Britain further, he states. Moreover, 'with an army over their heads, a colony will never thrive, or be of any use to the parent country'. Once again Thom describes the inevitable decay political injustice brings: such a society 'will quickly decline, and come to nothing' (*ATAT*, 40–41).

The principal injustice to which the colonists objected, of course, was taxation, a grievance that Thom overlooked in the early war sermons except when delivering broad criticisms of government's financial extravagance. In *From Whence Come Wars?*, however, he argues that Britain should nurture and protect its colonies and nothing more, it being understood that such 'mild rule' will lead to advantages all around: 'If a kingdom . . . sees . . . an infant-state, in danger of being crushed' (as had happened in the Seven Years War), 'and . . . interposeth to defend and protect that weak or infant-state; and . . . in fact exalts it to opulence and grandeur, it doth not, however, acquire any right to demand or exact by force any return, any pay or tax for their voluntary kindness' (*FWCW*, 10–11).

For Thom, the agency that can end the injustices of the American war is 'the people'. The most prolonged appeal to them occurs in *Achan's Trespass*:

> Even in the most despotic governments the last appeal is to the people: the people may by their cries and endeavors, find means to remove the patrons and tools of corruption from about the throne, by inquiries into misconduct, they must . . . oblige the Statesman to shake his hand from the taking of bribes. (*ATAT*, 22)

This sermon, however, suggests that 'the people' will act through Parliament, which Thom considered a flawed institution. 'When any part of the public revenue hath been purloined, or misapplied; or where unexpected disgraces in war have happened, it behooves the uncorrupted part of the legislative body to strive that the guilty may be detected' (*ATAT*, 28). Of greater significance than his appeal to Parliament is his granting legitimacy to Congress and local American assemblies. Such 'great and respectable bodies' of citizens, embodiments of the voluntary companies he urged on Scottish farmers and emigrants, must be conciliated (*RTT*, 14). Their legitimacy, and Parliament's, derives once again from 'the people, the bulk of the people, . . . tillers of the soil [and] artificers' (*FWCW*, 15–16). These men of middling rank with a stake in the country, here as elsewhere, will be 'those who contend for the interest of liberty or virtue, of the public good, of the human species' (*FWCW*, 31).

In suggesting means of redress for the people, Thom characteristically hesitated to go beyond petitioning the executive or legislature. In *Revolt of the Ten Tribes*, however, he warns, albeit circuitously, against the doctrine of passive obedience that Whig humanists detested:

> Though subjects may judge they are aggrieved by some particular laws, and feel themselves over-burdened by a heavy yoke; yet, in ordinary cases, it is their duty to yield obedience to the lawful magistrate. I dare not say, that resistance is, in all possible cases criminal. This doctrine, absurd and slavish as it is, hath sometimes been fashionable in this country: it is not yet a hundred years since passive obedience and non-resistance was from many pulpits in Britain, weekly obtruded upon the easy credulity of an injured and abused people.

'The yoke must be intolerable', of course, to invite open resistance, but wronged subjects may rebel (*RTT*, 36–37). *Achan's Trespass*, moreover,

praises the 'wonderful skill and courage' of the colonists who have done
so, who have 'from dread of slavery, applied long, and with ardour, to
get themselves disciplined and trained in all the exercises of war' (*ATAT*,
24). As the war progresses, Thom justifies force more explicitly. Having
denied Britain's right to tax colonies, he argues that, when so taxed,
colonists can 'demand reparations and effectuate it by open force, . . .
without which right human society could not subsist' (*FWCW*, 12). All
three sermons make clear his preference for conciliation and compromise,
a preference dictated by his civic humanism and his evangelical Calvinism
alike. But his argument denying Great Britain's right to tax its colonies
and his defence of the colonists' organized, armed resistance put him in
the forefront of radical thought in his day.

IV

THE UNION OF CIVIC HUMANISM and evangelical Calvinism in William
Thom's works represents the intellectual eclecticism and sophistication
of some late eighteenth-century Popular party spokesmen. To be sure,
the failure of Puritanism in England meant that thinkers there 'for the first
time engaged in a fully secular discussion of their society and its destinies',
as did some prominent Scots (Pocock, *Virtue, Commerce and History*,
93). But in Scotland and the northern colonies of America, 'Puritanism',
although it certainly changed, continued to influence many intellectuals.
Calvinism was surprisingly supple and receptive regarding Whig ideology (Landsman, 'Witherspoon', 36–37, 40–42). In some Americans a
stern, circumspect Protestantism gave way to an 'amalgam of traditional
Puritan apocalyptic rhetoric and eighteenth-century political discourse',
leading to the civil millenialism of the Revolution (Hatch, *Sacred Cause*,
22–24). Even in England, Whig radicals with civic humanist principles
included some dissenting clergy, the Puritan remnant (Brewer, 'English
Radicalism', 328–29, 342–43). In Scotland, the more receptive among
the orthodox accommodated themselves to the changing ideas of the age.
They took up the new learning and its values but put them to work with
an evangelical agenda and with evangelical gusto. This process had been
underway when the young William Thom entered Glasgow University,
where professors with civic humanist predilections were already teaching
students who would later form the Popular as well as the Moderate
parties.[29]

Aside from his education, Thom would have encountered humanist,
neoclassical and republican ideas when visiting Glasgow. In describing
the spread of civic humanism, J.G.A. Pocock notes its appeal among
English 'urban and suburban Old Whigs' (Pocock, *Virtue, Commerce
and History*, 130; Brewer, 'English Radicalism', 323, 331). The same
point applies to the Scotsman William Thom, who led a suburban life

as minister of Govan, from whence he could view Glasgow's spires and grumble about the better paid clergy who held forth beneath them. In so far as the fluctuations of a developing commercial economy stimulated political awareness and discontent among the urban middle ranks, the minister's complaints about his stipend help to explain his radicalism. As the century approached its end, True Whig spokesmen increasingly appeared in the English mercantile and professional classes, including the occasional cleric, whether Anglican or dissenter, and Thom was an example of the same phenomenon in Scotland (*Short History*, 13; Brewer, 'English Radicalism', 330–31, 334–35). Despite what historians have to say about eighteenth-century thought as largely secular, Protestant clergy and some laity in the British Isles and the colonies, and not always latitudinarians or socinians, gained a wider, more effective hearing by adopting its ideas with secular appeal. They combined in their agenda humanitarian and religious causes with more specifically political or economic ones. Fear for the rights of English or Irish dissenters, or New England Congregationalists or Scottish elders and heritors helped to motivate them (Brewer, 'English Radicalism', 361).

All kinds of hostile publicists and a bigoted public often considered Calvinists dangerously radical and lampooned them as traitorous republicans. The accusation was often unfair, but as we have seen, the charge, once divested of its biting edge, applies to such votaries of radical whiggery as the evangelical Calvinist William Thom. The identification of republicanism and orthodox Reformed Protestantism applied to him is one that, fairly or unfairly, reached back to an assortment of figures from the past: some obscure like the Scottish Whiggamores who bequeathed their name to British radicalism, and some celebrated, like John Calvin himself, a gifted humanist and the foremost ecclesiastical dignitary of a republican city-state.[30]

Notes

Research for this chapter was supported by the American Philosophical Society, the Massachusetts Historical Society and Kansas State University.

1. Andrew D. Hook, 'Scotland and America Revisited', in *Scotland, Europe and the American Revolution*, ed. Owen Dudley Edwards and George Shepperson (New York, 1976), 85.

2. Robert Kent Donovan, 'The Popular Party of the Church of Scotland and the American Revolution', in *Scotland and America in the Age of the Enlightenment*, ed. Richard B. Sher and Jeffrey R. Smitten (Princeton, 1990), 81–82.

3. All three sermons were later included in *The Works of William Thom* (Glasgow, 1799). Unless otherwise noted, William Thom is the author of all publications cited in this chapter.

4. *The Autobiography of Dr. Alexander Carlyle of Inveresk, 1722–1805*, new ed., ed. John Hill Burton (London and Edinburgh, 1910), 110.

5. John Gibson Lockhart, *Memoirs of the Life of Sir Walter Scott*, 2 vols. (Philadelphia, 1838), 2:405.

6. *Annals of the General Assembly of the Church of Scotland, 1739–1766*, 2 vols., ed. Nathaniel Morren (Edinburgh, 1838–40), 2:102n.

7. J. D. Mackie, 'The Professors and their Critics (Glasgow University in the Eighteenth Century)', *Proceedings of the Royal Philosophical Society of Glasgow* 72 (1947–48): 46; Peter Jones, 'The Scottish Professoriate and the Polite Academy, 1720–46', in *Wealth and Virtue: The Shaping of Political Economy in the Scottish Enlightenment*, ed. Istvan Hont and Michael Ignatieff (Cambridge, 1983), 112–15; Ned C. Landsman, 'Witherspoon and the Problem of Provincial Identity in Scottish Evangelical Culture', in *Scotland and America*, ed. Sher and Smitten, 39–40; Richard B. Sher, 'Commerce, Religion and the Enlightenment in Eighteenth-Century Glasgow', in *The History of Glasgow*, vol. 1, ed. T. M. Devine and Gordon Jackson (Manchester, 1994).

8. Hew Scott, *Fasti Ecclesiae Scoticanæ: The Succession of Ministers in the Church of Scotland*, new ed., 7 vols. (Edinburgh, 1915–28), 3:412.

9. See the following letters from Thom in GUA: to Robert Simpson, 3 July 1750; to the rector and masters of the university, 14 Feb. 1751; and to Principal Neil Campbell, 9 March 1752—requesting repairs to the manse; and the correspondence relating to the stipend augmentation issue, beginning in June 1763. Thom refers to his low stipend in *The Motives which Have Determined the University of Glasgow to Desert the Blackfriar Church* (Glasgow, 1764), 29–30, and to low clerical stipends generally in *The Scheme for Erecting an Academy at Glasgow* (Edinburgh, 1762), 29.

10. Richard Sher and Alexander Murdoch, 'Patronage and Party in the Church of Scotland, 1750–1800', in *Church, Politics and Society: Scotland 1408–1929*, ed. Norman Macdougall (Edinburgh, 1983), 197–220.

11. Scott, *Fasti*, 3:412; Glasgow Presbytery Minutes, 1733–49 (CH2/171/11), Mitchell Library, Strathclyde Regional Archives. Ned Landsman has suggested to me that it was Thom's 'style' rather than his doctrine which displeased his hearers.

12. *A Short History of the Late General Assembly . . . Shewing the Rise and Progress of the Schism Overture* (Glasgow, 1766); *A Letter to the Author of the Case of Patronage* (Glasgow, 1783). I am indebted to Ned Landsman for identifying Thom as the author of these pamphlets.

13. Thom praises Gillies in *Motives*, 7, 13–14. Witherspoon's library, now in Princeton University Library, contains copies of all three of Thom's American War sermons as well as his *Answers* to Glasgow University in his teind or stipend case.

14. *An Enquiry into the Causes of the Decline of Religion* (Glasgow, 1761), 21–22; *The Trial of a Student at the College of Clutha* (Glasgow, 1768), 16, 33, 73; *Scheme*, 38–39.

15. *Motives*, 7; *Trial*, 11–12; *Enquiry*, 7; *Sober and Religious Conference Considered and Recommended* (Glasgow, 1799), 47; *RTT*, 8.
16. *The Task-Masters*, in *Works*, 227; *Short History*, 39; *Sober Conference*, 52.
17. *A Candid Enquiry into the Causes of the Late and Intended Migrations* (Glasgow, 1771?), 50–56. On the basis of remarks in *Information Concerning the Province of North Carolina* (Glasgow, 1773), 11, 12, 19, 25–26, and *Task-Masters*, 119, it is possible that Thom himself visited America.
18. John Gibson, *The Unlimited Extent and Final Blessedness of God's Spiritual Kingdom* (Edinburgh, 1768), 8–9 (quoting *Isaiah* 66.18) and 33. See also Alan Heimert, *Religion and the American Mind from the Great Awakening to the Revolution* (Cambridge, Mass., 1966), 102.
19. The phrase is J.G.A. Pocock's, in *Virtue, Commerce and History: Essays in Political Thought and History* (Cambridge, 1985), 93.
20. Paul Tillich, *The Protestant Era* (Chicago, 1948), xviii; Heimert, *Religion and the American Mind*, 60, 68.
21. Nathan O. Hatch, *The Sacred Cause of Liberty: Republican Thought and the Millennium in Revolutionary New England* (New Haven, 1977), 29, 343–44, 353; James West Davidson, *The Logic of Millennial Thought: Eighteenth-Century New England* (New Haven, 1977), 54.
22. *Task-Masters*, 195, 197, 199–200, 205–7, 209–11, 214, 220, quoting *Isaiah* 54.1 and *Revelations* 11.15.
23. The Westminster Directory enjoined the fast day preacher 'to quicken affections' and 'work the hearts of the hearers to the special business of the day'. *The Westminster Directory*, ed. Thomas Leishman (Edinburgh, 1901), 70–71.
24. See Richard B. Sher, 'Witherspoon's *Dominion of Providence* and the Scottish Jeremiad Tradition', in *Scotland and America*, ed. Sher and Smitten, 47.
25. See also John Brewer, 'English Radicalism in the Age of George III', in *Three British Revolutions 1641, 1688, 1776*, ed. J.G.A. Pocock (Princeton, 1980), 345–46.
26. See J.G.A. Pocock, '1776: The Revolution Against Parliament', in *Three British Revolutions*, ed. Pocock, 272, and *Virtue, Commerce and History*, 147.
27. *Information to Emigrants, Being the Copy of a Letter from a Gentleman in North-America* (Glasgow, 1773), 12.
28. *A Letter of Advice to the Farmers Land-Labourers and Country Tradesmen in Scotland Concerning Roups*, in *Works*, 440–41, 447–50.
29. Friedhelm Voges, 'Moderate and Evangelical Thinking in the Later Eighteenth Century: Differences and Shared Attitudes, *Records of the Scottish Church History Society* 22 (1985): 144; Jones, 'Scottish Professoriate', 90.
30. William J. Bouwsma, *John Calvin: A Sixteenth-Century Portrait* (Oxford, 1988), 3, 12–14; Robert D. Linder, 'Calvinism and Humanism: The First Generation', *Church History* 44 (1975): 3, 5, 7, 9, 13, 15.

Index